AMERICA'S FIRST HAMLET

By the same author

GOVERNMENT AND THE ARTS

FAMOUS AMERICAN COMPOSERS

Payne at about the age of fifty,
"an elegantly-molded, gray-haired gentleman."

America's first Hamlet

BY
GRACE OVERMYER

Washington Square

NEW YORK UNIVERSITY PRESS

1957

Manufactured in the United States of America

To

ELIZABETH KNOWLTON

critic and friend

ACKNOWLEDGMENTS

IT WOULD be pleasant to be able to give individual credit to the many persons, librarians and others, who have aided in digging out the facts contained in this book.

At the New York Public Library, where most of the supplementary research was done, great thanks are due to the specialists who preside over the American history division, the genealogy division, the art, music, theater and manuscript sections, and the rare book room; as well as to the young men in the Twenty-fifth Street newspaper annex who have cheerfully produced innumerable issues of the London *Times* and other British as well as American journals of as far back as 1800.

Numerous other literary storehouses have also contributed to the book. Of Payne manuscript material there are, in addition to the collection of Colonel T. T. P. Luquer (see Prologue), several main sources. The author has personally examined, besides the New York Public Library and New-York Historical Society collections, those in the Library of Congress, National Archives, Harvard Theatre Division, Library of Union College (Schenectady), East Hampton (Long Island) Library, and Chicago's Newberry Library. The many excellent manuscript items in the Huntington Library (San Marino, California) have been made available by letter and photostat. And in the same way several colleges and historical societies have supplied some manuscripts, as well as general historical data.

Acknowledgment is gratefully extended to these institutions and persons: American Antiquarian Society (Worcester, Massachusetts), Mr. Clarence S. Brigham; Boston Athenaeum, Miss Margaret Hackett; Boston Public Library, Mr. Zoltan Haraszti, Mr. Richard G. Hensley, Mr. E. M. Oldham; Boston Museum of Fine Arts, Mrs. Barbara N. Parker; Brown University, Miss Marion E. Brown; Cleveland Public Library, Mr. L. Quincy Mumford, now Librarian of Congress; Columbia University, Dr. Lewis Leary; Duke University, Miss Pauline Cone, Mr. John P. Waggoner; East Hampton

Library (and Payne Museum), Mrs. Ruth Sterling Benjamin, Mr. Morton Pennypacker; Franklin and Marshall College (Lancaster, Pennsylvania), Mr. Herbert Anstaett; Georgia Historical Society, Mrs. Lilla M. Hawes; Harvard Theatre Collection, Dr. William Van Lennep; Henry E. Huntington Library, Dr. Herbert C. Schulz, Mr. Tyrus G. Harmsen, Mr. Theodore Heinrich, Mrs. Margaret Truax Hunter, Mr. W. A. Parish; Library of Congress, Mr. David C. Mearns, Mr. Clyde S. Edwards, Dr. Elizabeth McPherson, Mr. George A. Schwegman, Jr.; Maryland Historical Society, Dr. Harry Ammon, Mr. Fred Shelley; Massachusetts Historical Society, Mr. Stephen T. Riley; National Archives and Records Service, Dr. Carl L. Lokke, Mr. Almon R. Wright; Newberry Library, Mrs. Ruth Lapham Butler; New York Historical Society, Mr. Wayne Andrews, Miss Geraldine Beard, Mr. Louis J. Fox, Mr. Wilmer T. Leech; New York Public Library, Mr. Archibald De Weese and general reference staff, as well as Mr. John Morrison and Miss Jean Mc- Niece, manuscript division, Dr. John D. Gordan, Berg Collection, Miss Gladys Chamberlain, Music Library, Mr. Paul Myers, Theatre Division; Pennsylvania Historical Society, Mr. R. N. Williams 2nd, Mr. R. L. Sutcliffe; Princeton University, Mr. Alexander P. Clark; Providence Athenaeum, Mrs. Annie C. Cooper; Tufts College Library, Miss Eleanor Atherton; Union College, Mr. Codman Hislop, Mr. Helmer C. Webb; University of Illinois, Miss Alice S. Johnson; University of Pennsylvania, Dr. Arthur Hobson Quinn, Mr. Frederick L. Jones; University of Rochester, Mr. John R. Russell; University of Virginia, Miss Louise Savage; Valentine Museum (Richmond), Mrs. G. S. Snydor; Weidenthal Collection (Cleveland), Mr. Leo Weidenthal; Yale University, Mr. Robert S. Metzdorf, Miss Barbara D. Simison.

Also: Birmingham (England) City Museum, Dr. Mary Woodhall; British Museum, Mr. E. J. Dingwall; City of Liverpool Public Library, Mr. J. H. Hodson; Covent Garden Opera House, Mr. John Greenwood, Mr. Michael Wood; National Portrait Gallery (London), Mr. J. F. Kerslabe; Walker Art Gallery (Liverpool), Mr. Frank Lambert. Also Mr. Basil Francis, London; Mrs. D. Fletcher Howe, Honolulu.

Also: jacket picture of young Payne as Hamlet, from a portrait by Charles R. Leslie, Boston Museum of Fine Arts.

CONTENTS

Acknowledgments 7
Prologue: Legend and Man 11

Part One: 1791 and earlier to 1813

1. East Hampton: Home of Forebears 19
2. New York: Home and Family 26
3. Boston: Home and School 33
4. The Wonder Boy 43
5. The Boy Playwright 54
6. The Collegian 66
7. Master Payne, Actor 76
8. Young Roscius Tours America 88
9. Corlaer's Hook: Home Between the Acts 98

Part Two: 1813 to 1832

1. American Roscius in England 109
2. Emelia Von Harten 119
3. The Emerald Isle 131
4. The Home Folks and the War 135
5. Two Cities: Two Plays 139
6. One Man versus Two Managers 150
7. *The Tragedy of Brutus* 159
8. Troubled Interlude 172
9. Summer at Sadler's Wells 177
10. *Virginius*, Another Tragedy 186
11. Prison Diary 190
12. The Song Is Written 202

9

13. The Song Is Sung   211
14. Collaborators   223
15. Genteel Triangle   238
16. Looking at London from Paris   257
17. London: Final Years   267

Part Three: 1832 to 1852 and later

1. Benefits Remembered   277
2. *Jam Jehan Nima*   289
3. Indian Suite: Contrasting Movements   297
4. Home Theme, with Variations   311
5. Cherokees East and West   320
6. Entr'acte: Washington and New York   330
7. Mission to Tunis   337
8. Matters Official and Unofficial   353
9. Inevitable Hour   365
10. Precious Dust   374

Notes   389
Appendix: Specimens of Payne's Writing   415
Bibliography   423
Index   433

PROLOGUE: LEGEND AND MAN

JOHN HOWARD PAYNE was an able and many-sided man, a very unusual and engaging personality, a famous figure of his time. Outstandingly he was a pioneer in the theater, probably a more active and important one than any other American of his period. Yet today he is remembered solely for the authorship of "Home, Sweet Home," and the man is little more than a legend—one which begins and ends with the familiar hearsay that the home song's author "never had a home."

This is a legend that has lent itself to much elaboration. In the latter half of the nineteenth century, when the generation of Payne's contemporaries was no longer alive, the sentimentalists got to work picturing him as they felt the author of "Home, Sweet Home" must have been. They made him a solitary wanderer gazing longingly into cheerfully lighted windows; they made him a street beggar standing humbly, hat in hand, while a gay throng passed him by; or they placed him in bucolic surroundings with a vine-clad cottage in the background. Whatever the setting, they managed to convert him into a saint, complete in everything but halo, and they often decorated their printed effusions with borders of flowers and birds and other innocent and lovely things.

Actually, Payne was a man of broad experience and of diverse undertakings and achievements. He was an actor, a playwright, a minor poet, an original if unstable editor, a champion of the rights of the American Indian, and a United States consular official.

As a precocious boy actor he was the earliest American to become a stage idol in his own country and the first native player to enact the role of Hamlet. Subsequently the first American performer to appear on a European stage, he was also the earliest American playwright to have works produced abroad. He lived for years in London

11

and Paris, knew the London theaters from stage door to box office, and was associated with most of the British stage celebrities of his time.

Outside the theater, the activity that chiefly distinguished him was his effort to obtain justice for the Cherokee Indians. This in its own way was as important as his theatrical work, although of much briefer duration. His later government service brought him into contact with official Washington and many of its contemporary notables.

There may be several reasons why a career so significant has long been little known and generally underestimated. For one, Payne's principal work reversed the usual order of American pioneering: while his countrymen at home were absorbed in pushing back the wilderness frontier, he was living abroad and blazing a trail into the strongholds of an established art. For another, the field of that pioneering was one which many nineteenth-century Americans regarded with disfavor. Achievements in the theater were thought of little consequence, and scant attention was paid to what the earliest American accomplished there.

Further, there is the indubitable fact that Payne possessed one personal trait that militated against him. Throughout his life he was a bad financial manager, lavishly extravagant and never able to free himself from debt. This defect brought him enemies and detractors in his lifetime, and may have served to becloud his memory.

Yet Payne grows appreciably in stature as his life and work become known. He possessed a clear and independent mind, much charm, and a variety of talents. As an actor he displayed marked if uneven abilities, unless we believe the contemporary critics wholly lacking in judgment. As a playwright, and chiefly as an adapter (his plays being usually based on his own translations of the current French output), he provided the English and American theaters with half a hundred or more dramatic works. Nearly all enjoyed a measure of success, several were outstanding hits, and a few held the stage for half a century and longer.

Payne's skill as a dramatic craftsman was generally recognized by his contemporaries. Charles Lamb, no mean judge of things theatrical, when he tried his own hand at play-writing remarked (in a letter to Mary Shelley, September 26, 1827): "I need some Howard Payne to sketch for me a succession of artfully succeeding scenes, to say where a joke should come in or a pun be left out, to help me get my personae on and off."

That Payne was gifted also as director and producer we have only recently discovered, though there is evidence that this may have been the greatest of his talents.

It has been possible to write this extensive biography of Payne, including important details of his background, largely because of his own and his family's penchant for saving letters. This, on Payne's part, may have become a habit early in life as a result of his brief career as a mercantile clerk in precarbon-paper days, when careful businessmen had hand copies made of all letters and filed in bound volumes known as letter books. In after years Payne kept in this way a great many letters to and from himself, and he quite impartially included family letters, business letters, love letters, and letters asking for loans. In addition there are in various collections numerous unbound letters of Payne and the members of his family.

The letter books and many other personal and business documents were found among Payne's effects, after his death in Tunis, by two of his successors in the American consulate there. The earlier of these, W. P. Chandler, apparently enjoyed reading the private papers and scrawling crude but sometimes informative comments in the margins. Chandler's successor, Amos Perry, some years later gathered together all the material that could then be found and forwarded it to Payne's relatives in New York.

At the present time most of the family letters, several diaries and scrapbooks, and much of the correspondence of the London and Paris years, including about seventy letters in the handwriting of Washington Irving, are in the possession of Payne's grandnephew, Colonel Thatcher Taylor Payne Luquer of Bedford Hills, New York. Repeatedly consulted throughout the preparation of this work, Colonel Luquer has responded with invariable courtesy and helpfulness. Much of the manuscript material supplied by him, as well as a good deal of that from other sources, is here published for the first time.

For all the abundance of original material, however, there are points about which we might have fuller information. It seems likely that many documents were lost in Tunis or elsewhere. It is also possible that there are scattered items still in existence—perhaps valuable ones—that may yet come to light.

Payne has been the subject of three books that can be called biographical works: the full-length biography by Gabriel Harrison (1875), the story of early years by Willis Tracy Hanson, Jr. (1913), and the appreciative analysis by Rosa Pendleton Chiles (1930). (See Bibliography, p. 423.) None of these covers Payne's career completely, although all are valuable, being based on a careful study of facts.

Supplementing the books and manuscripts as source material are innumerable newspaper and magazine articles. Old newspapers have proved a veritable mine of reliable information. A careful study of the dramatic news and theater advertisements of the period of Payne's London activities has supplied factual data of great value. Of the periodical writing all the way from 1806 to the present, some is useful and informative; but there is also much of doubtful authenticity, its "facts" ranging from appallingly garbled statements to out-and-out fabrication. Mary Caroline Crawford's remark (in *The Romance of the American Theatre*), that "more untrue things have been printed of Payne than of any other American, with or without a stage background," seems entirely justified.

The author's greatest challenge has been awareness of a widespread prejudice against Payne. However this may have originated, it has been fostered and spread, not by Payne's biographers, but mainly by a few sophisticated writers who have mentioned him incidentally in comments on the old theater, or in some other historical connection. To these writers Payne the man was "a magnificent poseur," Payne the actor completely insignificant, Payne the writer "an irresponsible hack" whose works were "flimsy fabrications" and hardly worth mentioning.

We are convinced that such immoderate judgments are based at best on a very superficial acquaintance with the subject. Often they have no basis at all except hearsay; but they have nevertheless been accepted and carelessly passed on. At a few points in this book, some statement or implication reflecting such attitudes has required special comment; but for the most part it has seemed sufficient to present the facts, allowing the reader to form his own conclusions.

This book is in no degree fictionized biography. It is in large part a chronicle of situations and events, emotions and thoughts, long hidden away in old letters, diaries, and records of various kinds. Every effort has been made to depict Payne as he was, against the varied background of the times and places in which he lived and worked and the many persons with whom he was associated. A fascinating though complex task is that of turning a legend into a human being!

Part One

1791 AND EARLIER TO 1813

[1]

EAST HAMPTON: HOME OF FOREBEARS *

NEAR the remote tip of Long Island lies East Hampton, one of the loveliest of American villages.

Home for generations of Payne's maternal ancestors, East Hampton was once believed also to be his birthplace. But of recent years this pleasing part of the Payne legend has had to yield to the more convincing claims of the City of New York.[1]

This village, nevertheless, is as likely a background for the world's most famous home song as can well be imagined; and undoubtedly it played a part in shaping the mind of the man who wrote "Home, Sweet Home." For here he often came on visits in his childhood—visits marked by memories of fragrant pines and the ocean's distant music; of long summer days of play among the sand dunes and tall grasses; of evening's stillness and candlelight, in the secure protection of kindred and family friends.

Here, too, in later years, Payne loved to revisit favorite haunts; and through long association his name has become a part of the community's folklore.

East Hampton today is a fashionable suburb bordered by wealthy estates, but the village itself is much as it was in earlier times.

Today, as a century and a half ago, the heart of the town is a broad green parklike way called Main Street, flanked by magnificent trees. Along this shaded road may still be seen a few, if only a few, of the buildings Payne knew as a boy. One of these, with steeple and bell and flagstone porch, is the old Clinton Academy, with which his father was once connected. Another, across the way and well back

---

* The notes to Part One begin on p. 389.

19

among the trees, is the small colonial salt-box house preserved as a Payne memorial. And at the far end of the street is the ancient hillside cemetery, grass-grown, serenely peaceful in its quiet beauty, its headstones reflected in the pond where the slope merges into the village green.

These charming relics are not the only reminders of the past still observable in East Hampton. Family names which have been noted in fading inscriptions on the gravestones appear again in signs on Main Street's shops and inns. For here, as in most pioneer communities, all the oldest families are related. Here, from the town's beginnings some century and a quarter before the Revolution until the advent of nineteenth-century innovations, it was usual for East Hampton girls to marry East Hampton boys.

There were, of course, exceptions, even in the eighteenth century. And it is with the consequences of two of those—two marriages which brought entirely new blood to the village—that this biography deals.

Of the two adventurous immigrants to break the local marriage tradition, one arrived within the Revolutionary period. His name was William Payne; he was a native of Eastham, Massachusetts, thirty-three years old, a widower and childless. By occupation he was a teacher, a pursuit not usual at the time except for ministers.

William Payne had come to East Hampton for a very special purpose: that of calling on a young lady. She was Sarah Isaacs, age nineteen, a daughter of Aaron Isaacs, the town's only Jewish citizen. A few weeks earlier Sarah had accompanied her father on a business trip across Long Island Sound. In the Connecticut town of New London they had stopped at the postoffice, and there Sarah happened to open the door just as a stranger entered. That stranger was William Payne.

In the following year, 1780, the Long Island girl was married to her middle-aged suitor from Massachusetts; and this is the union responsible for "Home, Sweet Home," for in its twelfth year it would produce John Howard Payne.

Payne's grandfather, Aaron Isaacs, was the earlier of the two outsiders who came to call and remained to found a family. When he arrived the community was still called Maidstone, and its widely scattered houses had thatched roofs.

Isaacs, originally from Hamburg,[2] had lived in England before coming to America. From the relatively urban settlement of New York, more than a hundred miles away, he had ventured into the wilds of Long Island; and there a village girl proved the attraction which determined him to end his wanderings.

Married to Mary Hedges and merged into the clan that was old East Hampton, Aaron Isaacs built his house on a farm near the eastern end of the Island. There he reared his children, about a dozen of them, and there he prospered until the Revolution swept away most of his property. Then even his cautious habit of keeping his books in Hebrew, even the presence of his son Aaron Jr., the cordwainer, on the community muster rolls, could not keep most portable possessions from being carried off.

Aaron Isaacs, as a grandchild recalled years later, "was esteemed an honest, very kindly man by all who knew him." Though he is often described as a converted Jew, there are records which indicate that he did not embrace Christianity until some time after his marriage. Then came a year of great religious awakening in East Hampton, when both Aaron Isaacs and his wife joined the Presbyterian church. Concerning the conversion of Isaacs there is still preserved a copy of a letter dated March 17, 1764, from the Reverend Mr. Buell of East Hampton to the Reverend Mr. Barber of Groton, Connecticut, which contains this spiritually illuminating as well as historically interesting statement:

> Grace, Mercy and Peace by all in Heaven and Earth is come down by way of Influence upon and in the hearts of the people of East Hampton. . . . Among the rest we have a Jew, that I have reason to believe is now a true believer in the Messiah.[3]

The wife who shared this spiritual experience with her Jewish spouse was a daughter of the local aristocracy. For Mary Hedges was descended on both sides from the community's founders. Her father, Stephen Hedges, certainly possessed a family claim—perhaps as a direct descendant—upon that William Hedges mentioned in the history books as one of the eight original proprietors of East Hampton.

Her mother, Experience Talmadge, was a great- or great-great-grand-child of Thomas Talmadge, intrepid Puritan refugee from England, whose son, Thomas Jr., helped establish East Hampton in 1649, and who, being, as all historians state, "a man of education," became the town's first recorder.

In connection with the Talmadge line there is a romantic tale, confirmed in part by genealogical records. According to it a de-scendant of Thomas Talmadge was rightful heir to a British noble-man, the Earl of Dysart, and, had Experience been a son, the title and wealth of the Earl would have fallen to the American branch of the family. Since, however, she was only a girl, with younger sisters but no brothers, the rights reverted to heirs in Britain.[4]

Did Experience dream of pleasures and palaces that might have been hers had the laws of succession been as kind to girls as to boys? Or did she remain content with her life as a pioneer daughter? There is no answer to these queries. All that is known is that Experience Talmadge became the wife of Stephen Hedges, that she was the mother of Mary Hedges Isaacs, grandmother of Sarah Isaacs Payne and hence great-grandmother of "Home, Sweet Home."

On the paternal side also Payne was descended from earliest Americans. Indeed, it was only a year after the *Mayflower* that his father's first American forebear arrived in the New World.

That was Thomas Paine (of no known relationship to the famed Revolutionary Thomas), who came from Portsmouth, England, landed on Cape Cod in 1621, and later shared in the settlement of Eastham, Massachusetts.[5] Of the sons of this Paine, one was the grandfather of Robert Treat Paine, a signer of the Declaration of Independence, and another of William Payne, the father of John Howard. The variant in the spelling of the name was adopted by William Payne when his philological studies convinced him that "the letter *y* instead of *i* was in accord with the primitive and cor-rect orthography used by his progenitors on the other side of the Atlantic."

William Payne was a posthumous child. Shortly before his birth in 1746 his father, an officer in the Colonial army as well as a mem-ber of the Provincial Legislature, had been killed in one of those

futile wars between British and French on American soil. The young
widow soon remarried and moved to Nova Scotia, leaving her infant
son to be brought up in Massachusetts by the Reverend Joseph
Crocker, a Congregational minister. That choice, probably prayer-
fully made, proved for the good of the child, since the chosen guardian had a son Philander Crocker, a student at Harvard, and by him
the orphaned boy was provided with an education considerably beyond that usual at the time.

Later this boy, before deciding on teaching as his work in life,
spent some time preparing to be a doctor. As there were few, if any,
American medical schools in those days, his studies were carried
on in the office of a friend—Dr. Joseph Warren, subsequently a
famous Revolutionary hero who lost his life at Bunker Hill.

In his eventual career as teacher William Payne became a spe-
cialist in languages and elocution and started a school in Boston,
but this was forced to close by the turbulent conditions of 1775.
Removing to Barnstable to work as a tutor, he there met and married Lucy Taylor, but this wife lived only a year. His marriage to
Sarah Isaacs occurred three years later; and while the second alliance was undoubtedly a marriage of love, it is certain that William
Payne still cherished the memory of his first young wife, since for
her he named his oldest child, Lucy Taylor Payne. A minor detail
this, perhaps, but it has in it some of the sensibility that is the essence
of "Home, Sweet Home."

Of the nine children born to William and Sarah Payne, John
Howard was the sixth. The five older—Lucy, her brother William
Osborn, and the sisters Sarah, Eloise, and Anna—were all natives
of East Hampton: that is definitely established. When they were all
quite young the family moved to New York; and the question
whether the sixth child arrived before or after the move was made,
has been the basis of a birthplace controversy, revived from time to
time.

It was on the supposition that John Howard was a native of the
Long Island village that the quaint little house on East Hampton's
Main Street was originally selected as the Payne memorial museum.
Legends had long associated Payne's name with this place, and in

1910 Gustave Buek, a Brooklyn man of means and sentiment, bought the house, restored and to some extent modernized it, improved the grounds, and supplied the antique furnishings, which, with framed letters, portraits and other mementoes, now add artistic to the historic interest of its interior. On the death of Mr. Buek in 1927 the town of East Hampton voted bonds for purchase and preservation of the place. Though actually it is not known that Payne or any of his immediate family ever lived in this house, the long connection of his forebears with beautiful old East Hampton makes the location there of a Payne shrine altogether appropriate.

The exact age of the house is not known, but it is of a type erected early in the eighteenth century, when man's comfort was still largely regulated by Nature. Facing south for the warmth of the sun, it is two stories high in front and is protected on the north by a long sloping roof that runs down to one story above the kitchen windows. The shingled outer walls have the weather-beaten hue which fits so well into a rural landscape; the entrance is canopied by a lush wisteria vine, and the lawn protected by a picket fence. Within, the huge fireplace with spacious oven, the small, many-paned windows and uncomfortably steep little stairway, all are marks of an early era. Unlike some Payne memorials, this one is kept in the pink of condition—wood and metals shining, ruffled curtains white as new snow. Altogether it is a peaceful, gently romantic spot, thoroughly in keeping with the spirit of "Home, Sweet Home."

Each year this house attracts a few thousand tourist visitors, among whom there is occasionally one who wishes to cross the road to the cemetery and view the grave of Grandfather Isaacs. But here a disappointment is in store. For there is widely reputed to be inscribed on Aaron Isaacs' tombstone this slight paraphrase of a Biblical line:

"An Israelite, indeed, in whom there was no guile." [6]

It would be pleasant to believe that these words represented the feeling of fellow townsmen toward Payne's grandfather, so it is something of a shock to find the alleged sculptured tribute entirely lacking. The brownstone slab which marks the grave bears only this simple inscription:

In memory of Mr. Aaron Isaacs
who died September 11, 1797
in the 75th year of his age.

The story of the Israelite inscription, however, was once widely accepted and has been printed and reprinted many times. Today its origin seems a mystery, though it may not be an entire fabrication. There seems a possibility that the present headstone may long ago have replaced an earlier one which did have the eulogistic marking.

The other East Hampton relic most closely connected with Payne history is the Clinton Academy, now also a museum, though not of Payne mementoes. Founded by New York's Governor George Clinton in 1784 and chartered three years later, this was the first academy (in the sense of secondary school) to be officially authorized in the state. Previously there had been only one accredited institution—the Kingston Academy, actually ten years older than Clinton, but not incorporated until a decade later—to bridge the gap between the elementary school and the university; and most students residing in New York State who aspired to Columbia, Harvard, or Yale had to obtain their preparation from private tutors.

The location of an important educational institution in the sequestered village of East Hampton is credited to the presence there of well-qualified teachers. One of them was the Reverend Samuel Buell, who became the Academy's principal; and another was William Payne, a preceptor in Clinton Academy during most of his East Hampton residence.

The eventual removal of the Payne family from East Hampton to New York may have been caused by what seemed better opportunities in the city. Certain it is that his departure from Clinton Academy was no reflection on Preceptor Payne's work there. This we know by a cordial testimonial addressed to him by Principal Buell (the same who had welcomed Aaron Isaacs to the Christian faith), which, after praising Mr. Payne's "judicious and well-adapted mode of instruction, assiduity, fidelity and good government," assures him that "we should have been highly gratified if you could have made it consistent with your interest and have seen it your duty to have accepted our present invitation to continue with the Academy. We regret the necessity of your declining it, while we indulge a hope that you may return to it in some future day." [7]

Signed "Your affectionate friend and fellow servant," this letter is dated September 30, 1790. It therefore proves that whatever the date of his departure for New York, William Payne had resigned his official connection with East Hampton fully eight months before the birth, on June 9, 1791, of the son destined to cast a romantic aura about a family and a town.

[2]

NEW YORK: HOME AND FAMILY

WHATEVER the anxieties of the parents, attending the family's migration from East Hampton to New York, the trip was doubtless a lark for the children.

Lucy, eldest of the brood, was about ten years old at the time, and her brother William eight; while the three little stair-step sisters, Sally, Eloise, and Anna, had been in the world six, four, and two years. Had there been a baby brother on this trip—and such a brother as he turned out to be—that circumstance would hardly have been forgotten by Lucy when, late in her life, she prepared for posterity her little *History of the Family*, modest source of much valuable information. Penned on ruled notepaper in Lucy Payne Osborn's own hand, this little memorandum—its final pages missing —sheds the most convincing light upon the question of her famous brother's birthplace of any document in existence.

"My father and mother took with them to New York, five children, my brother William the only boy," is one statement of this record. And another: "Two brothers and a sister were born in this [the New York] period."

The two brothers were John Howard, whose birth date coincides with the family's first year in the city, and Thatcher Taylor, born five years later. Between the two was the sister referred to by Lucy —Eliza Maria, who died at the age of four.

Since their removal to New York was naturally a momentous event in the family, it is to be regretted that Lucy does not tell us how they traveled, when the journey began, or when it ended. It seems likely, however, that the trip was made by water, and, if so, it may have consumed no less than a week. For this was at the beginning of the last decade of the eighteenth century, and there was as yet no stagecoach line through the panorama of forest, dotted here and there by a pioneer town, which was the Long Island of the period, although Long Island Sound was an important lane of travel.

At Sag Harbor, on an inlet of the Sound and about seven miles from old East Hampton, was a wharf erected in 1770, which, during the frightening days of '76, had been "crowded with emigrants" [8] fleeing the Island for the safer shores of Connecticut. That wharf was connected with the village by a road, which "came through a pine swamp and ran so close to the bluff that at high tide one wagon wheel would be tilted up and the other depressed in the water."

Along this precarious way we may imagine Grandfather Isaacs driving a wide-wheeled farm wagon and well-fed team, as he accompanies his daughter and her family to the wharf. Their boat is waiting for them. Probably it is an arklike barge, equipped with sails and large enough to accommodate the family and all their household goods. As soon as the wind is favorable it slowly moves off, and grandparents, uncles, aunts, cousins, and friends wave as long as a speck can be seen.

The Paynes' second son is said to have been named for his father's friend Dr. John Howard, a Revolutionary veteran who lived in Smithtown Branch, Long Island. William Payne sometimes made trips from New York to East Hampton, probably traveling on horseback, and, the story goes, was accustomed to stop overnight at the home of Dr. Howard. On one of the visits, in June of 1791, the traveler reported the birth of another son and asked his host to suggest a name for the child.[9] The doctor presumably proposed his own.

This name, we know, was duly confirmed when John Howard Payne was two years old; for there is a record of his being christened, together with his brother William and four sisters, on July 24, 1793, by "a minister of the United Presbyterian Congregation in the City of New York." [10]

During their residence of nearly ten years in New York, the Paynes moved frequently. This may reflect the financial condition of the family; for the teaching profession, never, of course, very lucrative, was doubtless less than usually so in the case of William Payne, a hard-working man who gave much and asked little in return. It may be, also, that the father sometimes received his pupils in his home and sometimes outside and changed his residence to accommodate himself to that condition.

The New York Directory for 1791 contains this entry: "Paine, Wm., teacher of the French and English languages, writing, arithmetic and mathematics, 4 Great Dock do." And in the New York *Journal and Patriotic Register* for May 28, 1791, less than two weeks before the birth of John Howard, appeared a quarter-column advertisement of this teacher's plan of "Academical Instruction," of which "the terms, etc., may be known by enquiring in Great Dock Street at No. 4."

The name Great Dock Street was to be changed to Pearl Street [11] a few years after this advertisement appeared, and if we assume the house numbers to have been changed at the same time, 4 Great Dock Street is translatable as 33 Pearl Street, where, according to Payne's early biographer Gabriel Harrison, stood the house in which John Howard Payne was born.

Harrison, who himself grew up in New York, tells of having had 33 Pearl Street pointed out to him by his father as Payne's birthplace shortly before the house at that number was demolished, in 1832. The house was not large. It must have been fairly bursting with children, what with the six young Paynes and their father's pupils besides. It was only a temporary residence of the family, however, which soon sought other and probably more spacious quarters.[12]

As this was long before the day of the American public school, and even considerably in advance of the free school movement, the academies kept by William Payne must have had an important place in old New York. Very little is recorded about the schools of that time, and it adds interestingly to our scanty information to know where this pioneer teacher lived and taught in the closing decade of the century. The city directory supplies this information by listing five different addresses for "Payne, schoolmaster," usually of his combined "academy and house," within the ten-year period.

It can be seen then, that the author of "Home, Sweet Home" had not one, but several, childhood abodes; and if, as is often alleged, a mental picture of early home did inspire the famous song, it must have been a highly composite one. Indeed we must conclude, especially from what we shall learn later of the man, that the song was a tribute less to a particular dwelling place than to something deeper. Home was the family; home was where the folks were.

Moreover the creator of the song spent the first eight years of his life, except for annual visits to East Hampton, not among strictly rural surroundings but in what, even then, was the American metropolis. New York was, of course, a metropolis by comparison only, being, with its 60,000 inhabitants at the close of the century, but a few thousand above its nearest competitor, Philadelphia. The settlement originally called Nieuw Amsterdam had nevertheless become a very active, very cosmopolitan little city, especially along the bustling water fronts, separated by no more than a few short streets from any part of the then inhabited town.

Only two blocks from the juncture of Broadway, Bowling Green, and the Battery, 33 Pearl Street, in preskyscraper days, doubtless commanded a magnificent view of the harbor. From this and their other early New York homes, the Paynes could probably see tall-masted, ocean-going ships resting in the East River docks, where they towered above the ferries and brigs and sturdy Dutch sloops designed for the local river traffic. When errands took any of the family to busy, poplar-bordered Broadway—a straight, wide street among narrow and crooked ones—they must often have passed groups of sailors in the native garb of many parts of Europe and the Orient, chattering in a dozen tongues as they scurried along.

On evening strolls the children and their father probably visited

near-by Wall Street, which future great avenue of finance had only
one bank,[13] although, with several churches and many steep-roofed
Dutch-type houses, it was one of the finer residential streets. At the
corner of Wall and Broad streets the strollers may have paused to
view the impressive colonial structure known as Federal Hall, in
which Washington took the oath of office in 1789 and which for a
brief period had served as the nation's capitol. And they doubtless
noted another neighborhood landmark made famous by the first
president: Fraunce's Tavern at Pearl and Broad, where, the Revolution ended, Washington met the officers who had served under
him, "shook each man by the hand and bade him farewell." This
tavern, since restored and still in use, was only two short blocks
from the first New York home of the Paynes.

Not only in Pearl Street, but wherever they lived in the town, the
Paynes, like all other families, had only such facilities as today
seem primitive. For their main water supply they doubtless depended
on a back-yard well or cistern. If this ever proved inadequate, the
older children may have been sent with buckets to one or another
of the town's wooden pumps, to be found frequently at intersections
of the cobblestone-paved streets. Their homes had no bathrooms or
plumbing of any kind, but neither had anybody's; and as for heat-
ing, they doubtless thought themselves fortunate if the various houses
they lived in had fireplaces in most of the rooms.

Schoolmaster Payne may not have been able to afford a private
equipage, but it is to be hoped that his children sometimes had a
chance to travel beyond the pavements and into the adjoining countryside. For the great natural beauties of the island that the Indians
named Manahattani had not yet been sacrificed to greedy "improvements," and where the streets ended, the peaceful country roads,
the woods and streams, the farms and fields and jutting brown-gray
rocks began. Some of the farms were fine estates, with mansions
looking out over the rivers from both sides of the island; and in
between, for many miles, lay a magnificent natural playground of
the greatest variety and beauty.

Wherever they roamed and whatever they saw, it is probable that
little in their environment was lost on the young Paynes, for they

were all remarkably precocious. In school they doubtless set a stiff
pace for their father's other pupils, though they were not exclusively
a family of little bookworms. They enjoyed such homely pleasures
as would delight less gifted children; and not the least of these was
the trip each year to Grandma's and Aunt Esther's in East Hampton.
That visit was naturally made in the summertime, and later, around
Thanksgiving, Grandpa could be depended on to return the call. He
always brought with him, so Lucy remembered all her life, "a great
round basket filled with doughnuts and other good things to make
us happy to see him." [14]

The second Payne boy, Howard, as he was usually called at home,
was delicate as a child, and it is not surprising that in the way of
scholarship the parents expected less of him than of some of the
others, notably the brother William and the sister Eloise.

William Jr. was indeed a remarkable boy. When Howard was five
years old this big brother, then thirteen and a half, whose father had
"taken pains to make him a perfect master of arithmetic and the
French language, as well as of penmanship and accounts," and who
had "also made good progress in Latin," [15] was adjudged old enough
to go out into the world and earn a living. He went to Baltimore to
work in the countinghouse of William Taylor, the brother of his
father's first wife.

The early launching of young William Payne may have been
necessary, for the family was still increasing, and the father's teaching income was doubtless still small. This supposition is confirmed
by one letter from William to his sister Lucy, in which he speaks
of "the narrowness of my father's circumstances," meaning, of
course, financial stringency. "My father had intended and often
said," this letter confides, "it was the pinnacle of his wishes that
I should be educated at Harvard College." This was an ambition
never to be realized, though William was amply justified in the
"vanity" that he confesses to Lucy, but probably would not have
voiced outside the family, "of thinking that I possess more penetration than is common at my age."

Travel, even between the larger towns, was irregular, expensive,
and slow—the journey by stage from Baltimore to New York required four days—and William was rarely able to get home on a

visit. He wrote frequently, however, and his letters give us a key to the character of the family.

"Letters are the messengers of the heart," wrote the affectionate and doubtless homesick boy, who, in a later letter to Lucy, would declare: "The time absent from Mother has served to increase my affection." He also reminds Lucy of "the advantages we enjoy over the common run of children, how much more attentive our parents are and how grateful we should be to them."

In August of 1796 the father, writing from 29 Ann Street, tells William, who had then been away four months, of "an accession" to the family, and asks him to suggest a name for a new brother. William suggests Thatcher Taylor—Thatcher for the family of young William's best friends in Baltimore and Taylor for his employer, who was indeed almost a relative, being the father's brother-in-law by his first marriage. It was of this third son that the father would write to William Taylor a few years later, in 1802: "Our youngest son, Thatcher, is now almost six. I began with him about a year ago and have never seen one single instance of greater proficiency at that age."

Although John Howard does not figure in the earliest letters exchanged between the absent brother and the home folks, there are references that tell us something of the interests and achievements of the sisters, particularly Eloise. Scarcely less clever than the boys, the girls of this family possessed more than the usual feminine accomplishments of the time, particularly intellectual ones. They wrote graceful, polished, elegantly phrased letters and were proficient in French at an early age. Lucy, Sally, and Anna, however, all cheerfully acknowledged Eloise, the third sister, as most gifted of them all.

It is to Eloise, then nine years old, that William writes, not long after his departure from home: "I received your very pretty letter. . . . I recollect you used to be very forward in French and suppose you are quite a French girl [by now]. You ought to have written to me in that language." Later William tells Lucy of "having written to Eloisa in Italian."

Eloise, throughout her life, was to be famed beyond the family circle for her brilliance. As a young girl she was noted especially for "a remarkable proficiency in Latin" and of the superior capacities of her later years many carefully preserved letters bear evidence. One who reads them today is impressed by their literary excellence.

While they resided in New York, the father of these extraordinary young people seems to have achieved a wider pedagogical fame. Boston had heard of him and had "sent a committee, including Stephen Higginson and Col. Perkins," [16] to persuade Mr. Payne to move to that city and start a boarding school. Accordingly, near the last year of the century, the family—now, in the absence of the oldest son, consisting of the parents and six children, and this time certainly including John Howard—left New York for a new home in the Massachusetts capital.

[3]

BOSTON: HOME AND SCHOOL

THE BOSTON habitation of the Paynes is known to have been in Atkinson Street, around the corner from Federal and adjacent to the building that housed the Berry Street Academy, of which institution the father had become headmaster. Here, in what was almost a combined residence and school, John Howard lived from the age of eight to the age of fourteen; and this was the most enduring home that he would ever know.

It must have been in the autumn or late summer of 1799 that the kindly and scholarly William Payne arrived in Boston with his still youthful though doubtless somewhat weary wife and their six precocious youngsters. Since there was no other public conveyance, they presumably made this trip in one or more of the "stage wagons" operated by the New York-to-Boston line. This ran three times a week, starting at four in the morning and "performing its route through to Boston in four days, in carriages, all hung upon springs, and with good horses and roads better than they have been before."

The Berry Street Academy was a boarding school and was co-educational. From references in family letters it is evident that the boarding pupils and the Paynes lived together as one family. One of the earliest students was John Gorham Palfrey, subsequently a noted scholar, minister, and historian, who as a motherless lad had been "put to Berry Street" at the age of eight and was at one time Howard Payne's roommate.

Writing many years later, this distinguished alumnus provided the information that the school was located "in the street crossing from Atkinson to Federal Street." [17] Half a century after publication of this statement another authority described the academy as "a little old wooden building at the corner of Berry and Sister Streets" [18] and adjacent to Federal. The latter description of the school building is probably accurate, for William Payne himself is authority for the statement that "our place of literary instruction . . . was erst an ordinary stable." [19] Despite this fact, the academy for a decade was an active institution, to which various prominent New England families entrusted promising offspring. [20]

Neither Berry Street, Sister Street, nor Atkinson Street is found on a modern map of Boston proper. The name Berry Street, it is known, was later changed to Channing Street in honor of William Ellery Channing, leader of American Unitarianism, whose church in Federal Street was very near the school. Even Channing Street, however, was doomed to disappear; although today a small wooden sign at an alleyway near Federal Street, in Boston's financial district, bears the inscription "Channing Place," and this may mark the approximate location of the old school.

Although his wife was a devout Presbyterian, Headmaster Payne had become a Unitarian. He was among Channing's earliest followers in Boston, and was closely associated with the committee of citizens that called the noted minister, then only twenty-three years old, to the Federal Street pulpit. In February 1803 William Payne, writing to his daughter Lucy, absent from home on a visit, remarked: "Our Honourable Committee have succeeded in their overtures to Mr. Channing and his Answer in the Affirmative was read this day to us. Early in April is talked of for his ordination."

Channing's church was not the only historic spot with which the young Paynes had familiar contact in Boston. The old Statehouse—then probably still in active use, although the new edifice on Beacon Hill had lately been erected—was only a few blocks from where they lived. Faneuil Hall, that noted structure designed to combine ideally a public market and a public forum, was also near. Another neighboring landmark was the residence of the elder Payne's kinsman Robert Treat Paine—"a two-story gambrel-roofed mansion at the corner of Milk Street, with gardens reaching back to Federal Street." [21]

We may assume that the Berry Street Academy maintained the scholastic standards for which William Payne had become noted. That its regimen, however, was not one of all work and no play we know from more than one current record. The headmaster himself, in the same letter to his oldest daughter that tells of the acquisition of Channing, remarks: "Your sisters have fallen into rather more parties of amusement than heretofore"; and further: "A course of Particular Instruction which I had set a-going . . . has been entirely superseded by the indispensable demand for all our Young Ladies at Assemblies, Balls, Jambs and various kinds of Racket."

There is also the statement of another notable pupil, Catharine Maria Sedgwick, who would become one of America's pioneer woman novelists. In her early teens Miss Sedgwick spent part of a winter at "Mr. Payne's academy" and recorded in her memoirs that she could not devote herself exclusively to study because of the numerous social diversions. These were apparently no infraction of the Academy's rules.

There was one extracurricular activity at Berry Street definitely related to the academic work and that was the school theater. This was William Payne's particular province. He had always taught elocution, both because of his high regard for dramatic literature and because of a belief, stemming no doubt from his days as a medical student, that declamation was good for the health. From such beginnings he had developed an active interest in things theatrical, which led to establishment at the Academy of "a mimic theatre, with stage, curtains and pit." [22]

This was at a time when many good citizens, retaining a bias of colonial days, still looked down upon the theater. Not only had the Continental lawmakers frowned on the institution, but during and after the Revolution, Congress had passed resolutions to discourage the acting of plays and "to prevent theatrical entertainment, horse racing and such other diversions as are productive of idleness." [23] William Payne, however, was a liberal thinker. He could see no evil in a side course which delighted the pupils at the same time that it increased their appreciation of good literature. The widely published statement that he shared the current prejudice against everything connected with the theater is certainly erroneous.

The performances at Berry Street, usually called "exhibitions," became more and more ambitious. Sometimes scenes of current plays were enacted, with costumes borrowed from the Federal Street Theatre just across the way. All this was a development of far-reaching consequence to the headmaster's second son, John Howard, whose later career as an actor and playwright is directly traceable to these beginnings. From the age of twelve little Howard was given roles in the productions at the school.

The stage seems to have had a peculiar fascination also for Howard's older brother and sisters. At a considerably earlier date—indeed, before the family moved to Boston—the letters of the absent brother William make several references to theatergoing. On his way to Baltimore William had stopped in Philadelphia, and from there he reports to his sister Lucy that he has seen two theatrical performances, one of them *The Grecian Daughter*. William comments on the acting, but says that his employer, Mr. Taylor, "strongly objects to my visiting the plays." Lucy replies with enthusiasm and tells William that she is going to see *The Tragedy of the Fatal Marriage*, to which her brother remarks: "I am glad to see that I am not singular from our family in attachment to theatrical entertainment." He adds: "I think it the best possible school for morality and knowledge of the world. My father always told me so, and that if he could afford it, I should attend the theatre constantly." [24]

As for John Howard, he was soon evincing a desire to experience life professionally from the other side of the footlights. In theatrical

publications that had come his way he had read about the English
boy actor William Henry West Betty, who from the age of eleven
had been creating a sensation in London and Belfast and was said,
indeed, to have achieved a European fame "second only to that of
Napoleon." In London, Pitt was reported to have adjourned a session
of the House of Commons to allow the members to attend a performance by the English boy actor. In Boston the booksellers' windows
were filled with portraits of young Betty as Romeo, as Tancred, even
as Hamlet.

Master Betty, as he was called, became Howard Payne's idol.
"Waking he thought, and sleeping he dreamed, of the laurels of
Betty. He studied, recited and attitudinized, and the vision of weeping boxes and shouting gallery and pit filled his mind." [25] He
wanted to be the Master Betty of America, and "devoted himself
to the reading of plays and the study of dramatic character."

Before he became almost exclusively interested in the theater,
Howard had had other enthusiasms. He was brilliant, like the rest
of the family, though less devoted to study than his brother William
had been at a like age or than the younger boy, Thatcher, was promising to be. He was, besides, more adventurous than either of his
brothers, and displayed a restless originality at an early age.

Picturesquely and perhaps strangely, in view of his peaceful disposition and background, one of Howard's first enterprises was military. At eleven he had organized a little militia company and become its leader. It consisted at first of boys living in the neighborhood of his home, from which it took the name Federal Street Band.

Still in existence, excellently preserved, clearly printed, and distinguished by a literary elegance that betrays their authorship are
several leaflets of this band. One contains the statement that "membership is open to any young gentleman of decent behavior and respectable connections"; another the declaration of the band's object,
"to find a peaceful substitute for the kind of exercise which is frequently detrimental to the morals of such as are not better provided
for." If this be priggish, it at least is not the kind of sentiment that
juvenile delinquency is made of; and in its aims Howard Payne's

little militia might be called a forerunner of the Boy Scout movement.

The military tradition was strong in post-Revolutionary Boston, and parades were matters of public pride, marchers wearing the three-cornered hats and knee breeches of the heroes of Concord and Lexington. On one grand parade day, July 4, 1802, the procession through the town, bands playing, standards flying, had a new and striking feature. In perfect formation following the adult soldiers came a company of young boys, uniformed in blue and white "in exact replica of the Boston Light Infantry," [26] and led by a rosy-cheeked lad of eleven, in plumed helmet, sword by side—Captain John Howard Payne. The thrill was instantaneous. The little company, and especially its leader, forthwith became the idols of the town. It was the first instance of young Payne's attracting wide and admiring attention.

Even while he drilled the Federal Street Band young Payne's literary ambitions were manifesting themselves, and a year or so later he formed the acquaintance of one Samuel Woodworth, a youth from the neighboring town of Scituate, who had come to Boston to learn the printing trade. Woodworth possessed an authentic gift for ballad writing and was later to become famous for his poem, "The Old Oaken Bucket," which with its opening line, "How dear to my heart are the scenes of my childhood," is a more direct tribute to the sights and sounds of early youth than Payne's widely celebrated song. "The Old Oaken Bucket" achieved a place in school readers and was also set to music, and ranks among the most appealing home songs in the language. [27]

Precocious Howard Payne, at thirteen, found a congenial confederate in the virtually grown-up Samuel Woodworth, and when Samuel, at nineteen, launched a little magazine "for the improvement of youth of both sexes," called *The Fly, or Juvenile Miscellany*, Howard became assistant editor. Put forth under the collective pseudonym, "Simon Scribble and Company," the small periodical was published fortnightly and continued for twelve issues—a fairly long life for an effort of its kind at that time.

Notwithstanding its stated dedication to the interests of youth, little in *The Fly* would appeal to boys and girls of the twentieth century, except possibly an occasional quiz column on such topics as geography and mythology. Most numbers contain sketches of famous persons, ancient or contemporary, and very serious articles and poems on such adult abstractions as "Hope" and "Love," a surprising number of them labeled "written for The Fly."

It is suggested that the little publication may have come by its somewhat cryptic name from the fly of a theater. Both young editors were theater-lovers, and a column of general theatrical news appeared in every issue. One number had also a report of "an exhibition" (meaning theatrical) at the Berry Street Academy and commended particularly two of the school's youthful performers, "Master Palfrey" and "Master Payne." There is no way of knowing who wrote this complimentary notice, whether Woodworth or perhaps Payne himself, but Harrison states that Howard at this time had begun to attempt theatrical criticism "which the papers sought."

Whatever his efforts in other fields during the Boston period, Howard was finding himself, through performances at his father's school, more and more admired as a fledgling actor. His growing stage ambition reached its apex with a performance at Berry Street attended by a member of a professional acting company, who, according to Harrison, was "so struck by the boy's personal beauty and remarkable dramatic talent" that he at once called on William Payne and offered to take charge of his son and "to give him all the instruction in his power for one-half the emolument that might be derived from a two-year engagement." The offer was declined. Harrison further declares (and this part of his account has often been reprinted, both with and without credit) that as a result of this episode "Shakespeare was tucked away from his view, Beaumont and Fletcher were hidden among the cobwebs in the rafters of the attic, Congreve was lost."

This statement is chiefly responsible for the widespread belief that William Payne was averse to the theater *per se;* but it seems not in keeping with what we know of the man that he would oppose his son's ambition in quite so arbitrary a way. Not only is it certain that the elder Payne had a high regard for the drama and the art of acting: he must also have realized how much his own interests and tastes contributed to Howard's aspirations, as well as to the fascination the theater held for his other children. Nevertheless the serious suggestion that his young son be embarked upon a theatrical career was an unexpected result of his liberal attitude. He was not prepared to carry a theory so far in practical application. But Howard was "headstrong," whereas his brother William was tractable, and the father was doubtless confronted with a delicate problem in discipline.

Suddenly, in the midst of excitement over Howard's budding fame, the pleasant life of family and school was rocked by tragedy. Word came from New York of the death from quinsy of the oldest brother, William. Not yet twenty-one, William was well launched on a more than promising career. At his work in Baltimore he had done so well as to be sent to New York, and there had soon become a full partner in a mercantile firm. But for all his business success it was characteristic of the young idealist that he should have written (in a letter to Lucy) shortly before his premature end: "I shall never be an exclusive merchant. Never will I be lured by Temptations of Avarice. Nature and Habit have implanted in my heart a contempt for Wealth."

The taking away of young William at the threshold of his maturity was an inexpressible sorrow to his parents. His father speaks in a letter of "the magnitude of a parent's loss of such a son" and adds: "I am exceedingly distressed for his afflicted mother, whose heart was actually involved in his existence." No member of the family could be with William in his illness, and it is probable that before word of his death could reach distant Boston he had already been laid away "in Mr. Gellston's vault in Dr. Spring's old church in Wall Street." [28] The worthy dust of this excellent young man was long since mingled with the foundations of the great, thundering city.

William's death was his parents' third bereavement, as two little daughters had died at the appealing age of three or four. When the family moved to Boston they left in New York, doubtless with many a pang, the little grave of Eliza Maria, "in an old church yard near City Hall, on the Tammany Hall side." The other little sister, Elizabeth Mary, described by her father as "a very promising child," was born and lived her short life in Boston. It was a day when families were large, child diseases not well understood, and the deaths of young children frequent. In keeping seven of their nine children to adulthood, the Paynes were more fortunate than many; but the death of young William was a blow from which neither parent would ever fully recover.

William Jr. was still alive at the time his brother Howard's first stage offer came. Family letters were no doubt exchanged about the matter, and it is quite likely that William's Baltimore employer, William Taylor, with his expressed bias against the stage, had some weight with the boys' father in discouraging Howard's ambition.

Mr. Taylor, a sincere friend of the family, had begun to interest himself in Howard as a possible successor to his brother when William's excellent work in the countinghouse first pointed to his advancement to a higher position. If one Payne boy was a good accountant, another would be, Mr. Taylor doubtless reasoned. He expected any one of the Payne children to be a prodigy, so in Mr. Taylor's view, the fact of Howard's extreme youth was no deterrent to his candidacy for future connection with the firm.

Howard was indeed a prodigy, but of a kind that neither his own father nor Mr. Taylor supposed. William Taylor had first written about Howard when the lad was not quite eleven, and William Payne's reply, dated May 10, 1803, is a candid and enlightening appraisal:

> The mention you so kindly make of our second son is indeed flattering, and we can only hope that he might be equal to what you are willing to suppose he is. He is forward in his education but too considerably short of his brother's advancement at the same age to equal in any good degree what might be expected of him. . . .
>
> The powers of his mind are good and his disposition favorable to early acquirements, but he has been unfortunate in the point of health. His last illness has been the slightest, he has lately recovered and is now going on as I could wish. But he is capable of light service only and is by no

means equal to the management of a regular set of books. Whenever he may be, I am confident that it will be a great excitement to him as it was to his brother, to be employed by your counting house.

This last line may have been added, understandably, out of politeness. It seems, however, to have indicated a sincere belief that the second son would follow in the footsteps of the first, although perhaps less brilliantly. The idea that any boy of eleven might be thought "equal to the management of a regular set of books" does not appear to have seemed preposterous to either William Taylor or William Payne.

The references in this letter to Howard's health, and especially the comment "his last illness has been the slightest," help confirm the boy's somewhat sensational later statement that during three years of his childhood he had suffered from the disease known as St. Vitus' dance.[29] This is a disease that in children is usually curable, and Howard Payne certainly recovered outwardly, though his general health may have been permanently impaired by the early affliction. It must have been in his eighth, ninth, and tenth years that he was the most seriously affected, for at eleven he was leading the little militia, at twelve he made his first amateur stage appearances, and by the time he was thirteen was helping edit *The Fly* and reputedly contributing to adult newspapers.

The father's letter to Mr. Taylor about Howard was written two years before William and Sarah Payne were overwhelmed by the loss of their oldest son. It was a year after that grievous event that John Howard, at fourteen and a half, left home as William had done when a year younger. Howard did not enter Mr. Taylor's employ in Baltimore, however. Instead, he went to New York to work for R. B. Forbes, his late brother's partner.

It may be asked how the parents who had so lately lost a beloved son could send forth another at so early an age. Financial necessity probably had something to do with it. And, too, Howard, apparently recovered from the indispositions of his childhood and entering adolescence, was increasingly a problem. It was necessary to find something to occupy his energy and his too active mind. His parents doubtless hoped that mercantile employment would cure him of his interest in the stage as a career and at the same time serve to launch him on a useful way of life. In that, however, they were mistaken.

[4]

THE WONDER BOY

"An example of precocious talent, the like of which I doubt whether this country has produced, and the object of adulation such as I have never known to be bestowed upon any other young person." John Gorham Palfrey in Boston *Evening Gazette*, May 29, 1852.

WITH his coming to New York to work in September 1805 Payne began his life of wandering. Now for the first time he was homeless.

The office of his employer, formerly the firm of Forbes and Payne, was at 65 South Street. At this point the celebrated Street of Ships is met by Wall Street, which comes to an end there on the water front.

Facing the broad, cobblestoned causeway to the docks, where ships of all nations were arriving and departing, this was a fascinating location. Packets from Liverpool sailed regally into port with passengers and mail; merchantmen from the Orient unloaded their spices and silks to reload with the solid produce of the New World. For many a youth all this would have held great attraction. But young Payne's interests were not commercial; neither, apparently, were they nautical.

"I have been an unconcerned observer in the bustle of the city," he wrote in his first letter to the home folks. "Since that moment when I parted from the best of parents (perhaps forever!) I have felt myself, as it were, destitute, forsaken and alone."

Though thus forlornly it began, the New York period was to prove for the lonely lad one of unexpected brilliance. Within a few months he was to achieve such premature prominence as few boys have ever been so unfortunate as to experience. He was to be sought by young and old, admired, applauded, advised, and abused. He was to become *news*, talked and written about all up and down the Atlantic Coast and as far inland as the country then extended.

None of this, however, was anticipated when, "a rosy-cheeked boy with his collar open and tied with a black ribbon," [30] he first entered the South Street countinghouse, mounted a high stool before a slant-top desk, and with an inward if not an audible sigh, opened the big ledger before him.

If discipline had been an object of the boy's parents in sending him to New York to work, in that they were strongly abetted by his employer. R. B. Forbes [31] was a stern taskmaster. He perceived at once that the new bookkeeper was not a copy of his brother, who at twenty had been made a full partner in the firm. Perhaps Mr. Forbes had hoped eventually to have another Payne boy as a partner. If so, he very quickly changed his mind. No doubt he was hearing rumors that the younger Payne was more than a little stage-struck; and he turned the screws of discipline the tighter. "Mr. Forbes is to others kind and gentle; to me he is inattentive and almost insolent," says one of the early letters to the family.

Nevertheless the boy worked hard at the bookkeeping job. He tried to apply himself to a task to which neither his head nor his heart inclined. At night he went back to Pearl Street—but to No. 86 this time—where was located Mrs. Saltonstall's boardinghouse. There he was the youngest of "three or four gentleman boarders," and to his great dislike the fellow lodgers called him Jack. From this it is apparent that he had elected in his new life to be known by his first instead of his middle name.

In the years the Paynes had lived in Boston New York had grown and changed. Broadway now had street lamps, even above Canal Street.[32] The old-time residential sections of the Battery and Wall and William streets had burst their bounds, and there were now "many handsome new homes" and "tiled and corniced brick houses" in Greenwich Street. And there was another notable change in that the town pumps were falling into disuse (though thriftily preserved for emergency), since the city's water supply now came from the

Manhattan Waterworks, by which the water was "raised by steam and carried to a reservoir in Chambers Street, whence it was conveyed by pipes to every part of the city." [33]

Neither waterworks nor water front, however, had much attraction for John Howard, but there was a point in between which drew him like a loadstone. That was the Park Theatre on Park Row, facing the large open space where the foundation had lately been laid for New York's still-standing City Hall.

It was in the direction of the theater that the boy's eager footsteps would always have carried him when the day's work at the office was done, but for two considerations: first, his funds were limited; and second, the requirements of his work—sometimes twelve hours a day, six days a week—were not conducive to theatergoing. For in those days the doors opened at five o'clock, and the curtain rose at half past six; [34] and, like the double-feature picture houses of a century later, the theater gave the audience its money's worth, with two full plays, a main piece and an afterpiece. Since the first play was the more important, one who could not be on hand when it began had to miss the best part of the show. And John was often unable to arrive until the first half had nearly ended.

The uncongenial office grind went on for two or three months before the turning point came, and on the twelfth of December we find the boy writing to his father: "I am now almost a fortnight without advices of any kind from Boston, and this has served to heighten the gloom of my present situation, which, I assure you, is even more tedious than anticipated." By Mr. Forbes, this letter states, the new clerk is prohibited "under the most strict orders, *every amusement* and even denied the possibility of obtaining the *means* of indulging in any sort of recreation." He then tells of having bought a newspaper, the *Evening Post*, in order to read the theatrical news and describes the anger of his employer on learning of this. "With Mr. Forbes I can never be happy," this letter concludes. [35]

Very soon afterward he seems to have found what might have been a way out of the unhappy situation, for he tells his father of having received an offer to appear on the stage once a week: "I can get an engagement which will yield a handsome profit, which I should insist upon devoting to the interests of the family." Apparently his father advised against acceptance.

Denied one opportunity of escape, John sought another, though just when he found time to launch his first independent venture is a mystery. By his own statement, typical of his literary style at the time, he was "often obliged to watch the glimmerings of the midnight taper" and to "pen his lucubrations in the hours usually devoted to repose."

These "lucubrations" were to grace the justly celebrated little *Thespian Mirror*, which, seemingly out of the nowhere, first appeared in the stalls of the booksellers on December 28, 1805. As the first number was prepared in three days, John must have spent his first homeless Christmas in a novel manner.

New Yorkers of the period were avid newspaper readers. During the first decade of the century more than a dozen newspapers were published in the city, then of 80,000 inhabitants, and of these at least seven were dailies.[36] Among the more prominent were the venerable *Daily Gazette and General Advertiser*, established in 1785, the *Commercial Advertiser*, first published by Noah Webster in 1793, and the *American Citizen*, more recent but equally influential. Two newer dailies were the *Morning Courier*, edited by Washington Irving's brother Peter, and the *Evening Post*. The *Post*, established in 1801 by Alexander Hamilton, was in 1805 still associated in the public mind with Hamilton's sensational end the year before.

To readers accustomed to a mélange of advertising and politics in the public prints a new and refreshingly different periodical was a welcome surprise. The *Thespian Mirror* was the city's first publication devoted exclusively to the theater, and had it had a longer life, it might be ranked as an important pioneer.

A tiny eight-page sheet about 5 by 9 inches, it was attractively printed on paper of good quality, and it promised to be weekly. Its news, critiques, and sketches of stage personalities were dignified and written with an elegance of style then highly approved; and, to add to the piquancy of its sudden appearance, it was altogether anonymous. Nobody dreamed that the originator and editor was a fourteen-year-old boy who sat all day on a high stool in a countinghouse, endeavoring to bend his poetic mind to the dreary subject of mercantile bookkeeping.

"Chiefly intended to promote the interests of American drama," so its opening number stated, "and to eradicate false impressions respecting the nature, objects, design and general tendency of theatrical amusements," the little publication was politely presented "to the enlightened citizens of New York." (This has been twisted by a twentieth-century writer into the statement that Payne's declared purpose was "to enlighten the citizens of New York" [37]—merely one example of the careless distortion to which he has so often been subjected.)

The *Mirror's* "Entertainments of the Week" section contains items that are engaging as theatrical history. A current attraction was "Sheridan's opera of *The Duenna*, which possesses sterling merit and is attractive without extraordinary aid from the actors," according to the boy editor. James Fennell, a British tragedian who for some years had been connected with the Philadelphia Theatre, was on a visit to New York and had been "prevailed upon to run through his principal dramatic characters on our stage." Mrs. Jones and Mrs. Johnson, local stars whose particular brightness seems not to have been dimmed by the similarity of their none too distinguishing names, were delighting theatergoers in varied repertories ranging all the way from Shakespeare to *Country Girl, Poet in Petticoats,* and *No Song, No Supper; or, the Lawyer in the Sack.*

The public had reason to admire these two celebrated ladies of the stage. Mrs. Johnson, wife of one of the managers of the theater, was "a tall, beautiful woman, whose taste in dress made her a model for the belles of the day." Mrs. Jones, a singing actress from the Haymarket, London, was a half sister of the later celebrated English actors Henry and James Wallack. "Youthful, petite in person, with a pleasing face and exceedingly sprightly," [38] she was highly regarded as a comedienne, and one of her most popular roles was Little Pickle in *Spoiled Child*, a play without which no repertory at the time was complete. She was also something of a sensation for having once scandalized the good citizens of Boston by appearing in a "breeches part."

Not content with purveying news alone, Payne essayed some criticism. There is this bit of advice to a would-be interpreter of Romeo:

> Reading and literary information are essentials to a good actor; and a perfect acquaintance with at least *one language* is indispensable. The celebrated Kemble is said to have bestowed months, and indeed years, upon a single character. It is not unmeaning words, words, words, that he commits to memory—it is ideas, ideas, ideas.
>
> Lady Montague relates an instance of a lady at Constantinople who fell in love with a *dictionary*. If this gentleman could form a like attachment and take advantage of the passion by correcting his accent and pronunciation, he would give pleasure where he now offends propriety.

There are also comments upon the appearance of the "dramatic works of Mr. Dunlap" [39]—opinions in one respect many years ahead of the time:

> If foreign plays are printed, sold and reprinted in America, where is patriotism, that the exertions of native genius are discouraged? Where sleeps the public spirit, which gives the literature of its country to lumber the shelves of the booksellers? Why is native genius allowed to waste itself in obscurity when editions of foreign publications are multiplied in our city?

And most ingenuous of all the *Thespian Mirror's* contents is the youthful editor's panegyric on the stage:

> It cannot be denied that the STAGE is calculated for purposes at once the most laudable and useful. From its glowing and impressive representations, the Tyrant is induced to relax his wonted severity, the hand of Avarice is opened to the generous influence of Benevolence; the wantonness of the profligate is succeeded by philanthropic thoughtfulness; the asperity of Misanthropy is softened into charity and cheerfulness; the conscience of the criminal is struck to repentance.

This is summed up at another point in a declaration strongly reminiscent of young Payne's revered brother William: "The stage is the epitome of men and manners and the teacher of virtue and morality."

From what a lofty height was this youth approaching the work which would occupy the best years of his life!

New Yorkers who obtained a copy of the first *Thespian Mirror* sang its praises and eagerly awaited the second, which duly appeared on the first Saturday in the new year, 1806. A third followed a week later, and with each issue curiosity grew as to the source of the engaging new publication. Except for the printers—Southwick and Hardcastle, conveniently located at 2 Wall Street, just around the corner from his place of employment—John had shared the secret only with "three young men in the office" [40] and a few contributors of poems, but it was bound eventually to leak out. Immediately the young editor found himself the object of such flattering attention as to make pale the praise he had received in Boston as boy actor and as leader of the Federal Street Band. It was not the flattery of the undiscriminating, however, but was joined by persons regarded as among the town's intellectuals.

It is sometimes stated that Washington Irving was of this number, but Irving, abroad at the time, could not have made Payne's acquaintance until some time in the ensuing spring. That Irving's prominent and affluent friend Henry Brevoort, nine years Payne's senior, did seek out the young celebrity, we know by the following formal note:

To Mr. Payne
  Mrs. Saltonstall's
    Pearl Street
Dear Sir,
  I did myself the pleasure of calling at your Lodgings this evening; finding you absent, I take the liberty without apologizing of addressing a line to you. Will you do me the favor of taking with me an unceremonious and friendly dinner tomorrow at Thompson's B House corner of B Way & Cedar St?
  If you are not particularly engaged, you will confer additional pleasure by calling at 12 o'clock, as I am very desirous of having a familiar tete a tete for an hour or so before dinner, as well as to make you acquainted with a young lady who has importuned me to see you.
                    I am
                      Dr Sir
                        Yr. fd. &c
                          Henry Brevoort Junr.
Saturday Evg.
  8 ocl'k: Feb 1. [41]

Though the mails were still conveyed overland by post rider or horse-drawn coach, news of some kinds spread rapidly from town to town in those days. Philadelphia was soon agog about the *Thespian Mirror*, and the *Port-Folio* of February 4, 1806 in its column of New York correspondence, declared: "The little editor of the *Thespian Mirror* is almost the only topic of fashionable table talk" and followed this with what is apparently the first printed reference to Payne's later widely celebrated physical charms:

> This miraculous youth possesses a person short for his age, yet well-proportioned and graceful; a large, blue eye of the most unusual sweetness and expression and a complexion of the most susceptible delicacy. His voice is music itself.[42]

Boston also had heard about young Payne's new activity; but the home folks were almost the last to know of their boy's sensational fame. Three months after the first appearance of the *Thespian Mirror* his sister Eloise wrote in some agitation to Catharine Sedgwick that "Brother Howard's late schemes in the city were totally unknown to us until after they had been for some time the subject of conversation in our town. You may judge of our astonishment. We observed that the approbation and even admiration of some individuals were excited—this by no means set our minds at ease. We knew not how the minds of the judicious and discerning were affected."

No small part of the family's concern was for the effect of all the excitement on John's health. "You know the terrible malady with which he was afflicted for three years," continued this letter of his earnest sister, who was further dismayed that not only his journalistic feat "but even his personal appearance" had been publicized.[43]

John was sublimely unconscious of his family's anxiety. After the secret of the *Mirror* had become public property he wrote his father about the new venture, declaring that he had embarked on it "because my mercantile life grows hourly more irksome," but adding dutifully: "If I can bear it till I hear from you, I will."

He had considered at first a publication to be called *The Pastime*, for the exclusive perusal of youth, he tells his father, but had decided that "something new, something striking, is necessary 'to take,' something keyed to the prevailing love of pleasure." Optimistically he was calculating on 500 subscribers at $2. "The deduction of expenses from $1000 will leave *something*. That something will be devoted to the purposes of the family." This second reference to his wish to assist the family suggests financial difficulties at home, though undoubtedly the best assistance he could reasonably hope to give would have been in taking care of himself.

The *Thespian Mirror's* first notice in the *Evening Post* (the paper which had caused the altercation with Mr. Forbes) seemed equivocal, but it was to have important consequences. That famous paper was edited at the time by William Coleman, a political follower of Hamilton and an opponent of Jefferson. Coleman was a peppery individual, whose vitriolic writings had once caused him to be challenged by a rival journalist to a duel, although it was never fought. He was nevertheless regarded as a man of integrity as well as of literary tastes; and it so happened that before entering journalism he had studied law in the office of William Payne's cousin, Robert Treat Paine.

Noting the appearance of the *Thespian Mirror*, Coleman had remarked that the *Post's* Criticus lacked time for adequate comment in the current issue, but promised to provide that later. The boy editor read this with perturbation, aware that his first number had contained a few inaccuracies. He hastened to write the editor of the *Post* begging him to be merciful in view of his own "extreme youth . . . being under 14 years of age." (Here, according to authentic family records and every other statement of the matter ever made or authorized by Payne, he was making himself out a year younger than he actually was.)

Interested though incredulous—and he would have been scarcely less so had he thought John only instead of under fourteen—Coleman wrote the *Mirror's* editor inviting him to tea the same evening at his home, 30 Hudson Street. "Perhaps the visit may be serviceable to the young gentleman in his future progress," the invitation added.

John accepted the pleasing summons, but in so doing he reckoned without Mr. Forbes. That stern gentleman had naturally heard by now about his clerk's outside occupation, and his wrath can be imagined. He only piled the work the higher, and on that particular evening John was kept so late at the countinghouse that he could not get to Coleman's home in time for tea. When he did arrive, his none too patient host had gone out.

The seeming social lapse was forgiven when John called the next morning and explained. Mr. Coleman quickly perceived what Mr. Forbes had not: that here was a lad of exceptional gifts, whatever his attitude toward bookkeeping, "as amiable in disposition, ingenious in behavior and correct in sentiment as wonderful in talents. It required an effort on my part to keep up the conversation in as choice a style as his own." Coleman also had the discernment to see that the boy, although so precocious, was naturally immature, at once overripe and underdeveloped. What he needed and deserved, Mr. Coleman felt, was further education. Would not John like to go to college? John would, but his father could not afford to send him. Mr. Coleman was not himself in a position to finance a college education for the youth, but he set about finding someone who was.

Shortly after the visit Coleman, through the columns of his paper, delivered himself of this encomium:

> In my judgement we have scarcely anything in the annals of letters that is superior to the prosaic production of this youth. Boys have sometimes appeared who wrote pretty, nay good, verses at an early age; but nothing can be found in the youthful efforts of Cowley, Pope, Milton and Chatterton evincing a strength of mind superior to the ordinary and daily production of this little lad I now do myself the pleasure to notice.

Then follows Coleman's revelation that "three years of his little life have been, as it were, blotted out by disease, having during that period labored under what is called St. Vitus' dance."

This is the only direct statement yet found of the nature of Payne's early physical disorder; and publication of it at the time might seem unfortunate. But nothing written or said appears to have been damaging to the prodigy, and soon Coleman was writing William Payne of a proposal that a fund be established "to give your son a college education and have him finish with a law course. Or to find him a situation in some lawyer's office, under some gentleman whose character and professional celebrity would be security for his having every advantage, both mental and moral, and in whose family he

could reside." Among interested persons Coleman mentioned Dr.
Hosack, the physician whose fame had been enhanced by his attendance upon the dying Hamilton the year before; Judge Pendleton, an eminent jurist, and "a number of gentlemen of equal respectability and fortune." [44]

Eventually the several prospective patrons dwindled to one not
originally mentioned: John E. Seaman, "a merchant of the first respectability" who had been a friend and admirer of young William
Payne and was therefore especially well disposed toward the younger
brother. Like everybody else, Mr. Seaman was charmed by John
Howard. Not only did he gladly consent to send the boy to college:
in the enthusiasm of first acquaintance he even suggested adopting
the prodigy and making him his heir. Mr. Coleman, however, sagely
counseled postponement of adoption, at least until the projected college course was completed.

While John's unsolicited benefactors planned, the *Thespian Mirror* continued to appear each week. This was against the advice of
Mr. Coleman, who felt that the combined duties of editor and bookkeeper were too great a tax on the boy's health. Here again Coleman
was wise, but John did not think so. Within a few weeks he had become a sensation, not only as editor, but as author of a play that
he somehow managed to put forth early in February. Quite naturally
he had formed an exaggerated idea of his own importance.

When Seaman likewise counseled against continuance of the theatrical publication, however, the advice was heeded; and in the thirteenth issue of the *Mirror*, dated March 22, 1806 (and incidentally
the first to carry Payne's name), is the statement that the editor
"has resolved to relinquish his editorial duties in order more particularly to devote himself to studies, which may promote his future
usefulness in life." This issue pays high tribute to "one to whom he
feels obligations he cannot express" (Mr. Seaman), but makes no
mention of Mr. Coleman.

The omission was perhaps unintentional, but it was apparently
not unnoticed by the *Evening Post's* editor, who in the next issue
of his paper commented somewhat caustically that the *Mirror's*
early numbers had been better than the later. He also took occasion

to remark, of young Payne's theatrical criticisms, that "they have served, they could serve, no other purpose than to make him enemies"—an ironic judgment, for Coleman, in an early talk with Payne, had observed that the *Mirror* dealt too much in praise, and had advised more criticism.

As it turned out, the thirteenth was not the final *Thespian Mirror* after all. A real valedictory issue appeared two months later (on May 31) and reading it, one cannot but feel that it may have been brought out especially to make amends to Coleman. For in this number is printed the entire original correspondence with the *Evening Post* editor, "together with every acknowledgment to which his kindness is so justly entitled."

This was in essence a public apology, but it is doubtful if the disgruntled Mr. Coleman was entirely mollified. In fact, from too great enthusiasm at the start Coleman had now gone to the other extreme. Seaman, however, remained convinced of John's ability and worth, and willing to provide the practical means of advancing his career.

[5]

THE BOY PLAYWRIGHT

PAYNE's first play and its reception, though overlooked by previous biographers, constitute, in the opinion of the present writer, one of the most significant episodes of his entire career.

It was before his *Thespian Mirror* had been in existence two months that the astonishing youth burst forth with this new achievement, the original play *Julia; or, the Wanderer, a comedy in five acts*. It was performed at the Park by a group of the city's best actors on February 7, 1806.

The question of when the twelve-hour clerk found time to write it is baffling. According to a statement in the press—one which, in view of his known activities at all other hours, it seems reasonable to accept—*Julia* was "wholly written and copied in the space of seven evenings." And as the play was performed immediately upon completion, the labor must have included the longhand copying of the various parts.

Following the custom of a time when every newspaper carried contributions signed by Latinish pseudonyms, Payne presented his play under a *nom de guerre*. "Written by Eugenius, a gentleman of New York," said the notices. The public soon learned, however—indeed, everybody seems to have known in advance—that the playwright was that fourteen-year-old boy, scarcely more than a child, who had sprung into fame within a few short weeks and had already earned for himself the extremes of praise and blame.

However *Julia* may rank as an actable work for the stage, the play, when read, is fast-moving, witty, amazingly penetrating in thought: on the whole a very striking manifestation of talent. Its production, however, was far from successful, and despite some warm defenders it was so violently attacked in the press, chiefly for "indecorous incidents" and "objectionable language," as to be withdrawn after a single performance.

Being a satire on life in general, *Julia* needed no particular period or locale. Its scene is "a country town and vicinity" and its time "36 hours." Its characters (there are seventeen of them) are outwardly two-dimensional, but that is all they are supposed to be—so many animated paper dolls skipping about the stage in a series of mirth-provoking incidents, but spouting sprightly lines, which prove that the farcical creatures have substance after all.

Julia, the heroine, is that most conventional of stage creatures of the period, an orphan girl, beautiful of course, sublimely innocent, and aged sixteen. Stolen from home in infancy by her uncle, a cruel, miserly, interest-compounding country squire (here Payne gets in some delicious digs at respected commercial practices), Julia has been brought up by a neighboring farmer who loves her as a daughter, though his spiteful wife casts her out upon the world.

The curtain rises on "an opening in the forest." The time is "sunrise, hunters in the distance." One of the hunters is Frederick, a truly noble youth and inevitably Julia's affinity, who in the opening speech tells his companion, the mischievous rake Ranger: "I am heartily tired of the chase. . . . It hurts my feelings to see the poor animal torn to pieces. I doubt, Ranger, whether we are not violating the laws of humanity." To this, Ranger sets the shocking tone of the piece by replying: "Oh, damme, Fred, none of your philosophy."

Ranger, in fact, says "damme" several times in the play, and that alone may have been enough to damn it with an audience of the time. In addition there is the indubitable fact that some of the play's humor borders on the *risqué*, and, from a youthful applicant for public favor, that was altogether too much in the New York of the good year 1806.

When Julia, "an angel and unprotected," is discovered "wandering alone in a forest at sunrise" (which, as Ranger remarks, "may be virtue, but whip me if there is any prudence in it") that lighthearted profligate at once tries to kiss her. From this and implied worse consequences Julia is saved by the intervention of the noble Frederick.

Julia finds refuge in the home of a "man of benevolence"—actually her own father, brother to the miser who has stolen her in infancy, though with the usual imbecility of stage parents of lost children, the father fails to suspect her identity. Now enters Harry, nephew to both the philanthropist and the villainous miser. Another impish character, quite out-Rangering Ranger, Harry soon spreads the tale that the wandering Julia is the mistress of his parsimonious uncle. And for a counterplot there is Ranger's courtship of Maria, Harry's sister, who surprisingly develops into a thoughtful and highminded character, while fitting neatly into the merry plot.

The play proceeds through a series of hilarious incidents. Harry's tricks directed against his mean uncle include dropping the old fellow through a trap door into the basement (where luckily he lands on a bed) and bribing discharged servants to set his barns on fire. It is all pure fun, of course: nobody is seriously injured, the villains repent, the good are rewarded, and Julia and Frederick are betrothed with everybody's blessing.

It is obvious that a dramatic story such as this could become the acme of banality unless performed with the same kind of tongue-in-cheek whimsicality as had gone into its writing. Despite a distinguished cast—the "modest, delicate and amiable" [45] Mrs. Jones in the title role, the company's two actor-managers, Young and Tyler, as Ranger and the benevolent uncle, and as Frederick "Hallam junior," member of the famous family credited as founders of the theater in America [46]—apparently not all the players understood the play. According to at least two statements in the press, some of the performers changed lines to suit themselves, thus perverting and destroying meanings—a liberty they might not have taken had the author been a person of mature years instead of "a little boy."

For several days following the single presentation, which was on a Friday night, the play's merits and demerits were debated in the press. We are not told whether the audience was large or small, but one unfriendly commentator gives us an engaging picture of the young author (his "susceptible complexion" doubtless a little pinker than usual) "modestly seated in a stage box, where nothing could have escaped him, not even the hisses of condemnation, as judiciously bestowed as could have been expected."

Previously, the first critique, adverse, though mild compared with some to follow, had appeared in Peter Irving's *Morning Chronicle,* which not only found the piece "destitute of that delicacy of which the simplicity of our manners and the purity of our morals demand a scrupulous observance," but also concluded that "in its present condition, it will not, unless we are mistaken, *go down.*"

Payne's friend Mr. Coleman, the *Evening Post* editor, whose ardor, we have seen, was cooling, had apparently been warned in advance and had found himself unable to attend what was to have been the first of several performances; but the *Post* reprinted the comments of the morning paper as "perfectly just, so far as we could judge, from what we heard in the tearoom."

Now, what might Mr. Coleman have observed had he seen and heard the play himself, instead of repeating the opinions of others? Perhaps a glance at a few scenes will suggest an answer, though any selection of excerpts from *Julia* must omit others equally facetious and at times piquant. After the Act I opening episode in the forest we come to

Scene 2, the house of *Longville* [benevolent uncle]. *Longville* and *Dennis* [Irish tavern keeper] are discovered.

Longville: Well, Dennis, I have considered the sterility of the season and the pestilence that has prevailed . . . and shall not only abate your rent but forgive it.

Dennis: Och, upon my soul, sir, I wount take it. I cleared 13 and 9 pence last year that rightfully belongs to your honor, but Mrs. O'Dennis that loves to paint her nose, crept into the bar . . . and spoilt all the year's savings.

Longville: Here, Dennis, is a 50-pound note: use it as you please— your improvements about the house are worth that much to me.

Dennis (looking out): Och, hulaboo, do you see that pretty crature coming here? The very image of St. Mary herself—och, the lambkin. Mrs. O'Dennis, were you only put out of the way now, that I might look on a pretty face!

Enter *Frederick*, leading *Julia* [just rescued from the dishonorable intentions of *Ranger*].

Longville: I am happy to see you—this is a stranger I have not had the pleasure of—

Frederick: An unhappy wanderer, sir, whom I found this morning as I was pursuing the chase. . . . I have taken the liberty to commend her to your patronage and protection.

Longville: You give me pleasure, Frederick. She shall have a shelter under my roof. . . . The friendless and destitute have a rightful demand on every man.

Julia: Your kindness overpowers me. I can only speak my gratitude with my tears.

Dennis (coming forward): Och, my soul—beauty should never cry a tear. Take a 50-pound note, my dear creature, and wipe them pretty eyes of yours.

Longville: Dennis, this is a guest of mine.

Dennis: A pretty woman in tears is every soul's guest. . . .

Act II, scene 4. Outside *Dennis's* tavern. *Ranger* and *Harry* discovered drinking.

Ranger: Let us think of Diana [Julia]. What is your report on the case?

Harry: She is under the roof of old Longville and never ventures out but in company with him.

Ranger: That is bad, but we will look over the vocabulary of intrigue for a remedy.

Harry: You have a head, my lad, there's no doubt of success. . . . Suppose we could see her out alone—what's to be done?

Ranger: Look ye. Old Longville rides out every evening . . . no doubt our fair one will be a companion with him. I know his route. I will set upon him with a brace of servants and get the old man secured. While I am carrying off the prize, *you*—you must suddenly rush upon us: this will necessarily induce a quarrel, the issue of which will be your death. Then, if you can't manage for yourself . . . you will never be hung for your wit.

Harry: Bravo, give me your hand, my dear fellow! But what the devil can induce you to make such a sacrifice of happiness for me?

Ranger: Sacrifice? Why, Hal, I wouldn't give the novelty and romance of this adventure for all the girls in the world. My pleasures consist in their eccentricity. . . .

[Another scene. *Harry* and *Ranger* again meeting.]

Harry: But how goes the affair of my sister Maria? You'll make a pretty-looking husband.

Ranger: Our guardian, forbidding me the house, keeps Maria locked up.

Harry: Is there no window, door or scuttle? No hole through which a man might pass?

Ranger: I never thought of it. . . . But suppose I contrive to place a letter in the hands of Maria, requesting her to feign illness, and attend her in the garb of a physician, advise a little exercise in the garden, have my postchaise at the gate, slip into it and off. . . . Luck, luck, there's Maria's chamber maid now. I'll call her.

Chamber Maid: La! Your honor is very strange to me. I'm sure I never seed you before.

Ranger: Sit down, my pretty girl. I want to make a bargain with you (seats her in a chair).

Chamber Maid: I hope your honor has no intentions. . . . I shall scream.

Ranger: Women's fears and expectations are eternally putting ideas into a man's head he otherwise would not think of. I want you simply to carry a letter to your mistress. . . .

Act III, scene 2. Another part of the street. Enter *Maria* and *Ranger*. [*Maria* has learned that it was *Ranger* who tried to seduce *Julia* in the forest.]

Ranger: I trust, Maria, you do not suspect my honor.

Maria: I have had serious reasons to induce me to do so.

Ranger: I submit to it. Suspect everything but my honorable intentions towards you.

Maria: And when a man despises the sentiments and opinions of the world; when he puts no value on his moral character, tramples the laws of society and private virtue . . . is it sufficient to satisfy the fears and anxieties of the woman who is about to put her happiness at his disposal, that he singles her alone from his profligacy? To the whole sex ungenerous, would you not laugh at my credulity could I believe you constant, alone, to me?

Ranger: Your rebuke reaches my heart.

Maria: Yes, but through an unworthy channel. . . . It is the sordid wish of possessing my person which gives them their force.

Ranger: You pursue my thoughts into all their recesses. What can I do to merit your approbation?

Maria: Repent, discard your vices.

Ranger: I will begin by discovering the retreat of Julia . . . by your assistance we can avert the machinations of your brother, who is now her only persecutor. . . .

Maria assumes male attire, releases Julia from Dennis's tavern, where Harry has secreted her, summons Frederick and Longville (now revealed as Julia's father), and thus hastes the happy ending.[47]

These, at least are high lights of the action, though there are numerous other lively episodes. And it cannot be known, of course, that the quoted lines give a true account of the play as acted, since the author's public defenders complained of "numerous mutilations of the language." The first of them was Criticus, whose letter in the *American Citizen* on the Monday after the performance declared this fault "so great as to destroy the connection of incident and to place in jeopardy the reception of the play."

An even stronger exonerative effort followed—a column and a half in the *Commercial Advertiser* signed "Theatricus." It was prefaced by a statement of the editor that, although he had not seen the play, he believed it to have been "severely and unwarrantably attacked," since "in the opinion of several gentlemen of intelligence and judgment and taste, who have perused it in manuscript," it was *"a very respectable production."*

Theatricus was among those "honored by perusal of the play before it was performed." Now he complains that he "hardly knew it under the disguise thrown over it by the actors," whom he found "so palpably deficient in their parts as to paralyze every effort of grace."

It is doubtful, however, if this strong defense did not do the author more harm than good, for Theatricus proceeded to dissect the individual actors, who, since they were the best the city then afforded, were doubtless accustomed principally to praise. This may have been especially true of that universal favorite, Mrs. Jones, whom Theatricus pronounced "wholly incompetent, except in songs and even in them, imperfect." Payne's own *Thespian Mirror* had repeatedly lauded Mrs. Jones, and it was apparently with her vocal talents in mind that he had created the character of Julia, who is made to bemoan her fate in song.

Theatricus, apparently apprehensive that the author's youth might be against him, calls him "a young man of about 21," but, even so, advises him "not to be daunted by attacks" and concludes: "Should the respectable part of the population be influenced by the little wits of the day to withhold the requisite culture from this native germ, it will be a new instance of many examples of neglect which genius has experienced on our shores."

Almost before the ink was dry on this eloquent plea the "little wits" had triumphed, and through the evening papers of Tuesday the 11th the managers of the theater "respectfully informed the public" that Eugenius, on the advice of friends, had withdrawn his play.

Thus, besides the disappointment of artistic failure and the shock of public disapproval, Eugenius suffered material loss, for the second performance was to have been his "benefit." In those days, when neither playwrights nor actors were regularly or adequately compensated, benefits were quite the accepted order, and through them, even the greatest of theatrical persons were not averse to recouping the routine losses of their precarious trade.

Julia; or, the Wanderer was damned, never to be revived; but that part of the population most deeply offended by the play's unconventional originality could not let the matter drop. Curatii was the next pseudonymous critic to rush into print; he also through the

Commercial Advertiser, which was not averse to presenting both sides.

This observer's approbation of Eugenius's action in withdrawing the piece "could have been given in silence had not some person, calling himself 'Theatricus' attempted its vindication." Hence Curatii feels called upon to declare it "not only a negative production, deficient in every requisite to amuse or interest, but replete with criminal sentiments and indecorous observations."

Curatii was mild, though, compared with Thespis, to whose reply to Theatricus the *Evening Post* next day allowed more than a column of vituperative comment. First accusing Eugenius of having himself written the Theatricus letter, then owning this to be an error and withdrawing the accusation,[48] Thespis none the less blazes away. He complains of the "indecencies and smutty incidents with which the play is adorned," its "combination of stilted and indecent language with absurd and formless plotting . . . incidents offensive to the cheek of modesty, [which] ought to meet the chastisement of undisguised opprobrium." Eugenius is advised to "dismiss a portion of that unbecoming vanity which leads him to overrate his capacity and misapply his talents in a manner that can neither be valuable to society nor profitable to himself." [49]

While the arrows of condemnation thus showered about him, what must have been the feelings of the boy who was misfit bookkeeper "from 8 in the morning until after 8 at night" [50] and editor-author-playwright at all other hours? One, we strongly believe, was the mixed emotion of gratitude toward his champion Theatricus and dismay at the offense that friend might have given those other warm friends, the actors.

The controversy came to an end when the *Evening Post* of February 14, "with undissembled pleasure," gave space to a "well-written, very proper and very well-timed note of the author of *The Wanderer*" addressed to the managers of the theater, in which he absolved the actors from the general abuse:

> The performers are entitled to my warmest gratitude . . . and I am doubly indebted to Mrs. Jones for her care and anxiety to make the character of Julia meet with success. . . . Rest assured, gentlemen, no one has your success more at heart than Eugenius.

To Thespis, severest of Eugenius's critics, we are indebted for a query of some penetration. Obliged to admit that the play "no doubt is a surprising production for a youthful genius," this self-appointed judge nevertheless observes that "no small part of the astonishment is aroused" by the question as to where the prodigy could have learned so much sophistication ("such vile episodes and the language in which to clothe their meanings" is the way Thespis puts it).

Today the language does not seem vile, though it is still surprising that a fourteen-year-old could create characters to mouth lines so worldly wise as these: "He could not possibly appreciate her worth unless he suspected her virtue." "An obliging girl is worth all the wives in heaven." "There's not a pretty, blushing Diana between this and paradise who does not love a rake from the bottom of her heart." "What signifies the loss of one girl? The country's full of them." "Yes, the avarice of man will discover villainy when every other means proves abortive." "A vain show of wit you were at a loss to dispose of. An itching to make another appear ridiculous."

But not everything in the five acts of *Julia* is so lightly cynical. A few of its characters give voice to thoughts with quite a sober sound: "I despise a power built on the basis of riches. Money may oppress honest integrity for a time, but it will soon escape its grasp." " 'Tis thus the sanguine wishes of the heart deceive the indulgent eyes of a lover, and we see a thousand virtues in the object of our adoration which exist nowhere but in our fancy."

There is, besides, a priceless bit of humor in Maria's "The very thought of a doctor makes me feel better." And this is followed by a striking mock-poetic outburst, whimsically enough assigned to Harry at the height of his sportive revenge against his uncle:

> Thou bright moon and jovial stars! Peep through the blanket of the sky and shout applause! Old Boreas, too, with solemn blast and strong reiterating, bear the trembling echo to the astonished south!

The author's astonishing discernment is not all that impresses the reader of Payne's first play. One feels a genuine creative spark in the young playwright; but it was a spark quickly extinguished by the storm his effort aroused. And this rebuff may have caused a more than temporary thwarting of ambition. The force of adult opposition may then and there have robbed the overwrought and physically delicate boy of something that he would never regain: it may, indeed, have had an inhibiting effect upon his whole later life.

This little play, a spontaneous emanation, was like a flower brought to bloom by a premature spring day, only to be blasted by an ensuing freeze. Payne would remain self-willed, temperamental, and filled with ideas and plans; but this experience may have implanted in him an unconscious distrust of his own creative powers from which he would not recover easily, if at all.

Unfortunately, the adverse reports of this play have far outlived favorable judgments, and today most writers who mention it at all either refer to it slightingly or echo sentiments of the author's disapproving contemporaries. It is evident that most of the later critics have criticised without reading the play.

An exception is Arthur Hobson Quinn who obviously *has* read *Julia,* since his *History of the American Drama* (1923) provides a summary of the plot and pronounces the work on the whole "remarkable for a boy of 14 to have written." On the other hand, G. D. O'Dell manifestly had not read it when he passed judgment on it in his *Annals of the New York Stage* (1927).

First quoting the press comments pro and con, O'Dell then remarks of Peter Irving's verdict: "This was pretty bad but was not undeserved. The wonder is the management would stage the thing. . . . I feel it unnecessary to go further into the scandal"—the word "scandal" suggesting that this authority accepted reports that the young playwright had produced something improper. Though later, in the same work, O'Dell makes observations indicating a better acquaintance with Payne's activities and speaks of him with respect, even admiration, this historian's amended judgments are less conspicuous and less generally read than his condemnation of Payne's early effort.

Two of Payne's biographers also make comments that denote a greater familiarity with *Julia's* generally bad repute than with the play itself. Rosa Pendleton Chiles calls it Payne's "only offense," and declares that she finds all his other work "of acceptable nature"; and Gabriel Harrison even lists *The Wanderer,* a comedy if ever there was one, among Payne's tragedies: and there is no intimation here of irony.

For those who may wish to judge for themselves it is well that Payne published his play, and with it an introduction written in the third person to state that "the animadversions made on it" were his "chief inducements to putting it to the press. If it should be found that he really deserves all the censure he has received, he will not oppose his feeble genius to the decision of the public taste."

Then the embittered young man has a word for the critics. He has "learnt to despise those who condemn a performance in general terms:—the rancor of the gall into which their pen is dipped betrays its own malevolence; but he reveres those who, impartially canvassing the faults of an author, give a clue to mend them."

Except as "Eugenius, Gent." the author's name nowhere appears on the printed copy, though the title page names David Longworth, the printer, as "proprietor of the book" (apparently the first of Payne's many bad bargains where plays were concerned), and the back page is utilized to advertise the wares of other playwrights, with their full names given.

Did Eugenius continue his hated work at the countinghouse throughout the *Julia* episode? As he had no other means of support, it seems likely that he did, though the tensions there must have been mightily increased.

In April his new-found sponsor, Mr. Seaman, arranged for John Howard to have a vacation trip to Boston to see the family. After his four months of dazzling eminence, the quieting, if perhaps too affectionate, influence of the home folks was doubtless very welcome. He returned to New York in time to put forth the final issue of the *Thespian Mirror* and to complete arrangements for the college course, by which his well-meaning friends hoped to make an untimely genius into a useful citizen.

[6]

THE COLLEGIAN

EARLY in June of 1806—just a year before the launching of the first steamboat—a river boat, descriptively named the *Swan*, left her Manhattan Island moorings and began her calm, deliberate, almost motionless progress up the Hudson. Low and square, with broad white mainsail, the sloop slid slowly along, past the farms and country seats facing the riverside, their rose gardens in full bloom; past the Jersey Palisades and the northern tip of wooded Manhattan, leaving the little city far behind. In four to six days, barring head winds or a calm, she was due in Albany.

Besides the usual cargo of liquor, tea, fabrics, and factory wares destined for the thinly populated upstate areas, she carried a few passengers. These had paid for the New York-to-Albany trip "including three meals a day with spirits . . . passenger providing own bedding," about five dollars each.[51]

Heading the list of the passengers was a Revolutionary hero and later mayor of New York, Colonel Marinus Willett;[52] and "he and his lady," in the words of one of the group,[53] were "very agreeable company." There were also "two female passengers," unidentified but described as "equally pleasant," and two young men. Of these, one was Charles Brockden Brown, who has a place in literary history as the first American novelist. The other was the sensationally celebrated boy editor and playwright, John Howard Payne, handsome, eager, just past his fifteenth birthday. He was enroute to Schenectady to enter Union College. The others were bound for Montreal.

Whenever the *Swan* made a stop to await more favorable winds, as she did eight times, the young men went ashore for long walks in the hills. One who has ever imagined the beauties of the Hudson River country before the wide encroachments of White civilization may well envy them. Payne, writing to his father, declared: "the passage through the highlands is sublime and original. I have never found anything more striking, nor can a more magnificent prospect be imagined."

Though Brown, in his middle thirties, was more than twice as old as Payne, the two had become at once great friends: congenial friends, with a world of things to talk about. Brown, who found in his young companion "a heart naturally pure and tractable and a taste for the wise and good," [54] may have understood the precocious boy better than many people did, for Brown himself had been a prodigy, who was said to have read Latin and Greek at the age of eleven. His four novels, which only scholars read today, were at the time attracting some attention in literary England.

Young Payne, however, was not so happy as might be supposed. He was far from averse to going to college, but he had not wanted to go to Union, which was too far from urban attractions for his liking. Although by the time the trip began he was largely reconciled, he had previously written his father that he looked upon going to Union "as I should to enter the State's prison for the same term." To this his father had doubtless replied with the calm of maturer years, for John's next letter home refers to his parent's remark that "one should be happy in any situation" and declares that this philosophy has had "no trifling effect in producing my acceptance of the Schenectady plan." [55]

Union College, founded in 1795 and hence fairly new, had been chosen after much discussion among young Payne's friends in New York. His direct financial backer, the merchant John E. Seaman, had originally favored Princeton as being—of all contrary reasons! —"far removed from the seducing and baleful influences of a large, commercial city like New York." [56] This was in the first flush of his enthusiasm for the lad, when he had wanted to adopt him, and Seaman had then offered to provide a riding horse for the boy away at school. However, it was pointed out that Princeton was not yet so far away but that John could mount his horse at any time and ride in to the "seducing and baleful" city. Seaman at length agreed with the rest. No horse at all, and a college several days from New York by boat or coach, would be more likely to achieve the object in view: an object not only educational, but at least in part disciplinary.

Although in his first letter home John had described Albany as "but a poor, shabby-looking little clump of houses," there he was soon surrounded by the elite of the town and countryside. Among the prominent citizens who welcomed him was the lawyer Robert Sedgwick, whose sister Catharine, the novelist-to-be, had once been a student at the Berry Street Academy. And through the Sedgwicks Albany's Mayor Van Rensselaer also became John's friend.

If the boy's parents and supporters had considered him a problem as he climbed aboard the *Swan*, they had reason for amazement and real anxiety by the time he reached Schenectady. For not only did he feel justified, before incarcerating himself in school, in lingering several days in Albany: he also decided—and this despite the fact that he had been provided with only $20 above original traveling expenses—to accompany the rest of the party to Montreal.

John was generally blamed for undertaking the Montreal detour, although the idea had been suggested by his companion, Colonel Willett, and except for expense, it does not seem to have been unreasonable. There was surely time for the excursion, as the new school term did not begin till fall. The Montreal coach arrived, and he saw his friends preparing to depart. It was incredible that they should go on without him; and, happily unmindful of consequences, he boarded the coach with the rest.

The happiness, however, was short-lived. Travel by stage, with stops for meals and lodging, was more expensive than travel by sloop had been, and the $20 was soon gone. "Added to this," as he wrote to a friend, "a dispute with a fellow passenger resolved me to stop at Glen's Falls and I would go no farther." By a series of remarkable manipulations he returned to Albany. "I had to borrow from the driver for the trip to Albany and from a landlord to pay the driver," he records.[57]

A letter from Mr. Seaman awaited him in Albany, and it was not a pleasant one. His patron, greatly displeased that he had not gone directly to Schenectady, declared that he "would be trifled with and imposed upon no longer." This letter contained no money, and the stranded youth was obliged to wait while explanations were made

and a truce effected. The extravagant tastes and bad management
in money matters which were to cause him so much grief in later
years were already manifesting themselves, and his Albany expenses
somehow mounted to $90, a very large sum in those days. His good
friend the mayor assumed this debt, but Mr. Seaman was not told
that it had been paid. Thus was created a fresh misunderstanding,
far-reaching in its consequences.

So many and such dreadful reports had reached Schenectady
ahead of the new student that when he arrived at last, well over a
month after starting, the college authorities must have felt that they
had a young wild man on their hands.

Dr. Eliphalet Nott, under whose "particular care and direction" [58]
the new pupil had been placed, was then in his second year as president of the college—a post that he was to fill for the amazing period
of sixty-two years. Already noted as a progressive educator, Dr.
Nott, against the counsel of the conservative, was introducing many
novelties. (Later he would add civil engineering and a scientific
course and would institute student government.) [59]

John's patron, genuinely alarmed by true and untrue reports, now
wrote to Dr. Nott of young Payne: "You are the only person who
can save him from destruction . . . if you, sir, can reclaim this
youth and by any means whatever supplant a love of pleasure by
a love of study, you will confer a high obligation upon his friends
and render an essential service to his country, for talents like his,
if properly directed, will do much good in arresting the dreadful
evils which await us from the increasing and desolating effects of
democracy."

Even without the added responsibility implied in this remark
about democracy, it is said that Dr. Nott was "reluctant to undertake
the moulding and instruction of so unusual a youth," [60] but when
once he had accepted the assignment he made a thorough job of it.
Not only did he assume personal tutorship of the new student: he
even had him share his own rooms, secluded from the rest of the
student body.

It was an arrangement first dreaded, but later entirely pleasing
to John Howard. For all his temperament, he was a genial lad,

readily appealed to by a firm and really intelligent approach. Because his interests were far more adult than those of most boys his age, he probably found Dr. Nott congenial. John writes his father: "I am his companion at college, his 'chum,' as they say, and even share his bed.[61] These distinctions are most gratifying." For Dr. Nott's soothing intervention in the Seaman matter, John declares: "Dr. Nott is an honor to human nature. With Dr. Nott I can be happy *anywhere*."

School began at last, and its regimen was austere. There was, first of all, the schedule of hours, which John described in a letter to his sister Eloise, without superfluous comment:

> 5, rise; 5½, prayers (after which classes return to recitation rooms); 8, breakfast; 9½ to 11, study in rooms; 11, recitation; 12, recreation; 1, dinner, recreation till 2; 2–4, study in rooms; 4, recitation; 5, prayers; 5½, tea; recreation till 7; 7–9, study in rooms; 9–11, devoted to anything agreeable in rooms. No student out of rooms after 7; no light to be seen after 11. A professor is constantly visiting the rooms to see that the laws are fulfilled. . . . On Sunday, no intercourse is allowed without, and very little within, the college walls. The students attend church in procession. One professor goes to each place of worship and any student may follow him.[62]

The arrangement of courses at Union seems odd to us today. Under the old curriculum a first-year student was plunged into such subjects as "Virgil, Cicero's Orations, Greek Testament, Lucian, and Roman Antiquities," in addition to "Arithmetic and English Grammar"; whereas "Geography and the Use of Globes, History of America and of American Revolution" were not undertaken until the second year.[63] Dr. Nott may have altered this system, but the dead languages were still required.

John, like his brothers and sisters, was proficient in French. Latin and Greek he apparently found difficult, for he wrote his father that the use of a Greek grammar in which the rules were printed in Latin was "so dispiritingly burthensome that we become exhausted with construing the grammar ere we ascertain its application." [64]

West College, in which John shared the president's quarters, was a new three-story stone structure with cupola and spire, built in

Italian style and truly magnificent for its day. Most of the students lived less elegantly in Long College, a row of brick buildings on near-by College Street. These buildings were no doubt heated by fireplaces, and some of the dormitories may not have been heated at all.

There was time for such extracurricular activities as literary societies and the school paper; and during his early months at Union the future author of "Home, Sweet Home" offered the editor of that publication a piece of work that, in view of later developments, seems significant. It was a poem entitled "Home, Dear Home," in which, as he wrote the family, enclosing a copy, "the pleasures of home are reduced to doggrell." The verses had been written during an acute attack of "violent remitting fever," accompanied by one of those fits of "despondency and blue devils" to which this fifteen-year-old was subject. Serious in tone and exalted in feeling, this poetic effort, except for its main theme, bears no resemblance to its very famous successor.[65]

It was not enough merely to contribute to the school paper. This young man must start a paper himself. Here was the opportunity to utilize an idea that he had had in New York for a paper called *The Pastime,* "a spirited auxiliary to the cause of polite literature"; and from it he hoped to make a profit. Most of the students had pocket money, and John reasoned that they would be willing to subscribe to his paper at a dollar or more a session. With the income thus to be earned he dreamed of helping the family at home as well as of paying off some embarrassing old debts left over from the New York period.

Weekly except for several brief suspensions, *The Pastime* was to prove the longest-lived of any of Payne's fugitive journalistic ventures. It began February 21, 1807 and ran for twenty-one issues, the last dated June 18, 1808. In format, arrangement, and general content it strongly resembles its predecessor, the *Thespian Mirror,* but not in details of subject matter. Here, instead of theatrical affairs, the predominating themes are writing and writers, especially poetry and poets; and though lightened by campus jokes and bits of humor, *The Pastime* seems to indicate that the mental recreation of college

boys in those days was on the serious side. There are several references to the work of Payne's distant cousin Robert Treat Paine Jr.,
a rising poet with whom John Howard has established a warm friendship.[66]

Financially *The Pastime* was not successful. Shortly after the final
issue John wrote his father that he had had "250 subscribers at $1.50
each," but that "most of them are out of town, some said the paper
was irregular and refused to pay, and others would pay at the end,
but few gave me the money."

He had other money-making ideas, ingenious but impractical and
naturally beyond the capacity of a schoolboy to carry out—even a
boy of his one-sided brilliance. He might, remarkably enough, have
performed the literary part in the main, but of the all-important
business requirements he had no conception. One plan, soon abandoned, which he confided not only to the family but also to Henry
Brevoort, was that of compiling *The American Plutarch*, "a profitable and amusing compendium of American biography" to be issued
anonymously and "made to sell."

John needed money, certainly, and that not only because his expenses exceeded the yearly stipend of $250 (fairly liberal for the
time) provided by his patron, but also because Mr. Seaman was not
disposed to pay a debt of $300 contracted in New York in connec-
tion with the *Thespian Mirror*. The situation became serious, and
Dr. Nott, in an effort to relieve the young debtor of "obstructive
visitors, who are daily reminding him of their claims and demand-
ing satisfaction," wrote for advice to the Albany law firm of Sedgwick and Bleecker. To their suggestion of a subscription to raise
the $300 Dr. Nott replied: "I should fear the consequences of afford-
ing Payne assistance in any way which would lead to public observation. . . . His acquaintances have contributed to make him
giddy—the folly of others may in great measure be plead as an
apology for his own." To John's father Dr. Nott wrote kindly,
omitting critical comment:

Though he has contracted debts and spent money unwisely, he is not dis-
sipated nor inclined to any vice. It is not easy for him to reduce his ex-

penses to those of other boys. He has associated with men, is constitutionally liberal, has an extensive correspondence, and wishes to own as well as read every new book.[67]

During his first year at college, John's parents had intended to pay him a visit, but his mother's failing health made traveling impossible. Accordingly Mr. Seaman, partly mollified, enabled John Howard to spend his first school Christmas with the family in Boston, where he "tasted again the pleasures of home, of all pleasures the most delightful." [68]

On his next vacation, in the spring, for which also he was indebted to Mr. Seaman, John paid a visit to New York, with side trips to such faraway places as Newark, Trenton, and Philadelphia, traveling of course by stagecoach "over roads like the devil's turnpike to the infernal regions." [69] He was now sixteen and much attracted by pretty girls, in whom the inland cities apparently abounded. He had a gay time.

Perhaps he felt somewhat conscience-stricken not to go again to Boston to see his ailing mother, but he did take time from social diversions to write her a long letter. It is a letter full of acknowledgements of his own faults, full of resolutions to do better. "You have had reason to believe me deficient in moral sense. The passionate temper and promptness to anger and resentment have lost me many a friend and cost me many a pang. . . . You have held up my brother William as a perfect model for my imitation. I *will* imitate him."

The letter ends with an avowal, which, however trite it may sound to the detached reader, was doubtless very gratifying to the recipient: "I shall never cease to attribute all that is good in me to the early care and admonitions of my father and yourself."

It is good to know that John paid this attention to his mother, for she was to live but a few weeks longer. She died on June 18, 1807 at the age of forty-seven. To the absent son her death was a staggering blow. If he had been homesick before, he was now plunged into deepest gloom. To his father he writes: "To me, now, since Mother's death, all nature seems speechless; the flowers have lost their color

and perfume, the heavens are black and the trees seem motionless." [70]
The Pastime was delayed a week, and when it appeared it contained
the stilted, pathetic effort of this boy, surrounded as he was by
"those who, having never known affliction, know not how to pity or
console it," to pay a fitting tribute to his lost parent.

The private tutelage of Dr. Nott had ceased during John's second
year at school, and at his own request he had been transferred to
the regular student body. Now Dr. Nott would write to William
Payne: "With respect to his application, I presume it has been as
great as any of his friends could wish. With respect to company,
I believe he has seen none in his rooms and he visits none in town.
His Pastime is his only amusement, though this work is perhaps too
great a burden."

John would break out of this cloistered habit to take part in a
theatrical performance given as a feature of the 1808 commence-
ment exercises. The play performed was *Pulaski*, written or adapted
by a fellow student, Henry Warner, and presumably built about the
career of Count Casimir Pulaski, the Polish patriot who had fought
in the American Revolution. John was a hit in the role of Lodoiska,
the only female character.

It may be asked why the boy who was already a playwright did
not write the school play. And the answer may be that the painful
New York experience was already having an inhibiting effect. Or
that the reputation of that effort was undeservedly such that John
was not encouraged in playwriting even by Dr. Nott, who, at a time
when most colleges still frowned upon the theater, displayed unusual
liberality in allowing a play on the campus at all. Whatever the
reason, the erstwhile dramatic author did write the epilogue, which
furthermore he recited, clad in Lodoiska's curls and flowing skirts:

> Stay, gentlefolk, one moment longer, stay—
> I come to ask you how you like our play. . . .
>
> Tell me, ye beaux, are your affections free?
> You need not answer, for I plainly see
> That you're all dying for the love of me!

Ladies, do you no indignation feel
That Lodoiska should your lovers steal?
Be calm, dear ladies, set your hearts at rest,
You shall retain your beaux and make them blest!
For, lest a late discoverer damp their joy
In time I'll tell them that their fair's a boy!

A boy in petticoats? Nay, do not stare,
For girls in breeches are not half so rare! [71]

John's interest in theatrical matters, which may have been temporarily dampened by the reception accorded his original play in New York, was considerably revived by this performance at college, and it was one of several developments that were to determine future events. Others were his father's financial difficulties and the renewed strain of John's relations with his patron. At length, with his usual impetuosity, he writes to Mr. Seaman suggesting that "our connections shall cease entirely," and further, somewhat grandly: "What I have received from you I shall consider a loan. When I am able, you shall be paid."

Neither the threat nor the promise seems to have been taken seriously by his sponsor. He remained John's friend, and certainly was never repaid the thousand or so dollars, a large sum at the time, that he had spent on the boy, who, regardless of Mr. Seaman's attitude, was determined to leave school and go on the stage.

Back in Boston, John obtained his father's "reluctant, slow and weeping leave to try his fortunes on the stage"; [72] and this perhaps may be taken literally, for William Payne was sadly broken. Only a year after the death of his wife his daughter Sally, only twenty-one and her mother's namesake, had succumbed to the dread disease consumption; and in addition to bereavements his monetary affairs had reached a crisis. It had become impossible for him to make the Berry Street Academy a going concern financially. (Was John's lack of business acumen a direct inheritance?) The son felt confident, however, of his ability to earn enough money on the stage to pay his father's debts.

While waiting for his theatrical plans to take shape, John again

turned briefly to journalism. A connection with a Boston paper was
not allowed, however, to divert him from his main course. In his
spare time he worked at preparing his roles for the stage and re-
hearsed them at home, probably in the evening, to an appreciative
audience of one: his roommate, John Gorham Palfrey. This we know
on the reliable evidence of Palfrey himself:

> In 1808 his father had fallen into unprosperous circumstances. I was still
> a member of the family and shared Howard's room, along with the office
> of prompter and critic, while he ran through each mode of the lyre, the
> diapason of histrionic passion. At the same time he conducted the Boston
> Mirror for Oliver and Munroe (the latter since editor of the Baltimore
> Patriot).[73]

Palfrey's statement is confirmed by the Boston *Mirror* of November 5, 1808, which contains announcement of "a formal connection
with the editor of a paper formerly published in Schenectady, New
York (that sprightly miscellany, The Pastime)." The combined
Mirror and *Pastime,* now declared to be "the same," is a more promising publication than either of Payne's previous journalistic undertakings. Its format is larger, and its content, though similar, is varied
by some news of the world in addition to theatrical items, essays,
and much poetry. It also actually contains some general and theatrical advertising, indicating that there was a business office this time.

All of which suggests that Payne was learning the ropes of practical journalism and that this might have been a good place for him
to remain. However, it was only a passing occupation, entirely secondary to his real ambition—that of embarking upon acting as a
career.

[7]

MASTER PAYNE, ACTOR

THE WINTER of 1809 in New York had been one of steady
cold and good sleighing. February's lengthening days brought that
ancient, sweet promise of spring, as well as the opening of the snow-

clogged roads for intercity travel; and among the intrepid passengers on an arriving Boston coach was young John Howard Payne, returning to New York to make his formal debut as an actor.

Since the production just three years earlier of Payne's ill-fated *Julia* there had been changes in the theatrical life of New York. The talented and charming Mrs. Jones had died; [74] new actors from England were constantly being added to the roster of an already crowded profession, and new theatrical enterprises were springing up in the rapidly growing city. There was a troupe specializing in "rope dancing" at the Italian theater, corner of Broadway and Reade Street; while at Mechanics' Hall, Broadway and Park, "narrative pictures," a French importation, were being shown. [75] These, however, were minor efforts, since the real center of stage life was still the theater at 23 Park Row, its façade extending from Ann to Beekman Street, and its spacious auditorium and huge stage reaching back to Theatre Alley.

Not long before Payne's debut the Park had been completely remodeled within. [76] Now, officially rechristened the New Theatre but still known to the public as the Park, it was opening its doors on the evening of February 24 for the first professional stage appearance of the prodigious youth who, though he had become a somewhat controversial figure, was still the most celebrated boy in America.

For his initial role the boy actor had had the good judgment to choose a real boy's part: Young Norval in *The Tragedy of Douglas; or, the Noble Shepherd*, by the "Scotch Shakespeare," John Home. [77] This play, grand in manner and stately in meter, had first been performed in Edinburgh more than sixty years earlier and was still a favorite in Britain with serious actors and actresses—particularly actresses, for the role of Lady Randolph, the hero's mother, had added to the laurels of both Peg Woffington and Mrs. Siddons. Appearing in that part with young Payne was Mrs. Twaits, a rising young star regarded as a tragedienne of particular talent.

The year 1809 was not the most propitious time for the launching of a theatrical career in the port city of New York, for by reason of the government's embargo on trade with England—precursor to the War of 1812—many ordinarily prosperous persons were complaining of hard times. Payne, constitutionally unlucky, was to feel the effects of this edict, but not at his opening. On that particular February evening "the house was unusually thronged and alive with expectation." [78]

This was apparently one of the occasions described by Gabriel Harrison on which "the old and the young, the beautiful and learned" left their "strings of carriages for blocks all up and down Park Place" and crowded into the theater. Within, Harrison further recalls, "there could be seen in the boxes, servants of private families, dressed with the most scrupulous care, with the white napkin fixed around the right arm above the elbow, holding the reserved seats until the party they represented came to claim them." What happened to the servants after their employers arrived we are not told, but this was a day when servants "knew their place," so they probably had to be satisfied with having contributed to the picturesqueness of the scene and incidentally enjoyed a glimpse of the remodeled interior.

For the Park in its new attire was little short of magnificent. The lower lobby was "a handsome colonnade . . . lighted by glass lamps between the columns," which mirrors doubled in number. The ceiling was "painted as a dome, with panels of a light purple and gold mouldings"; and at either end of the lobby was a fireplace, shedding, this evening late in winter, what was doubtless a welcoming warmth.

To William Dunlap, who had lately resigned the management, we are indebted for this description of the Park's remodeled interior: "The boxes accommodated upwards of 1600 persons and the pit and galleries, 1100"; and "there was an improvement over the plan of all other theatres in that the box fronts, instead of being perpendicular, fall in at the top, giving room for the knees." Those convex fronts were "divided into panels, blue ground with white and gold ornaments; a crimson festoon draped over each box and the lower ones lighted by 10 glass chandeliers, projecting from the front and suspended from gilt iron brackets." There were also "four private boxes with rooms to retire to on the stage," and "a beautiful effect was produced by a large, oval mirror, reflecting the whole of the audience in the first row."

The house, Dunlap also states, was "extremely well lighted" (patent oil lamps being doubtless a great improvement over candles), and "in every part spectators might both hear and see the performance." We must regret with him, however, that the revamped auditorium omitted one picturesque feature of the old: "a large box in the center of the second tier, directly in front of the stage, capable of containing two or three hundred persons and called 'The Shakespeare.' This box was the resort of the critics, as the pit of the English theatre had been in former times."

The large audience on this brilliant first night has now had time to inspect the decorative minutiae and to read and reread the brief playbill:

Young Norval	Master Payne
(his first appearance)	
Old Norval	Mr. Huntington
Lord Randolph	Mr. Tyler
Glenalvon	Mr. Rutherford
Lady Randolph	Mrs. Twaits
Anna	Miss White

Promptly at a quarter of seven the leading lady's husband, Mr. Twaits—himself a celebrated actor, though he has no part in *Douglas*—appears before the curtain and recites the prologue. This is a poetic tribute to the star of the evening, written especially for the occasion by Joseph D. Fay,[79] a prominent lawyer of the city, who not only admired young Payne, but also may be said to have loved him as he would his own son. Throughout the evening Judge Fay, as he is called, stands behind the scenes with John Howard's father, who has traveled from Boston for the event. With them is another faithful friend, none other than young Payne's former patron, John Seaman, a man capable of both giving and forgiving.

The curtain rises on "the court of a castle surrounded by woods." There, to her faithful servant Anna, Lady Randolph laments the loss eighteen years earlier of both her noble husband and her infant son, as well as her later "forced marriage" to Lord Randolph, who must now go to war, leaving her unprotected against the attentions of her unlawful suitor Glenalvon. "Amid thunders of applause"[80] a young stranger in Highland plaid, "with sword drawn and bloody," enters to report that he has just saved Lord Randolph from "four armed men, killing two and donning the warrior's attire of one" of the slain. To the lady's demand to know his identity the youthful voice rings out (most thrillingly, according to contemporary accounts):

> My name is Norval; on the Grampian Hills
> My father feeds his flocks.

"How blest the mother of yon gallant Norval," sighs Lady Randolph; though in good old storybook style it is soon revealed, through the appearance of Old Norval, the foster father, displaying jewels discovered eighteen years earlier on his foundling son, that the youth is her own long-lost child:

> *The Lady:* My son, my son,
> I am thy mother and the wife of Douglas!
> *The Youth:* Oh, heav'n and earth! How wondrous is my fate!
> Art thou my mother? . . . let me kneel!
> *The Lady:* Arise, my son! In me thou dost behold
> The poor remains of beauty once admir'd! . . .
> Thou art the rightful heir
> Of yonder castle and the wide domains.
> *The Youth:* To be the son of Douglas is to me inheritance enough!

This bliss, of course, cannot last. The jealous Glenalvon suspects Lady Randolph's interest in the stranger, and, Iago-like, poisons the mind of Lord Randolph against his wife:

> This distinguished dame
> Invites a youth, th' acquaintance of a day,
> Alone to meet her at the midnight hour.

The stranger's death is plotted, and in the ensuing combat Young Norval (now Douglas) is mortally wounded, but only after he has slain the villainous Glenalvon. Offstage, Lady Randolph plunges over the cliff, and Lord Randolph goes off to fight the Danes, "hoping he never shall return."

It is indeed a sad piece, and the audience that night was particularly appreciative of the "deep and poignant effect of the closing scene," in which Young Norval, bravely murmuring "I feel a

little faintness, I hope it will not last," expires in Lady Randolph's
arms.

After it was all over and cheerfulness restored by the afterpiece,
High Life Below Stairs, there was a supper for the young star of
the evening at the home of Stephen Price, who, with Thomas
Abthorpe Cooper, "the unrivaled tragic actor," was co-manager of
the theater. Cooper and Price [81] were not sentimentalists, but businessmen destined to succeed in their ambition to make the Old Park
pay. They had brought out Master Payne on the chance that he
would prove commercially profitable, though they may have considered him something of an experiment.

Cooper, now thirty-five and at the peak of his career, had long
been greatly admired by young Payne. Though English-born, Cooper
had become the most important stage personage in America, which
would henceforth be his home. Self-assured and physically powerful, he shone in numerous tragic roles, "despite a faulty memory
and careless study"; [82] and for some years it had been his custom
to perform in New York on Monday and Wednesday nights and in
Philadelphia Friday and Saturday, "driving his own fast horses"
between the two cities. Payne, when he decided on a stage career,
had recited to Cooper Antony's oration and the conversations of
Brutus and Cassius, and Cooper had been only mildly enthusiastic.
He judged that Payne "might succeed as a youth," but would not
predict that he would go farther. Now, however, here was Master
Payne hobnobbing with the great Cooper on equal terms.

Though Payne at the time was in the latter half of his seventeenth
year and almost old enough, at least by later standards, for the
designation Mr., he was still being astutely billed as Master Payne.
"Boy actors were a novelty," remarks Dunlap, "and we have seen
none since who equaled Master Payne. . . . The young gentleman
was sixteen years of age, small for that age and looking still younger.
His face was remarkably handsome, his countenance full of intelligence and his manner fascinating. He performed Young Norval with
credit and his succeeding characters with an increased display of
talent."

In launching his succeeding characters, however, the young actor was somewhat delayed, for the strain of the debut had been very great; and the *Commercial Advertiser* of February 27 announced that "owing to the indisposition of Master Payne, *The Tragedy of Mahomet* is necessarily postponed until Wednesday next." It was one of the handicaps under which Payne launched his career that any actor—and particularly a star—must perfect not one, but several, weighty parts.

There were no schools of acting in those days, no counselors against attempting too much or beginning at the top—suggestions that probably would not have been welcomed had they been made. Payne was his own director, his own teacher and coach. Fortunately he had the intelligence not to cast himself in swashbuckling or heavy villain parts, but usually in roles suited to his age and physical type.

When able to appear again he enacted at intervals of three or four days, five leading roles in dramas highly esteemed at the time, though scarcely known today. They were Zaphna in Voltaire's *Mahomet,* Tancred in James Thompson's *Tancred and Sigismunda,* Rolla in Sheridan's *Pizarro,* Octavian in *The Mountaineers,* and the lad Achmed in John Brown's *Barbarossa.* In the last he was especially successful, and it was the one play of the series that, "in consequence of a great number of applications," [83] he repeated.

It is reported that except for the first of the young actor's performances, the house "was not numerously attended." After all, Payne was not yet Cooper, though there were many admirers of the younger actor's talent, and the general public was friendly. That public made amends when, on March 15, he appeared for his own benefit as Romeo. Though winter played an encore that night in the form of a heavy snowfall, everybody who had not yet seen the prodigy turned out, and his receipts totaled nearly $1400 [84]—the equivalent of several times that amount a century later.

Dramatic criticisms in the press were still signed with pseudonyms or not at all, and apparently they were free-lance contributions. Again Master Payne was news, and for more than a month he shared with "Mr. Madison's inaugural address" and editorials on the "odious embargo," the somewhat scanty newspaper space that could be spared from advertising.

Though there was an occasional rhapsodic outburst, the critical comments were in the main judicious in tone, and their consensus was to be borne out by later judgments: namely, that the boy's greatest assets were natural intelligence and taste. His most notice-able defect was declared to be a voice unequal to the demands of a theater the size of the Park. "Let him habituate himself to de-claiming aloud, and ever, like Demosthenes, visit the seashore and address the raging waves," grandly advised the *Evening Post*. "His voice is sweet but not forceful, for it is the voice of 16," said the *American Citizen*, which also found him "not skilled in the use of his feet—a circumstance which injures his appearance, and, whether he will or not, diminishes the effect of his performance." This writer none the less reminded readers that the youth was "the *first* theatrical genius our nation has produced." This was a fact worth remarking, for most of the leading actors on the American stage of the time were actually of British birth.

Inevitably there were comparisons to that other boy actor, Brit-ain's Master Betty, and an authority unidentified even by a pseu-donym declared:

> I have seen Master Payne as Douglas, Selim, Zaphna and Octavian, and can truly say I think him superior to Betty in them all. There was one scene of his Zaphna which exhibited more taste and sensibility than I have observed since the days of Garrick. He has astonished everybody.[85]

Some of the press comments refer to Payne as "young Roscius," [86] and this sobriquet, later altered to "the American Roscius," would follow him through the rest of his acting career. In England young Betty had been called "the infant Roscius," and Payne himself was perhaps responsible for the prevalence of the term in New York, though not for its application to himself. In the *Thespian Mirror* and other writings he had repeatedly referred to Cooper as "the American Roscius," somewhat unaccountably, since Cooper was British.

At the close of the engagement, however, Payne's friendly rela-tions with Cooper were to go into reverse. This mischance, though in part the result of dissatisfactions probably smoldering for some time, had its immediate cause in an incident that occurred when Payne was packing his trunks to leave the theater. There, by agreement with the management he had been supplied with costumes made for him,[87] and had been allowed to wear the ornaments belonging to Cooper, as he, at least during the term of Payne's debut, was exclusively engaged in managerial work.

In the costuming of the roles that both Payne and Cooper preferred—those of historic or imaginary noblemen, chief reliance of the serious drama of the period—such ornaments as plumes, heavy chains, epaulets, ruffs, and gauntlets, as well as all varieties of weapons and shields, were of course indispensable, and Payne had naturally supposed that the accessories were part of the costumes. On packing his wardrobe he found, to his dismay, that all the ornaments had been removed, and "with childish impetuosity and self-importance" [88] called Mr. Price and demanded to know what had become of them.

This little flare-up seems to have been disastrous for Payne, since it gave Cooper and Price the excuse they may have been looking for, to block the future progress of the young actor. Whatever the cause, the Park's management turned against Payne, and the boy actor left the scene of his triumphs minus both ornaments and good will and in a state of mind that can perhaps be imagined.

With the insouciance of a veteran, young Roscius accepted the bad with the good, replaced the ornaments out of his own pocket, finished packing his "dresses," as theatrical costumes were then called, and took the coach for Boston. In that city, where he was still remembered as youthful captain and boy editor, he was now warmly welcomed as stage star.

Here again he opened as Young Norval, and the occasion was notable, if for nothing else, by reason of the prologue written by that distant cousin, Robert Treat Paine Jr., himself something of a celebrity. This Paine had long been a devotee of the theater and was the first American to become a professional dramatic critic.[89] Reputedly a hardened man of the world, he had earned by his temperamental and somewhat irregular ways, as well as by the crime of marriage to an actress, the displeasure of his father, the judge.

Paine the poet was nearly twenty years older than Payne the actor, but the two had much in common intellectually and had been in correspondence for years.

Of the many poetic tributes to John Howard Payne the Boston prologue, particularly its closing stanza, has most nearly the ring of authentic poetry:

> An humble weed, transplanted from the waste,
> Formed the proud chapiter of Grecian taste,
> Chance dropp'd the weight; the yielding foliage twined
> And drooped, with graceful negligence inclined.
> Sculpture a model saw, to art unknown,
> Copied the form, and turn'd the plant to stone;
> The chisell'd weed adorned the temple's head,
> And gods were worshipped where its branches spread!
> If, in our Norval, candid judges find
> Some kindred flower, to grace the stage, design'd:
> If, to the pressure fortune has imposed,
> You owe those talents art has ne'er disclosed;
> If, like the graced Acanthus he appear,
> Be you Callimachus—be Corinth here! [90]

It was in Boston at this time that Payne made so bold as to add Hamlet to his repertory, thus becoming the first American ever to enact the role.[91] Though he chose his own parts, he probably had little to say in the selection of supporting actors, but here the local company gave him an Ophelia worthy of note. She was a young English actress, regarded as particularly talented, whose name was Elizabeth Poe, or, as in those formal times she was more generally called, Mrs. David Poe. For later generations the most interesting fact about her is that she had left at home a three-months-old son named Edgar—the great Edgar Allan Poe of the future.

Mrs. Poe not only appeared as Ophelia to Payne's Hamlet, but also played with him as Palmyra in *Mahomet* and as Juliet to his Romeo; and at the close of his regular Boston engagement he gave for her benefit a special performance of *Pizarro* in which she played Cora to his Rolla.[92]

Of all impecunious stage families there probably never was one more in need of a benefit than the Poes. For David Poe was another young man penalized for marrying an actress. After he chose the stage in preference to law, financial assistance was refused by his relatives, Maryland citizens of good standing.[93]

It is particularly pleasant to imagine Payne and Mrs. Poe as the Veronese lovers. The familiar complaint that it is difficult to find a Romeo or a Juliet young enough to seem appropriately cast in either part, who is yet an actor of sufficient understanding to play the part intelligently, may have been dispelled when those two appeared in the familiar roles. Payne, not quite eighteen, was just the right age for the ideal Romeo, and Mrs. Poe, though she was twenty-two and the mother of two young children, is said to have been petite and very youthful in appearance. Probably she could look the part of the fourteen-year-old Juliet without overtaxing the make-up art.

Mrs. Poe must also have been a vocalist of some ability, for several times she is listed on the same bill with Payne not only as actress but as singer. She was, besides, an important participant with him in an extra production following the conclusion of his regular engagement. This began with *Lovers' Vows; or, the Natural Son*, Payne acting Frederick and Mrs. Poe Amelia, continued with several vocal numbers by Mrs. Poe, and ended with an extraordinary musical afterpiece:

A Grand Operatic Drama in 3 acts
LODOISKA; or, the Captive Princess
Princess Lodoiska, Mrs. Poe.[94]

This "grand operatic drama" may have been an adaptation by Payne of the play *Pulaski* given the year before at Union College, in which he had played Lodoiska, the female role now assigned, with the addition of songs, to Mrs. Poe. As to what music was used in the new production, or who supplied the instrumental accompaniment, there is, regrettably, no information.

In the ten days' interval between his last regular Boston appearance and this double bill, it is reasonable to suppose that young Payne had been very busy with adaptation and production-planning for which, as later events were to prove, he had much talent. For besides bringing out the operatic drama, whatever its origin, he probably made at this time the adaptation of *Lovers' Vows* that he was to use thereafter.[95]

Although this play by the German, August Kotzebue, had been frequently performed in America in translations by Mrs. Inchbald and Benjamin Thompson, Payne had never been satisfied with either currently used version. He therefore made his own composite version. The result, printed in Baltimore before the end of 1809, is usually listed as Payne's first published play, though he gives scrupulous credit to the original author and to both earlier adapters.

It was before his appearances in this play with Mrs. Poe, and before the operatic drama, that a Boston citizen sent the New York papers a comment that, by its sincerity, carries conviction:

> Master Payne, we are told, finishes his engagement at our theatre this evening. We are happy, as much for the reputation of the town as for his individual interest, that the house Monday evening [probably Payne's benefit] was full and overflowing. It was a small remuneration for the delight and satisfaction he has given the town.
>
> The claims of this judicious young performer are not obtrusive or adventitious. He increases in interest and gratification every time he appears. . . . In delineating character he shews excellent discriminatory powers; and, which is highly useful as well as pleasing, he gives a correct pronunciation of the language of the author.
>
> We understand he has volunteered his services for the benefit of Mrs. Poe. This circumstance, and her merit, we hope will insure her a bumper.[96]

With Hamlet added to his acting parts, as well as Edgar in *King Lear* and Lord Hastings in *Jane Shore*, young Roscius was back in New York by the middle of May.

During his absence Cooper had returned to the stage for ten nights, playing some of the same roles that John Howard had essayed, and it is not to be supposed the established actor was trying to prove himself inferior to the novice. In fact, the rift between the two had not healed. Payne declares that they "did not speak," and amusingly describes "the great and little Roscius, brushing by each other on Broadway, keeping up all the dignity of two tragedy heroes." [97] More seriously, he says that he found on returning "a strong party formed against me, and it consists exclusively of

Cooper's parasites," and speaks of "the injury to my pocket and reputation on account of not fawning to Mr. Cooper and the manager."

In these circumstances it is surprising that Payne was allowed to return to the Park at all. Yet he did play a second engagement of seven performances, although "on the most niggardly terms ever offered a poor player, one-half the receipts of the seventh night for playing six." As it turned out, though, this was more successful financially, and probably artistically, than the first engagement had been. Boston had provided needed experience, and the warm endorsement of Bostonians now supplied prestige. No longer a mere novelty, "little Roscius" was beginning to show signs of becoming a solid attraction. He averaged "above $500 for each regular performance and $755 for the closing benefit, extraordinary for the season." For a very young man he was doing very well; so well, in fact, that "great Roscius," at last sensing a potential stage rival, may have had an added motive for blocking his advance.

[8]

YOUNG ROSCIUS TOURS AMERICA

AFTER his second New York engagement, the stage of his home town seemed closed to young Payne, because of the break with Cooper and Price. There was nothing to do but go on tour.

Beginning experimentally in the summer of 1809, the touring continued for nearly three years, with such fluctuations of fortune that the strolling player himself would declare: "There is no breeze so variable as the 'aura popularis.' Sometimes my pockets were so full that I could hardly carry them. Again, I had not a farthing to pay for sewing up the rents my affluence had caused." [98]

The play was indeed the thing in those days, despite the cruel uncertainties of the acting profession and the lingering shadow of the blue laws. Music as a separate attraction had not yet achieved a wide following in America, and it is probable that the theater had proportionately a greater importance than it would possess a century later. The larger towns maintained playhouses, and there "managers followed the custom of engaging a stock company of from 10 to 30 players, more than half of them men, in which group there was usually one outstanding actor or actress to play the leading roles." [99] Even the most active theatrical centers, however, had neither the population nor the wealth to support highly paid visiting performers for long seasons or on return engagements after their novelty had worn off.

In addition to these fundamental difficulties, which any actor would have encountered, Payne was to find as the touring progressed that the New York rivalry was far-reaching and had resulted in "a very powerful combination arrayed against him, for the purpose of preventing his obtaining engagements in various theatres." [100]

He set forth in late summer, apparently without plan, and his first stop was Providence. It has often been stated that the Rhode Island city had no theater at the time and that Payne's activities there consisted of giving a dramatic reading. But local newspapers of 1809 contain a number of advertisements of the Providence Theatre and announce performances by Master Payne, as Hamlet on September 4, and on September 11 as Octavian in *The Mountaineers*.[101] There is also a family letter which refers to his having played in Providence "three times to very brilliant houses." It must not have been financial brilliance, however, since Hanson is authority for the statement that "with only a shilling" Payne drifted on to Baltimore.

Though lately outdistanced by New York in population, Baltimore had many proud and wealthy citizens who, like most upperclass Americans of the period, were keenly interested in the theater. Among them was an influential group that resented the treatment Payne had received in New York, rose to his defense, and provided the practical means of restoring his prestige.

"What a society I recollect on my first visit to Baltimore!" he would write years later. "What an endearing welcome! I hope to have it in my power some day to give a picture of what was surely the Augustan Age of Baltimore . . . when all its hearts seemed to me so warm and all its minds so brilliant." [102]

There, at the old Holliday Street theater (where "the attraction was the acting, not the scenery, of which the less said the better, nor the comfort experienced by the audience, since the seats were long, uncushioned benches without backs"),[103] Payne quite literally staged a comeback. That was during the last two weeks of October 1809. Although by agreement with the management he was paid for only one of the performances—his benefit—that one was so profitable that "in a fortnight he had $1500 in his pocket."

The press of the Maryland city was enthusiastic, so much so, indeed, that Washington Irving, perusing the journalistic transports, felt called upon to write his young friend warning him against the "cant and fustian" of newspaper comment and advising him to leave Baltimore as soon as possible, because "you cannot excite more attention, you cannot gain more notoriety and applause, but you may cease to be a novelty, curiosity may be satisfied." [104]

This was good advice, but Payne did not need it. He had had the good sense, two months earlier, to write to William Warren, then managing both the Baltimore and Philadelphia theaters, proposing a short stay and making other sage suggestions:

> To me it seems good policy to limit all engagements to seven nights, and, if justified, to repeat a visit of the same length at some distant interval of the same season. . . . Prior to anything else, I should choose to understand that the plays are to be *thoroughly* rehearsed before representation . . . and that the female counterparts should be given to persons as petite in figure as myself.

(This last refers to an occasion when the heroine, a buxom girl, had to be carried off the stage by the none too sturdy hero—to the considerable amusement of the audience.)

News of his Baltimore triumphs traveled to Philadelphia by every coach. Success succeeds, and in December the Philadelphia management felt safe in engaging him for ten nights in a repertory of nine different works, Young Norval to be given twice. Once again he was the wonder boy.

"From the first enunciation of Master Payne's expected arrival" one Philadelphian heard on the street such comments as "He is superior to Cooper," "He speaks better than Fennell." Or such a colloquy as this, overheard in the lobby of the theater: "You have been in England, sir, don't you think Master Payne superior to young Betty?" "I don't know, sir, never having seen young Betty." "I think he is much superior." "You have seen Master Betty, then, sir?" "No, I never have, but I am sure of it. I have heard a person who was in England say so."

So persistent was the comparison of the young American to the British boy actor that a leading journalist felt constrained to re-mind his readers that "Payne lacked many of the advantages en-joyed by Master Betty." The youthful Roscius of England had, "from his very infancy," said this writer, "been in a state of the best discipline." From the time he was five years old young Betty had been "exercised in the daily recitation of poetry by his mother, who shone in private theatricals." Later he was "prepared for the stage and tutored by an excellent preceptor. By his father, one of the best fencers in England, he was improved in gracefulness of attitude." [105] Of Payne, on the other hand, the writer lamented that there was "not a man in America capable and willing to instruct him."

As a theatrical center Philadelphia was important. Its theater, with stately colonnaded front flanked by impressive wings, extended ninety feet along Chestnut Street and had a seating capacity of 2000. It possessed many up-to-date features: superior dressing rooms, greenrooms, a well-stocked wardrobe, and "the first wardrobe-keeper in America." [106]

Philadelphia also supported an exclusively theatrical publication, the *Mirror of Taste and Dramatic Censor,* whose comments, more judicious than some of the journalism of the day, it is possible to take seriously. In young Payne its editor found an individual who could not be described simply or dismissed lightly, and, while "re-fusing to join the multitude in burning vile incense under the boy's nose," succeeded in being for several pages both constructively crit-ical and very complimentary. For surely, despite unfavorable re-marks upon the young actor's walk, the inadequacy of his voice, and the stiffness of some of his gesticulations, there is high praise in the general summation: "The performance of Master Payne pleased us

so much that we have since derived great enjoyment from the recollection of it."

It was this critic who provided, too, an oft-quoted tribute to the
youthful actor's personal appearance:

> Nature has bestowed upon the young gentleman a countenance of no mean
> order. What is now wanting in muscular expression is in great measure
> supplied by the eye, which glows with animation and intelligence, and at
> times SPEAKS the language of a soul really impassioned. . . . A more
> extraordinary mixture of softness and intelligence was never associated
> in a human face. The forehead is particularly fine.[107]

The fame of the "young gentleman" suffered no diminution
throughout the Philadelphia engagement, and when he concluded
as Romeo for his own benefit, the theater was so crowded and in all
accessible places "there was so much pressing, confusion and ill-
mannered noise and struggle and rudeness" that few but those in
the front boxes could hear or see the play out.

The all-important figures for this benefit Payne gave in a letter
to the Boston manager John Bernard, dated December 23, 1809:
"My ten nights here terminated with a benefit of $1408. The best
of my other nights, $1376, to Hamlet. . . . Placide wants me at
Richmond by the 16th of January." [108]

Richmond proved a gratifying encore to Philadelphia, and in the
southern city a flying visit of ten days produced for young Payne
$1700—an amount surpassing anything ever before bestowed upon
a stage personage by that community.[109] This is the more remarkable
in view of the fact that Richmond then had fewer than 10,000 inhabitants. Its theater, however, was among the important ones of the
country, and the wealthy planters with their bevies of fluttering, be-
ruffled females, willing to drive many miles for an evening's entertainment, were substantial and dependable patrons.

But for all his triumphs, the stage was losing its glamour for
Young Roscius, whose written comments about this time reveal the
boy who a few years earlier had described the theater as "the teacher
of virtue and morality" now completely disillusioned. In a letter to
one friend he declared:

The interior of a playhouse, if it does not represent an epitome of the whole world, shews at least that part of it which is most bare and ludicrous. It is not nearly so pleasing to unravel the mysterious causes of the thunder and lightning in the theatre, and to find out what brings the ghost up from the bottom of the stage and lets him down again, as it is to explore the secret springs which activate the mock Jupiters of the drama, who dress themselves out in paper crowns and imagine they are real emperors.[110]

And to another: "The *judicious few* are very few indeed. They are always to be found in the theatre like flowers in a desert." [111]

He nevertheless played return engagements in the northern cities, appeared in Charleston's beautiful little playhouse with its "handsome pediment, palisaded courtyard, circular-front stage, and three tiers of boxes with Venetian blinds," [112] and traveled on to Petersburg and Norfolk. Despite disillusionment the young actor was still giving his best to his work, to judge by a Norfolk reviewer's comment: "After the first entrance, modestly saluting the audience, he appeared to forget them. No breaking off abruptly in the midst of the most interesting speech to thank the audience for applause, no ogling of the boxes as he came on or went off the stage."

Returning from the South, he ran through his repertory in the embryonic "Washington City" in a playhouse later converted into a saloon and under conditions more primitive than he had encountered anywhere else. The Washington engagement, however, was notable for one circumstance. There in the audience nightly, drinking in the soliloquies of Hamlet, lamenting the sad demise of Norval, and pondering the ancient tragedy of Romeo, was an eleven-year-old boy, one Billy Corcoran,[113] who in later years would contribute importantly to the perpetuation of Payne's fame.

If it were possible to make a minute study of these years of Payne's barnstorming, it would provide an illuminating picture, not only of the pioneer American theater, but also of traveling conditions of the period: the long, jolting journeys by stagecoach over "devil's turnpike" roads and the even greater hardships of tedious, sickening passages by water.

Overland, between the East Coast cities, though roads were far from smooth, routes were defined, coaches ran on schedule, and wayside accommodations for horses and humans were often models of good management. It was on venturing into the interior that one jolted endlessly for days through the incredible depths of primeval forest, over roads that ranged from grass-grown paths to stony chasms, forded streams or risked frail skeletons of bridges, and rested in inns that were often little more than log huts, to be hailed gratefully at nightfall and left thankfully at daybreak.

These, however, were the accepted, indeed the only modes of travel by land, and on the early tours they may have seemed to the youthful thespian part of the fun; but with repetition their grimmer aspects impressed him.

A lap of one inland journey took him into "the wild and desolate mountains of Virginia, where it is as difficult to receive intelligence from a place no more than ten miles away as it would be to get a letter from the moon." [114] And a boat trip down the Atlantic Coast he thus described to a Charleston friend:

> I sent you a few lines by the pilot who conveyed our ship out of harbor. That ship was literally another ark—such a confusion of sounds and manners could never have existed except in the little wooden world of Mr. Noah. Pigs, Deers and Parsons, Geese, Women and Players; Sheep, Chickens and College Students, all pent up together for 12 days of blessed captivity. In the morning we had exhortations and psalm singing; at noon, reading and sleeping; at night, gales of wind, praying and sea-sickness.[115]

What a miracle it must have seemed at journey's end to come upon trim little cities, homes with the appointments of gracious living, matrons and maids in silks and crinolines, and provincial scholars so conversant with the classics of dramatic literature that the actor did not dare forget his lines!

For Payne the difficult and sordid travel experiences were often canceled out by high personal adventures; for wherever the visiting celebrity went, he was the object of flattering social attention. In Richmond on the occasion of his second visit he was entertained at the plantation home of one Colonel Mayo, to whose daughter Maria, a famous belle, the guest addressed a set of verses that managed to attract wide attention. It is indicative of the glamorous reputation of Miss Mayo—who later became the wife of General Winfield Scott —as well as of the kind of sensational fame surrounding Payne, that these verses were "unceremoniously taken" from his room in a Georgetown hotel and "published in nearly every newspaper from Alexandria to Boston." [116]

In Washington, fresh from this southern tour, the young actor was an interested guest at one of the White House levees or "drawing-rooms," as they were called, presided over by the President's wife, the "tall, majestic, queen-like" Dolly Payne Madison. These evenings were official weekly affairs, but Payne went at the personal bidding of Mrs. Madison, who was always especially friendly because her own name had been Payne.[117] And it was through the charming Miss Mayo, then on a visit to Washington, that the White House invitation was extended.

Payne, by this time, had seen a good deal of "high society" and may have been somewhat blasé, but he recognized the White House function as something special and sent a report of it home to the family: "On Wednesday, December 10 [probably 1810] called to see Miss Mayo. She told me that Mrs. Madison had expressed considerable regret at my neglecting to attend her levee last week and that she had been requested by Mrs. Madison to invite me to the levee this evening."

Though obliged to improvise a formal costume "from a coat, small-clothes and a waistcoat, borrowed from Richards, and a black waistcoat borrowed from Appleton," Payne promised to attend. Arrived at the mansion, he found two large adjoining rooms opened for the function, which he described in some detail:

> The visitors mob in the centre or sit around the sides, and are much more ceremonious than at private parties. Mrs. Madison sits by the side of the fireplace at the upper end of the larger room to receive her company, and after they are assembled, moves familiarly among them and has some pretty remark for every lady and some agreeable reply for every gentleman.
>
> Madison is "a little man in black," not more than 5 feet 5 inches, with a neatly powdered head and club queue. He is remarkable for always making the last bow. He inclines his head in true dancing-school fashion—

his arms dangling by his side, and at every fresh bow stepping off. . . . I was particularly struck by the cunningness of Madison's physiognomy. To an indifferent observer he would appear absorbed in state matters, while the more watchful will detect his active eye glancing by stealth to every corner and at every face. Mrs. Madison always darts a sly glance at one while she appears devoted to another.

All the officers of State and of the Army & Navy & members of the Senate and Congress and all foreign Ministers, convene at these festivals. . . . Some Members of Congress from the wilderness were dressed in boots and pantaloons, but the etiquette of small-clothes and stockings is much more universal at the drawing-rooms than at other parties.

Tea, coffee, wine and small refreshments were handed round. . . . Some of the young ladies sung and played the piano. . . . The company drops off just as they choose, and without form. At nine they begin to retire.

The levees give great employ to the Hackney Coaches. Hack hire to and from the Capitol to Georgetown is cheap, being only half a dollar, though double the stage fare, which is a fipenny bit a mile.[118]

After Washington Payne returned to Baltimore, where, though he complained of "dining parties, ladies' parties, all the etcetera of frothy, insincere attention," he found "a girl of purest heart, beautiful as spring and romantic as a young enthusiast's dream. I fell almost in love."

"Almost in love" seems to have been a chronic state of the susceptible youth at this time. Indeed, according to both Harrison and Hanson, Payne at a slightly earlier age had even become engaged to "a Boston lady," though the engagement was broken because of objections by her parents. As to her identity, there is evidence that she was Rebecca Power—(not of Boston, but of Providence)—who previously, by an early marriage, had become Mrs. Air.[119]

This Mrs. Air is the subject of romantic little poems by Payne and others, with plays upon the name *Air,* and she is mentioned by both Payne and his sisters in several letters. "Mrs. Air, lovely creature, has been admired by everybody," Payne wrote Eloise from Boston early in 1812. And a really significant letter is one from him to Mrs. Air herself, written a few weeks after that, which declares:

At Providence I risked a seat in the mail coach for a quarter hour's talk with you. Your absence never before gave me half the concern that it has since we parted at Roxbury. . . . I will not betray your confidence, but as to burning letters like yours, that is out of the question. I will treas-

ure them and they shall comfort me when I have no other comfort left.
Though the feelings which prompted them may subside or change, yet
they will hereafter remind me that such feelings once existed to make me
happy.[120]

Years later, referring to Mrs. Air's marriage to a Doctor Tillinghast of Providence, Payne wrote from London to his sister Anna:
"To Mrs. Air pray offer a remembrance as affectionate as may become anyone to send a lady, who has, as you say, 'a doctor husband.' I shall now open and place before me a little mother-of-pearl
box she gave me years ago, with the word 'Air' inscribed in the lid.
It conjures up numberless recollections of Providence and the past."

It is well that the touring had provided some gratifying incidents,
for theatrical life was certainly not becoming easier. Cooper, the
New York actor-manager, had gone abroad and was complicating the
already cutthroat conditions in the American theater by "sending
over actors at a deuce of a rate." [121] In addition Payne was to encounter professional jealousy in other managers who were themselves actors.

In Richmond in 1811, occurred two tragic events that temporarily eclipsed for Payne his private misfortunes. One was a terrible fire on the night after Christmas, which destroyed the Richmond theater, "killing 66 persons, including the governor of the
state and the president of the state bank." [122] The other was the
death earlier in the same month of Payne's esteemed actress friend
Elizabeth Poe. "By the death of this lady the stage is deprived of
one of its brightest ornaments," was the brief and feeling tribute of
the Richmond *Enquirer*. It is a verdict that we who have come after
are disposed to accept on the evidence left to posterity through her
greatly gifted son.

Payne was back in Baltimore when news of these disasters reached
him. And almost simultaneously came word of the death of his talented and eccentric kinsman, Robert Treat Paine Jr. This was a
blow, and with characteristic generosity Payne wrote the widow,
offering not only to obtain publication, in her interest, of her husband's works, but also to give a Boston benefit for her. He even
added the suggestion that Mrs. Paine "reflect upon the expediency"

of placing her two little boys "in charge of my father, to board and educate them free of charge."

None of these offers seems to have been accepted, and that, in the case of the last, overimpulsive one, was especially fortunate.

[9]

CORLAER'S HOOK: HOME BETWEEN
THE ACTS

FINANCIAL reverses in Boston had finally resulted in William Payne's closing the Berry Street Academy and returning with the family, or what was left of it, to New York. There for the next few years it was joined intermittently by the wandering member, John Howard.

Howard—for with his return to the bosom of the family we restore the name he was usually called at home—had turned over to his father for the payment of debts the substantial profits of early theatrical appearances, and would use later earnings to help provide a house for the reunited family group.

The new habitation was located in what in the early years of the nineteenth century was a suburban section of New York: the point of land adjacent to Grand Street, jutting into the East River and known, then as now, as Corlaer's Hook.[128] The northward surge of Manhattan's increasing population had compelled the opening of this and other outlying districts approached by new highways blasted through the island's rock-bound surface. Howard described the location to a friend:

> The spot on which our domicile stands is remarkable both for its history and appearance. Its nickname is derived from Antony Van Corlaer, the famed trumpeter, who makes such a figure in Knickerbocker's History of New York. The road which leads to it from town is cut between two hills which appear to have been torn asunder by some giant quake. . . . The only constant society we have is the Lord of the Manor (one of three

patriots who received swords from Congress), lately appointed mayor of the city. He is about seventy-two years of age and was one of Washington's favorites.[124]

New York's mayor at the time was none other than the distinguished Colonel Marinus Willett who had been one of Howard's traveling companions on the famous 1806 trip up the Hudson. Colonel Willett, later described by Howard as "one of the worthiest men that ever existed," owned the house in which the Paynes resettled in New York, was their nearest neighbor, and became a devoted friend.

In addition to William Payne himself the family now consisted of the oldest daughter, Lucy, the younger son, Thatcher, a boy in his teens, and "Aunt Esther" Isaacs, who had come from East Hampton to live with her relatives. Eloise and Anna were absent, for they, though only in the early twenties, had struck out on their own and were conducting a boarding school in Newport.[125] William Payne, no longer young, resumed the work of teaching in New York, mostly as "tutor of young ladies and classical teacher of young gentlemen preparing for college." [126] The new pupils were received in his home, where the brilliant boy Thatcher was his father's assistant.

The combined earnings of the family, however, including Howard's lavish but irregular contributions, were not large. William Payne wrote his daughter Anna in July of 1809: "We live frugally, in the strictest sense, but our house is convenient and our furniture genteel."

Flushed by the triumphs of his early tours and overflowing with riches, Howard returned from time to time to New York, and on his visits home the house in Corlaer's Hook shook off the dull calm of the schoolroom and became the scene of varied activities. The newfound wealth, of course, never lasted long, for in addition to meeting his own obligations and assisting the family, he spent anything that was left on friend or stranger.

Back at home in the autumn of 1810, he found himself considerably involved in affairs attending the visit to New York of the famous British tragedian, George Frederick Cooke. Though the Amer-

ican stage of the time was actually cluttered with actors from England, Cooke, regarded in London as rightful heir to the crown of
Garrick, was the first acknowledged star to be imported; and the fact
that he was brought over by the actor-manager Cooper must indicate that theatrical affairs in New York were solvent, despite the
embargo. Furthermore, Cooke was certainly in a class to outshine
even Cooper as an actor, though the latter may not have feared
the competition of a man twenty years his senior and too much ad-
dicted to drink.

Cooke's opening at the Park on November 21, 1810 as Richard
III, his greatest role, was the occasion for one of those near riots,
not unusual in American stage history, when, by way of honoring a
celebrity, less favored sections of the populace would swarm around
the theater in such numbers that ticket holders found it difficult to
enter. On this particular night "the throngs were so great that many
were pushed through the doors without paying. . . . Many ladies
were taken round to the back door, on Theatre Alley, and introduced to the boxes from behind the curtain." [127]

A firsthand account of this demonstration has been supplied in the
memoirs of one of the earliest imported English actors, James Fennell, himself once a brilliant ornament of the London stage, who for
some twenty years had been following a decreasingly successful
American stage career, interspersed with even less happy attempts
to get rich in a salt industry.

At the time of Cooke's arrival Fennell, greatly reduced in resources, had been ill for some weeks at the Corlaer's Hook home
of the Paynes, where of course he had been taken by Howard. There
the sick man was "watched over day and night by his young friend,"
and "no one could experience more tenderness of attention than was
shown me by this amiable family." [128] Yet it was neither the nursing
nor the friendliness that, according to his own account, "resusci-
tated" Fennell, but excitement over the arrival of his old colleague
Cooke.

No less lavish as host than as nurse to sick and needy friends,
Payne, Fennell records, had taken "thirteen places in a front box
for a party of ladies and gentlemen he had made up" to attend

Cooke's opening; and Fennell, "though still in a very debilitated state," determined to go along. Arriving at the theater an hour ahead of time, Payne and his party "found the street jammed with humanity, and as we drove up, there was a general cry that we could not enter. Some of the ladies were alarmed, and after waiting about half an hour, one ventured the attempt under the care of Mr. Payne and myself, the rest went home. We struggled through the crowd and at last gained our places." The intrepid lady is, unfortunately, not identified.

It was through the friendship of Cooke that Payne briefly achieved re-entry to the New York stage, though undoubtedly the coming of the English star added considerably to the difficulty of the young American's obtaining engagements there or elsewhere. For now Cooke was the sensation, and the price he demanded and received was so high as to dwarf the earnings of all other actors in the country.

Whereas Payne's first two years of acting had brought him the considerable sum of $13,000,[129] Cooke, *for his first seventeen nights* in New York, including $1878 for his benefit as Cato,[130] realized a total of $17,578; and despite his reputation for inebriety and unreliability he was eagerly sought by all the managers in the country, while the public everywhere clamored to see him.

In addition to this, Cooke though ostensibly friendly, showed unmistakable signs of jealousy, and claimed illness when billed to appear as Glenalvon to Payne's Norval. "To have a boy called in to support him wounded his pride so severely that he could not conceal his irritation as to its cause," says Dunlap; though the more likely cause of resentment in this case, was that one so famous should be *called in to support a boy!* Cooke did consent to appear as King Lear for Payne's benefit, with Payne as Edgar; but this was near the end of the season, and the receipts, $857, were less than Payne had often earned unassisted.

Cooke's star would soon wane, but its luster lasted long enough to constitute another misadventure for Payne, who had apparently spent all his earnings and had been trying, even before Cooke's arrival, to supplement his income by activities unconnected with the stage. "I am sick of the theater and of everybody connected with it," he would write. "In less than two years I hope to take an eternal farewell of the profession."

For some time bookselling had appealed to him as a professional second choice, and on December 24, 1810 we find him writing several letters from the Corlaer's Hook home about a contemplated change of occupation. One is to Philip Nicklin of Philadelphia, whom Payne tells of his plan to start "a kind of reading room, entitled Literary Exchange, which, when I get it a-going, can be managed by my father, while I am attending to my theatrical affairs, not to be given up immediately." There is also a circular letter which he sent to eight publishers, requesting copies of periodicals for "a literary institute" and "every new pamphlet, political, literary or scientific, the moment it appears."

The reading-room idea was a good one and should have been practicable, for the expanding city was beginning to need an institution to supplement the work of the old Society Library, founded in 1754 and still the only public reading room. Payne's preparations had been thorough and intelligent, but as usual he had overlooked or been too optimistic about the very important item of expense.[131] No doubt he invested too heavily at the outset and had to pay the penalty: new debts just as old ones were being canceled, and a whole new flock of creditors to mar his reputation and make his life miserable. Later he stated that persons who had disapproved of his connection with the stage had offered to assist him in the new enterprise, but that such friends were found wanting at the critical time. The reading room was abandoned, and a now realistic Roscius took to the road again.

The absent sisters, as well as the folks at home in Corlaer's Hook, had been deeply concerned over Howard's adversities, and Eloise, with the affectionate devotion typical of the family, offered out of her slender earnings to assist her prodigal brother. To his credit, he did not accept the offer, and in November 1811 he wrote to Eloise: "Anything you can *conveniently* spare, you will oblige me by sending to our father; for myself, I can scrape along well enough. The kindness of your offer to me shall never be forgotten, even though I do not avail myself of it."

This is a cheerful letter, for now things seem to have taken a turn for the better, and he adds: "The difficulties which have given you so much concern are disappearing and I have two engagements, one of 12 nights in Philadelphia and the other for 12 nights in Boston, which must yield a handsome profit—enough to carry us through another year." [132]

With ready hopefulness as well as improvidence, Howard purchased a new wardrobe for Philadelphia, but there his bright hopes were soon dimmed. Wood, the manager, "seemed to share the animosity of the New York theatrical crowd," and "placed every obstacle" in the way of the young actor,[133] who now reports: "The world frowns on me . . . my constant prayer is for fortitude. . . . I feel, however, the value of every trifling attention and the sting of every trifling neglect."

From Boston, likewise disappointing, he wrote his sister: "My success here is so inconsiderable that were I not blest with some trifling fortitude, it would have made me, combined with other disappointments, wretched beyond endurance or description."

This sad letter must have reached Eloise at a very sad time, for two days before it was written, William Payne, the kind and faithful father, had been fatally stricken with palsy in the schoolroom. Only two months earlier, with determined optimism, he had sent this New Year's greeting to William Ellery Channing: "Another anniversary, my dear friend, finds me surrounded by the comforts of health, competence and friendship."

There is no question of the accuracy of this statement on the score of friendship, for William Payne had many friends in addition to his own children; but there is evidence that his health and material circumstances left a good deal to be desired. His courage, however, was of that old-fashioned kind which feels that there is no deception in exaggerating the hopeful side of things. Offered wine by the doctor first called to attend him, William Payne, his powers of speech departing, "made a gesture of thanks and offered to drink the physician's health." His reply, when informed by Thatcher that things were going ahead in the schoolroom, was, "I'll drop in when I am better." Apprised by the physician that the illness might last a long time, the dying man managed to murmur: "Then I will have to bear it." [134]

The letters of Lucy and the other children during the four days that their father lay stricken are almost too touching to be read by alien eyes. Lucy records "many feeling acts of friendship." Catharine Sedgwick and Eliza Verplanck spent whole days at the Payne home and "were unwearied in their services," and "the gentlemen of the Association of Teachers" sent Henry Sedgwick to state that "if we needed pecuniary aid the Society would be happy to serve us."

Of these offers Lucy was not immediately obliged to avail herself, for Howard, on learning of his father's illness, had somehow managed to forward funds. "I am very glad you sent me money," Lucy tells her brother in the letter bearing news of the father's death.

On Monday, March 9, 1812 the *Evening Post* contained this notice:

> Died, on Saturday evening, Mr. William Payne, in the 65th year of his age. His friends and acquaintances are requested to attend the funeral from his late residence, corner Cannon Street, between Grand and Broome Streets, Corlaer's Hook, Tuesday afternoon at 4 o'clock. The members of the Society of Teachers of the City of New York, in particular, and also the teachers of the city in general, are requested to attend.

Howard came with all speed by mail coach, but could not arrive until after his father had been buried in the old Friends' Cemetery on Second Avenue,[135] not far from his home. Though he "succeeded in suppressing every external indication of feeling until he reached New York, Howard, in a letter often quoted, tells of this homecoming:

> When I entered our house and my eye glanced on those objects, every one of which brought my departed father before my eyes, reason became extinct, and I surrendered myself to tears and sorrow. But grief was not my only sensation. I recalled a thousand instances of waywardness which I had never looked upon as wayward before. . . . How essentially would it improve our future peace of mind could we always treat our associates as if they were trembling on the verge of eternity and would exist no longer than we saw or spoke to them! [136]

Its helmsman gone, the house in Corlaer's Hook struggled to right itself. It devolved upon Lucy, at thirty, to assume the office of pilot. As first mate Thatcher, now sixteen, became director of the school, though the Association of Teachers appointed a man to act as principal.

Eloise and Anna were urged by Lucy to leave Rhode Island and set up a school in New York, in order not only that the family might all be together, but also that the two minor brothers might have the protection and guidance of their sisters. "We have their characters to mold for time and eternity," she wrote.

Good Lucy would soon learn that her solicitude for both brothers was wasted. Thatcher would remain steady without guidance; whereas Howard, nearing twenty-one and with a small world of experience behind him, had only reached the threshold of his career of wider roaming.

It was the year after his father's death that with the financial backing of a group of Baltimore friends,[137] Howard left New York to try his fortunes in Europe. He would be gone for twenty years.

Part Two

1813 TO 1832

[1]

AMERICAN ROSCIUS IN ENGLAND *

THE WAR of 1812 was mainly a commercial war. The issue of human freedom being involved but indirectly, it was not a struggle to stir the souls of poetic young men, generally unmindful of politics.

Nevertheless, it was a war between England and the new republic of the United States; and when the *Catherine Ray* docked at Liverpool after a stormy passage of thirty-five days, Payne found himself in what was technically enemy territory. Aside from formalities, however (the war being unpopular with the people of both countries), the enemy was friendly. Formalities in this case included internment in Liverpool of the *Catherine Ray's* seven American passengers pending examination of their passports—a process that required two weeks.

Marched off to the borough jail on landing, the Americans, "at the special intercession of influential inhabitants," were quickly transferred to cheerful and commodious quarters. Payne wrote his brother and sisters:

"His Worship," the mayor, who is a genteel sort of man, treated us with great politeness and indulged us with permission to be removed to our present lodgings, which are delightful, and for which we are permitted to pay five guineas weekly (liquor and washing not included). . . . The only thing that interferes with our comfort is confinement within the massy gates, but our apartments in the home of the governor are as pleasant as could be wished for.

Finally released from his elegant prison "by means of the Barings," [1] Payne proceeded to London, where he was joined by his

---

* The notes to Part Two begin on p. 394.

friend and countryman Henry Brevoort. Together they spent several days viewing "the wonders of that great Babel."

This was London—London of the Abbey, the Tower, the Palaces, and Parliament Houses; the London of a million inhabitants, ten times as large as New York. For the two Americans there were probably numerous comparisons. The Thames, with its many masts, may have recalled the scene from New York's South Street. The four great bridges may have reminded the visitors that their own Hudson and East River were bridgeless. But the most signal advance over things American was to be seen when evening came and the street gas lamps made old London almost as light as by day. Here indeed was something new; for while New York had been only talking about gas, London (except for such conservative areas as Berkeley Square, which still clung to oil and wicks) had been glowing in the new illumination for some six years.

It is probable that important introductions accompanied the sight-seeing, for Brevoort, Howard wrote the family, was "hand in glove" with Walter Scott (not yet Sir Walter); with Jeffrey, editor of a pugnacious literary sheet the *Edinburgh Review*, and with "all the literati." Byron, England's most distinguished literary figure, whose *Childe Harold* was then the talk of two continents, Payne was to meet some time later. He expected also, so he wrote his sister, to be introduced to Coleridge, who had produced "The Ancient Mariner" but was still to give the world "Kubla Khan"; to Robert Southey, later poet laureate, whose "Battle of Blenheim" had been recited in America as well as England for more than a decade; and, probably most important of all from the standpoint of the American Roscius, to John Philip Kemble, dean of English actors.[2]

So much for the outward picture. Actually, if Payne had made his New York debut at an unpropitious time, he had come to London at one even more unfavorable. For England was doubly at war, her long struggle against Napoleon, then at its height, so overshadowing the American revolt as to make the latter relatively unimportant. Wars notwithstanding, such institutions as the theater were carrying on in the British capital—partly, perhaps, in obedience to the wishes of the Prince Regent, who, since the mental breakdown of his father, George III, had been the acting monarch.

The funds provided by Payne's Baltimore patrons were not, of course, unlimited, and he knew he had to get to work. For all his dissatisfaction with acting as a profession, he was experienced in no other, and it was therefore necessary to try to break into the London theatrical world. There was naturally the hope that in a new and vastly larger field he would encounter fewer personal jealousies and consequent obstructions. He was apparently still unaware that he was the first native of the New World to attempt an acting career in the Old. At home he had followed a profession that was still in a pioneer state; here he was to be a lonely alien pioneer in pursuance of an art as old and honored as any in the kingdom.

Though London in the early nineteenth century had numerous minor theaters, there were but two classed as legitimate: Drury Lane and Covent Garden. These were the Theatres Royal, existing under patents granted by King Charles II, which gave them exclusive rights in the field of regular drama, as distinguished from "gymnastic" and variety exhibitions. Both dated from 1660, but Drury Lane was traditionally the older, perhaps because it still occupied its original site; whereas Covent Garden had been moved from its first location in Lincoln's Inn Fields when rebuilt in 1732.[3]

The two were not far apart. "Drury Lane is in sight from our front, and Covent Garden from our back windows," Mary Lamb once recorded.[4] Both were situated in the section of the city known as Covent Garden, former site of the gardens of Westminster Abbey or Convent.

In 1813, when Payne first saw them, each of the great theaters was housed in a new and expensive structure, both having recently been rebuilt after destruction by fire in the first decade of the century. The fire that razed Old Drury had occurred on February 24, 1809, the very night of Payne's debut at the Park in New York; though of this coincidence he may not have been aware, and it probably had nothing to do with his decision to try Drury Lane first.

Among his several distinguished new acquaintances it would seem that Payne might have found one or more to sponsor his London debut. Apparently, however, he sought no such assistance, nor was any offered, and it was through his own unaided efforts that he obtained an entrée to the British stage.

On April 5, 1813, little more than a month after his arrival, he addressed a letter to the Drury's manager, the Honorable Samuel Whitbread, who was not only a power in the theater but also a Member of Parliament, an ardent social and financial reformer, and author of an idealistic Poor Law bill. As this was in the obedient-and-humble-servant era of business letter writing, when the ultimate in politeness was expected, Payne's manner of addressing this dignitary does not seem unduly flattering:

> Sir: From your openness, urbanity and independence as a public character, I am confident that you must be incapable of taking offense at the respectful address of a stranger. . . . I am an American, recently arrived in this country. My pursuit is theatrical. It is my wish to appear at Drury Lane Theatre as soon as may be convenient, and, being unwilling to risk the possible contumely of agents . . . I have taken the freedom to request your aid. . . . Higher considerations than the attainment of pecuniary reward excite my desire to play in England. . . . But, lest my playing might prove unworthy of a refined British audience, I should wish to make my earliest efforts without being publicly known.[5]

Whether or not this courteous communication would have been effective at the height of the winter season, we know that in June of 1813, two months after it was written, the young American made his bow on the stage of Drury Lane Theatre. Peter Irving, then on a visit to England, traveled from Birmingham to London for Payne's debut and wrote him a few days in advance of it: "It may be some comfort to you to know that you will have friends present on Friday. I therefore mention that I have taken places and that Brevoort and myself and some good fellows will be there to support you in your hour of trial." [6]

The friends from home were not the only persons in that first-night audience with a deep personal concern for the debutant's success. The marked personality of the young actor from America had already attracted the notice of numerous Londoners, and he was constantly making new acquaintances and friends. This had its difficult as well as its advantageous side, and soon Payne was finding himself involved in personal situations that must have been distinctly distracting. Nevertheless he carried on.

He had hoped that his introductory London appearance might be in Voltaire's *Mahomet,* as the character of the youth Zaphna was one in which he particularly fancied himself. The management, however, felt that it was safer to bring him out in what had been his initial role in most American cities. Accordingly, it was in the bonnet and kilts of Young Norval that he first essayed a London appearance. His wish to be judged solely on his merits was respected, and the advance bills merely stated that the part of Norval would be "enacted by a young gentleman, his first appearance in London." Neither the name nor the nationality of the young gentleman was revealed.

Whatever their practical wisdom, these precautions were nothing if not self-effacing; yet Payne was confronted by personal jealousy at the start. Cast as Lady Randolph was one of Drury's leading actresses, Miss Smith by name, who instead of trying to exalt that nondistinctive cognomen chose to dishonor it. At the one rehearsal allowed she objected to Payne, first on the ground of his acting. This complaint being overruled, for he was undoubtedly well cast and experienced in the part, she then frankly avowed that the presence of a novel actor would "take the attention of the house" from her own performance. It is probable that before the advent of such young actors as Payne and Master Betty to impersonate Norval, the role of Lady Randolph had been the chief attraction of *Douglas.*

On the evening of Payne's debut Miss Smith feigned illness. A substitute was quickly obtained from the rival theater, Covent Garden—one Mrs. Powell, a distinguished tragedienne who was not only letter-perfect as Lady Randolph but also possessed of a fame so well established that she could risk competition. Although the lateness of the substitution meant that the young actor from abroad had to make his first appearance before a foreign audience face to face with a stage mother whom he had never seen, the change was fortunate for John Howard. Mrs. Powell proved really kind and generous. "While the house was ringing with the thunders of applause for the death scene, the great Mrs. Powell, as she leant over him, was exclaiming in an exultant whisper, 'There! Do you hear that? Do you hear the verdict?' " [7]

Though at first "slightly startled by the staid tone of the London press reports" of this performance, Payne later realized that he "should have been elated to find himself treated so indulgently." [8]

Indulgence, however, can hardly have been what caused the *Weekly Dispatch* to declare it "remarkable that a youth from a remote country—a country nearly 200 years behind us in the improvement of every art—should have the courage to come before a London audience under every possible disadvantage."

Nor can mere politeness have inspired the observations of two others as to the young American's regard for historically correct costuming. This, despite half a century of endeavor on the part of a few, was a consideration still disregarded by many of London's leading actors, who were not censured for appearing in the fashionable attire of the moment, no matter what part they were playing.[9] Later, in planning productions, Payne was to do what, even in nineteenth-century London, was almost pioneer work, by stressing the importance of correct period dress on the stage.

Now the London *Globe* found it "rather remarkable that the Highland bonnet, which is exceedingly graceful, should have been introduced on our stage by an American." And the London *Day* dwelt at some length upon the correctness of the new Norval's attire:

With respect to Mr. Payne's dress, nothing could have been more classically elegant and appropriate (if we except the sandals). . . . The modern military bonnet, not worn in Norval's time, was most judiciously thrown out and an ancient Scotch bonnet, with the eagle and plume, used in its place. The ancient and characteristic Scotch dagger, with a knife and fork attached, was also fastened to Mr. Payne's belt and produced a novel effect.

It was particularly characteristic, and what we especially remarked as a novelty of great importance, that the dress was not changed, as has been customary. The history of this dramatic action certainly does not justify the change made by any of Mr. Payne's predecessors.[10]

There were other observations, covering a considerable range. The American's pronunciation, "especially in words containing the vowel *a*," seemed provincial to Britishers, and "a little study for correcting faults in enunciation," as well as "the aid of a dancing and fencing master for acquiring graceful attitudes," was recommended. On the score of acting ability both praise and blame were administered, and one critic concluded: "This young gentleman makes a fairer promise than any juvenile actor we have ever seen."

The phrase "juvenile actor" was doubtless particularly pleasing to the Drury Lane management, for the mysterious newcomer was promptly revealed as "Master Payne of the New York and Philadelphia theatres." The term "Master," which had been reluctantly dropped in America even by managers, may have seemed justified by the youthful appearance of the slim blue-eyed boy, although between his first and second London appearances he would celebrate his twenty-second birthday.

Douglas was repeated before a considerably larger audience, and in it was a venerable American who remarked that he "had not been to the theatre since the time of Garrick." [11] This was Benjamin West, who for many years had blazed the trail in England for American artists of the brush as Payne was now opening the way for those of the "sock and buskin."

In the early nineteenth century, West was regarded as dean of American painters, in both England and America, and for some years had held the exalted post of president of the Royal Academy. He had lived in England throughout the Revolution and had been a friend of George III without, at the time, losing caste at home. Even today this fact seems less reprehensible when it is considered that the best trait of that discredited monarch was his devotion to the arts.

American pupils were still flocking to West, and Payne had apparently visited the famous studio, for he wrote a friend in America,[12] mentioning among the old master's pupils Washington Allston, "who has succeeded beyond the most sanguine hopes," Charles R. Leslie, "who daily increases in merit and reputation," and "young Morse, the son of Dr. Morse, the geographer," who "has gained quite a reputation for his painting." This was Samuel F. B. Morse, later to become one of the most distinguished of American painters and to achieve an even greater eminence as inventor of the telegraph.[13]

Charles Leslie, one of the new arrivals at the studio, accompanied West on this visit to the theater, by which the older artist was delighted. "Our young Roscius," he declared, "far exceeded my expectations. . . . His action was graceful and his voice very fine; his dress picturesque and perfectly adapted to his figure." [14]

After his two *Douglas* performances, Payne would appear once as Romeo. Supporting him on this occasion was the eminent British actor, William Robert Elliston, as Mercutio. Elliston, described as "the exponent of the gentleman in comedy," though sufficiently versatile to appear in tragedy as well, was one of the actors, who "refused to bow to the natural, his dress consisting of blue coat, white waistcoat and white knee breeches, whatever the character happened to be." [15] This was Payne's first contact with that eccentric man, who in years to come would often loom up in the American's path. Also in the *Romeo* cast that evening, although in minor parts, were the Wallack brothers, later founders of the famous Wallack stage family of America. James Wallack was then only eighteen, while Henry was twenty-three.

The London theaters soon closed for the summer, but not those in the other English cities, and the first week of July found the American Roscius, with his bulging theatrical trunks, boarding a coach for Liverpool, where handbills had been distributed proclaiming:

The public is respectfully informed that
MR. PAYNE
The Youth Whose Theatrical Celebrity
On the American Stage has been unequivocally Confirmed
by his Recent Successes at the
Theatre Royal, Drury Lane
Is Engaged to Perform
A few Nights Only.[16]

When inhabitants of the port city read this impressive announcement the subject of the broadside was speeding toward Liverpool at the astonishing rate—allowing for refreshment stops and change of horses—of seven to nine miles an hour. For here as in America that mighty animal the horse was still the *sine qua non* of all land travel. Even kings and queens, even statesmen and high churchmen, even merchant princes glittering with new-found wealth, had to depend on equine strength for ground transport of their persons and belongings.

In the cities two-horse teams, clattering over the cobblestones, drew iron-tired omnibuses and hackney coaches—the streetcars and taxicabs of the day. For inland travel four horses were usually required to carry four adult passengers and their baggage from town to town. Some coaches were two-deckers, either with outside accommodations de luxe for privileged persons in fine weather, or with space allowed on top for second-class sight-seers to ride precariously with the baggage.

There were of course differences between the British and American coach systems, which the stranger from abroad probably noted. In England the roads between towns, being shorter and more frequented, may have been somewhat better, with fewer rocks and ruts, mudholes and washouts. Furthermore the English coaches, all licensed and carefully numbered, also had names—The Hero, Prince Regent, Duke of Norfolk, Queen Charlotte. And here, as in America, the mail coaches were the express trains of the time; they drove the fleetest horses, their stops on long journeys were fewest, and passengers who were hardy enough might cut their travel time by riding with the mails throughout the night.[17]

Whatever travel discomforts may have attended Payne's journey from London, we know that Liverpool was the English city which took him to its heart as had Baltimore at home. A new portrait of him by the eminent American artist John Trumbull [18] was in Liverpool's summer exhibition, attracting many visitors.

Liverpool, furthermore, was the home of one of the most distinguished of nineteenth-century art patrons, William Roscoe. Because of him there was a graciousness in the art life of the commercial city that no other English town possessed. As Payne himself remarked, Liverpool seemed indebted to Roscoe "for the chief elegancies of its civilization." For Roscoe had encouraged and helped many artists, and his other beneficences were so numerous that eventually they would exhaust his wealth, though this calamity had not befallen the community at the time of Payne's visit.

Roscoe singled out John Howard for special attention. "He came from his country seat to call on me without a letter of introduction," Payne wrote to a friend. "He is coming to see me act and bringing all his family." [19] As the Liverpool Maecenas was the father of ten children, this must have meant quite a box party.

The performance so honored was *Hamlet* for Payne's own benefit; and here again he met Elliston, cast as the King. The Queen Gertrude was Mrs. Glover, another luminary, who has gone down in dramatic history as "England's leading comic actress," [20] though she too could "double" in tragedy, being versatile, as were all stage persons of the time. Julia Glover was the mother of several young children, whom she supported by her acting. Later she would become a close personal friend of Payne.

The Liverpool *Hamlet,* though not very profitable after management fees and other expenses had been paid, was in other respects most successful. At its close the young American, in the words of the city's *Mercury,* "unexpectedly appeared in *persona propria* before the curtain" and made the first of those informal talks that would henceforth be expected of him. His reception in Liverpool, he declared, had "forced him to forget" he was a stranger. "Under existing circumstances [obviously a reference to the war], I must feel and feel sensibly, the magnanimity of spirit, which, disdaining national distinctions, can hail even the humblest member of the family of the arts as a brother and a friend." [21]

Offers from the smaller cities poured in upon the young star, and he soon became familiar with the main coach roads to Birmingham, Brighton, and Buxton, to Stourbridge, Manchester, and Leeds; but despite so much activity, the financial rewards were hardly sufficient to pay for transporting his stage wardrobe from place to place.

"I have plenty of business, but get nothing out of it," he wrote. Indeed, outside the larger cities, England held for those in the acting profession no more promise of continuous support than had the United States; and in general the British economic situation was less favorable than the American. The people loved the theater, certainly, but all too few could pay the price.

That the two wars had much to do with the state of the theater seems probable, though in the summer of 1813 the Napoleonic situation was beginning to look more hopeful. At Buxton on August 18 Payne found "the town very full" and "hoped the engagement would pay expenses." He reported in a letter to John Trumbull: "In the course of the evening, when the mail came in, the manager came forward and *read the newspaper to the audience,* containing news of Wellington's latest victory, which was cheered, and 'God Save the King,' sung in full chorus."

In Manchester Payne heard a note that must have sounded oddly familiar. There one critic, harking back considerably, compared the now nearly mature young man to Master Betty and adjudged the American's acting "quite equal if not superior" to that of the British boy star.

This raises an interesting question: What had become of that other wonder boy? Was he aware of Payne's existence? Did the two ever meet? On these particular points we find no answer, but it is known that a year or so before Payne came to England, Betty had left the stage to enter Christ College at Oxford, though later he would return to acting for a time.

But now, in England, the British and the American Roscius were being compared, not at all to the detriment of the American. "In graceful attitudes and the pantomime of the art they are nearly equal. . . . In treading the stage the palm must be given to Mr. Betty [but] in expression of countenance and conception of character Mr. Payne has by far the advantage." [22]

To Payne it may have seemed worth crossing all the oceans to find himself thus matched against his former idol.

[2]

EMELIA VON HARTEN

WHILE America's youthful pioneer of the theater was being weighed in the scales of an older civilization he was also having a personal adventure to rival any he portrayed on the stage.

That was a "romantic friendship" with Emelia Von Harten, a young matron who fell in love with him.[23] Emelia was American-born; Von Harten was a wealthy German who had his business office and when not abroad, his home in London.

The time was early April. Payne had been in London less than two months and was still dazzled by the attentions of celebrities, and perhaps still somewhat awed by the urban magnificence of the great Georgian houses of the famous West End, when he was invited to dine at one of them, the elegant Von Harten home in Weymouth Street.

The invitation came through an American acquaintance, James Biggs,[24] a lawyer and government official, with a brief letter of his own:

> My dear Payne: I enclose you a note which I have this moment received from our amiable friend, Mrs. Von Harten, who has invited us to dinner tomorrow. I mean to accept . . . myself, as her society is one of the greatest pleasures I have in London, and the pleasure will be much increased by having you with me. As your company is so much in demand, and so much desired, I have apprised you of Mrs. Von Harten's wish thus early, that you may not form another engagement.

The enclosed note was correctly formal:

> James Biggs, Esq.
> My dear Sir:
>   If not engaged, I shall be most happy to have your company at dinner tomorrow at six o'clock.
>   Being unacquainted with Mr. Payne's address, I must beg you will present my respects to him, and in my name, request the favor of his company with you.
>
> I remain, dear sir,
Yours respectfully,
Emelia Von Harten.

Emelia was twenty-three, a year older than Payne, and was, like him, prematurely schooled in life's vicissitudes. Hers, indeed, had been the harsher experience, for she had previously been married, when scarcely more than a child, to an unnamed American, who, Payne records, had "forced her from a boarding school" at the age of thirteen and after marriage had treated her "in a manner so shameless as to deprive her for months of reason and permanently to impair her constitution." On coming to England she had left in

America two little daughters, who were not yet returned to her. All these circumstances, besides "the absence for 18 months of her husband and the total uncertainty of his return," no doubt induced "the graceful solemnity of deportment" which Payne remarked on their first meeting.

Almost immediately he found himself admitted to Weymouth Street on the footing of a friend, "to which character the lady soon added the endearing appellation of *brother*"; and it is the letters of Brother Howard and Sister Emelia, together with a statement prepared by Payne for an American friend, which constitute the record of this extraordinary affair. Emelia's, often several pages in length and filled with frank expressions of tenderness, are sprightly and engaging. Though usually detailing, as she says, "the important history of nothings," they have a pleasing literary quality; the boarding school from which she had been "forced" must have been a good one and she an apt pupil. Payne's are briefer and more formal, and frequently remind her of her duty to her husband.

Near the beginning of the friendship, which developed quickly on the romantic side, Emelia became gravely ill, and physicians and friends feared a return of mental disturbance. She was "once seized by a violent paroxysm of illness, preceded by an expectoration of blood. In her wild hysterics no person was permitted to approach her but myself," Payne records. "She reclined in my arms. I trembled for her life, and left her with sad forebodings that I might never again see her living."

It was Brother Howard who, after some days, succeeded in dispelling the gloom, and as reward she asked him at parting to kiss, not her hand, but her lips; which "unreserve of deportment, nearly always in the presence of others" (Emelia's household included at least two female companions) "became," despite Payne's scruples, "habitual."

The dangerous practice had apparently a curative effect, for soon Howard "had the satisfaction of seeing the head raised which had drooped with sorrow, and the pale countenance lighted by the smiles of returning hope. . . . Our intimacy, it is true, daily increased and we saw each day distinctly into the minds of each other." Privileged to associate "with a lady whose manners were refined and playful, whose conversation was enlarged and sentimental, it is but natural that I should feel more than an ordinary delight in her society. . . . But there are bounds prescribed between the sexes, notwithstanding the most unreserved friendship, which we with one accord made a law to ourselves, and which I am religiously sure she would ever be the last to transgress."

Gifts, accompanied by sonnets, were exchanged. Her birthday in May and his in June occasioned poetic outbursts on both sides and a gift from Emelia to Howard of a red morocco box,[25] which he kept all his life. He describes this box as having his name "engraved on a gilt plate on the top outside" and containing within a portfolio "concealed beneath a lid by a leaf, faced with white velvet and decorated with a painted wreath, and in the middle, the initials, J.H.P., formed of painted flowers."

There was time in those busy, delightful weeks for Howard to bring his noted young friend Charles Leslie to Weymouth Street to paint Emelia's portrait. This was begun without fee, in the hope no doubt of a large one later; but the lovely Emelia was painted out upon Von Harten's eventually pronouncing the image "not as handsome as the original."

It was in this "dispensation of affairs" that "the long-wished-for husband" at last arrived in England. "The wife flew to his arms and her bliss became complete."

Payne had no reason at the time to think that the bliss would not continue. In fact, in a letter from Liverpool where she had gone to meet Von Harten, Emelia declared that "the reunion with George was like a transition from darkness to light. This morning finds me cheerful and animated, with feelings of exquisite happiness. My heart is light as air."

Von Harten's reception of the "amiable young man" who had done so much to restore Emelia's health was cordial in the extreme. He promptly extended welcome in a letter expressing pleased surprise on finding Young Roscius "one of the friends I wish to see at all times in Weymouth Street. . . . I was not unacquainted with your good self in America, but without the fortune of making myself known. . . . Nothing will be more acceptable than your society at any hour when you'll favor us with it."

The frequency of the young actor's calls at Weymouth Street in the scant three months between the first visit and Von Harten's return had not, of course, been unobserved. Indeed, it was very soon after his Drury Lane debut that Payne wrote to James Biggs about "alleged insinuations concerning Mrs. Von Harten and myself. So far as Mrs. Von Harten is concerned, the courage of innocence will protect her. She, dear little enthusiast—so kind-hearted, so generous and so guiltless—has suffered enough, and I fondly hope that those who know her worth will shield her from calumny. But should *I* be slandered (and you know what London is)—I am fully determined to stop the wrong in its infancy." [26]

The return of the master to Weymouth Street was not to resolve the perplexing situation, however; and to Howard's probable amazement, when next he hears from Emelia, she makes a strange avowal: "I blush to own it, but my feelings toward Von Harten have changed. . . . When he held me in his arms, it was your face I saw, not his."

And soon after, she writes: "I dream incessantly of my Howard" and suggests "a private mode of communication." To this, Howard, "though almost robbed of the power of self-possession," replies:

We must have no more clandestine correspondence. . . . Whatever pleasure your love under other circumstances might afford, it is more than improper for me to hear such expressions now. . . . Our attachment, Dearest Friend, has hitherto been pure, but if the flame is fanned by further expressions of tenderness, it will consume us both.

Imploring Emelia not to imagine that he "supposes her capable of dishonor" or himself "prompted by self-exaltation produced by the avowal of your affection," he adds: "Could I uncase my heart and show you the effort by which this letter and a triumph over unhallowed emotions has been achieved, you would no longer conceive it impossible to conquer such feeling."

"You have saved me, Howard, and I adore you for it," writes Emelia in reply. But the effort is too much, and again she is gravely ill. This justifies open resumption of correspondence, fully approved by Von Harten, and occasional meetings.

Renunciation, especially in love, is not a popular theme with moderns, and Payne's attitude may not be readily appreciated today. A generation that knows how to die magnificently demands, while living, emotional satisfaction. We have a word which includes the voluntary sacrifice of love: the all-too-convenient word "Victorian."

In 1813, however, Queen Victoria had not yet been born; though the period preceding her had maintained standards in some ways equally rigid. Howard, unlike Emelia, was obedient to those standards, and whether or not one believes him guided also by motives which transcend them, may depend upon one's estimate of the depth of his feeling for Emelia. Certainly it was the part of prudence not to become involved; but the consistency of his conduct in a situation of such staggering difficulty suggests that the complex character had unexpected reserves of strength.

Whatever he may have felt, he was obliged to go on as if circumstances were less complicated. It was in the shadow of the fantastic adventure that he made his London debut and followed it with his late summer tour to Liverpool, Birmingham, and the smaller English cities.

On this tour he hears almost daily from Emelia, but to judge by her remonstrances his replies are much less frequent. When he is slated to appear as Romeo ("that vile character for the actor, which everybody abuses, and yet everybody wishes me to play oftener than any other") to the Juliet of the rising young British star Miss Booth,[27] Emelia writes: "On the 30th you will play Romeo to Miss Booth's Juliet. I will at 7 o'clock take up the book. I will read every part. I will fancy myself Miss Booth. I will fancy myself in the garden at daylight, and then I shall smile, as I see you do now. . . . 'Romeo, Romeo, wherefore art thou Romeo?' or, as I should rather say to Miss Booth, 'Wherefore art thou Juliet?' "

In another, a particularly engaging letter, Emelia turns the mirror on herself:

Howard, my amiable brother, there is a twinge of conscience troubling my bosom, from which I cannot escape. Certain reflections have come to me which almost induce me to wish I had written less *warmly* than I have in *some* of my letters to you. When our correspondence began, I resolved always to write freely and unreservedly. I *have* written freely—so freely—

that, in short, I don't like to recollect *how* freely. Not that I repent having expressed anything that is expressed. I have meant to be without concealments, to be as familiar with you as with my own thoughts. . . .

The meaning of it all is simply this—I am apprehensive of having fallen in your opinion through an apparent want of delicacy or proper reserve. And yet, I would rather, if you please, avoid entering into any vindication or deprecation upon the subject. It is a cause which may not stand trial, and if I can get out of it by a spontaneous, what, I believe the lawyers call *nolle prosequi* from your thoughts, I would rather take that as an acquittal, consider myself triumphantly discharged by it, and forthwith enter upon a new score.

"Who could help overflowing with tenderness to such a woman?" asks Payne in a letter to James Biggs.

Howard declined another Liverpool offer "for the sake of going back to London." He may have returned because he was sick and discouraged, or because the earnings of touring were not half adequate to meet the demands of his expensive mode of living. Or he may have had the hope of bettering matters financially with the start of the winter season by appearing again on the London stage (for months he had been trying for Covent Garden). Or, drawn against his will and better judgment, he may have returned in response to repeated invitations of both Emelia and Von Harten to come and stay with them at their country home, Drayton Green, until Payne's prospects should improve or until he could make an adjustment of his affairs and leave the theatrical profession for some other.

Von Harten himself had written: "Come live with me three, six, twelve months, or as many years. Do not ruin yourself by becoming a strolling player."

As matters developed, this entirely impersonal issue—disapproval by Von Harten and a group of his friends of the role of strolling player and Payne's defense of the practice with the argument that "Charles Kemble and others have done the same thing"— would soon become one cause of coolness between the two men. Another was the fact that to Von Harten's tender of financial assistance [28] Payne had offered the countersuggestion that he be aided in a theatrical management in America—a plan which the older man quite rightly thought impractical and dangerous. A third cause was the silly superscription that a playful friend named Hawkes had placed on the outside of one of Payne's cautious letters to Emelia: "A tear from Young Roscius and a kiss from Tom Hawkes"—a little joke which Von Harten might have brushed off lightly had not the envelope been passed around among his business associates. Apparently Von Harten did not become aware that the friendship of his wife for the young actor had caused a torrent of gossip until it reached flood stage.

For Payne "it was a hard effort to fly from such fascinations" as the Von Hartens' proffered hospitality, and he reluctantly consented to be their house guest for a time, but cautiously stipulated that not much sociability was to be expected of him as he would be greatly occupied with work. Emelia, overjoyed by the acceptance, went to his lodgings in Firth Street and removed his belongings, including a closetful of books, to her country home.

He would pay but one visit, and that a very brief and unhappy one, to this house and the apartment in it that the servants had named "Mr Payne's room," yet many years later he would recall that experience and his sensations as "like a sick man's feverish and paralyzing dream" with impressions "burnt into my brain," where "the scars remain." [29]

Of the outward incidents of the visit he relates: "What I remember of it is a long horseback ride from London in the dark, an arrival at the house while both host and hostess were absent, an evening's waiting for them and a withdrawal, through weariness of body and spirit, to the chamber prepared for me; a formal meeting at breakfast, where the conversation, though polite, was not cordial; and a departure, obviously unregretted by both."

Payne was too young and too impetuous to realize the value of silence in strained situations, and wrote Von Harten asking for an interview by which he might exonerate himself "from having given just cause for the recent change in your deportment." Von Harten replied with sarcastic candor, and Payne countered with warmth, injudiciously flinging back some of the former expressions of friendship. Actually, in all the circumstances, Payne's defense of himself was justified, but Von Harten was in a mood to be incensed by it.

Then the final spark was touched off by Von Harten's discovery of Emelia's dressmaking bill, to which had been added, through error, a charge for the making of three theatrical costumes "for Mr. Payne." It was Emelia who had introduced Howard to the dressmaker, and Emelia who had called for and dispatched the costumes to him during his tour, but an American patron of Payne's actually paid for the costumes.[30] The incident, however, tardily awakened Von Harten to the fact that something had been going on. He naturally suspected the worst and in his wrath rose to defend his honor as a husband.

On December 2, 1813 Payne is found in his room at the Tavistock Hotel preparing for his esteemed Baltimore friend and patron, J. N. D'Arcy, then in London, and "in consequence of the express solicitation" of Mr. D'Arcy, "a very confidential narrative of the romantic friendship between Emelia and myself."

The affair, this narrative states, "now promises to assume serious shape." Serious, indeed! Von Harten's valet, secretly dispatched by Emelia, has brought the warning that his master is threatening to challenge Young Roscius to a duel. And Emelia has written: "For God's sake, don't, don't fight Von Harten!"

James Biggs also writes of rumors of an impending duel; and the confidential valet comes again to report that he has heard "a friend in consultation with Von Harten declare that as an honorable man, he was bound to leave either his own or Mr. Payne's body on the field."

Now calmly, John Howard puts down, for D'Arcy as intermediary, facts "to be used in the worst event, privately, for the information of my family in America"; facts "without which death or accident would render it impossible, should these papers get among strangers, to correct misapprehension." Though "at first determined to tell the whole story with fictitious names," he has concluded that the use of actual ones might be "indispensable to my future vindication." Again his chief concern is for Emelia:

Whatever ill treatment I have received at the hands of her husband, the lady herself has the most absolute claims to my regard, esteem and respect, and even my affection, and in all that relates to her and myself I feel bound to observe the most scrupulous delicacy.

In the course of the narrative, some new and singular views of the human character may be presented to your mind, and you will discover the ardor of an excentric and sensitive nature, often striking out of the beaten path . . . but I am sure nothing ought to be construed to indicate a departure from the loftiest principles of strict purity and unsullied virtue. This acknowledgment is due from me to the lady.

There is forbearance in this, for poor Emelia, again nearly deranged, had begun to write reproving letters, and they must have made unpleasant reading.

Barring, of course, the dreaded outcome of threatened combat, the bizarre affair would seem to have reached its climax—but no. One more amazing circumstance remained to be discovered by Payne at the height of the imbroglio: namely that Emelia had actually not been married to Von Harten until some weeks after his return from abroad!

This was another revelation of the dressmaker, who reported having received in midsummer, orders, apparently anonymous, "given with an air of delirious excitement, for the most beautiful wedding dress that could be made, without limitation of price." And on the day after delivery of the dress she had noted "the appearance in Weymouth Street of Mrs. Von Harten's carriage, with the coachman and footmen wearing wedding favors."

After much searching "from church to church," Payne, accompanied by the dressmaker, finally found a parish register with this record:

> Marriages solemnized in the Parish of Mary le Bone, in the county of Middlesex
>
> George Von Harten, a bachelor, and Emelia Jenkins, a widow, were married in this church by license, this 14th day of July, One Thousand Eight Hundred and Thirteen.[31]

A day or two after this astounding discovery, Payne received another message from the country place, Drayton Green—this time a letter not from the lord or lady, but from their confidential servant: "Mr. Von Harten appears in better temper. I have not heard any more on the subject of fighting, and I think the storm is over."

Perhaps it was because Von Harten knew that his own position was not unassailable that the challenge was never made. Or the innocence of the suspected lover may have been proved by the husband's discovery of his wife's letters in the red morocco box, still reposing in Mr. Payne's room in the country house. Or Von Harten may have noted this passage in Howard's letter to Emelia, after the fateful visit to that house:

Consider our separation a blessing to us both. Placed together, we might have forgotten ourselves. Heaven has intervened to save us from temptation.

At all events, the danger of a duel passed, and the year 1814 found Young Roscius free to embark upon his tour of Ireland, with new dramatic triumphs and fresh attractions for his young and susceptible heart.

Whatever his other romantic interests, however, Emelia cannot have faded quickly from his mind; and on his intermittent visits to London he kept in touch with events at Drayton Green by paying occasional calls at the dressmaking establishment, center of information for both parties to the strange affair. Through one of the girls employed there and by her connivance with the Von Harten servants, the red morocco box containing the letters—probably both Emelia's and his own—was finally returned to him.

The rest of the Emelia story Payne sketched briefly in the summary which he completed many years later. To round out the Von Harten episode it is included here, although it overlaps the later narrative.

"In March, 1815, I went to France and was back and forth from France to England from that time till the spring of 1816, without ever hearing Mr. or Mrs. Von Harten mentioned, except when I called at the dressmaker's, and then very little was said. I understood generally that a liberal establishment was still kept up at Drayton Green, where the house was largely visited and expensive parties were given.

"In June, 1816, Mr. Biggs, calling upon me, observed, 'Wonders will never cease! Have you heard anything of your friend Von Harten latterly?'

" 'Not a word,' I replied."

Mr. Biggs then recounted that, Von Harten's affairs having become involved, he had been cast into the King's Prison for debt and "could only be released on a certificate of bankruptcy." With ready forgiveness Payne at once wrote Von Harten expressing deep concern:

> I could not listen with indifference to the account of a calamity befalling you; and, regarding this as the time to forget that a disagreement of opinion has so long separated us, take the liberty to offer my humble services in any way in which they may be converted to your advantage. My power is very limited, but whatever I can do I beg you to command.

Von Harten's grateful answer came at once, with assurances of his own and Emelia's continued friendship. It also told Howard that since October Emelia had been "in possession of her two lovely little girls. After their arrival, unaware that such calamities could befall me, we thought ourselves truly happy, without any earthly wants, except a little better health for her. She now lives in a small cottage at Acre Lane, Chapham, where she will be happy to see you; and if you pass this way and are not alarmed by the word *prison*, I shall be happy to shake hands with you."

Payne promptly called at the prison and afterward went twice to see Emelia. On the first visit he was "eyed suspiciously" by a strange servant who, obviously thinking him a creditor, turned him away.

Emelia was greatly changed; and what, nearly forty years later, Howard recalled of his own deportment at their meeting was "not satisfactory" to him. "It must have appeared cold. If it did, it was from emotion so excessive as to paralyze the power of expression, and to create a callous and stony manner." As for poor Emelia, "she was for some time as if in a strong ague fit and shook from head to foot. At length conversation began, but it was general and without allusion to the past."

Half a year later, in December 1816, Howard, on his travels, was overtaken by a sad letter from Von Harten, who, though finally released from prison, was bowed with grief:

You know by the public papers, undoubtedly, that on the first instant, at 12 noon, my beloved Emelia ended her dreadful sufferings in my presence. . . . You know what I have lost! [32]

You also have lost a warm friend. Her daily journals, where you, my dear friend, are much mentioned, will convince you of her sincere regard and affection, and in that I fully unite, with the warmest heart.

His debts of honor finally discharged, Von Harten intended to take the little girls—"my children," he called them—to America and to settle "probably near New York." But this plan was changed, and for another year he remained in London, lodging for a time in the house where Payne resided—the two men connected by a tragic bond that had once so violently divided them.

Von Harten with the girls did finally quit London, but, according to the only available account,[33] for Hamburg, not America. And with him departed Payne's last contact with another unhappy episode of his early life.

[3]

THE EMERALD ISLE

PAYNE's Irish tour in the summer of 1814 was as unrewarding financially as everything else he touched on the other side of the water but it enlarged considerably his histrionic fame abroad.

Furthermore, to his triumphs as an actor was added the forming of friendships with some of Ireland's leading literary and public personages, notably the poet Charles Phillips and the statesman Daniel O'Connell. It is said also that Payne had the privilege in Ireland of helping to launch the larger career of Eliza O'Neill, who was later to become Britain's leading tragic actress and, until her marriage to an Irish Member of Parliament and subsequent withdrawal from the stage, to fill the void caused by the retirement of Mrs. Siddons.

Payne's association with Miss O'Neill, though brief, is note-worthy. He performed with her in Dublin, Waterford, and other Irish cities in the same varied repertory that he had enacted five years earlier in Boston with the lamented Mrs. Poe: *Hamlet, Barbarossa, Jane Shore, Lovers' Vows* (possibly his own version), and the inevitable *Romeo and Juliet.* And several times the two appeared together for Miss O'Neill's benefit or his own.[34]

Certainly Payne was impressed by the exceptional talents of this young Irish actress, "who cried more naturally than any other, tears [seeming] wrung from her heart." He "urged her to give up play-ing in stock," according to Harrison, and to set her aims for a career suited to her ability. Harrison even avers that "this was the starting point of her brilliant fame." Some credibility is given to this state-ment by the fact that Payne, with an astuteness for recognizing talent in others, was always generous about proclaiming it; and that it was not until after the Irish girl's appearances with the American celeb-rity that she made her triumphant London debut.

It is known, however, that Eliza O'Neill, who by her acting since the age of eleven had helped her actor-manager father in the support of a large family,[35] was on the road to recognition at the time Payne appeared. The year before, in Dublin, Limerick, and Cork, she had played with the very distinguished John Philip Kemble, who had taken back to London the report of "a very pretty girl, with a touch of brogue on her tongue, great talent and some genius." [36]

In the Irish cities at the time, theatrical performances had to be sponsored by the mayors. In Cork at the Theatre Royal, George's Street, when Payne first visited it, the performance was announced as "by permission of the Right Worshipful Sir David Kent, Mayor." There, before "a most fashionable and elegant audience," a very full program was given. It began with *Douglas,* starring Payne and O'Neill, and concluded with the two in "Shakespeare's celebrated afterpiece, *The Taming of the Shrew"*; and "between the play and the farce" (in the words of the broadside) "an occasional address, written by Charles Phillips and recited by Mr. Payne." Assuredly actors in those times earned their meager pay.

Sometimes, indeed, as in the town of Waterford, they were not paid at all. There a double bill including *Lovers' Vows* and *The*

Mountaineers was given "by permission of the Worshipful Henry Sargent, Esq., Mayor," and the following announcement adorned the playbill:

> The theatrical season having proved very unsuccessful and the most part of the company finding themselves destitute of the means of quitting the stage honorably, the mayor (to whom they return their sincere thanks), has assented to their performing Thursday night only, and Mr. Payne has kindly offered his services without any emolument whatever.

Payne's Irish engagements with Miss O'Neill included one in May and another later in the summer. For the second she had apparently been booked in advance, for the playbills carried this statement: "Mr. Payne has politely volunteered to accommodate Miss O'Neill by postponing his performances until completion of her engagement." [37]

However difficult his circumstances, Payne was never immune to the charms of an attractive woman, though he seems in his early years to have been somewhat reticent on that point. We have it on his own later statement that he "fell desperately in love" with Miss O'Neill,[38] but despite considerable prodding at the time he did not write as much to the family. Neither had he the year before in letters to the home folks, made the slightest reference to the Emelia affair, though he had meant for them to have the whole story had he fallen in a duel with Von Harten.

Rumors of some romance, however, reached his brother and sisters in New York, together with reports of his Irish appearances with the later celebrated Miss O'Neill, and they correctly assumed that she was the current object of his affections.

"Did you do nothing in Ireland but hunt the red deer and say civil things to that Irish girl?" asks a letter from his sister Eloise; and his brother writes: "Eloise tells me that you are going to bring home a little Irish bride, and of course we laugh and busy ourselves wondering how she will look." And later Thatcher reports that "Mr. Randolph mentions to me that there was an actress of great attractiveness performing and that you looked upon her with more than admiration." [39]

This was the elderly David Meade Randolph of Richmond, who

returned to America from England early in 1815. Mr. Randolph certainly knew about Emelia, for he had been entertained at the Von Hartens' and had, furthermore, gone to their country place to retrieve some of Howard's property left there. In reporting to the family, however, Mr. Randolph may have sought to clear Howard of implication in an adventure with a married woman by confining the rumor of romance to "an actress." That, of course, was the truth but not the whole truth.

Even a year later Howard's brother inquired apprehensively: "I wish you would let me know something about this O'Neill business, of which I have heard so much, so variously and so vaguely." [40]

It seems certain that Howard made no reply to these queries. And it is even more certain, from brief and scattered references in his later diaries that, very soon after Emelia, the charms of the lovely Eliza *had* caught his reawakened affections on rebound. In addition to the confession of having fallen "desperately in love with her," there is also, in a journal of much later date, mention of a conversation with some European friends of which he relates: "I told them about my love for Miss O'Neill." [41] How far that feeling was reciprocated, if ever revealed, is a part of the story that has been lost.

After his final appearances with Miss O'Neill, Payne went to Killarney with his new friends O'Connell and Phillips, both of whom heaped such praises on the American as are impressive, even allowing for a bit of blarney. Said O'Connell: "I never had the honor of conversing with a young gentleman of more liberal mind, more affable and interesting manners, or a taste more cultivated and refined." [42]

The tribute of Phillips to the visitor was in reply to a toast at a dinner in Payne's honor: "To be associated with Mr. Payne must be, to anyone who esteems private virtue and personal accomplishments, a source of peculiar pride, and that feeling is not a little enhanced to me by recollections of that country to which we are indebted for his qualifications."

This laudation of Young Roscius is embodied in Phillips's "Eulogy to Washington"—an address teeming with admiration for

American achievements and institutions—widely read in the United States in pre-Civil War decades.

Had Payne returned to London in June of 1814 he would have found the staid old city and its usually phlegmatic inhabitants in such a state of excitement as only patriotism could evoke.

The windows of Piccadilly were "a blaze of beauty and fashion." Balconies were "ornamented with festoons and rosettes of white ribbon, intermingled with laurel leaves." Streets were "crowded with people in whose hats and bosoms white cockades and sprigs of laurel were conspicuous." Carriages of the nobility "paraded up and down, with servants wearing white ribbons and laurel, and the colors of England and France intermingled." The King of France arrived in London, "preceded by 100 gentlemen on horseback and horse trumpeters in splendid gold lace dress," and the train was met by the Prince Regent in the "royal state carriage with eight cream-colored horses." [43]

The meaning of it all? Why, the news that the Allies had entered Paris, and that Napoleon had abdicated. One of England's wars, the greater one, was over. Now only those doughty Americans remained to be disposed of!

[4]

THE HOME FOLKS AND THE WAR

IF THE NEW complexities of life during his first year abroad had made Payne unmindful of the war still waging between his own country and England, that would not have been surprising. In the generally apathetic atmosphere of London the war no doubt seemed shadowy, faraway. Even in the United States, awakening had been slow; though the protracted conflict came finally to have grim realities for the home folks, and of these the expatriate was reminded by a letter from his sister Eloise. [44]

It was written September–October 1814 and received by Howard near the end of the year. After his adventure with Emelia, his infatuation for Miss O'Neill, and the strange and baffling experiences of the British stage, this message from home must have seemed like a voice from another world.

Eloise wrote from New York, to which she and Anna had returned to establish themselves in a day school at 346 Broadway. Their Rhode Island boarding school had had to be abandoned, when most of the pupils were taken home by their parents, with the outbreak of the war.

More than any other development of that strange war of 1812, the event that turned the tide of American sentiment completely was the near destruction of the national capital. "How will you feel on hearing the fate of Washington?" the sister's letter asks.

> Many a gay hour have you spent in the capitol, of which, like the sacred temple of Jerusalem, it may be said that not one stone is left upon another.[45] Mrs. Madison, stepping into her carriage, when she saw destruction of the building was inevitable, said to Jacob Barker, "Save the portrait of Washington, if everything else is lost." And Jacob actually carried it in his arms, three miles, to a place of safety.

Even New York was threatened:

> There is much consternation in our city. We have no reason to feel ourselves secure from attack, the outcome of which must be very doubtful. The chances are probably against us, and yet we are very quiet, and I might say, insensible. All business is at an end and all conversation of military affairs. It often surprises me to observe how soon the mind becomes accustomed to scenes and ideas, at which but a little season before it would have shuddered.

How was all this affecting family and friends? Eloise provides the answer in a budget of notes combining the personal with the military:

> Washington Irving is aide to the governor and writes all his orders and dispatches. Fay is a militia officer; Brevoort, a captain; Jarvis is raising a company.
>
> Thatcher, our gallant boy, not liable to be called for six months, has joined a company composed of some of the finest young men of the city, and in his new uniform looks quite like an incipient hero—dress makes

no unimportant part of a soldier—gray pantaloons, short coat commonly called coatee, with black buttons, black velvet collar and black cord crossed over the breast, a gold star on each side of the collar, and a plain, round hat, quite unornamented. The colors are gray silk, with the U. S. arms in black and the motto, "Our Country."

Preparing to help defend the city, young Thatcher, the letter continues, "expects daily to be ordered into camp in Brooklyn, where citizens of all ranks are working on entrenchments. . . . He shews me every day a fresh blister on his hands, and I hope they may be his only wounds. Col. Willett asks about 'John' whenever I see him. The war seems to have given him a little renewal of his youth and vigor. A few weeks since, he made quite a speech to the citizens assembled in the park. He was quite delighted with it himself and made Lucy read it over."

Then there are more peaceful items.

> Mrs. Air begs to be remembered to Howard with unfeigned regard. . . . Your poetical friend, Maria Mayo, is about to be married to a very rich and very dull gentleman of Philadelphia—$15,000 per annum.[46]
>
> Aunt Etty said yesterday, and her ready tears accompanied the words, "I wonder if Howard wouldn't like to have Aunt Etty make him some milk toast?" Many and many the times she has pampered her darling boy.

Generous and affectionate, like all the Payne family letters, this one cannot conceal the writer's displeasure that apparently Howard has not written home since spring. But inasmuch as Howard, in a somewhat earlier letter to Aunt Etty, not yet received in New York, complained that he "had not heard from the girls for nine or ten months," we must conclude that the war was interfering with communications on both sides.

Howard's letter from Liverpool, when finally received, would be found to accompany a gift of morning caps for his aunt, "procured for me by a couple of lovely ladies of Manchester, ladies of the first fashion and exact *fac similes* of their own morning headdress." But when Eloise wrote, there had been no word from Howard for many months, and to her the lapse could not seem merely incidental to wartime conditions. "We have almost abandoned hope of ever hearing anything more of you except from other pens than your own. . . . It is not kind, it is not brotherly!" scolds the sister at one point. Quickly, though, she tempers this complaint:

> Think what we lose if our brother desert us! . . . We dread that you may be ill, for we cannot suspect that you are negligent. . . . Six months is a long and melancholy period for conjecture to perform her busy work! The ship, John Adams, brought 1200 letters. When I saw the announcement I thought 500 of them must be for us, and could hardly have waited for the postman in more painful impatience if his knock had been on my heart. No letters, however, and we are sadly disappointed.

Eloise had double cause for awaiting the foreign mail in a state of palpitation, as certain of her references indicate: "I have received letters from Mr. W., dated London, June, in which he speaks of your still being in Ireland. . . . I wish you would adopt some method of communication with [through] Mr. W. . . . by this means we might hope to receive information respecting your health, etc."

The "Mr. W." was Thomas Warner of New York, a promising young Presbyterian minister, later for many years a professor and chaplain at West Point, to whom Eloise had become engaged.[47] Mr. W. had gone abroad a year earlier, as we know by a letter of Thatcher to Howard (October 28, 1813) which contains the remark: "This will be handed to you by Mr. Thomas Warner, a gentleman in whom we all, and especially Eloise, feel a peculiar interest."

That Thatcher, with the return of more settled conditions, expected to begin the study of law in the office of Thomas Warner's brother Henry[48] is another revelation of Eloise's letter. It was this same Henry Warner who, years before at Union College, had written the play *Pulaski,* in which Howard Payne had appeared.

Near its close, Eloise's wartime letter contains more military items. In retrospect they can be seen as actual history in a few brief sentences:

> Sept. 16th: The British are repulsed from Baltimore and their general killed (General Ross, the same who commanded the forces in Washington).
> Sept. 23rd: The Baltimore conflict has terminated gloriously for us. . . .

The enemy are repulsed from Pittsburgh with great slaughter. . . . Pendants waving gaily from every eminence. This is war!

Oct. 20th: Now all very quiet from any expectation of attack upon our city.

These were significant developments—indeed, they were victories more important than the Americans probably realized. Soon after Eloise's letter reached its destination, Howard in London doubtless knew, as his family in America did not, that in the Flemish town of Ghent, only a few days removed from London by swiftest sailing ship and fleetest horseback courier, the treaty of peace between England and the United States had been signed. But the news of that signing took more than three weeks to cross the Atlantic, and the greatest engagement of the War of 1812—the bloody Battle of New Orleans—was fought after the war had officially ended.[49]

This tragic fact is one of the familiar ironies of history—sad commentary on the sport of transoceanic warfare while steam navigation was in its infancy, the future father of the telegraph still an art student, and the destined inventor of the underwater cable not yet born.

[5]

TWO CITIES: TWO PLAYS

WHAT must have been the relief in England when the war clouds lifted on both sides: across the Atlantic, the American claims satisfied; across the Channel, the danger of invasion past! Travel restrictions were soon removed, and in the early spring of 1815 Howard Payne joined the throngs making the crossing to Paris.

The 225-mile journey from London to Paris required several days, and Payne accomplished it near the middle of March. Hence his arrival in the French capital almost coincided with that of another tourist of some eminence—none other than Napoleon Bonaparte, escaped from his temporary exile on the Island of Elba and returning to reproclaim himself Emperor of the French.

Into what a frenzy would the American visitor directly be plunged: the whole city in an uproar: everywhere the tricolor, marching soldiers, blaring bands; along the boulevards shopkeepers nervously taking down the still-new royal signs to restore the emblems of the Empire; in every square orators hoarsely shouting to crowds that hardly paused to listen; in the streets citizens of all ranks joining the clamorous rabble in *"Vive l'Empereur! Vive l'Empereur!"* [50]

It was a short-lived tumult, to be terminated three months later by the Battle of Waterloo and Napoleon's defeat and permanent banishment to St. Helena; but the excitement may have been the more hysterical because built on a frail foundation. Altogether this was a memorable spring and summer in which to pay one's first visit to the city on the Seine.

But Payne had not come to Paris for political thrills. He had come, as any traveler comes, primarily to see the city; and for him, its particular attraction—the theater. Though his financial resources were probably very slight, he had, as he wrote his brother, a definite plan for making money "by giving some sort of English recital— Half Acting, Half Concert, Half Everything, to make it lucrative." In preparation he was armed with letters of introduction to various notables, including the celebrated Mme. de Staël, Helen Maria Williams, an Englishwoman noted for her writings on French politics, and Talma, the most eminent French actor. Excitement over Napoleon's return, however, kept Payne's plan from being so much as launched, though at least one of his letters, that to Talma, was to yield important results.

The name of François Joseph Talma is little known to Americans today, but in the early nineteenth century it was familiar to theatergoers everywhere. For not only was Talma among the greatest of contemporary tragedians, he was also a man of broad social interests, which at that time inevitably meant political ones. Long attached to the century-old *Comédie française*,[51] he had become during the Revolution the leader of the antiroyalists in that company—actors who broke away from the original organization, though they would later be reunited with it. This group was recognized by Napoleon as constituting the National Theatre and given the name Théâtre de la République de France. An association of actors distinguished for high artistic standards, it was also keyed to the economic needs of its members and had a profit-sharing and self-governing plan which might serve as a model, even today.[52]

Politically, Talma's ardor was such that it is a wonder he escaped the fate of his Revolutionary associates, Danton, Chénier, and Desmoulins, who had gone to the guillotine in the terrible days of '94. But Talma survived, to become a pioneer in advocacy of realism in stage scenery and costuming and to fight long and hard for theatrical reforms later universally accepted.

Howard Payne paid a call on Talma, who at once manifested a great liking for the young American. "Talma has been profuse in kindness," Howard wrote Eloise in June. "He wants me to travel with him, 1800 miles, through France, for 3½ months."

This attractive offer was not accepted, however, because the great actor provided still other advantages for the visitor, and those had for him more interest. Through Talma the National Theatre extended to Payne the freedom of the house, and the other theaters followed suit.[53] This privilege provided an opportunity to see every play then showing in Paris, free of charge, and Howard preferred to remain in the city.

These unusual courtesies he acknowledged in a tactfully worded letter, written in French, in which instinctively he did the right thing, declaring them "a tribute more to my country than to myself" and "to the progress in the New World of a branch of the liberal arts, of which no American representative but myself has appeared on this side of the ocean." [54] This letter made such a favorable impression, even in the midst of current excitement over the war and Napoleon's return, as to be published in the newspapers, together with a biographical sketch of the *Roscius Américain*. The *Mercure de France* of about the same date also published an article declaring: "Paris contains at this moment the first tragedian of the United States, Mr. J. Howard Payne."

The visitor from abroad entered into a correspondence with Talma about his theories of acting. Payne, whose stage walk had often been criticized even when his interpretations were praised, apparently sought Talma's advice with a view to overcoming the defect. The great actor's reply, signed "Your true and affectionate friend, Talma," must have given Howard considerable comfort:

> The graces of the *danseuse* are not requisite in tragedy . . . choose rather to have a noble elegance in your gait. . . . The first rule is to be deeply impressed with the character and the situation of your personage and all his surroundings, until your imagination is imbued with him and your nerves agitated to a proper condition. The rest will follow: your arms and legs will properly do their work. . . . If it is a historical personage you propose to represent, know well the history of the man and the events of the times he lived in, even before the period of the dramatic action, of which he is one of the characters.[55]

This counsel too was gratifying, for from his earliest appearances Payne had known the necessity of studying historical backgrounds: indeed, that may have been part of his father's teaching.

Here in Paris that summer Howard Payne found himself in the midst of history, very important history, in the making. A slight, inconspicuous figure, he moved through the crowded streets past throngs of excited visitors from the provinces, and made his way into the theaters past gay young army officers in resplendent uniforms, so soon to be besmirched by the mud and blood of Waterloo.

Always the play must go on: hence the current commotion meant no lessening of the opportunity to see the best of French stage attractions and to observe how Paris theaters were conducted, and their likeness or unlikeness to London's theatrical ways.

"London has eleven theatres, Paris only ten, and all inferior to the London theatres in gorgeousness, though better in other respects," is one of Payne's observations.[56] Another concerned the classifications of French theatrical fare: "In Paris, every quality of audience has a different establishment, appropriate to its quality and taste. There is one theatre for the lovers of show and pantomime; another for the lovers of Shakespeare. Should the national theatre in the Rue de Richelieu dare to produce a *mélo-drame*, even the powers of Talma could not protect it from indignation." [57]

One "mélo-drame" especially popular in Paris that summer was

La Pie Voleuse (*The Thieving Magpie*), by the French playwrights Caigniez and Baudoin. Its story is of a farmer's servant girl convicted and sentenced to be hanged for thefts committed by a magpie. The play opens on an idyllic scene, with the maid happily setting a picnic table under the trees; but tragedy looms when the company assembles and finds that the spoons have been stolen from the table. Suspicion, accusation, and imprisonment of the maid follow, but just as sentence is pronounced the real culprit is discovered, and amid great rejoicing the maid is released and married to the farmer's handsome son.

That so simple a play could have been a sensational Paris hit may seem strange, until it is considered how well it suited the mood of the times. It had the right elements of danger and suspense; and ended with the miraculous triumph of virtue, in which audiences wanted to believe. Furthermore, it was given with attractive outdoor settings and enlivened by music and dancing.

Payne must have been particularly impressed with it, for as an exercise to improve his everyday French he chose to make a translation of this play. Thus, all unknowing, he was entering upon the work which would chiefly engage him for nearly twenty years.

He still expected to return to the London stage as an actor, and when at length he could tear himself away from Paris, went back to England for that purpose; not however, until the close of the famous Hundred Days between Napoleon's return and the disaster of Waterloo, when Paris had begun to settle back to normal ways.

Since Payne's appearances two years earlier at Drury Lane, that institution had undergone great financial difficulties. The services as advisory committee chairman of the Honorable Mr. Whitbread, an overconscientious man, had been terminated by his suicide, caused, it was said, by worry about Old Drury's tangled affairs. His place had been taken by the Honorable Douglas Kinnaird, a member of the nobility, who was by profession a banker. Kinnaird was a friend of Lord Byron, another director, who had declared that being a member of Drury Lane's committee was "a bitter business." [58]

Payne, back in London, called on Kinnaird and was cordially

received. "He said spontaneously," Payne wrote later to the Drury Lane directors, "that I had not had a fair chance under the old Committee, and that the new one would bring me out under the proper advantages." [59] There was no specific offer, however, and when the conversation turned to Paris Payne mentioned the translation he had made of *The Thieving Magpie,* whose fame had already reached London. This at once interested Mr. Kinnaird, who declared Payne's translation better than a version of the same play lately received from a London playwright and unfortunately accepted.

Impressed also by Payne's knowledge of the French stage, Kinnaird suggested his returning to France to look out for novelties which might be suited to Drury Lane, "until there should be an opening to bring him out as an actor in a way that might do him justice." [60] Nobody can wonder that Howard was encouraged, even flattered, by this offer.

The manager of the rival London theater, Covent Garden, heard of Payne's translation of *The Magpie* and offered 125 pounds for it "with leave to make such changes as the theatre might feel necessary." Payne consented, and "the play was quickly put into rehearsal." Thus, quite without trying, the young American, now age 24, had begun simultaneously to serve both of London's leading theaters. With a translation accepted by Covent Garden and an assignment to acquire material for Drury Lane, he returned happily to Paris.

"But what of copyright?" it may be asked. The answer is that if there were international copyright laws at the time, they were largely disregarded. Playwrights were apparently glad of the prestige of having their works translated and presented abroad, even without monetary gain to themselves. This attitude was, at least initially, to the advantage of the adapter, though he also was the victim of the lack of legal restrictions, and had little or no redress if what he adapted was misappropriated.

In his preface to the play, which he entitled *Trial Without Jury; or, the Magpie and the Maid,* Payne tells us that it was "based upon a story of unquestioned authenticity, in which a servant girl, convicted of thefts committed by a magpie, was actually hanged," which sad event "led to the Expiatory Mass of the Magpie, celebrated in Paris in early times in atonement for the awful error." [61]

The French play built on that incident, however, ended happily, and so did the several English versions that reached London soon after Payne's return. Since Paris liked *The Magpie*, London wanted it, for the value of a new play was gauged in England by its popularity abroad. London, in fact, thought so well of this play that in the fall of 1815 English adaptations were introduced at three different theaters at almost the same time. The first appeared at the Lyceum in August; those of Drury Lane and Covent Garden followed a few weeks later. All three remained in the repertory throughout the winter and were repeated intermittently for many years. The Italian composer Rossini even made the story the basis of an opera, *La Gazza Ladra*, whose overture is still played.

As to the authorship of the various London versions: The Lyceum adaptation is known to have been by that theater's playwright-manager, Thomas J. Arnold. Drury Lane's has been attributed to Thomas Dibdin, though the prolific playwright did not claim it; and an amusing letter of Lord Byron to the publisher, John Murray, reveals that in all probability it was the work of an adapter not mentioned by any other authority. Byron asks:

> Will you publish the Drury Lane "Magpye"? Or, what is more, will you give 50 or even 40 pounds for the copyright of same? I have undertaken to ask you on behalf of the translator. . . . Mr. Concannon (the translator) would be delighted and will pay his washerwoman.[62]

With the "Drury Lane 'Magpye,'" however, this history is less concerned than with the version given at Covent Garden. Payne's early biographers credit him with that adaptation, but printed editions of the Covent Garden version, now available, attribute it to a London playwright, Isaac Pocock, a man somewhat older and more experienced than Payne then was in adapting plays for the stage. This has naturally led some students in the field to deny credit to Payne; but letters have recently come to light which indicate that the early biographers were correct, after all. The most important

of them is a letter from Payne to Jonathan Meredith of Baltimore
(May 16, 1816) that contains this statement:

> The manager of Covent Garden gave me 125 pounds for my Magpie piece,
> and the translation was immediately put into the hands of one of this
> theatre's hack writers, and some time after, my Magpie came flying out,
> with Mr. Pocock announced as author.

Evidence that Pocock may have used Payne's translation as the
basis of his adaptation, with sufficient alterations to claim authorship, is provided by a comparison of the printed version with Payne's
manuscript. Here we find that Pocock used different names for most
of the characters from those given them by Payne and also made
some changes in dialogue, but the sequence is almost identical.

The *Theatrical Inquisitor* of September 1815, in its comment on
the Covent Garden *Magpie,* contains this tantalizing hint: "A share
in its production is said to be due to Mr. Payne, the American
Roscius—*thereby hangs a tale.*" There are also two letters from New
York received by Payne a few months later. From Thatcher Payne:
"Your plays have reached here . . . Pie Voleuse on the Boston
stage . . . without being attributed to the author." And from Joseph
D. Fay: "I have laughed over the Magpie, when I hadn't dreamed
it was your language that so moved my mind." [63]

As these references prove, it had not taken long for word of the
successful new piece to reach the United States; and before the end
of 1816 not only the Boston theater but also the theater in Philadelphia, managed by William Wood, was producing "this delicate
little drama with an excellent cast." Characteristically, Wood "offers
the receipts as a test of public opinion—$1118, $730, $641, $580"
(a first week's nightly earnings, perhaps, though Wood does not
explain).[64] None of this profit, of course, was shared by Payne, or
indeed by the original authors, though presumably they had been
paid for the Paris production.

While London's theatergoers were shuddering over the threatened
sad fate of the maiden whom Payne named Rosalie (the other adapters called her Annette) and rejoicing in her just release, the fledgling playwright had returned to Paris. There, in accordance with his

agreement with Mr. Kinnaird, Payne was engaged in preparing an altogether different play, his first to be sent over for Drury.

It was a three-act melodrama by Frederic du Petit-Méré, *Le Vol; ou la Famille D'Anglade*. Entitled in English *Accusation; or, the Family of D'Anglade*, Payne's version was first enacted at Drury Lane February 1, 1816, and though it did not have a long run in London,[65] it was to prove an artistic success and to win high praise for the young American. Here he is known to have triumphed over a well-known British playwright, James Kenney, who had made an adaptation of the same play, but who "had the fairness to concur with the public and papers and to admit Payne's production superior."

Payne required less than a week to make his adaptation of *Accusation*, and it was performed in London before the original French work had seen the light of the Paris or any other stage. He therefore had no previous performance on which to base details of the production, but he accompanied his translation with "such complete directions for scenery, costuming and stage business, that with the assistance of an able scene painter, one Mr. Greenwood, it was produced on the tenth day after its arrival from France." [66]

The story of *Accusation* is a mystery, hardly raw enough for modern taste and with overtones somewhat too moralistic, though well suited to audiences of its own time, in which "robbery, blackmail and false accusation are visited upon a wealthy philanthropist and his faithful wife," although "suppressed virtue triumphs in revealed innocence at the end."

In his preface to the published play, Payne gives credit for its success to the members of the cast, who were all to be associated with his future efforts. These included "the estimable and accomplished actress" Mrs. Glover, with whom he had appeared on tour; James Wallack, who more than twenty years later would establish the first Wallack theater in New York; and Fanny Kelly,[67] that noted London actress to whom Charles Lamb is known to have proposed marriage.

In that same introduction Payne reveals a bit of his own philosophy by stating that "the leading object" of his alteration has been "to present the graces and dignity of conjugal love" (which observation, if naive by later standards, at least indicates his sincerity in the Von Harten matter), and "to hold up for the admiration it deserves, the sublime and disinterested constancy toward the unfortunate and suffering, which endears and ennobles the female character."

These somewhat heavy observations are to a degree offset in the play by a few lines given to minor characters. One declares Mme. D'Anglade "a downright she-dragon of virtue." Another pronounces the epigram: "Cheat a man and he'll remember you"; and a third, "Among all the rogues in this roguish world, your preaching rogue is the most ridiculous. This man would rob a church, but wants the courage to break in the door." The play on the whole is not humorous, however, but it had qualities that the London public liked.

The unusual lighting effects produced in *Accusation* were especially noted by an important publication, the *European Magazine*, in comments suggesting that the stage possibilities of that still new illuminant, gas, were realized in this production as they had not been before. Though gas for lighting theaters had been used since 1803, its introduction had been gradual—first in foyers, then in the auditorium, and last of all on the stage.[68]

Here are Payne's suggestions for lighting in the first two acts:

Act I—A beautiful sunset has taken place. Twilight has succeeded. The stage has grown gradually darker. The distance is filled with boats, in which all the company bestow themselves to depart. . . . Music playing all the while.

Act II—The elegantly appointed study of M. D'Anglade. . . . Two windows opening on a garden. When curtain rises, it is morning, but shutters still closed . . . shutters are opened and garden appears; it is broad day.

And these are the *European Magazine's* comments: (Act I) "The gradual decline of evening, with advancing clouds to usher in the night, was admirably executed, and the returning gondolas, with Chinese lanterns, were beautifully effective"; (Act II) "M. D'Anglade's study was in the true spirit of French decoration; and the opening of his windows to gardens, illuminated by the effects of a meridian sun, was a novelty deservedly approved."

Such effects, of course, are nothing to comment upon today, but in 1816 they were far from common if not completely new to the

London stage. On other details of the production of *Accusation* the same issue of the *European Magazine* comments: "When it is considered that the play was publicly exhibited on the tenth night after its translation was received from Paris, we are at a loss to comprehend the elegance of the scenery, classically adapted to its presentation."

Harrison gives Payne and the scene painter all the credit for these much praised achievements. That may be too much, for Payne was not present, and the effects could not have been accomplished without able stage management. On the other hand, Thomas Dibdin, Drury's stage manager at the time, claims all the credit for himself and gives none of it to Payne: [69] an assertion equally unfair.

Now back in Paris, Payne was obliged to miss all performances of *Accusation,* and it was several weeks before he learned how sensationally successful, even though short-lived, his second effort had been. Had he read what "a London monthly reviewer" had to say of his work as an adapter, he would have had great cause for encouragement:

> Mr. Payne, a writer already known to the public by some excellent productions, has increased his literary distinction. He has had all the difficulties of stage translation to encounter, and has overcome them with singular skill. His arrangement of the scenes is admirably theatric, his additions happy and his language entirely above the usual vulgar tongue of translation—at once more forcible and refined, expressive and elegant.[70]

Discussing briefly "the merits and difficulties of transferring the *chefs d'œuvres* of the foreign stage to our own," this writer concludes that "there is no good reason why French sentiment should not be allowed to dazzle, without prejudice to our native drama."

"French sentiment" had come to the London boards for a protracted stay, and more and more, London managers were to demand adaptations of Paris hits—to prefer them, indeed, to original work. This preference was to Payne's loss, for he undoubtedly had talent as a dramatic writer, and had he expended half the effort in producing original plays that he lavished on adaptations, he might have achieved noteworthy results. Circumstances, however, plus perhaps, his own disinclination to undertake original work, were to keep him for years at the task of adaptation, for which he never received much recognition, or even monetary reward in keeping with the value that his plays nearly always had for managers, publishers, and even actors.

That he was to profit little himself had begun to be demonstrated in his early dealings with Drury Lane. When he submitted *Accusation,* he wrote Kinnaird asking for an advance of 300 pounds—100 for the completed piece and for each of two others on which he was then working. Kinnaird wrote an order for 200 pounds, stating: "It is done from myself as a loan, for which I consider that I have a claim on whatever may become due from the theatre." Payne was never to realize another cent from this piece, so highly praised in London, and a few months later he learned that it had been sold to Stephen Price, manager of the New York theater, for only thirteen pounds! [71]

[6]

ONE MAN versus TWO MANAGERS

ABOUT Payne's dealings with the London managers, statements of some twentieth-century writers have clearly been made with too little regard for implications. The belief that he "quarreled with managers" has become almost standard, especially as applied to his negotiations with the chairman of Drury Lane's directing committee, the Honorable Douglas Kinnaird. Here the inference is that the blame was entirely Payne's, and the merits of the case have never been considered.

It is true that the charge of disagreement between the twenty-four-year-old American and the directing head of England's greatest theater is based on statements of Payne himself. [72] One is a remark in a letter to his brother: "I was reduced to quarrel with the Honorable." Others have been found in a diary and in a letter to Daniel O'Connell. These are accepted as accurate. In consistency, then,

Payne's record of his early dealings with Drury Lane Theatre, as incorporated in his 1816 *Statement to the Drury Lane Sub-Committee,* must also be credited. This is composed in the main of letters exchanged between himself and Kinnaird, copied by Payne into one of his letter books. In some instances there are outside proofs of the factual correctness of these letters.

So far as can be gleaned from a careful study of this long and complex correspondence—which began most cordially—the truth seems to be that Payne, in executing Kinnaird's oral order to "go to Paris and look out for novelties for Drury Lane," so far exceeded any expectations Kinnaird had had in making the suggestion that embarrassments and misunderstandings naturally ensued. And Kinnaird, on his part, somewhat irresponsibly, but surely without intent to deceive, wrote enough encouraging letters to keep Payne working hopefully for many months, although, as it turned out, almost fruitlessly so far as his own interests were concerned.

At the time he began work on *Accusation* Payne had in hand two other plays—*Man of the Black Forest,* a melodrama, and *Visitandines,* an opera. The second had previously been translated into Italian, Spanish, and German, but his was the first English version. On completing these translations he sent them to Kinnaird, together with elaborate production details.

With *Man of the Black Forest:* 16 full-length drawings of costume
3 finished drawings of scenery
stage business marked throughout
music arranged throughout for performance—overture, scores and parts
3 sketches of scenery for scene painter

With *Visitandines:* words throughout adapted to French music
2 finished drawings of scenery
14 orchestral parts
(the musical score, 150 pages; the singing parts, 52 pages, of manuscript) [73]

Talma wrote Kinnaird about these efforts: "The productions are more perfectly arranged as to action, scenery, costuming and every accessory of the least consequence, than any plan yet offered, or that perhaps ever will be offered, to a theatre. . . . Having been a witness to Mr. Payne's labor and sacrifices, I must declare he could not have done or suffered more if the theatre were his own property." [74]

Partly on his own responsibility, but certainly in the reasonable expectation of being paid, Payne had gone ahead with all this work. In addition to the two then submitted, he was at work on another musical play, *Joconde,* and was also deeply engaged in his own adaptation of Voltaire's *Mahomet,* in which he himself expected to appear.

In connection with *Mahomet* his exertions were extraordinary.[75] Heretofore in performances of that play in which he had appeared he had had to depend upon English versions then available; but now in the great Imperial Library of Paris he found the chance to dig into original sources and perhaps improve on what had been done by earlier translators. He found a work on Mohammed by an Arabian author who had lived only fifty years after the prophet, and found in Paris a man capable of translating it. He himself made extensive researches into the arms and costumes of the period and "furnished an entire recomposition" of the play.

Also, being nothing if not forehanded where the spending of money was concerned, he provided himself with a correct costume for the role of Zaphna, Mohammed's ward, which he hoped to enact again. Payne, as we have seen, had played this role in New York and elsewhere and had wanted to make his London debut in it. Now he was negotiating with Kinnaird to be brought out in this part. Kinnaird, however, though he had originally proposed Payne's reappearance at Drury Lane, accepted without enthusiasm the suggestion of his acting Zaphna.

About other matters Kinnaird was for a time generally agreeable. Two months before the première of *Accusation* he had written Payne: "I write this to say, have you anything new? Nothing but novelty will bring money. Yours faithfully, Douglas Kinnaird."

There is also a letter of the following month in which Kinnaird, though not encouraging about *Man of the Black Forest,* expressed himself as "delighted with 'Visitandines'" and "entertaining highest hopes for it. . . . I think you might do 'Joconde' as you have done this." And a few days later he wrote: "Pray do 'Joconde' in the same way." It was not until some months had passed that Kinnaird reported " 'Man of the Black Forest' definitely rejected"; " 'Visitandines' accepted, but not for this season; 'Joconde' ordered, subject to rejection if disapproved."

It was two months after the première of *Accusation* that Payne again returned to London. Although he had begun to have misgivings, he felt himself still in the service of Drury Lane, and consequently dispatched a messenger to Mr. Kinnaird with the revised *Mahomet* manuscript, "stage business marked throughout," together with voluminous notes and in addition, these other items picked up in Paris:

> A collection of 592 prints of costume (7 volumes). Music purchased from the Emperor of Austria's band (some of his most admired original pieces). Manuscript letter book, 35 pages. Five pieces of manuscript, Austrian music.

Accompanying this collection, was the statement that he, Payne, had "organized a system whereby every accessory to pieces which might be desirable could be completed in ten days." Also that he had "written M. Frederic, author of 'D'Anglade,' offering him conditionally terms for a regular engagement, to furnish me exclusively for Drury Lane, all works in manuscript." [76]

Kinnaird, perhaps somewhat overwhelmed, did not reply promptly; but when Payne wrote requesting "an explicit understanding before involving myself further," the manager invited the impetuous young man to breakfast to talk things over. The host, so the guest afterwards recorded, "evaded the subject of the articles brought from Paris," but an important item of the conversation was the observation that "Zeal, however much the Committee might esteem it, could never be rewarded." [77]

To this rebuff, Payne asked "to be considered only as an author, without regard for other exertions." He had worked six months and had spent $2000, but the enthusiasm of the free-lance playwright was no match for the persuasive technique of the banker turned

manager, and the breakfast interview left Payne completely unsatisfied. The following day he wrote Kinnaird a letter which, although
it pointedly asked for a decision about the manuscripts, ended with
the fair but unwise confession: "My transactions in Paris were dic-
tated by a thoughtless enthusiasm for which it was wrong to have
anticipated reciprocation."

There was no reply, and Payne, after waiting a month for the
return of his various materials, addressed a less conciliatory message to the Committee.[78] This communication reviews the entire nego-
tiation, asks what has become of the manuscript of *Visitandines*,
"accepted in December," and of *Joconde*, "ordered in January" by
Kinnaird. It also asks for a consideration of the merits of the case.
Perhaps this constitutes a quarrel, though it is hard to see how any
person in like circumstances could have done less.

Whatever the opinion of the Committee, this letter was apparently
tabled, along with Payne's manuscripts and other property; and for
two more months he waited vainly for an answer. It was only after
he began an almost daily bombardment by letter of the Committee's
secretary that the answer arrived. It is the typical, cool reply of en-
trenched authority to an unarmed individual who has a plea based
on moral but not on legal grounds:

> They [the Committee members] regret that you should have ventured
> into any expense they do not feel themselves justified in defraying; but
> they are decidedly of opinion that you have not established in your state-
> ment any claims upon the Sub-Committee, beyond the amount of re-
> muneration of "D'Anglade" [*Accusation*], which has already been dis-
> charged.

A day or two after receiving this reply Payne called by appointment at the office of the Committee's secretary, only to find the theater's lawyer there ahead of him. As Gabriel Harrison sums it up,
"Payne felt himself too unfriended and alone even to dream of
further struggling."

News gets around, even in a city of a million inhabitants; and
the report of the American playwright's dilemma soon reached Old
Drury's rival, the theater in Covent Garden, whose manager, Henry
Harris—the man who had bought the Magpie piece altered by

Pocock—dropped in for an informal talk with Payne at his lodging. This was the beginning of a second managerial impasse which would prove almost more difficult than the first.

Harris "expressed regret at the conduct of the rival house and offered an engagement, both literary and theatrical, which would be put in so specific a form as to render disappointment impossible." For Payne's services "in selecting and sending over plays from Paris" Harris offered 300 guineas (about $1500) for the season and "stipulated to bring him out as an actor, with further and independent compensation, and allowing him to select his own plays and characters." Under the literary part of the bargain Payne was "to acquaint the Covent Garden management with all the novelties which might appear abroad." Should a free translation be required, he was to make it and receive fifty pounds, "with the further recompense of about $1000 if an adaptation was desired." [79]

This seemingly generous offer was quite naturally accepted, but it did not work out as expected. In fact, as a consequence, we now see Payne really engaged in a first-rate quarrel. In view of his Drury Lane experience, it might seem that he would have asked the Covent Garden management for a contract; but it is doubtful if contracts were used in the unbusinesslike business of the theater of the early nineteenth century.

He went back to Paris in August 1816 at his own expense, and there opened a correspondence "between Covent Garden and the Parisian theatres, authors and artificers upon advantageous terms." Returning to London, he spent the next few months, as he later reminded Harris, in a combined editing, publicity and submanagerial job at the theater. It was responsible work that could be entrusted only to a person of specialized experience, as well as very ready intelligence, but it involved much that was onerous.

"A voluminous correspondence, foreign and domestic, was left to my management," Payne recounted. "I was called upon to produce articles for the press, to read all the printed plays and crabbed manuscripts from France, sometimes three in a day; and in the evenings to support new pieces and new actors." For all these "varied and troublesome services," Payne complained that he was paid "the prodigious sum of 3 pounds, 13 shillings [about $23] a week." In addition he received 50 pounds for four translations of Harris's ordering (not 50 pounds each, as originally agreed)—"and not literal translations, but adapted for performance." [80]

When it came to fulfilling the promise about bringing out Payne as an actor, Harris stated that he "wanted to reserve Payne's appearance until it might be made with a certainty of creating a sensation" —a stipulation no doubt flattering had the delay not seemed to Payne unnecessarily long. He was well pleased, however, when finally the suggestion was made that he appear in a play called *Adelgitha* with Miss O'Neill, now at the height of her fame. This was professionally gratifying, regardless of the state of his heart respecting that lady.

The performance first billed, with Miss O'Neill in the title role and Payne as leading man, was postponed because of Miss O'Neill's illness. After that, first one and then another of the actors was unable to appear, and there followed a series of postponements, to Payne most humiliating, with the play announced for nine different dates but never given at all.[81]

During Easter week it was usual for the London theaters to close, but the custom was not followed in the provinces. There managers improved the opportunity to call in acting talent from the city, and in the spring of 1817 Payne was invited to perform at Bath, where formerly he had appeared successfully.

Here his opening role was Zaphna in *Mahomet, The Impostor*. Doubtless he wore the new Paris costume, and he may also have utilized, at least in part, his own adaptation of Voltaire's tragedy. He was well received in this and other roles, and despite his three years' absence from the boards, seemed actually to have staged a comeback.

Returning to London, he found—perhaps to his surprise—"all the other actors announced as ready" for the delayed performance of *Adelgitha*. But this time it was Payne who was not, for he had sprained an ankle in alighting from the coach. He made other stage appearances that year, but none in London. In October, on the return of Miss O'Neill from France, he was most flatteringly called upon to support her at Shrewsbury in a special performance of

Otway's *Venice Preserved; or, A Plot Discovered.* Here the advance bills announcing Miss O'Neill had this postscript:

> The manager begs to add that . . . on the Immediate Knowledge of Miss O'Neill's intention to act in his theatre, he departed for London, for the Express Purpose of engaging a Gentleman from Town to sustain the Opposite Character with her; and has the honor to present
>
> Mr. Howard Payne
>
> who has recently added to his established fame by his successful performances at Bath. Mr. Payne is author of a Tragedy (just published) called Accusation, and acted with very great applause at the Theatre Royal, Drury Lane.[82]

During this revival of his own acting career Payne had apparently discontinued his connection with Harris. Perhaps that unhappy partnership would not have been resumed had not Payne, the following year, found himself, again to his surprise, billed once more to appear at Covent Garden in that play of many postponements, *Adelgitha,* with Miss Somerville announced for the role formerly assigned to Miss O'Neill. He wrote to Harris forthwith:

> I confess I have been inclined to hope this was a projected surprise on your part to shew your intention of still enabling me to redeem myself with a public, to which I have been so often pledged. If I am right, I consider it very kind of you. If I am deceived, of course I shall be exposed to the implication of having myself caused the announcement, and must lose no time in publishing a proper contradiction.[83]

Whether or not this performance was given, some part of Harris's conduct here gave rise to fresh complaints from Payne, to which Harris replied by offering the American, whose acting career in England was now encouragingly revived, all the roles usually played by the celebrated Charles Kemble, with whom Harris was temporarily at outs. But Payne, conscious of devious motives and wary of complications, refused to have anything to do with such an arrangement.

The upshot was an exchange of angry letters. Payne, accusing Harris of "worse than faithlessness," declared: "I cannot but believe some secret malignity interposes to warp your mind and poison your good will. I wish to convince you that, though injured, I will not be insulted. . . . You may now shelter yourself under the security from legal compulsion derived from my implicit reliance upon your honor."

Harris retorted that Payne's letter was "coarse and rude" and averred that what he had promised was that "should Mr. Payne succeed in an eminent degree as an actor—act more than one part for any number of nights—he would have an added 100 pounds per annum." [84]

Beyond this, we have nothing of Harris's side of the story.

There were private tribulations too for Payne. It was in the midst of the perplexing anxieties concerning his negotiations with Drury Lane that he re-established contact with the Von Hartens; and it was when his dissatisfaction with Harris's treatment was acute that word came of Emelia's tragic end. Whatever Howard's feelings for Emelia were or ever had been, that message could not have failed to darken the horizon further.

At the climax of it all, Payne had to pull himself together to receive his eminent friend Talma, who came to London late in May to deliver an address at a dinner celebrating the retirement of John Philip Kemble. For all his humbling experiences, Howard Payne probably knew Talma better than did most London actors. Under difficult circumstances he was obliged to do his best to repay the courtesies he had received on his first visit to Paris.

"Talma reached London on May 28, and visited Covent Garden in the evening with a party conducted by Mr. Howard Payne, a gentleman who merits and possesses his most distinguished regard," said the *Theatrical Inquisitor*. And later that paper reported: "Mr. Payne attended Talma to Drury Lane Theatre."

Howard, in his letter to "Dearest Eloise" written at about this time, makes no mention of this honor. Nor does he refer to his difficulties in any but the most general way: "Upon the future I cannot speak distinctly, because the necessity for daily labor to produce daily resources, greatly impedes the soarings of ambition and prevents one from doing many grand things, merely because nature forces us to follow the fashion of eating and drinking, and both cost money."

An extraordinary fact about Howard Payne was that, no matter how great his financial embarrassments, he was usually able to send gifts to relatives and friends. With this letter to his sister he sends " 'Manfred,' a new poem by Lord Byron," remarking: "probably yours will be the first copy in America." He adds: "I also send you from the beginning *The Literary Gazette*." [85]

This is a long letter, containing comments on many prominent British stage personages. But of the meanness of the managers it says not a word.

[7]

THE TRAGEDY OF BRUTUS

DURING the early years of Payne's long struggle with the London theaters a new star had appeared on the British dramatic horizon, one later proclaimed as of the first magnitude: Edmund Kean.

Kean brought something different to the British stage, and for popular acceptance he had come at just the right time—in an era of postwar disillusion, when traditions were flouted and novelty was demanded. Kean, furthermore, had the advantage of appearing in a period of slight competition. Cooke had gone to America and died there; John Philip Kemble and his sister, Mrs. Siddons, were on the eve of retirement.

Payne had had an eye on Kean ever since that barnstormer from the provincial theaters, snubbed for his poverty and scoffed at for his originality, had electrified Old Drury by playing Shylock in a manner stubbornly his own. That was in 1814. Four years later Payne's fortunes were to be linked with Kean's in circumstances highly creditable to both, though with immediate consequences more fortunate for Kean than for Payne.

Kean, some five or six years older than Payne, is described as "small of stature, of mobile countenance and fine eyes." [86] His mother was a strolling actress; his paternity, never definitely established though some admirers alleged that a certain nobleman was his father.[87] Such upbringing as he had had was at the hands of an uncle, a ventriloquist, assisted by a friend who had sent the boy to school a few years. An actor from the age of three, when he had portrayed a baby Cupid, later a tavern dancer and a tumbler in a circus, Kean was thoroughly hardened to the trials, indignities, and tawdry triumphs of the itinerant player's life.

"A magnificent uncut gem," Talma called this British actor. Payne, who noted in Kean's stage manner a strong resemblance to Cooke, declared that Kean "by flashes, like Etna, is always emitting evidence of a hidden fire, which at times flashes forth to astonish you." But Washington Irving pronounced this judgment: "Kean to me is insufferable. He is vulgar, full of tricks, a complete mannerist." [88] Irving's, however, was a minority opinion. Lord Byron was an ardent Kean devotee, as were many other contemporary notables; and history has given him a place among the great British tragedians.

After his mistreatment by Harris at Covent Garden, Payne was able quickly to retransfer his allegiance to Drury Lane, which had again changed managers. Though there was still a directing committee (from which both Byron and Kinnaird had resigned), the active management had been assumed by two of the Kembles, Charles and Stephen. Full brothers of John Philip and Mrs. Siddons, though Charles was some twenty years younger, these two Kembles were quite unlike in appearance and temperament. Charles, himself a distinguished actor though somewhat overshadowed by his own family name, was a handsome and amiable gentleman. Stephen, described as "a man so fat that he could play Falstaff without padding," was probably unfitted for most roles, and frustration may have soured his disposition. The brothers were at one, however, in upholding the polished and scholarly Kemble tradition in acting, which was everything that the crudely brilliant Kean was not. It was perhaps for this reason that Kean, after sensational successes in London and on tour, now found his progress temporarily slowed down and himself accepted by the reorganized Drury as "an experiment." [89]

Viewing the situation, Payne felt that what Kean needed was a new vehicle—something other than the Shakespeare roles in which he had always excelled, still a tragedy in the grand manner which by its novelty would restore his languishing prestige. Proceeding as always on impulse, Payne quickly set to work and in a period of weeks produced an adaptation of a play, that not only re-established the popularity of Kean, but also pulled Drury Lane Theatre through a severe financial crisis. This play by its full title was *The Tragedy of Brutus; or, the Fall of Tarquin.*

Payne had read several plays in English and at least one in French on the subject of Brutus—not the Marcus Junius Brutus who was one of the assassins of Caesar, but the earlier, half mythical Lucius Junius Brutus who lived in Rome some five centuries before the Christian era. One of the two first consuls, this Brutus, according to what is a combination of history and legend, expelled the Tarquin kings from Rome and established the republic; and, for their part in conspiring against the state, condemned his own sons to death.

Around this dramatic subject several plays had been built, but none previous to Payne's had been successfully produced. Payne derived the materials of his play from five of the earlier ones. Of these, *Lucius Junius Brutus, Father of His Country,* by Nathaniel Lee, seventeenth-century English dramatist, had been produced in 1681, but is said to have had only three performances because it gave offense at court. Voltaire's *Brutus, A Tragedy* was first produced in France in 1730, but was never notably successful, even when later performed with the young Talma in the cast; though Talma's connection with the play may have accounted for Payne's interest in it. The other three plays used in part by Payne were translations and adaptations of Voltaire: William Duncombe's *Brutus,* produced at Drury in 1734 and soon withdrawn, and the versions of two later Englishmen, Hugh Downman and Richard Cumberland, both of which had been printed, but never acted.

Out of this collection Payne, now aged twenty-seven, evolved what was to prove "one of the most successful and long-lived tragedies written in English in the nineteenth century." [90]

Payne's *Brutus,* with Kean in the title role, was first produced at Drury Lane on December 3, 1818. The date of the première was fortunate, as the Royal Theatre, which had been darkened during several weeks of mourning after the death of Queen Charlotte, consort of George III, was officially reopened on that night.

When the play begins, Lucius Junius, Roman nobleman, rival to the Tarquins, murderers and deposers of his family, has himself escaped death by feigning idiocy and has become the enemy's official jester. In this advantageous disguise he

> prattles shrewdly, with such witty folly
> As almost betters reason.

The Tarquin queen, Tullia, in the words of Cumberland, adopted by Payne, gives the jester his new name in this wise:

Tullia: Hark thee, fellow,
          How art thou call'd?
Lucius: A fool.
Tullia: Fool, for thy nature,
          Thou answerest well—but I demand thy name.
Lucius: Nothing but fool.
Tullia: His faculties are brutish:—
          BRUTUS shall be thy name.
Brutus: Thanks to your grace.

Whether or not her naming of Brutus is true to history, Tullia should have been more careful, for every Tarquin knew that the Sibyl had foretold that a fool would set Rome free.

In Payne's play, Brutus is given one son instead of two; and it is the love of that son, Titus, for Tarquinia, the Tarquin princess, that causes him to join the enemies of Rome and thus to earn the death sentence, pronounced by his own father. This is the central theme of the play. The episode on which the plot turns is the celebrated rape of Lucretia, beautiful and virtuous wife of one of Rome's defenders. The Tarquin prince, Sextus, boasts that he has violated the noble lady, and Brutus, aroused by the foul deed, throws off his idiot's disguise, "assails the wretch Sextus, with indignant curses," and swears to avenge Lucretia and free Rome from the usurpers. "The people join him, proclaim Brutus consul, shut the gates of the city against the tyrants and destroy their palace."

The play has much of the savagery of what Payne and his prede-

cessors conceived as a barbarous age. Upon Brutus himself, since
the Senate would have spared his traitorous son, devolves the awful
responsibility of giving the signal for the death of Titus "by the
axe." That is a trial before whose terrors even Brutus quails—as
Payne, in a section of the dialogue entirely original with him,[91]
makes manifest—but which, with stern devotion to higher duty, the
head of state must meet.

Stunned, incredulous, when the terrible task is thrust upon him,
Brutus gasps:

> The Senate hath to me referred the fate of Titus? . . .
> That boy, my Titus, was my age's hope,
> I loved him more than language can express;
> I tho't him born to dignify the state. . . .

Then, steeling himself:

> . . . he hath betray'd his country—
> That is a crime, which ev'ry honest heart
> That beats for freedom, feels!

In the closing scene "lictors, their axes turned edgewise toward
him," lead Titus before his father and a conference of senators and
citizens.

Brutus: Romans, forgive this agony of grief. . . .
> I will perform all that a Roman should—
> I cannot feel less than a father ought! . . .

> Well, Titus, speak. . . .
> Tell me, my son, art thou prepared to die?

Titus: Father, I call the powers of heaven to witness,
> Titus dares die if so you have decreed.

Brutus: They will, my Titus:
> Nor heav'n nor earth can have it otherwise. . . .
> It seems as if thy fate were preordain'd
> To fix the reeling spirits of the people
> And settle the loose liberty of Rome. . . .

> Poor youth! Thy pilgrimage is at an end!
> A few sad steps have brought thee to the brink
> Of that tremendous precipice whose depth
> No thought of man can fathom. . . .

I must myself ascend yon sad tribunal—
And there behold thee meet this shame of death—
With all thy hopes and all thy youth upon thee. . . .

Go—meet thy death with a more manly courage
Than grief now suffers me to show in parting. . . .[92]

The directions for the close are laconic: "Titus is led off stage to the place of execution; Brutus reascends the tribunal. . . . He rises, waves his hand, convulsed with agitation, then drops to his seat and shrouds his face with his toga."

"Justice is satisfied and Rome is free!" he cries as the curtain falls.

This is indeed a monstrous denouement, and one not easy to associate with the as yet unborn classic, "Home, Sweet Home." Kean, however, without foreknowledge of Payne's destined master stroke, was delighted with the play and its possibilities for tragic acting. When he first read the manuscript the tragedian declared that it could not be improved upon, though Payne felt otherwise and kept it a few days longer for polishing. On the eve of the opening performance the playwright wrote the star about the interpretation of the awful closing scene. Though advice to Kean on such a matter was perhaps superfluous, Payne's letter illustrates the thoroughness of his planning, as well as his feeling for music as dramatic background.

After Brutus waves his hand, a breathless pause. The trumpets sound three notes, short, abrupt and each lower than the last. A roll of drums follows, then 4 flutes . . . breathe a momentary dirge, followed by another roll of the drums.

At the third note of the trumpet, Brutus sinks down, hides his face in his mantle and remains petrified in awful torpor until the second roll of the drums, which follows the dirge; then starts up wildly, rushes in frenzy down, looks out toward the place of execution with such an expression as no one living but yourself can imagine or give, then utters the hysterical outburst which terminates the play. . . . All this music and business need not occupy two minutes.[93]

Payne himself had expected to enact the role of the hapless son of Brutus, but was dissuaded by Stephen Kemble, who declared it improper for an author to appear in his own play. This decision was unfortunate if Payne really wanted to continue to act, for, as it turned out, the role would have given him an opportunity—the first he had had—to play one part repeatedly and thus become established with the London public as an actor.

For *Brutus* was performed at Drury Lane twenty-three consecutive times in December and over fifty times the first season—a long run for any play at the time, when repertory was still the rule and few pieces were repeated on successive nights.[94] Later Kean took it to Paris, and both Cooper in New York [95] and Wood in Philadelphia were performing it with good profit to themselves, before the play was a year old. It was, furthermore, to hold the stage in both England and America for more than half a century. Leading tragedians unborn or not yet established at the time of the première, including Edwin Booth, John McCullough, and Edwin Forrest, would star in it in America until well after the Civil War. In February of 1886, when the play was nearly seventy years old, Edwin Booth gave four performances of it in New York—the last that are recorded.

"The character of Brutus was performed with great ability by Mr. Kean," said the *European Magazine* of the drama's first performance. "The transition from seeming idiocy to intellectual and moral elevation, was powerful, natural and unexaggerated."

It must indeed have been a test of any actor's ability to play this part convincingly. More warmly human and more humanly tragic is the character of Titus, caught between loyalty and love; and as if to compensate for his cruel fate, Titus is given some of the play's best lines. These, in the Drury Lane performance, were spoken by a young actor designated on the program as D. Fisher. That versatile actress Mrs. Glover, who had had a leading part in Payne's *Accusation,* was the regally ruthless Tullia, doubtless very handsome in "white train dress, scarlet toga and gold tiara." Young Henry Kemble, son of Stephen, took the role of Sextus, though his father had at first opposed his appearance in that offensive character —an objection withdrawn when Henry was chosen also to read the prologue.

The scenery was elaborate and varied. It included Roman streets, ruins, and encampments as well as the Forum, where, over the body of Lucretia, dead by her own hand, Brutus delivers an address strongly reminiscent of Antony's oration at the bier of Caesar. There were also palaces of the barbaric Tarquins, and an equestrian statue which, as a detail of the action, had to be destroyed by lightning.

All the plans for the scenery and sets were made by Payne himself, and he also supervised the making of the properties and costumes. His notes show researches into the construction and decoration of Roman altars and homes, with period furnishings and utensils; designs of soldiers' tunics and senators' togas, colors worn and weapons carried by persons of various ranks and on various occasions; as well as specific instructions for the costuming of every leading character.[96] Though he could not avoid a few anachronisms, noted by the press, he had at least tried to achieve historical accuracy—an effort unusual in the London theater of the time, as we have seen. In the general haste and excitement he provided some of the properties out of his own pocket, with the result that he "finished Brutus surrounded by duns and in absolute penury" being, on the day of the first performance, "obliged to obtain a pound from a pawn broker, not to be without money on such an occasion." [97]

The first season's production of *Brutus* brought thousands into the treasury of Drury Lane and enriched Kean by "fifty pounds a week extra," [98] no mean augmentation in the theater of the time. Payne, for his authorship (or compilation) of the sensationally acclaimed five-act drama was paid during the first season a total of 183 pounds, 6 shillings—"less than the regular recompense for a successful afterpiece." [99] And from its innumerable performances of subsequent years in London and all other places he would never receive a cent.

The playbills of *Brutus* did not even bear the name of the adapter, although the names not only of the actors but also of all persons responsible for the "scenery, machinery, decorations and incidental music" were meticulously stated. This listing of others concerned in the production may have been an innovation of Payne's, whereas omission of his own name may have been in accordance with custom.

Authors' names seldom if ever appeared in play advertisements, and it was not unusual for press reviews to make no mention of the author.

Harrison and others, however, recount a circumstance that seems decidedly a personal slight. "Despite the fact that the play had been expressly written for Kean," it was falsely reported that the playwright himself aspired to the lead ("was intriguing for the pasteboard crown," as Harrison puts it). This may have been the reason that Kean, "whom Payne had so largely served, treated him with marked neglect, and, to the astonishment of all the performers, publicly presented Mr. Stephen Kemble with a gold snuff box, bearing the last scene of 'Brutus' engraved upon its lid, but took no notice of the author, notwithstanding that Payne had previously presented Kean with the very toga he wore and showed him how its folds should be adjusted in the true Roman style." [100]

In addition Payne was accused of plagiarism, despite the fact that his introduction to the play, published a week after its première, contains this plain statement:

> Seven plays on the subject of Brutus are before the public. Only two have been thought capable of representation, and those did not long hold possession of the stage. In the present play, I have had no hesitation in adopting the conceptions and language of my predecessors, whenever they seemed likely to strengthen the plan I had prescribed. This has been so done as to allow no injury to personal feelings or private property. Such obligations, to be culpable, must be secret.

The report of plagiarism nevertheless became widely current, and it was specifically charged that Payne had "taken most of his plot and language from the play of the late Mr. Cumberland," the only one of the earlier Brutus dramas with copyright unexpired. It is true that Payne was greatly indebted to Cumberland—more than to any other—but he had been particularly careful to avoid involvement there. Several weeks before the first performance he had sent the *Brutus* manuscript to one George Nicol, "the king's bookseller, an early and constant friend of Mr. Cumberland and the proprietor and publisher of his play," requesting that gentleman "frankly to say whether he had any fault to find with any part of my conduct, either in making the quotations or with the mode of their avowal." And Mr. Nicol's reply, with apologies for not calling in person since he was "obliged to be much at Windsor," was "to express how much I am satisfied with your conduct in putting part of it [the Cumberland play] for representation." [101]

The press generally knew that the reconstructed play was Payne's, though the plagiarism charge, according to Harrison, had been originally printed in a responsible organ, the *London Literary Journal*. That paper in its next issue made a denial, apologized for the error, and declared: *"Brutus* is undoubtedly the production of Mr. John Howard Payne. The construction differs thoroughly from any former treatment of the story and the present production is exceedingly creditable to the poet . . . a young gentleman of much actual merit and of great future promise. . . ."

Denials, however, seldom have the force of the damaging charges they are intended to refute. Many people knew the truth, but others remained unconvinced. Payne's long-time friend Washington Irving, then in London, was asked by Thomas Moore what all the commotion was about.

"Why," replied Irving, "Payne has given credit in his play to six authors from whom he has taken hints; and because he has included a seventh, from whom he has borrowed nothing, they have raised against him a hue and cry of plagiarism." [102]

Irving was not always pleased with Payne, but was sure to be encouraging when he could see his young friend making good use of his talents. There is an amusing note from Irving to Payne, undated, but probably written in connection with the opening of *Brutus*, asking for "orders" (that is, free admissions) for himself and two young artist friends, Charles Leslie and Gilbert Stuart Newton. The note reads:

Dear Payne: I know you have many applications for orders, but know they cost you nothing and you are anxious to have your friends present. I mean to get Newton and Leslie to accompany me and make a party to persuade folks not to hiss.

If you can furnish us with orders—so. If not, we will go at our own expense and consider ourselves at liberty to hiss as much as we please.

We will call at your lodgings on the way to the theatre; if you have spare orders, leave them for us. I wish to hold out no menaces, but I have in my possession a cat-call which has been of potent service in helping to damn half a score of tragedies.

Yours truly

W. I.[103]

Payne probably had to risk the catcalls, for at the bottom of the playbills announcing early repeat performances of *Brutus* the management had had printed the usual warning picture of a hand, pointing to these words in large type:

NO ORDERS CAN POSSIBLY BE ADMITTED

The train of miseries attending Payne's noteworthy effort was not yet complete. In addition to being slighted, underpaid, and accused of literary theft he was also threatened with official objections—a serious matter in the England of those days, especially for a foreigner. According to a rumor, a brother of the Lord High Chancellor had said that the play was unconstitutional and ought to be suppressed. Payne eventually cleared the situation up by writing to the Chancellor's brother, Sir William Scott, a noted jurist, that he, Payne, "never conceived that I had introduced a single sentence which could give offense to the constituted authorities of the state."

Sir William's reply admitted that he had mentioned to his brother, "not in my official capacity but in the idle style of private gossip," having heard that the play "did contain passages calculated to produce democratic impressions." Although the learned gentleman would apparently have considered the production of "democratic impressions" a crime, he stated that he had not seen or read the play, that he accepted "the mode in which Mr. Payne attempted to do himself justice," and was "grieved by the consequences described." [104]

In a memorable letter to the Drury Lane Sub-Committee Payne took up the three matters of inadequate remuneration, alleged plagiarism, and political offense; but like his previous communication to that august body while Kinnaird was at its head, this letter remained for weeks unanswered. He accordingly had his plea printed, "under a pledge of secrecy from the printer," and dispatched a copy to each committee member.[105]

"Aware that all theatrical speculation is peculiarly uncertain," the playwright nevertheless had "indulged an expectation that, if benefits failed, I should not be suffered to lose. I was impelled to this belief by knowing that there is no recorded case of a great success, which has not met with a corresponding consideration from the theatre, whether previously agreed upon or not."

Continuing, Payne recounted his exertions outside the mere composition of the play and reminded the committee members that their own playbills confirmed their impression of its attractions. The personal note then injected by him was entirely justified, but it is doubtful if it did much to advance his cause with the committee: "The mind is unnerved for further great exertion when it is not allowed to derive adequate advantage from present success. If the greatest good fortune to the theatre confers no encouraging reward on him who causes it, even hope is deprived of incentive."

The committee finally read the letter, acknowledged that the recompense had not been liberal enough, and authorized the management to offer another benefit on the same terms as before. This letter must also have spoken well of the play, for Payne replied that he was "much flattered by the expressions with which you are pleased to compliment my efforts." Compliments, however, were not enough, and again he appealed for *better terms*, "begging leave to remind you of the pittance of my profit from my previous nights" (announced as benefits, though only a portion of the benefit was Payne's).

This appeal was as unavailing as the first, and on March 4, 1819 he closed the matter with this letter:

To the Subcommittee
in the Management of
the Theatre Royal, Drury Lane

Gentlemen: I have the honor of acknowledging receipt of your last letter, refusing to accede to my proposal for a free benefit in place of the one offered, upon terms which had failed in four previous instances to realize anything remotely approaching adequate remuneration. . . . I beg leave to say, after maturely weighing the effect which acceptance would produce, it seems a forlorn hope, which I must respectfully decline.

Highly successful for everybody but himself, Payne's *Brutus* was more than a box office triumph. As a dramatic work it was notable. Though little of the literary substance of the piece is attributable to him except in the closing dialogue, there the writing is quite on a par with the best of the earlier pages.

Nevertheless various critics and biographers among Payne's countrymen have seen fit to belittle the whole effort, and a few have seemed especially to approve the censure of Genest: "Payne's 'Brutus' enjoyed a success *vastly* beyond its merits." (The italicizing is Genest's.)

The pronouncer of this judgment, John Genest, was a former clergyman whose *Some Account of the English Stage* (1832), almost the only British theatrical history of the period, contains much valuable though badly organized information. His specific criticism of Payne for representing Horatius as an adherent of the Tarquins appears justified; though his suggestion that Payne might have avoided this error "if he had looked into Livy" is wholly at variance with a statement made by Payne years before Genest's criticism was written.[106] Furthermore, when it is considered that Genest, in his book, dismisses *The Marriage of Figaro* as "little more than the follies of the day degraded into an opera," it may be doubted if his animadversions on *Brutus* should be accepted as more than they were—merely one man's opinion.

There have been more considered judgments of *Brutus*, two on the part of Americans. One of these, William Winter, who lived while the play was still being performed, felt that it "produced the effect of a series of episodes in Roman history, rather than a single dramatic narrative," but found it "valuable for its tumultuous action, its splendid pictorial effects and its moments of pathos."[107] The other, a twentieth-century writer, Arthur Hobson Quinn, finds that Payne's greatest merit is his talent for selection and arrangement. "His prime characteristic was a capacity for borrowing what would be theatrically effective and reshaping it to make a new thing."[108]

The new thing created in *Brutus* was an impressively dramatic play. Few dramas of any period, original or adapted, outside acknowledged masterpieces, have had the qualities to endure for half a century.

[8]

TROUBLED INTERLUDE

"MY SUCCESS has obliged me to keep myself out of view," Payne wrote to a friend in 1819. To another: "The consequence has been ruinous. Creditors who were quiet before, become clamorous." And to a third: "All whom I owe money swarm upon me at once, attracted by the reputation of great wealth." [109]

This was the year following the London première of *Brutus*. For Payne, deprived of the just emoluments of that achievement, it was a year of desperate effort to launch a new project or to obtain a connection which might assure a living; and to these ends he wrote scores of letters. There are letters to managers offering plays (a tragedy called *Virginius*, completed within the year, is mentioned in several); letters to publishers proposing attractive but impractical projects ("a new monthly magazine covering the United States" is one); letters to theatrical friends in America suggesting his possible return; and, most of all, letters aimed at obtaining some British theatrical management wherein, as his own producer, he fondly hoped to avoid such experiences as had lately turned success into something more ironic than failure.

There is no questioning the sincerity of these diversified and sometimes badly aimed appeals. Reading them, one almost shares the agonizing headache of which their writer complains in more than one. Payne was apparently willing, or thought he was, to take any of several paths to financial self-redemption; but the managerial possibility was the one that he pursued with most conviction. Here there were two main opportunities: the Royal Theatre of Birmingham and the Olympic, a minor theater in London.[110] Both were managements that Elliston was on the point of relinquishing to become manager of Drury Lane, the younger Kembles having abandoned that venture.

Though especially talented in production planning, Payne was so deficient in business sense that the defeat of any effort of his to assume theatrical management may seem fortunate. Nevertheless the shifts and dodges of the inscrutable Elliston did little to relieve the headaches. Negotiations concerning the Birmingham theater, Payne wrote his brother, had proceeded so far that "an order had been sent for delivery of the key into my hands," when Elliston changed his mind. The Olympic opportunity was lost when both Elliston and Payne's financial backer withdrew at the last minute.

One bright detail in connection with these efforts is a very agreeable letter of recommendation written by Kean to the proprietors of the Birmingham theater. This suggests that any breach between the two chief *Brutus* protagonists had been healed. Kean "bears the strongest testimony to the competency of my worthy friend, Mr. Payne. His dramatic qualities have been tested in the severest, and also in the most successful manner in the production of his tragedy of Brutus, which has had such ample and almost unexampled success at Drury Lane." [111]

It was not until the fourth of May, 1819, that Howard found himself in a spirit to answer a letter from his brother Thatcher, received the previous December, "just in the midst of the tremendous fire of malevolence which was opened against the success of 'Brutus.' I delayed writing purposely at the time, because I hoped to have great good fortune to communicate."

Similar motives perhaps account for Howard's previous delays in writing to the family in New York, which was now receiving his cherished letters no oftener than once or twice a year. Though he may have been at fault here, his remissness was exaggerated by the general state of transatlantic communications. Mail "entrusted to the ship's letter bags" was often greatly delayed; one letter from Thatcher to Howard was not delivered until seventeen months after the date of writing. Furthermore, letters might be lost altogether unless committed to travelers for personal delivery—a burden apparently accepted as a matter of course by persons crossing the Atlantic.

It can also be seen by comparing dates that more than once an overdue missive of Howard's crossed one or more from his brother or sisters. Nevertheless, in nearly all the home letters, expressions of the most devoted affection are combined with complaints of his failure to write. This from Thatcher:

> You have so long been the life of our family circle that the memory of you still serves daily to recall the joy of our departed hours. Your picture stands over the fireplace, as it was wont, but we begin to imagine that we can trace in its fading colors the fading lineaments of that affection which we were assured by testimony stronger than mere profession was once ours.

True, the infrequency of the letters spared the family knowledge of the absent brother's tribulations ("If a man must be miserable he may as well be miserable by himself," he once remarked); but the anxiety caused by his long periods of silence was often acute. When more than a year had passed since the writing date of his letter most recently received, Eloise added to one of hers a bit that might have melted a stonier heart than Howard's:

> Aunt Esther goes up and down stairs, sighing like the gusts in autumn, and puts on her spectacles every evening to read the marine lists and see if you are mentioned in them. . . . From speculation and anxiety we have passed to the most painful solicitude. . . . We have never believed our brother could *live* and be insensible to every domestic claim.

Four days after this was written, a letter from the prodigal reached New York, conveyed by a returning traveler. Consequently the sister is repentant: "You must not be displeased by the plainness of my letters, dearest Howard. It is from a heart full of tenderness for you." She begs to be told "without reserve and without delay" if her brother is "in circumstances of distress of any kind."

They were fine, courageous, tender-hearted people, that family left behind—the kind of human beings that writers of a later period would almost have us believe never existed. Gentlefolk unsuited to life's meaner competitions, they were a pathetic little group, bound for years by financial restraints from which they seemed unable to free themselves. Though Howard was all too sure of their forgiveness, there can be no question of his love for them, and his hopes for prosperity and success always included some sincere if perhaps impractical plan for helping the family.

For some years the news from home had not been encouraging. Thatcher had continued to teach in order to provide for his sisters and aunt, though his progress as a law student was thus greatly impeded. His letters touch upon the situation:

> My dear brother, I never could fully appreciate the worth of your labors and your sacrifices, while yet a stripling, until the rude blasts which sweep through this desert of a world made me also wrap my mantle around me. . . . I am engaged seven to nine hours a day in teaching, for which I receive $1000 per annum, which, with what little remains of Eloise's business, keeps our heads above the waters of despair.[112]

Lucy had married a distant cousin, Dr. John Cheever Osborn, and as the wife of an exceptionally kindly man and the mother of two little boys, she would know a brief period of happiness. To Eloise's account of the Trinity Church christening of Lucy's first child, named for his grandfather, William Payne, Howard replied with much feeling:

> Could the spirits of our parents have hovered near the baptismal fount, they must have rejoiced. I could not have borne the scene. The recollection of that name . . . would have unmanned me, for as I write, my eyes are overflowing and my heart is bursting.
>
> I suppose the emotion inspired by the commencement of a new generation in a family is the same everywhere and in every mind. The extension of a line, though it be merely the extension of earthly existence, swells the bosoms of those even indirectly concerned, with a kind of epic feeling, because it resembles immortality.[113]

Two years later Lucy had lost both her children. Christened in New York's Trinity Church, Lucy's babies are buried there in the old churchyard.[114] Soon after the death of the second child, her husband died in March of 1819, in the West Indies, where he had gone in search of health.

Howard knew nothing of these sad happenings when he said in the letter of May 1819 to Thatcher: "You do not communicate to me any news of what is going on in New York. . . . Anna seems quite obsolete, and so do Lucy and Aunt Esther. . . . And I hear nothing from Eloise, who was formerly fond of writing. Is she married?"

No. The long engagement of Eloise to Thomas Warner was never to be crowned by marriage; and she, for years in failing health, was finally "obliged to renounce all occupations." In July of 1819 came the most crushing blow of all, in the death of this admired, beloved sister, "the pride of our family and the cherished idol of our hearts." Only thirty-two, Eloise had fallen victim to a malady akin to tuberculosis, greatly aggravated, no doubt, by disappointed hopes. Her death occurred in Lancaster, Massachusetts, where she had gone for treatment; and there the family's devoted friend John Gorham Palfrey later erected a small monument in her memory.

The "painful intelligence" of the death of this sister reached Howard in September, after a summer during which his misfortunes had multiplied. For nonpayment of rent he had been put out of the house where he had long been a lodger. He had even, for a time, "been reduced to the want of my daily bread." [115]

These circumstances may help account for the fact that his sister Anna's letter, with the shocking news of the death of Eloise, remained for two months unanswered. When he did reply he expressed a resignation unusual on the part of one still in the twenties and reflective of his own near despair: "When we daily feel the pressures of misery, the stings of life, which cannot be escaped, tears for the dead ought to be changed to rejoicing for a soul in bliss."

He begs Anna not to regard "the interval which has elapsed between your letter and my answer as any proof of the impression that letter made upon me. . . . My feelings were not in a state to suffer me to write immediately. As our family circle narrows, our hearts draw nearer; and the loss we have sustained, renders me doubly desirous to husband the domestic treasures still left to us."

His tribute to the departed sister is eloquent:

In the entire range of my recollection and reading, I cannot refer to any character . . . more entitled to exclusive admiration than our departed Eloise. In all the graces of the intellect, the coruscations of wit, the powers of fancy, she was at a very early age acknowledged to be without a rival.

As she grew in the higher accomplishments . . . having amassed an intellectual fortune equal to all the purposes of the world, she did not look down from the eminence as from a throne lifting her above her fellow creatures, but turned her gaze heavenward, making it a footstool to gaze more clearly on the skies. To die with a heart thus purified is to be rewarded. Added years, which would have made us happy in her possession, would have diminished her certainty of happiness.[116]

Later, writing to Thatcher on the last day of the year, Howard would make his only reference to the bereavements of Lucy:

I am sincerely grieved to hear of Lucy's afflictions, and trust she will not sink under them, but call into action all the energies of her peculiar fortitude. I . . . hope that the reliance upon providence which she always zealously inculcated, will sustain her own mind amid the dissolution of those new ties, which sometimes seem only to be given to convince us that, however deeply we may have suffered, even when misery may seem to have attained its climax, there may be sufferings yet unfelt, deeper and deeper still.

The past year has not been a source of much comfort to any of us. As for myself, I do hope that experience and maturer age will give me strength to improve my entire plan of life and make me worthy of better things to come. My mind dwells much upon some comfortable and respectable settlement in life. . . . I wish to make for myself a comfortable home and have you all about me.

This final letter of the year, addressed and sealed, was opened for "an addendum" recording two strange turns of fate in the field of his recent efforts: "We seldom know what we ought to wish for. On Friday last the Birmingham theatre was burned to the ground; and the very next day an attempt was commenced to reduce the minor theatres to concerns of no profit or value whatever."

[9]

SUMMER AT SADLER'S WELLS

MIDWAY of the twentieth century, when the Sadler's Wells Ballet, acme of the choreographic art, paid a first visit to America, its "fifty tons of scenery, costumes and properties" constituted "the greatest transatlantic haul in theatrical history." [117]

Could the shade of a onetime stage-struck boy of old New York have witnessed the clearing of the 7000 items at the Hudson River pier and the journey of the huge cargo through the modern city's congested streets, what would have been his wonderment and delight! For here was proof that a once humble institution, which more than a century earlier he had attempted "to elevate above a mere vehicle of amusement," had achieved an artistic triumph far beyond his dreams.

It was in 1820 on April 3, Easter Monday, that Payne took over the management of the "Musick House" at the mineral springs, then a few miles out of London, known as Sadler's Wells. The following November he was obliged to relinquish the project, but under him the little playhouse had had a new experience. For the first time in its history it had seen serious drama added to the "spectacular and pantomimic" for which the place had long been noted.

Sadler's Wells is probably London's oldest theater.[118] In fact, one authority suggests not only that it is the oldest still existing, but also that if traced to its very beginnings, it may even antedate the Globe. According to that interesting account, which has a not improbable sound, "long before Henry VIII" there was a building at these springs "to afford diversion to the water drinkers." [119] In the reign of Henry, this report continues, Protestant authorities stopped up the spring known as the "Holy Well," and it was discovered a century later by a workman employed by one Mr. Sadler, "a surveyor for the highways." [120] Sadler not only "planted trees and shrubs, and constructed a marble basin to receive the waters of the principal well," but also restored the entertainment features of the place by building "a long room with a stage at one end" and employing "posturers, tumblers and rope dancers." [121]

In its long intermediate career the theater at the Wells would know fluctuating fortunes; more than once declared "a place injurious to morals"; at other times reformed and patronized by kings. After the death of Sadler a weekly newspaper of the community called it "a resort of strolling damsels, half-pay officers, peripatetic tradesmen, tars, butchers and others musically inclined." That was in

1718 but a few decades later a new building for the theater was licensed by act of George II.

A writer who knew the place in the 1840's once recalled that it was reached "by a pleasant walk in summer time, over the fields to Hoxton." And some twenty years earlier the *London Magazine* had similarly recorded: "Took a pleasant stroll up to the theatre at Sadler's Wells. We hope that under the management of a gentleman (Mr. Howard Payne), so well acquainted with both departments of his undertaking, the literary and the dramatic, this theatre will soon flourish in all the pride of summer."

Another contemporary journal, the alert *Theatrical Inquisitor*, remarked of Payne's management: "A new era has dawned upon this establishment, which, having now fallen into the hands of a gentleman of tried histrionic and dramatic talent, may look forward to an equal measure of merit and prosperity." And toward the end of the season, the *Literary Gazette*, widely read by theatergoers, added its tribute:

> This is a pleasant little theatre which has gained our good word. Mr. Howard Payne has exerted himself to gratify the public and has succeeded. It is not a little flattering to the taste and ability of Mr. Payne that he procures such a large measure of popular approbation. The audiences seen at this little place have been both numerous and respectable and would grace any theatre.[122]

Payne's immediate predecessor in the management of the summer playhouse was the younger Charles Dibdin, son of the famous British song writer of that name and brother of Thomas Dibdin, who had been stage manager at Drury Lane when Payne's *Accusation* was performed there. At the Wells Dibdin is known to have continued or revived a celebrated practice of earlier proprietors by "allowing a pint of old port to each man in the audience." [123] Since the entertainment usually offered was "very monotonous," [124] this device had probably been used to draw a crowd.

Payne, however, had no use for such secondary enticements. His interest in the Wells lay entirely in the opportunity it afforded of conducting a theater after his own ideas. It was a bold undertaking, not only in view of intrinsic difficulties, but also because of the legal restrictions long placed upon the minor theaters. For in accordance with patents granted by Charles II, some century and a half earlier, to Drury Lane and Covent Garden, those two were the only London theaters licensed to produce regular drama,[125] at least during the winter months. The Haymarket, after years of effort, had obtained the privilege of producing plays in the summertime, when the two great houses were closed. All the others (excepting, at one time, the Lyceum, which was "limited to English opera and farces") were supposed to provide only pantomime or "gymnastic entertainment."

These restrictions, lasting until the middle of the nineteenth century, were much criticised and opposed, on the ground that they either discouraged effort and initiative or led to violations.[126] For like other laws too drastic to be enforced consistently, this one was constantly flouted. Occasionally the law would come down on a violator; but some of the minor theaters succeeded in putting on melodramas without hindrance so long as they called their offerings "exhibitions" or "burlettas"; or perhaps more importantly, so long as results were not good enough to offer serious competition to the Theatres Royal.

Payne cannot have been unaware of this situation, but fortunately he seems not to have regarded it seriously. That Sadler's Wells had long been known as the *summer* theater was in his favor. Perhaps even more so was the fact that, of all the theaters in or about London, it was the last from which the great patent houses would have expected even a threat of competition.

Payne's opening bill, although it included a melodrama, kept mainly to the Sadler's Wells tradition. It was a three-part attraction, and that also was approved by custom; for though other innovations might be welcomed, an evening's entertainment consisting of only one number would not have been tolerated.

This triple bill, "received with great applause by a numerous and overflowing audience," began with "an interesting new pantomime, 'Goody Two-Shoes,' followed by a new melodrama called 'Calas,' and concluded with 'The Cottage by the Lake; or, My Vassal's Dog,' in which the dog Bruin and a lake of real water were introduced." [127] The novelty was *Calas*, by the French dramatist Victor H. J. B. Ducange, whose *Thérèse* Payne would later make famous in England

and America. *Calas* was then showing in Paris, but had not previously been seen in London, and playgoers were glad of the opportunity to see it at popular prices at the Wells.

The other two items were of a kind more familiar to the usual Wells audiences. The "dog Bruin" number required those "elaborate aquatic effects" for which the Wells had special equipment— "an immense tank constructed under the stage and fed from the New River." Pantomimes, too, were often given at the Wells, but *Goody Two-Shoes*, which the *Times* described as new, merits special comment. Charles Dibdin, Payne's predecessor in the management, is credited as author of this pantomime,[128] based on a charming children's classic very popular in the early nineteenth century but unaccountably neglected today.

If it is true that Dibdin was originator of the idea of making *Goody Two-Shoes* into a pantomime, there is coincidence in a remark made by Payne only three months earlier in a letter to his sister Anna: "You and I, in our early days, were very much together, and the old times of the pewter equipage and Little Goody Two-Shoes returns upon my memory with redoubled interest, as new times and increasing years bear us farther from them."

So no matter who first thought of the pantomime, the new manager must have worked with real nostalgia on rehearsals of the story of little Margery Meanwell in her precious new shoes, faring forth to teach the village children, with her two baskets of letters—"26 big letters and 26 little letters," which "could spell all the words in the world." It would make a charming playlet for children or grownups of any period, and to judge by the many repeat performances announced in London papers it was exceedingly popular that summer at the Wells.

Playbills still preserved cover only the second half of Payne's season at the Wells, and that incompletely. These, however, are sufficient to give an idea of the variety and elaborateness of the performances undertaken, most of them announced as "entirely new," presented with new music, new scenery, new dresses and properties, and even new machinery. Of the "strong company" then performing at the suburban theater, one member was Joey Grimaldi, the famous clown, long a favorite with audiences there.[129] Before Payne arrived

Grimaldi had attempted briefly to manage the Wells, but soon returned to his old métier.

The Mountaineers was in the repertory that summer; so was the old tragedy *Douglas*, with Payne himself appearing in his famous role, Young Norval. There was also "a dramatic version of 'The Monastery' from a Scotch novel, 'The White Maid of Avendel,' very happily contrived and productive of a beautiful effect."

Of the new pieces the greatest number are described as melodramas, and that designation is suggested by their titles. Among them was *Man of the Black Forest*, one of Payne's translations rejected by Kinnaird. Others were *A Father's Curse; or, Guilt Discovered* ("much better performed than the majority of melodramas") and *Anne Boleyn; or, Virtue Betrayed*, the last ending bloodcurdlingly with "the procession of Anne to her death and the scene of her execution." [130]

Wells audiences of course were out for a summer evening's entertainment, and it would not do to offer exclusively serious fare. Hence every tragedy or tense melodrama was followed, for relief, by a minor piece called a burletta. *How to Live Without Money* and *Pay Today and Trust Tomorrow* are typical titles. *Robin Roughhead* was a comedy much approved, and so was "an irresistibly laughable extravaganza" called *More Ghosts Than One*. One afterpiece, *Not Invited*, later given with much success at the major theaters, is known to have been of Payne's adapting. It is probable that he arranged or rewrote others to suit himself; but this cannot be known, since neither authors nor adapters were then named on playbills.

Toward the end of the season, in what may have been the climax of all the purely dramatic performances at the Wells, there was presented an adaptation of Schiller's play, *The Robbers*, and in it Payne made another stage appearance, playing the part of Charles de Moor.

From various reports it appears that here, free from outside managerial restraints, he acquitted himself with special distinction. The *Theatrical Inquisitor*, which some months earlier had regretted "the obstinate fatality which has excluded Mr. Payne from a place in the theatre," [131] would now declare that "the spirit of Mr. Payne has been manifested in a production of no common order, to which not only the strength of the company but his own exertions are devoted." This publication advised London theatergoers to "embrace the opportunity of seeing 'The Robbers,' one of the finest specimens of German drama" (of which the British public at the time knew but little) and "a delineation of intensive passion, highly wrought character and powerful incident."

The bringing forth in a minor theater of Schiller's tragedy, "that tremendous production which had thrilled all Europe," was deemed "an effort which it required a spirit of daring enterprise to make," and the result on the whole "displayed a degree of good taste and of adventurous courage deserving of every encouragement. . . . The scenery, especially that of the conflagration, is very effective, and the dresses are throughout correct and elegant."

The manager's own impersonation of Charles de Moor, "though not a performance of superlative excellence," was "one which should gratify all those who have a delicate susceptibility of its histrionic beauties. For just conception of character, acute sensibility, deep feeling and impressive pathos, we know of no actor who surpasses Mr. Howard Payne; but in energy and fire, his physical powers do not bear out the suggestions of his intellect." [132] These judgments were heartily concurred in by W. Waltham, a London journalist, who on September 20 wrote to Payne:

> My dear Sir: I have written a critique of your admirable performance of Charles de Moor for the Statesman, which could not be inserted until this evening. Permit me, however, to advise you to take a glass or two of wine extra every night before you perform. Physical energy alone is wanting to render the delineation of mental power and highly wrought passion complete. [133]

These are the first recorded references by outsiders to what may have been the shattering effect of tribulation upon Payne's never very robust health; and this may hold the key to the whole mystery of his strange career.

Exciting things were happening in England during the summer that Payne directed the Wells. George III had died, and preparations were begun for the elevation of the Prince Regent to the throne. These events brought to a head the long-standing feud between George IV and his estranged wife, Caroline, whom the King had accused of adultery. When Caroline, who had been living abroad for years, returned to London and demanded the right to be crowned queen the King started proceedings against her.[134] Though public opinion favored her, her long trial, lasting several months, aroused great contention and even disorder. Hoodlum mobs sprang up on all sides, and for a time good citizens feared to venture forth at night.

Harrison relates that Payne, at Sadler's Wells, took a hand in the controversy by putting on several pieces which by implication upheld "the Queen," [135] as she was called. "The great political and moral subject that was agitating the most remote corners of the country and almost revolutionizing the metropolis" had even "found its way into this little place," the *Theatrical Inquisitor* observed. The venture was intrepid, but it did the place no good, since audiences were intimidated and stayed away from such performances.

The following year, however, Caroline, cleared of the charges but still not permitted to become queen, heard that the Wells had espoused her cause. Knowing nothing of the management, she lent her patronage to the little theater, to the advantage, of course, of Payne's successor. This unintended outcome was but another touch of irony in the career of Payne. It was not the first time, nor yet the last, that he would lay a foundation on which others would build profitably.

As Payne's management neared its close, the costumers, carpenters, scene painters, and others who had contributed to the success of the little theater under his direction not unreasonably wanted to be paid, and paid in full; and the box office receipts, though very gratifying, were simply not adequate. Poorer by $7000 than when he began [136] and unable to carry on longer on credit, he was obliged to resign.

A versifier connected with the theater later wrote a song called "A History of Sadler's Wells," which, after disposing of the era of Dibdin's gifts of wine to audiences, proceeded to the period of Payne:

Grimaldi in disgust determined to reign
But soon yielded the sceptre to young Howard Payne;
Yet somehow or other, his reign was cut short,
For managing was not at all Yankee's forte,
    And barring all pother, yet somehow or other,
    Payne managed one season in turn.[137]

Today we have begun belatedly to realize that managing—the planning and directing side of it—was very much "Yankee's" forte. It was on the financial side that he failed.

In his valedictory, a broadside written in the third person and dated November 4, 1820, Payne declared: "All his losses will be met with cheerfulness if he shall find as the result of his exertions that he has succeeded in elevating Sadler's Wells Theatre beyond a mere vehicle of amusement, by . . . those means of improvement in Literature and Life from which the Stage derives its Dignity and Value."

This was a high aim, and it would pay artistic dividends in the future, even though it could not pay the current bills. Records of immediately succeeding seasons at the Wells indicate that in some respects, chiefly the addition of stage plays to the variety programs, Payne had set a precedent. Perhaps it is too much—or perhaps it is not—to assert that his brief pioneering led to what is called "the Golden Age of Sadler's Wells" (1842–60), when Samuel Phelps succeeded in converting a theater "which for nearly two centuries had been the resort of the roughest audiences in London" into "the most legitimate temple of the drama." [138]

The work of Phelps at the Wells is still referred to as "a daring project"; but the fact remains that two decades before him, a young American had first explored the higher possibilities of London's oldest theater.

[10]

VIRGINIUS, ANOTHER TRAGEDY

To THE PERIOD of the Sadler's Wells experiment belongs one of the most disappointing experiences of Payne's London years: namely the failure of his play, *Virginius,* by all accounts a superior work and largely original, to find a producer.

Apparently it was the great success of *Brutus* that inspired in him —and, it happened, in two other London playwrights, John Sheridan Knowles and a third whose name is usually given as Barlow—the idea of writing a tragedy based upon the awful sacrifice of another Roman, Virginius. This is a tragedy even more terrible than *Brutus,* for Virginius, according to historians, killed his innocent daughter Virginia with his own hand "to save her from the lust of Appius."

The simultaneous revival by three playwrights of this ancient tale drew from a contemporary writer the observation that Brutus and Virginius were two Roman characters whom Shakespeare had over-looked. Perhaps Shakespeare would have agreed with the London critic who remarked incidentally, of "the sweet and dreadful story" of the Virginius plays: "We cannot say that we ourselves have much relish for these enormities of barbarous people of ancient times." [139]

Nevertheless the dramatic possibilities of the story were great; and each of the three playwrights, feeling that Kean alone could do justice to the father's role, had offered his play to Drury Lane. Payne's *Virginius; or, the Patrician's Perfidy* (the patrician being Appius) was promptly rejected by Drury, and later by Covent Garden also.

Knowles's *Virginius; or, the Liberation of Rome* was rejected by Drury, but accepted by Covent Garden. Only Barlow's *Virginius; or, the Fall of the Decemviri*—according to contemporary reports the least meritorious of the three—was accepted by Drury Lane, probably after Elliston learned that the rival theater was bringing out Knowles's play. The " 'Virginius' by a new author, a friend of Kean, although paid for in advance much more than had been paid for 'Brutus' after its great triumph," [140] had only a few performances, even with Kean in the cast.

The Covent Garden *Virginius,* however (Knowles's play), was successful. Knowles's dialogue was modern: he made his ancient characters talk like nineteenth-century men and women. This was novel and was generally approved, though there were critics then and later who felt that Payne's adherence to a classical idiom was better suited to the subject. But whatever the faults or merits of the style adopted by Knowles, his *Virginius* was to prove the making of both himself and the actor, William Charles Macready—cast in the title role originally intended for Kean—and was almost to rival Payne's *Brutus* in popularity and longevity.

Payne, struggling against odds at Sadler's Wells, had to be confronted in the newspapers almost daily with panegyrics of Knowles's effort, and to ponder what must have seemed to him a particularly unkind thrust of outrageous fortune. Hence it must have been gratifying to receive the praise of a London journalist who wrote proposing to review the Payne *Virginius* "in the *London Magazine,*[141] and to institute a comparison between it and its inflated as well as meagre rival."

This critic was that same Mr. Waltham who had advised Payne to "take a glass or two of wine extra" before his stage performances. Now he asked to be told "the sources from which part of it [*Virginius*] was compiled." [142]

The question was easily answered. Payne, in writing to Kinnaird more than a year earlier, had stated that his *Virginius* was "based upon an old play of Webster's" (*Appius and Virginia,* by the seventeenth-century dramatist John Webster); "the rest [except for plot outlines] is entirely my own."

What is probably Waltham's critique, since no other analysis of Payne's *Virginius* has been found, appears in the theatrical paper which by this time was called *Gold's London Magazine and Theatrical Inquisitor* (a familiar publication with a new prefix to its name, which sometimes causes it to be confused with the *London Magazine*). This review, printed in the December 1820 issue shortly after the conclusion of Payne's work at the Wells, should have done a good deal to assuage his sufferings over the unfortunate outcome of his brilliant managerial effort.

Mr. Waltham (assuming him to have been the author) is extremely warm in praise of Payne's tragedy and declares it "very superior to that of Sheridan Knowles," which he adjudged "by no means deserving of the degree of popularity attached to it."

We have no way of weighing this opinion accurately, for although Knowles's play is available in printed form, Payne's, except for a few pages which the *Inquisitor* reproduced, was never published, and even the manuscript seems to have disappeared. Furthermore much critical comment on Knowles's drama can be found, whereas what seems to be the sole surviving review of Payne's *Virginius,* is not generally known to exist. Hence its essential points should be quoted:

> For imagination, for feeling, for poetry, for energy, it is inferior to few plays which our age has witnessed. . . . Were not the partiality and stupidity of our theatres fully known and frequently experienced, it might surprise us to know that the tragedy has actually been rejected by both.

Concluding, this writer does "not hesitate to declare Mr. Payne's by far the best yet written on the subject" and further to aver: "Though it was rejected by the ignorance of managers, it ought to take a rank, and that not a mean one, in the dramatic literature of the country."

If a few lines from Payne's *Virginius* printed in New York after his return to America are representative of the play as a whole, praise is merited. Here Appius addresses the artist Fulvius:

> Painting gives a life to history
> And makes the visions of the poet real;
> It triumphs over time, restores the dead,
> Retains the rose which time or sorrow withers;
> Comforts sad hearts when they are torn asunder;
> And in this silent monitor, old age
> Sees what it was, and scarce believes the change! [143]

What his *Virginius* may have deserved, however, could not compensate Payne for the treatment it received. But his honest effort in bringing it forth was useful in restoring him to the regard of his most esteemed friend, Washington Irving.

Payne's extravagance and bad luck combined, even without the added burdens of the summer at the Wells, had involved him in financial obligations that he could not promptly meet, and his embarrassments had inevitably turned a part of the theatrical world against him. He was, as he himself said, "pressed down by a mountain of calumny and debt."

Aware that unfavorable reports were circulating, Payne, shortly before beginning work at Sadler's Wells, had written Irving expressing concern lest that friend be misled by what he might hear of "an alleged system of financeering, which . . . it is reported, I am pursuing with no other thought than that of raising supplies to be squandered." He then had high hopes that *Virginius* would improve his financial situation and redeem his reputation, for he added: "It will not be long, I trust, before the dinner-table cant regarding me undergoes a revolution."

Irving, in reply, expressed gratification at hearing that Payne had another tragedy in the making and begged him to "renounce the idea of my being prejudiced against you by the gossip of dining-out gentlemen"; though for the sake of honesty he was constrained to add: "I confess I did once think you acting inconsiderately and unjustifiably, in depending upon the casual assistance of others [seemingly] without any laudable object or definite pursuit—but this opinion was at once and completely destroyed by your telling me of your having a tragedy in preparation. You have no idea what an agreeable revolution took place at that moment in my feelings."

Payne must have told Irving some time earlier about disagreements with the Covent Garden management, for this note continues:

The letter to Mr. Harris completely confirmed my esteem for you. It gave me the whole story of your struggles here and shewed me that you had been busily engaged when others thought you idle, and that your difficulties had been occasioned by the faithlessness of others. . . . Instead, therefore, of suffering others to prejudice me against you, I have ever since taken pains to put your conduct and situation in a proper light.[144]

It was Irving's opinion that in view of Payne's accumulating difficulties in England, it might be advisable for him to return to America "and connect with a magazine." But Payne decided instead to try his hand at managing the Wells.

[11]

PRISON DIARY

PAYNE had to suffer severely for his summertime adventure at the Wells. Some of his creditors were lenient, but others obtained judgments against him, with the result that in the last week of the year he was committed to London's Fleet Prison for debt.

Half a century later England would abolish the custom of imprisoning a man for debt except when he had the means but refused to pay. Even by the time Payne found himself in the Fleet the conditions of incarceration were considerably more humane than they had once been, and prisoners who were respectable except for insolvency were allowed certain privileges.

The old Fleet Prison, so called because it stood near the east bank of the Fleet River on Ludgate Hill, had been destroyed by fire some forty years earlier and "rebuilt in a commodious manner." There was a "felons' side"—of which even then, perhaps, the less said the better—and a "masters' side," a rectangle four stories high that contained 109 rooms, "nearly all with fireplaces," and a courtyard for exercise. In addition, quarters outside but adjacent to the prison walls were provided for the privileged inmates under a provision known as Rules of the Fleet.[145] For the advantage of living in the Rules section a prisoner paid. Payne somehow obtained the funds for lodgment in this section, where his windows opened on an alley known as Boy Court. Here he was permitted to receive callers and upon obtaining a pass each time, was allowed at specified hours to move about the city.

Despite such favors, the incarceration and the failure it represented were matters of deep discouragement to Payne, who was aware that other men were still profiting from his earlier successful work. The period of his confinement, however, was to prove fortunate for him, though he little dreamed as much on New Year's eve when, with a splitting headache, he heard the bells of nearby St. Paul's and Westminster's midnight chimes proclaim the coming of the year 1821.

His head still ached on the morrow, but it was New Year's day, and the habit of decent observance had been acquired in childhood. "It is the consolation of helplessness and error that it can at least make good resolutions," he wrote in his diary on this January first.[146]

On the second day of the year his resolutions were specific. He would adopt a methodical course of study, would pay more attention to religion and to reading the Bible, and would exercise "more prudence, economy and punctuality," which might "produce advantages hereafter" and the punitive experience "be repaid by the change to which it may lead. . . . Others blame me exclusively, still I have laboured hard and suffered severely." One lesson learned he "would never forget—never to owe money to one's landlord. Little debts are always worse than big ones, they get a man more out of a good name and make him more hated and shunned."

There was a steady stream of callers at No. 1 Boy Court: actors, managers, playwrights, and creditors, in addition to a few who were just friends. One who proved a friend indeed was William Godwin Jr., son of the celebrated political philosopher. Young Godwin, then eighteen and employed as a reporter on the London *Chronicle*, dropped in to tea with the prisoner on the day after New Year's and later came several times to breakfast. He also looked after business matters for Payne and did much to obtain his release.

Another friend was John Miller,[147] the London bookseller, who made a specialty of American publications. And a third was the actress Julia Betterton, widely known in the acting profession by her married name, Mrs. Glover.[148] Though especially noted as a comedienne, she had appeared in a leading role in Payne's *Brutus* as well as in his early melodrama *Accusation*.

It is good to know that Payne had a generous woman friend in this time of need, even though a very temperamental one, twelve years his senior. Julia had suffered herself. Her husband, Samuel Glover, seems to have deserted her, and she was left the main support of five young children and a number of needy relations. Very much of a Bohemian herself, she was more lenient than some toward Payne's erratic ways with money.

His prison diary reports seeing much of J., his name for Mrs. Glover. The first entry concerning her is that of January second: "J. passed the evening here, together with Mrs. H." (not further identified). January 3: "J. sent Mrs. H. with four one-pound notes to settle with Harris [presumably a Wells creditor]. Kind and considerate! What would I do in my distress but for her!"

A real sacrifice, those one-pound notes must have been, for only a week later J. herself was in great distress. "The treasurer [of the theater] lent her ten pounds or she would have been destitute."

Early in his imprisonment Payne was painfully ill with a bowel complaint, and J., for all her own troubles, "sent a kind note, some rhubarb, some camphor julip and instructions."

The winter days were dreary. January 7: "A deep reddish fog all day, in consequence of which I had to have a candle to read by." January 9: "The fog was such all day as completely to exclude the light; the air was red and murky and I burned candles without intermission." January 10: "A death-like melancholy possessed me during the latter part of the day and evening."

Soon, however, an active mind came to the rescue of a troubled spirit. J. had lent him Moore's *Lalla Rookh,* and Payne remarked in his diary on "the delightful sensations of poetry . . . the delights of poetry and virtue are similar. . . . Poetry is perhaps the language of Heaven; while Virtue is the employment of the Angels."

From the sublimity of such observations, his mind descended to the more practical. What *could* he do to better his situation? The poverty of the prison library had driven him to peruse the National Spelling Book, and now he weighed the possibility of contriving a similar though more interesting work, one especially for American children. Wouldn't that perhaps offer a solution? He made a few notes for such a book. Then there was that historical work he had long had vaguely in mind. A few paragraphs were jotted down forthwith:

> The French Revolution has produced advantages to the world. It has given an impulse to inquiry. Like a vast volcanic eruption it has swallowed up myriads, but in cleaving the earth asunder, unshrouded treasures which repay to general science what it tore from individual happiness.
>
> When we look back upon the recent history of France, we regard it as a whole. We connect the fall of Louis fifteenth with the rise of Napoleon. We stand on a mountain and grasp disconnected domains with a glance. We do not consider that the dwellers in the plains below have very different feelings, and are operated upon by considerations which cannot arise to our perception. They behold in fragments. . . .

The year's first month was more than half gone before a solution of the prisoner's problem appeared, in unexpected form.

January 17: "At about one today I received a parcel from France, without name or letter . . . merely endorsed [postmarked] Havre, January 10, 1821." It contained two plays by Victor H. J. B. Ducange, the French dramatist generally referred to by Payne and his biographers as M. Victor—a man who had himself known what it was to be in prison, his offense having been not bankruptcy, but a tendency to speak too plainly on social and political matters to please the French authorities.

One of the plays, *Calas,* had previously been translated into English, and Payne had produced it on his opening night at Sadler's Wells. The other, *Thérèse; or, the Orphan of Geneva,* he had not seen before.

"I instantly left my history and read 'Thérèse.' It is admirably contrived and most interesting." It would make, he felt, an excellent piece for Drury Lane, where Elliston, as new manager, was eager for novelties.

January 18: "Sent shirt to pawn brokers and got enough money to buy a day's provisions and begin work on 'Thérèse.' " January 19: "I go at it with less eager anxiety and fear of rejection than I ever went to any work of the kind. . . . Finished first act and began second." January 20: "Finished second act. Did not put finishing touches to it till the watchman was calling past six!"

January 21: "Not well all day. Wrote 'Thérèse' till late at night. Passed a miserably sleepless night, counting the clocks, and when I slept the characters rushed through my brain, all conversing and speaking the emphatic passages." January 22: "Monday night. I have this moment finished 'Thérèse.' Was cooking gruel and spilled it on last page. The watchman is now calling 'gone half-past eleven o'clock.' I knelt down and prayed Heaven to make this bantling propitious to my extrication!"

The next day Payne wrote Elliston offering to call and read the play aloud, as he did not wish to trust it out of his own hands; besides, it was "so full of the rude blottings of first thoughts" that another could not decipher it at all points. After dispatching the letter by messenger, he indulged in a bit of recreation: "Went up to J.'s and had a snack—a sausage and potatoes and some porter. . . . She threw her old shoe after me for luck, and I, quite as bad, having put on my under waistcoat wrong side out, would not change it."

Elliston granted an interview, although "fatigued and jaded." He had read a play, an opera, and a melodrama that day. He listened to Payne's reading, taking a few notes on it, but seeming chiefly engaged in opening letters, giving orders, "writing a letter or two in the unimportant passages," and "walking back and forth to look in at the stage door, where a rehearsal was in progress."

By the time the reading was finished "the band were tuning their fiddles for the overture of the evening performance—'A School for Scandal,'" in which Mrs. Glover had a leading part. The harassed manager "took a snack," gave orders for Payne to be admitted behind scenes at any time, and then pronounced the verdict. *Thérèse* was too long: he wanted the leading male part, that of Carwin, the villain, cut out!

Payne felt "unimportant and somewhat disgusted." Though the area backstage was very cold, he "stayed behind all evening." Between the acts, "went to J.'s dressing room" for a little consolation and a warming cup of tea. Julia had had high hopes for *Thérèse* and could not believe that the management would not eagerly accept it. "What! Didn't he seem struck?" exclaimed this sympathetic friend.

Payne "waited to walk home with J., leaving the play with her to cut, and felt no further interest in it."

The unpredictable Elliston, however, was apparently one of those persons who say least when most impressed. At any rate, two days later he paid an unannounced call at No. 1 Boy Court. He had come to say, not only that *Thérèse* was accepted just as it was, but that it was to be produced immediately. Three men had been kept up all night copying the parts.

January 26: "J. rejoiced," says the diary.

Thérèse is a typical melodrama of the day, its heroine that stock favorite of early nineteenth-century playwrights, a blameless orphan girl. For this particular orphan the trials usual to one in her sad situation are augmented by the stigma of illegitimacy (proved false, of course, for contemporary taste would not have it otherwise), and upon her helpless head are heaped lying accusations of forgery and murder. The plot, as sketched by the *New Monthly Magazine*, is especially lurid:

> The play opens with the heroine under sentence of death for an offense of which she is guiltless. . . . Pursued by her traitorous advocate, who has effected her ruin, she is compelled to fly from the dreadful alternative of his hand or the scaffold. . . . A thunderbolt sets the pavilion afire, her persecutor murders her protectress believing *Thérèse* to be the victim. She appears as her own ghost and frightens her oppressor into confession and death. . . . Delivered from indictments and an odious suitor, she acquires a fortune and a husband.

Neither actors nor management found any fault with this improbable and tortuous plot, and when, two days after Elliston's call, Payne went in to the first rehearsal, he was able to report: January 27: "Well, today all seems lightening. Listened at green room door to reading. Heard them applaud and cry out 'beautiful' in some passages. J. delighted and full of congratulations. To dine with her [tonight]."

It was decided to produce *Thérèse* on the second of February,

almost before the copyists' ink was dry. Though Elliston was reminded that the second fell on a Friday, he replied that "no day
could be unlucky for this piece," which he declared "surer than
Brutus." The diary provides further backstage details:

January 27: "Went to the theatre, play being read. Directed scene
painters about the last scene. Walked up and down the stage half
the morning, nearly." Elliston, unusually friendly, made Payne
acknowledge himself as adapter. Fanny Kelly,[149] one of the best-
liked of all the actresses in London, was chosen to portray Thérèse.
W. J. Wallack was cast as the villain, Carwin, and his agreement
to act the part "the first 20 nights" Payne regarded as "proof
they expect a run." Twenty consecutive performances were rarely
achieved at the time.

Drury Lane Theatre was used for occasional concerts as well as
plays, and when Payne arrived for the second rehearsal he found
"all at six's and seven's in preparation for the oratorio" that evening—"the stage filled with scaffolding to support the musicians
[choral singers], the organ tuning, and in one room a singing rehearsal." Then follows a brief subordinate observation that suggests the state of musical culture in his homeland and at the same
time shows a new facet of the diarist's mind: "They were practicing
the beautiful oratorio music in the next room. What a treat it would
have been in America, even to hear such fine strains through the
wall!"[150]

The play and its concerns, however, were the main thing, and
Payne, the natural producer, records:

Great bother about settling the dresses . . . discussion about dancers
[a ballet of villagers in second act]. My wish to have them all different,
instead of being uniformed, like a company of soldiers, for they all come
from different families and would rather avoid, than study, uniformity.
Are tea parties and dances uniformly dressed in private life? . . . Actors
at these meetings are like children left to themselves at school.

February 1: "Could not attend rehearsal. Purification Day, no
court sits and a pass has to be signed by the court every morning."
February 2 (day of performance):

A scampering rehearsal. Miss Kelly wanted to be excused from attending on account of illness, but was persuaded by a note from me. Heaven help "Thérèse"! Everybody in a bad humor. . . .

We got through the piece late in the afternoon. All the company parted with little or no hope of success. Distracted myself, I was too sick and prostrated to leave the theatre; was invited to dine in Elliston's room, where I remained till time for the theatre to open. Increased headache.

Though theatrical people are notoriously superstitious, the old belief about a bad rehearsal and a good performance did not inspire hopefulness this time, in either actors or playwright. At curtain time Payne, all apprehension, found a place with friends in an upper private box. "The atmosphere of the house was unfriendly," says the diary. "The overture—one of Mozart's, which had been mistaken for something new—was hissed."

The setting of the first act, however, was applauded, "and the interest of the audience began to be excited. The applause was frequent and increased at every step, till, when the back drops fell, it became tumultuous and was repeated in three or four rounds." This was an unexpectedly good beginning, but there was still time for anxiety.

A long pause before the next act began. The people got impatient. I ran down to the stage, alarmed for the consequences. To this act there was not as much applause as might have been, until the close.

The third act, especially the scene between Fontaine [father confessor] and Thérèse, was tremendously applauded. Miss Kelly's acting of that scene was one of the most impressive pieces of acting I have ever seen. The play went off, to my utter astonishment. The third act was the triumph. I was congratulated by the performers and the performers congratulated each other.

February 3: "Well, 'Therese' has succeeded triumphantly and splendidly, and I am enjoying my triumph with my feet in hot water, a box of pills before me, a bowl of gruel and a terrific headache. Yet I cannot help remarking upon the contrast in the manner of my reception by the actors upon the stage last evening and the dreadful coldness with which I was treated on the same stage when 'Brutus' was produced. Miss Kelly thanked me for the little stage business I showed her, and Wallack thanked me heartily for naming him for the part of Carwin."

Every period has its fashions, in drama as surely as in dress, and in Payne's time, as in ours, many absurdities of the contemporary stage were carried off by magnificent acting. In *Thérèse,* a play that a modern audience would not take seriously, it was the talented Miss Kelly who made the preposterous plot seem plausible. As a result the play, according to Harrison, was hailed by a London journalist as "the best and most successful melodrama ever produced at Drury Lane." [151]

Thérèse was published within two weeks, and the first edition of a thousand copies sold out at once. Payne, in his prison room, composed a noteworthy preface. Acknowledging indebtedness to M. Victor "for the compliment paid so mysteriously," the adapter asks the author's indulgence of some alterations. This refers to certain cuts and particularly to a change whereby the charge of murder against Thérèse is delivered in her presence instead of while she is offstage. He believes M. Victor "would require no apology" could he have witnessed Miss Kelly's performance; nor does Payne believe the others in the cast will deem a particular notice of that lady "in the slightest degree invidious. Her fellow actors know her talent better than the public. They can observe it better. As she wrote in the pavilion the audience could not see her brushing the tears which blotted the letters as she was forming them . . . but in the closing scenes of pathos, all could share in the agonizing interest she excites, all could feel her acting was unaffected, irresistible."

Payne, well aware of certain limitations of the contemporary drama, adds some general comments:

> It is so necessary in productions of modern drama to consult the peculiarities of leading performers . . . that it seems almost hopeless to look to the stage as a vehicle for permanent literary distinction. An *acted* (or I might say more properly) an *actable* play, seems to derive its value from what is *done,* rather than from what is *said,* but the great power of a literary work consists in what is said and the manner of saying it. He therefore who best knows the stage, can best tell why, in the present temper of audiences, good writers so often make bad dramatists.

As characteristic of the period as the plot and phrasing of *Thérèse* was the custom of pirating and the surest proof of the validity of a hit was the extent to which it was copied.

Payne had been too much occupied on the night of the opening to observe two young men in the pit very busy with notebooks and pencils, one taking down the entire dialogue in shorthand while the other sketched the scenery. Less than a week later bills blazed forth the announcement of a *Thérèse* at the Royal Coburg, one of the minor theaters then maintaining a precarious existence.

Elliston and Payne went together to see the Coburg piece, and, despite glaring errors in the stenographically transcribed dialogue, Payne found the pirating "the most evident thing in the world, even to minutiae of the scenery, and its very faults." Even more convincing were the seventy-four cuts—compressions, he called them—"the very same lines [500 of them] always omitted in the very same places" as in his translation.

All this was too much for Elliston, who sought to obtain legal means of stopping the pirated work by injunction, though Payne thought it better to let the imitation die of its own weakness. He told Elliston he doubted "whether even the advantage of a triumph were to be compared with the effect of reviving the clamour against the supposed disposition to persecute the minor theatres."

Elliston nevertheless persisted, and the verdict in Chancery Court favored him and Payne. On a technicality, however, the lawyers for the Coburg management obtained permission to keep their piece in performance for a limited time, which happened to be long enough to affect somewhat the success of Drury Lane's. Further competition at once sprang up when Covent Garden came out with *its* version of *Thérèse*, and though the new orphan was named Henrietta, she was still M. Victor's tortured heroine. This adaptation was by Beazley, something of a master hand. No charge of piracy could be brought here, however, for Beazley had made his own translation, though perhaps assisted by Payne's, which by this time had been published. The situation brought this comment from the *European Magazine:*

> The competition of the theatres has sometimes been looked upon as likely to increase the public gratification, but they have now adopted a mode which makes this competition an exhaustive trial of public patience.

Even the Lord Chancellor, during the hearing on *Thérèse*, remarked of the general situation: "Disputes respecting theatrical property have become so frequent that it might be advisable to institute a separate court for deciding them." [152]

Drury Lane paid Payne 140 pounds for *Thérèse*, including copyright; and though Elliston himself was a poor businessman, he doubtless got a bargain. For not only did the play become a favorite in Britain: within two months Payne's adaptation was also published in New York, and it was played for many years in America. The great Edwin Forrest later adopted the role of Carwin and acted it frequently. A performance of *Thérèse* is known to have been given at the Walnut Street Theatre in Philadelphia as late as 1848, some twenty-seven years after the London première, and one in New York in 1853.[153]

Using the forty pounds advanced by the theater to settle a few obligations and pay court costs, and aided by young Godwin and a friendly lawyer, Payne finally obtained release from Boy Court. On March 1 he was able to write in the diary:

"Liberty! Delicious liberty!"

Two weeks later the diary tells what happened when he went to the theater to collect the remainder. Kept waiting for two hours by Elliston, with nothing to do but roam about the empty stage, Payne found a scene painter making copies of the Drury Lane backdrops. The man was at work on one depicting "the inside of the King's Bench, with a complete view of two sides of the very room I once occupied."

This somewhat incidental remark is an important disclosure, for it reveals that the recent adventure at the Fleet was not Payne's first experience with imprisonment for debt. Other evidence shows that the earlier one, in King's Bench prison, was probably brief and that it must have resulted from his disastrous dealings with Kinnaird in 1816. It explains certain references in letters of that year —one from Procter, the poet, who says, "I hope you got out of your scrape," and an even more significantly worded one from Charles Kemble regretting that he "cannot supply bail." [154]

Payne had gone to the theater in a mood to demand just payment for *Thérèse*, but found this ghastly reminder "as a sort of warning monition to take what I could get." He settled on Elliston's terms, and though he regarded the total as only half what the play should have brought, "anything under the circumstances was a godsend. . . . But here all my immediate hopes and resources terminate, and what have I to look for when this little is gone?"

In a few days this anxious query seemed answered. It is proof of the reputation he had acquired that proposals of collaboration came from two sources. Charles Horn, a German-born composer then quite active in London, who had supplied the incidental music for *Thérèse*, suggested that they write an opera on the subject of Psyche, and Payne eagerly began to plan the libretto. Simultaneously James Welsh, a prominent singer and manager, proposed a musical adaptation of the old play *Love in a Village*, with Payne to provide new dialogue.

And in addition to these crumbs of encouragement, Elliston, quite out of a clear sky, proposed sending Payne back to Paris, again as agent for Drury Lane Theatre. This necessitated reclaiming his trunks, now held by the second landlady within two years.[155] Payne took them to the quarters of the infinitely kind though often tempestuous J., whose outbursts were excusable, since she and her children had by this time been obliged to move into one large room.[156]

"Left 20 pounds with J. in answer to my request that she should take whatever share she wished," says the diary. "She shed tears at the idea of taking any portion of so small a sum in the circumstances."

On the whole, the prospect might have seemed much brighter had not the suggestions of the two musical gentlemen cooled—as such suggestions will sometimes—and had not the mercurial Elliston appeared to forget all about the Paris proposal.

> Elliston's conduct becomes guarded and inexplicable. He wants my assistance and does not want to pay for it; or to ask for it lest I should make him pay.

Nevertheless, creditors were again becoming persistent, and "the necessity of disappearance seemed to increase." J. assisted in preparations for Payne's departure from London, and early April found him out of the way of British bailiffs and, to outward appearances, once more free to bask in the beauties of Paris in the spring.

[12]

THE SONG IS WRITTEN

"The song was his career; the song is his monument."

THIS tribute to Payne by a contemporary who survived him, though eloquent, is only half accurate. "Home, Sweet Home" is indeed his monument, but, we know today, is by no means the sum of his achievement. Yet because of the song's lasting fame its appearance may still be regarded as the high point of his career. Oddly enough, this celebrated hymn to home was a product of the theater. It was designed as a soprano solo—nothing so exalted as an aria—for an operetta called *Clari; or, the Maid of Milan*, with text by Payne and score by Henry Rowley Bishop, who later became Sir Henry. Payne wrote the dialogue and lyrics in Paris nearly two years after the success of his drama *Thérèse* and his release from debtor's prison; and Bishop composed the music in London. Neither expected anything unusual to result from the joint effort.

Before the song was thought of there was for Payne a period of varied adventures, some of them of a kind to make debtor's prison seem luxurious by contrast. "After I got back to France things went on so hopelessly as to leave me in a state next to starvation, and I must have perished from want but for accidents," he later wrote his brother.[157] Such agreement as he had with the Drury Lane management was vague and unsatisfactory, but it was an assignment of a sort, and he tried to carry it out. To "Dearest J." he wrote of the unprofitable profits of "seeking something for Elliston." At the same time he was trying to establish contact with some of London's minor theaters, especially the Surrey. But this was for some time unavailing, and in a letter to Talma Payne told of having been "very unpleasantly situated and in deep distress, even by a series of misadventures, once cast into the streets for want of a night's lodging." [158] And later, in more detail, he wrote to Washington Irving:

> I suffered incredible hardships . . . for 3 or 4 months; want of food, want of raiment, want of bed—all in bitter, stormy weather. . . . Nothing but a strong sense of religion, which will, I hope, sustain me in every trial, prevailed over my paroxysms of despair, which made me pause on the banks of the Seine, wishing for the relief of any alteration, and thinking, with poor Oroonoko, "Whatever world we are next thrown upon cannot be worse than this." [159]

With Payne, however, bad times and better times were always fluctuating. Before his Paris troubles became so acute he had occupied for a time "the first floor of a small house with a garden at No. 16 Petit de St. Pierre, Pont aux Choux" (the quaint suffix, "Bridge of the Cabbages" suggesting a Bohemian neighborhood). This may have been a homelike habitation, but it lacked "the peace of mind dearer than all," to judge by a letter to a London friend:

> I am settled near the Boulevard du Temple, a quiet, out-of-the-way place, with a garden before it. . . . No companions but two little birds I bought of an old woman on the Boulevard; and scarcely a visitor but the Blue Devils. The birds are tame and run about the room . . . and the Blue Devils often accompany me on my saunterings about the streets.[160]

This place and the birds are also mentioned by Irving, who breakfasted there with Payne one morning late in April 1821 and recorded in his diary:

> The morning was fine and the air soft and spring-like. His casements were thrown open and the breezes that blew in were extremely gratifying. He has a couple of canary birds, with a little perch ornamented with moss. He stands at the window and they fly about the garden and return to their perch for food and for rest at night.

Irving, we may believe, chased away the Blue Devils at least for that day; and after breakfast the two Americans, quite at home in the foreign city, "strolled along the Boulevards, staring at groups and sights and signs, and looking over booksellers' stalls . . . Payne full of dramatic projects, some of them very feasible." [161]

The following July Irving, back in London to attend the coronation of George IV, agreed to perform some commissions for Payne. One was to submit to Drury Lane a little play called *The Borrower;* another "to call on Elliston and endeavor to impress upon his mind the necessity of sending me some money"; a third to attempt to make a magazine connection for Payne. The last was apparently Irving's idea, for he wrote: "I want to see you launched in general literature. I think you have an ease and gracefulness in your style which will be enough to make your way. Do try again, my dear Payne, and don't depend upon the drama for support." [162]

Irving gave a good deal of time to these efforts, but none was successful. *The Borrower* was rejected; the magazine editor who had promised to consider Mr. Payne promptly forgot to do so; and, worst of all, Elliston did not respond to the request for money and Irving had to report: "I find he has an agent in Paris at a weekly salary."

No such favorable arrangement, of course, had ever been made with Payne, who now tells Irving that at one stage of the negotiations with Elliston "he was to pay me for a week's work and then employed me for three months, without pay, into the bargain. My wants forced me to overlook two or three indignities and I sent him two pieces which he happened to want at the moment, 'Love in Humble Life' for (a promise of) 20 pounds down, and 'Adeline' for 30 pounds the copyright and 15 pounds every third night until it should reach 100 pounds." [163]

Both of these pieces were accepted, and their production within the same week of February 1822 seems to have marked for Payne the beginning of the better times recorded later that year in a letter to the family:

> My connection with the London theatres has extended. I am now on terms with more than one and have earned about 500 pounds by pieces uniformly successful. . . . I shall begin the New Year richer than I have been for a very great while. Have about 120 pounds before me and am out of the way of being gnawed at by creditors. This gives me a momentary independence, through which I trust I shall be able to complete various productions which are by me in the rough.

It was well for him that luck turned when it did, for during the spring and summer of 1822 several of his London associates came to Paris. The genial Charles Lamb and his unfortunate sister Mary chose to pay their only visit to the Continent that year; and "Mr. Payne, without grudge or grumbling," [164] as Mary later reported, conducted them about the city.

Mary was not able to enjoy the sojourn at the start, however, for she had suffered a recurrence of her mental illness on the journey, and Charles, leaving her in Versailles "to be nursed," came on to Paris alone. There he was joined by Payne, and we may form a pleasant picture of these two "doing" the parks and theaters and galleries together. They stroll along the boulevards, pause long at the bookstalls, and even slyly observe the more than casual interest of another sight-seer, later described by Lamb in a letter to Payne as "the Blue Silk Girl, who fell in love with you and whom I fell in love with." [165]

Some weeks earlier than the Lambs, James Kenney, the playwright, whose fair-mindedness distinguished him from some others in the profession, had arrived in France with his wife and children.[166] And when the summer was nearly over, came the composer Bishop, then Covent Garden's director of music, whose visit, in the light of subsequent events, was the most important of them all.

One of the theatrical attractions of that Paris season was a ballet entitled *Clari; or, the Promise of Marriage,* with choreography by a Frenchman, Louis Milon, and music by the German composer-violinist Rudolph Kreutzer (the man to whom Beethoven, a few years earlier, had dedicated *The Kreutzer Sonata*).

Payne had seen the ballet and was delighted with it. He had forthwith created original dialogue for the story enacted in pantomime by the dancers, thus making it into a play. He renamed it *Angioletta* and sent it to Watkyns Burroughs, manager of the Surrey Theatre in London. Burroughs immediately accepted the piece and brought it out. When Bishop arrived in Paris he too attended a performance of the ballet and pronounced it "one of the most interesting I have ever seen." [167] Possessed no less than Payne of the showman's instinct, Bishop conceived the ballet as the basis of a light opera, and, finding that Payne had already provided words for the dancing pantomime, suggested that it be readapted, this time from a play into an operetta.

Payne's letters to Bishop after the composer had gone back to London give the main points of the story. The first on the subject of *Clari* is dated October 1, 1822:

> My dear Sir: I have at last received a letter from Mr. Burroughs about "Clari." It has been produced by him with great success as "Angioletta." He seems desirous of retaining it but is willing to give it up if the relinquishment on his part can be of any real advantage to me, and it would be inconsiderate in me to disoblige him without obliging others and myself.
>
> It seems to have made a hit at the Surrey, but I do not think a night or two there can possibly injure it for any other audience. . . . You will see what the drama is, and if I can get anything by the transfer, let it be made. If not, it would be absurd to remove it from the course of actual success.[168]

By this time there had been more shifts in London's ever-changing theatrical scene, and Charles Kemble had become manager of Covent Garden. Kemble had apparently turned over to his musical director, Bishop, the entire matter of negotiating with Payne, not only about the operetta *Clari* but also other pieces, and Payne immediately submitted to Bishop two melodramas, *Ali Pacha* and *The Two Galley Slaves*, with the promise that *Clari* would follow. Because of "Home, Sweet Home" the little opera was destined to overshadow the other two, but there was nothing at the start to suggest such an outcome.

Ali Pacha was produced at once, somewhat to Payne's regret, for as he wrote to Charles Lamb, "I am rather sorry that my connection with that theatre [Covent Garden] should begin with such a trifle." But Lamb, though not enthusiastic, was not discouraging, either, and replied: " 'Ali Pacha' will do. I sent my sister the first night, not being able to attend myself. I saw it the third night and it was very satisfactorily received. It is going on steadily, I am sure, for many weeks."

For the second work, *The Two Galley Slaves*, just brought out successfully in Paris, Payne had had particular hopes, and with his translation he included suggestions to Bishop for putting it on immediately. But for all the urging, Covent Garden could not forestall Drury Lane, and the piece opened at both of London's leading theaters the same night. The *New Monthly Magazine* of December 1822 commented encouragingly:

> Two melodramas, "Ali Pacha" and "The Two Galley Slaves," have been enacted this month, from the pen of Mr. Howard Payne, and though the subjects are unpromising they evince uncommon dramatic skill. He is an excellent contriver of melodramatic situations, but he can do higher things, and we hope soon will enable us to congratulate him on something more worthy of his powers.

It was Payne's own proposal that the two melodramas and the still unfinished operetta be lumped together for payment, and on this point he wrote to Bishop:

> I will take 250 pounds for the three pieces, "Ali Pacha," "The Two Galley Slaves" and "Clari"; or 120 pounds for "The Two Galley Slaves," 100 pounds for "Ali Pacha" and 100 pounds for "Clari," engaging to complete "Clari" in any way you like. . . . As I hate bargaining I mention the lowest terms at once.[169]

This suggestion was not answered promptly, and Payne complained somewhat later in a letter to Charles Lamb: "Is it not teasing that I should not have had a syllable from the theater? They wrote to know what I would take for 'Ali Pacha' and the other pieces and I named my price. They give me no reply, act 'Ali,' alter it, and put another person's name to it." (The London *Times* had attributed *Ali Pacha* to another adapter.)

The theater's silence must have been further prolonged, to judge by Payne's acknowledgment of Bishop's reply when it finally arrived:

> My thanks for your obliging letter. Pray pardon the impatience of my last. Yours found me very ill with fidgeting and a severe cold. I will do "Clari" in any way that you and Mr. Kemble care to point out. You had better make marginal notes where you want songs and choruses and give me some hints as to what sort you would like to have.

That letter to Bishop was written about two weeks after Payne's complaint to Lamb, and it is interesting to note that in further preliminary arrangements for the piece that would contain "Home, Sweet Home" the eminent Charles Lamb had a hand. While waiting for Bishop's delayed letter, Payne wrote to ask Lamb's intervention with the theater, and Lamb replied: "I am a poor man of business, but command me to the short extent of my tether."

Though he stated that he had no acquaintance with Charles Kemble, Lamb accommodatingly addressed to his friend Henry Robertson, the Covent Garden treasurer, a letter "for Kemble to see" and reported to Payne that "Robertson, in the name of the management, has recognized to you the full ratifying of your having 250 pounds for Ali, The Slaves and another piece they have not yet received." (The piece not received was *Clari*.) Lamb added: "He assures me that the whole will be paid to you as soon as ever the treasury will permit it."

But the treasury was in no hurry, and if Payne had been fidgeting in October, he must have been "fit to be tied" by the following January, when, to judge by further correspondence, full payment for the three pieces had not yet been forwarded, and *Clari* had been sent back to the author for alterations. For now Lamb writes:

> Mary has seen Robertson who says that the piece which is to be operafied [*Clari*] was sent to you six weeks since by a Mr. Wooten, whose going was delayed, but he supposes you have it by this time. On receiving it back, properly done, the rest of your dues will be forthcoming.[170]

What alterations had been requested is not known, but the amusing close of this letter of Lamb's shows that Payne, in writing to his good friends Charles and Mary, had expressed his indignation toward the theater in no uncertain terms:

> Mary says you must write more *showable* letters about these matters, for what with all our trouble in crossing out this word and giving a clearer turn to t'other, and folding down this part, and squeezing an obnoxious epithet into a corner, she can hardly communicate their contents without offense. What, man, put less gall into your ink or write me a biting tragedy!

Despite annoyances, the months preceding "Home, Sweet Home" were notably productive ones for Payne. In fact, between February and November of 1822 six adaptations known to be his were performed in London: three at Drury Lane (*Adeline, Love in Humble Life*, and a revival of *Brutus*), two ("Ali and the Slaves," as Lamb abbreviated them) at Covent Garden, and one (*The Solitary of*

Mount Savage) at the Surrey. There may indeed, have been more, for Payne wrote Irving: "The manager of the Surrey has kept me in food and I have kept him in melodramas." And there is corroboration in a letter to that manager, written in August:

> You have acted two melodramas of mine, one pantomime and one one-act piece, being in all nine parts. . . . First I knew of one of them was the announcement in today's British press of the fifth performance. . . . I saw "The Armistice" spoken of in the British Monitor as one of the principal pieces to which your house owes its good character.[171]

Nowadays we should say that a young man of thirty-one who, after providing a great theater with two outstanding hits, was responsible for at least half a dozen new productions within a period of ten months and had numerous others in preparation was doing rather well, even though all the plays were adaptations.

But this young man was not greatly impressed, to judge by a further remark to Irving: "What it will all lead to, the Lord only knows. Nothing much, I fear." [172]

It was leading to "Home, Sweet Home."

The song, then, legends notwithstanding, was not written while its author, near starvation, was gazing darkly into the waters of the Seine. Rather it was a product of the more prosperous part of this Paris period.

Payne had perforce abandoned the little house with the canary birds some time earlier. Now improved fortune had given a lift to his spirits, and he had moved to a better part of the city. The new abode was a top-floor apartment in the celebrated Palais Royal, built in the 1620's by Richelieu for his official residence. It was a place of many historic associations, and Payne would add and give variety to them by writing "Home, Sweet Home" within its walls.

Originally called the Palais Cardinal, the Palace had acquired its royal name when Richelieu willed it to Louis XIII. It was the boyhood home of Louis XIV and later the property of the Duke of Orléans. After it lost its royal inhabitants there was joined to the original structure a great four-sided addition built about a magnificent garden or park. For the Parisians of prerevolutionary days this enclosure had been a favorite promenade, though later it would know grimmer uses, for there, it is said, the first revolutionary meetings were held and various public enemies were burned in effigy.

By the time Payne knew the place the gardens, with their fountains and flowers, "clipped trees and plots of turf," had been restored to their original beauty. A corner of the quadrangle was occupied by the Théâtre Français, and in the adjoining buildings the great, high-ceilinged ground floor rooms were given over to a fascinating variety of restaurants and shops. The upper floors were mostly let to painters, poets, and other artistic folk.

By descending a flight or two of stairs these tenants would find themselves in one of the finest marts in all Paris. Here were "shops of millinery and jewellry; coffee houses, bagnios, money-changers, gamesters; book-sellers, toy merchants, pastry cooks, florists." All were expensive, gay, "brilliantly lighted," with "a concourse of people never at an end" ("gamblers, sharpers and prostitutes among them"), "regaling themselves with feasting and music" and thronging through the arcades and out across the gardens.[173]

It was therefore quite literally "mid pleasures and palaces" that "Home, Sweet Home" was born. The time was the autumn of 1822. Irving, just returned to Paris, looked in on his old friend again and recorded: "Call on Payne. Find him in a sky parlor of the Palais Royal. Chat and dine together in a restaurant of the Palais." [174]

And it was from this "sky parlor" that Payne, writing to the home folks on the New Year's eve preceding *Clari's* advent, gave voice to sentiments much like those soon to be revealed through the song:

My yearnings toward Home become stronger as the term of my exile lengthens. I long to see all your faces and to hear all your voices. 'Twould do me good to be scolded by Lucy and to see Anna look pretty and simple and sentimental. . . . I feel the want of you, parts of myself, in this *strange* world, for though I am naturalized to vagabondage, still it is *but* vagabondage. . . . I long for a Home about me.

[13]

THE SONG IS SUNG

Clari, with "Home, Sweet Home," had its première at London's Covent Garden Theatre May 8, 1823. Payne, remaining in Paris, could not be present on the occasion of his most enduring triumph, but London's first-nighters were more fortunate. "A house crowded in every part" [175] followed the sweetly affecting story, which seems so quaint today, and first heard the famous song.

It would be a mistake to measure *Clari* by twentieth-century tastes in theater. The operetta belongs distinctly to a less sophisticated age. It was right for its time, as events would prove.

Clari is a rustic maiden lured from home by the Duke Vivaldi, a traveler through the Italian countryside. On the promise of marriage she has gone with him to his palace, but there the "splendid slavery of rank" prevents his redeeming the promise. Luxuries of every kind surround her, but Clari is disconsolate: she has been deceived by him she deeply loves!

Servants enter with rich gifts from the Duke. One brings a miniature of Vivaldi, which Clari, in sad rapture, clasps to her heart. Others come with gowns, jewels, the loveliest of Paris bonnets; but all these she casts aside. Finally, left alone in "a magnificent apartment of the palace," she sadly sings her song of home. To appreciate its effect upon that great, expectant première audience, we must not forget that these now so famous and familiar words had never been heard in all the world before:

> 'Mid pleasures and palaces, though we may roam,
> Be it ever so humble, there's no place like home!
> A charm from the sky seems to hallow us there,
> Which, seek through the world, is ne'er met with elsewhere.

Home, ho-ome, sweet, sweet home—
There's no place like home, there's no-o place like home!

Here Clari opens a cabinet and takes from it the simple country
frock she used to wear, gazes on it fondly, and resumes her plaintive
little song:

An exile from home, splendor dazzles in vain,
Oh, give me my lowly thatched cottage again;
The birds singing gaily that came at my call,
Give me them with the peace of mind, dearer than all!

Enter at this point Clari's maid, Vespina. "Bless me, ma'am," she
exclaims, "what a pretty song that was and how prettily you sang it!
Where might you have learn't that song, ma'am, if I may be so
bold?"

"Where I learned other lessons I ought never have forgotten," replies the chastened Clari. "It is the song of my native village, the
hymn of the lowly heart."

Act II shows "a garden splendidly illuminated, a theatre formed
among trees at the back." It is Clari's birthday, and the Duke, distressed by her unhappiness, has arranged a playlet in her honor.
The strolling actors assemble, Clari is led in by the Duke while the
stage audience rises and bows.

The play within a play begins, and Clari, who, as the servants remark, "has never seen a play in her life," becomes more and more
agitated as it proceeds. And well she may, for here on the miniature
stage is another country daughter enticed by a wealthy suitor away
from home and family. At length, as the actor-father is "about to
call down the vengeance of heaven upon his undutiful child," Clari
starts from her seat and throws herself at his feet, begging that the
girl be forgiven. The Duke is angered, the guests withdraw, and the
scene ends in planned confusion.

Clari's sadness is increased; likewise her pride and determina-
tion. She will endure this plight no longer. With the Duke conveniently called away, she seizes the opportunity to escape. She "brings
a scarf and fastens one end of it to the balcony railing, makes an
appeal to heaven and blows out the candles." Then before "letting

herself down by the scarf till her head sinks out of sight," she pauses to reassure any possible doubters: "I have been indiscreet, but I am not guilty."

She returns in safety to her home and sorrowing parents. There is no trouble with the mother, who knows, of course, that her child is innocent; but the father is implacable, and pleadings seem vain. Suddenly there is a great stir without, and the Duke, with several courtiers, enters. This Clari, little commoner, has displayed quite queenly mettle, so His Highness has found a way to circumvent legal barriers and now asks her hand in marriage. Thereby the father is finally won over, but only after a stormy scene in which he has threatened to shoot the suspected betrayer. The chorus chants "Virtue in her child rejoices," and all ends happily.[176]

In *Clari,* as in many greater works, minor characters and situations add appreciably to the value of the whole. The byplay and wise little jokes of the servants enhance the palace setting and do much to carry the action along. The entrance of the troupe of strolling players, some drunk and all hungry, is a very good piece of fooling. The playlet they perform has some unexpectedly charming lines. In the closing act Clari's fond, forgiving mother, her stern and sorrowing father, and the kindly village friends are truly "sympathetic characters."

The music throughout is of course indispensable, and the play as originally given contained numerous songs, though some were omitted from later performances. Payne, indeed, had provided so many that he wrote to Bishop: "I do not see where more songs could be got in without overloading the piece."

The main melodic line of "Home, Sweet Home" is heard in the overture, and reminders of it appear again and again throughout the score. For here, while Wagner was only ten years old, Bishop was modestly employing something very like the leitmotif.[177] Clari's song, after she had introduced it, seems to go wherever she goes. A few lines of it, to harp accompaniment, are heard in the play within a play when the daughter briefly becomes the counterpart of Clari. Suggestions of it follow the true Clari as she approaches the village, the flute now carrying the air, and she pauses to listen as if to her own thoughts. As she hesitates outside the house before facing her parents a chorus of happy villagers passes in the road, cheerily singing the song's opening lines. And at the close the neighbors group around to welcome the now tearfully happy heroine in a chorus through which phrases of the home melody are woven.

"You will probably know before this that *Clari* has had perfect success," the friendly James Kenney wrote Payne a few days after the opening. "There was no opposition and it stands fair for a run. As early as the first act I saw handkerchiefs employed upon the bright eyes in the dress boxes." It was even reported, Kenney added, that Mrs. Charles Kemble, the actor-manager's wife, had "wept torrents" over the little play.[178]

The compelling pathos of this first performance was a tribute to the talents of a young singing actress, Ann Maria Tree, who impersonated Clari and thus achieved the distinction of being the first person ever to sing "Home, Sweet Home." She was then twenty-two, and had a voice described as "a cordial, expressive mezzo-soprano, with much real feeling." [179] Doubtless especially sweet in "white morning dress of muslin, frilled," [180] Miss Tree as Clari was widely approved. The *Quarterly Musical Review* even compared her to Fanny Kelly, who, "previous to this melodrama, might be said to have had no rival in that species of acting which describes simple, natural feeling in its most natural and therefore most affecting manner."

Shortly before the opening Payne had remarked in a letter to Bishop:

I would have written largely about the acting of Clari, but I feared Miss Tree would have deemed it impertinent. I wish her safely through. . . . In the last scene, where Clari appeals to her father, considerable effect can be produced by her dragging after him on her knees. . . . And in order to fill in the time between his and the mother's speeches, by standing in an attitude of utter despondency.

Next to Clari herself the strongest individual in the little drama is her father; and fortunately for the operetta's initial success, the experienced John Fawcett appeared in the role of that severe but essentially loving parent. Fawcett continued to act Rolamo for years;

and it is further evidence of the attractiveness of the part that Charles Dickens, when he put on amateur performances of *Clari* some years later, himself chose to portray the father.

The press and critical journals were nearly unanimous in praise of *Clari.*

"Long and loud plaudits, accompanied by the waving of hats" according to the next day's *Courier,* greeted the "announcement for repetition" (then a first-night custom of the London theaters). "Assuredly the most successful and in many respects the most able production of the season at this house," said *The Drama or Theatrical Pocket Magazine* (May 1823). "The sentiments are very natural and pathetic and the situations not at all improbable. It does credit to the well-known dramatic talent of Mr. Howard Payne."

The *European Magazine* was impressed by the music, which it called "pleasing and in some instances delightful" but this judgment was mild beside that of the *Quarterly Musical Magazine and Review,* which pronounced the air of Clari's song "simple, sweet, touching, beyond any we almost ever heard." The *New Monthly Magazine* remarked chiefly on the text: "The words were supplied and ingeniously supplied by Mr. Howard Payne. . . . The last scene was extremely well-wrought and extremely pleasing."

Bell's Weekly Messenger, which admired the beauty of the scenery and felt that the story was "improved by the circumstance that Clari's elopement was not accompanied by her fall from virtue," said this of the sentiment expressed by her song: "The ballad is entitled to every praise. It is simple and sweet and expressed the longing, lingering tenderness with which the heart reverts to its best affections."

To the *Weekly Examiner* it seemed that "There are some points of nature which never fail of exciting sympathy, because the corresponding vibration is universal and eternal. . . . The piece made a great and deserved impression, despite the drawbacks of a hackneyed story and commonplace material."

Except for this partly adverse observation, it remained for the London *Times,* alone among the publications today available, to take a dissenting view and to avow the play unworthy of the composer:

> On such a drama as this Mr. Bishop has judiciously refrained from expending his happiest composition, for with the exception of Miss Tree's song, there is not a piece in it that will linger on the ear or be recalled to memory. . . . The overture is loud and startling, but we can say little else in its favor. The songs are commonplace and there is no concerted piece making pretensions to novelty.

With a considerable lack of prescience this comment concluded: "We do not think it will add to the reputation of the composer or bring much money into the treasury." [181]

The statement, often published, that *Clari* had only a few performances is entirely erroneous. In fact, it is one of the most egregious of the many false reports connected with Payne and his career. While it is true that only ten performances of the play are advertised in the London papers between its first night and the theater's closing for the summer, this does not take account of its later history.

For years immensely popular in England, *Clari* was performed times without number not only in London, but soon after the première in cities and towns large and small throughout Great Britain—current copyright provisions, or the lack of them, making this possible. In theater advertisements of the next few years the London *Times* records innumerable repeat performances of the operetta at Covent Garden. In 1824 Miss Tree took it to Glasgow and Dublin; in 1825, Mlle. Noblet appeared as Clari in Paris. In 1826, when the play was three years old, not only was Covent Garden still putting it on frequently, but the other London theaters had adopted it: the Haymarket, the Royal Coburg, and even Drury Lane. It also had a great run that summer at Sadler's Wells, whose advertisement day after day printed "Clari, Clari, Clari" in large type, and in smaller the statement: "No orders except the press can possibly be admitted, every night the rest of season." [182]

Meanwhile the London publisher John Miller had lost no time in issuing "Home, Sweet Home" separately, and estimates of the number of copies sold the first year vary considerably. A London musical publication of 1824, commenting on the popularity of Bishop's work in general, said: "20 of his pieces we know to have worn out three sets of plates, and of 'Home, Sweet Home,' written only last year, no less than 30,000 copies have been sold." [183] But Bishop's principal biographer states that 100,000 copies of the song were sold the first year; and that figure, whether or not correct, is the one most often quoted.[184] Neither Bishop nor Payne shared in the publisher's profits.

Of the two collaborators Payne fared the better financially. That he finally got the price he had asked for *Clari* and the two plays bracketed with it is indicated by his letter to Burroughs, manager of the theater that had brought out the play without the music: "I am desired by the Covent Garden management to acquaint you with their adoption of 'Clari,' as they take that and two other pieces and give me a round sum for the three."

If the round sum for the three was 250 pounds, then Payne was paid by the theater for *Clari,* and hence for "Home, Sweet Home," one third of that amount, or about 85 pounds. In addition James Kenney, acting privately for Payne, had sold the libretto to John Miller for 50 pounds. Hence the moot question of what Payne earned from his famous song does not seem difficult to answer: probably about 135 pounds. Apparently he was never to receive anything more for "Home, Sweet Home," but this is a greater amount than he is generally believed to have realized from it.

Kenney was an exceptionally good friend. In a letter to Payne four days after the première he detailed his negotiations concerning the libretto:

> Miller was near me at the opening and seemed disposed to buy, but wished to see what was offered by others. . . . I have been to Longman's, Simpkins and Whittaker's. The latter would make me no offer, but would hear mine. I asked 70, which they refused. I then offered it to Miller for 50, with 25 more in case of a run of 20 nights. He has taken it, and we all think you well off (times considered). I will remit next week.

Kenney also refers to changes in Payne's text: "Charles [Kemble] says he has paid for the alterations and it is wholly at your disposal."

That these changes were unauthorized and were not pleasing to

Payne is indicated by another letter of Kenney a month later: "Push on and never mind Clari. She should have been acted as you sent her, but she will do your fame no harm." [185] (Surely a prophetic comment, though we probably shall never know just what the play was like as Payne wrote it.)

Evidence of cutting is provided also by the official playbill of the royal theaters, issued a week after the première, which lists ten songs (solos, duets, and choruses) as the principal numbers of *Clari*,[186] and not a single song by the Duke is included, though to Bishop Payne wrote that he had given that character three songs. Even more songs were omitted later, and most printed editions of *Clari* available today contain only four songs, others five or six. The solo of Clari's maid, Vespina, "Love's a Mischievous Boy," which, next to "Home, Sweet Home," was the hit of the piece, is found in all editions.[187]

If Bishop, as the *Times* averred, actually "did not spend his happiest composition" on this work, the reason may have been less the slenderness of the drama than the slimness of his remuneration. It seems doubtful, indeed, if he was paid much, if anything, for writing the music of *Clari* above his salary as Covent Garden's musical director, and that was so small that he would resign in protest the following year. He probably did receive royalties from one number, "Sleep, Gentle Lady," cut from the score after the early performances and published separately.

Bishop was then the most distinguished British composer, so highly regarded in his own country as to be called "the English Mozart." Twenty years later he would be knighted by Queen Victoria. One of the founders of the Royal Academy of Music and for some years an associate conductor of the Royal Philharmonic, he was made a Doctor of Music by Oxford toward the end of his life. His more than 500 compositions included operas, glees, ensemble pieces, and "display songs," but for all his industry, he died poor. Whether or not he deserves oblivion, little of his work is known today except "Sweet Home" and one or two of the "display" numbers, notably "Lo, Here the Gentle Lark."

Bishop, who was five years older than Payne, is described as "reticent, quiet and slightly pompous." He often appeared "in cut-away coat, tight pants, huge white cravat and a collar which seemed to hold his head as in a pillory." [188]

The story is told of his meeting Rossini on the street soon after the première of *Clari*. The genial Italian, unable to recall the English maestro's name, yet greeted him cordially by humming the first line of "Home, Sweet Home": "Ah, you are Signor Da, da, *da*, da, de, *da*, da!" [189]

Payne liked and trusted Bishop. There is this remark in one letter: "I need not hint that I trust you to look a little to my interest in whatever is discussed about terms, though on that head I shall leave all to your sense of justice, only (entre nous) remember how close I was shaved by Mr. Stephen Kemble about Brutus."

And in another: "I hope you will make memoranda of the expenses you have been at in postage, etc., on account of what I have sent to the theatre through you. If the treasury has not paid it, I shall think you do me an injustice to deny me the opportunity of preventing my correspondence from becoming a tax on anything but your patience."

Naturally pleased to have been invited into collaboration by so famous a personage as Bishop, Payne had thus acknowledged the composer's initiative: "I cannot express to you how deeply I feel your kindness relative to my interests at Covent Garden Theatre. The only way I can acknowledge it will be by endeavoring to frame such a piece as may furnish your talents with fitting opportunities. This is not an easy matter, but eventually I feel certain of doing it." His suggestions to Bishop of subjects for operatic collaboration are clues to Payne's taste and judgment at the time:

> I have often thought that a very good thing could be made of Dr. Faustus. What a field for supernatural agency and a Macbeth sort of music! . . . Then there is Sappho. That's a good subject. All the poetry of Sappho that remains could be brought in well. Her "blest as the immortal gods is he," would be beautiful with music. . . . And have you ever thought of "Camille" by Marsollier and Dalayrac? [190]

The prolific Bishop had probably turned off *Clari* as fast and easily as possible. In fact, he always freely admitted that he borrowed from a previous work of his own the air of "Home, Sweet Home" and wove bits of it into the overture and other parts of the score.

Some years before the writing of *Clari* Bishop had been commissioned by a London publisher to compile a collection of national airs to be called *Melodies of Various Nations*. He duly executed the order, using authentic national melodies when he could find them. Inclusion of a Sicilian air had been specified by the publisher, but Bishop's researches revealed no national melody for Sicily. He therefore invented one himself; and it is this melody, with some variants and additions, that he later used for "Home, Sweet Home" and the score of *Clari*.[191]

The lyrics for *Melodies of Various Nations* were supplied by an Englishman, Thomas Haynes Bayly, and for the air which Bishop had invented for Sicily, Bayly supplied words that are a tribute to home. This may be what caused that particular air to be chosen for the later home song.

Despite plain proof, the origin of the melody was for some years the subject of controversy. There was first of all the theory that Payne had heard the air in Italy, sung by a peasant girl "carrying a basket laden with flowers and vegetables," and that, "having some slight knowledge of music," he jotted down the notes and sent them to Bishop.[192]

Though long discredited by the more critical, this pretty yarn has been widely printed, and many persons have liked to believe it. Two circumstances, however, almost conclusively prove it a fabrication: One, the fact that there is no record of Payne's having ever been in Italy until some years after *Clari* first appeared; the other, that his "slight knowledge of music" may be questioned. In fact, in his diary kept during rehearsals of *Thérèse* he stated that he "knew not a note."

If either of the collaborators first heard the melody originally called a Sicilian air sung by a peasant girl in Italy, it seems more likely that it was Bishop. There is basis for the theory of Italian inspiration in the operetta's Italian setting, its subtitle, *The Maid of Milan,* and its characters' Italian names. To be sure, the setting seems to have little or nothing to do with the story; but in the original, unaltered version it may have been more important.

It took *Clari* six months—longer than most of Payne's work—to cross the Atlantic for its first performance in New York; and on advance bills of the American première, November 12, 1823, Clari's solo was not mentioned. The advertising featured instead the British baritone Pearman with several solos as Jocoso, the Duke's servant, a major-minor character in the original.[193] After two or three performances, however, "Sweet Home" was discovered by the New York *Mirror*, which called the music "the most tender and beautiful we have ever heard" and further declared:

> The scene at the old home where the flute plays the air of "Home, Sweet Home" and Clari listens, is one of the prettiest incidents we have ever witnessed on a stage, and if we may judge by certain symptoms about the eyes of the audience, their hearts felt all its tenderness.

Authorities have differed as to the identity of the first American Clari,[194] although the singer who first appeared in the role in New York is plainly designated on the program as Miss Johnson. This fact and references in the dramatic news of New York papers of the time make it seem probable that she was Ellen Johnson, a harpist as well as a singer, and a versatile young actress. Records indicate that she was a daughter of that famed Mrs. Johnson, who had been one of the two great ladies of the New York stage in Payne's *Thespian Mirror* days.

A long line of American Claris followed within the quarter century that the operetta remained in vogue in this country, but it is doubtful if the play itself ever attained quite the popularity on this side of the water that it enjoyed for many years in England.

Both in the United States and abroad, however, Clari's song speedily achieved a life of its own quite apart from the playlet. In its early years it appeared on the programs of the greatest singers. So pronounced was its popularity in Europe, even after seven years, that the Italian diva Pasta persuaded Donizetti to incorporate a modification of the air in the opera *Anna Bolina*, which he composed for her.[195] It occurs in the final scene of that opera, where poor Anne's last prayer is set to Bishop's music. This use of the air is responsible for the myth that sometimes confuses Donizetti with Bishop as composer of "Home, Sweet Home."

Distinguished singers of a later time have also used "Home, Sweet Home," especially on British and American programs. Jenny Lind, who was three years older than the song, and Adelina Patti, who was twenty years younger, both sang it widely; while the person chiefly responsible for making it known beyond the Western world was Mme. Anna Rivere Bishop, estranged wife of the composer. Traveling more widely than most concert singers of her time, Mme. Bishop took "Home, Sweet Home" with her on a world tour, "including China, India and parts of Africa." Once, shipwrecked in the Pacific, her music and her wardrobe lost, she entranced an audience of natives and stranded travelers with the peculiarly pertinent song of home.[196]

Several copies of the lyric in Payne's pleasantly legible script exist in this country, but whether his original *Clari* manuscript—the words of the operetta without the music—is still extant cannot be learned.[197] The original score—the music without the words—in Bishop's hand, formerly for years part of a private British collection,[198] is now owned by the Eastman School of Music at Rochester, New York.

It is unusual in the history of famous songs to find the author of the words honored above the composer, but so it is with "Home, Sweet Home." Nor does this reversal seem unfair, inasmuch as Bishop's melody had been used before and it is the sentiment of the ballad that gives the song its universal appeal.

Lifelong familiarity has perhaps dulled us to both sound and meaning of this song, and a just appraisal is difficult. Yet Payne's words, when examined (or at least part of them, for the piece is admittedly uneven) are found to possess a good deal of originality and lyric merit. " 'Mid pleasures and palaces"—almost too hackneyed by now to admit of analysis—is perhaps a little theatrical; but "a charm from the sky seems to hallow us there" has imagination and a touch of spirituality. "The birds singing gaily that came at my call" is charming in its artlessness. If it were possible to imagine coming across this lyric today for the first time, those of us whose response to verse is not greatly influenced by period or school would say that here is a sentiment simple yet deep, expressed in a fresh and appealing way.

The popularity and fame of "Home, Sweet Home" through the years are beyond estimating. How important it was in England, at least up to the first decade of our century, is indicated by the remark of a British writer: "It is curious and a little disappointing to find that the author of these universally familiar words was not an Englishman, but an American."

For the average American of the late nineteenth and early twentieth centuries the song is so interwoven with school and family experiences that it is hard to imagine never having known it. It is one of those songs that have become a part of the language, familiar and meaningful, like a word in common usage—a part of life itself.

[14]

COLLABORATORS

"I HAVE lately been favored with another theatrical success, an opera called 'Clari,' " Payne wrote his sister Anna near the end of May 1823. With the letter he sent the family half a dozen copies of the play, but made no mention of the song. As yet he was unaware even of the attraction it would have for the London public.

In Paris all winter he had been working hard, and doubtless felt the need of getting away from city streets. On a trip to Versailles one fine spring day he had run across a cottage. Just the thing for summer. He rented it and forthwith became a suburbanite, retaining, with his usual lavishness, the Palais Royal "sky parlor" as a sort of office or as a place to stay when kept in town overnight. He reported to Anna:

I have taken a country place at Versailles in order to finish several works. . . . Fifteen pounds until January next. You have no house rent in New York so cheap . . . retaining apartment for purposes of business . . . so very cheap can do so without violating your injunctions of economy.

In the country he has room for them all, his brother and two sisters, this letter adds, and wishes they could visit him. In no great expectation of such pleasure, however, he is on the lookout for other companions—"a cat, rabbits, a large dog, pigeons, and a cock and hens." [199]

Payne did not remain a country gentleman for long. It is characteristic of his impulsive ways that he left the Versailles place after four months' tenancy and, having at the same time abandoned the sky parlor, removed his furnishings to yet another Paris apartment. The reason may have been that the coming of winter made country life inconvenient; or the move to the city may have been for the express purpose, when he himself should go back to London, of subletting to Washington Irving the new apartment, located at 89 Rue Richelieu in the heart of Paris.

Irving, far more practical than Payne, demurred at first. He wrote from Havre September 27: "My dear Payne: The situation you mention on the Rue Richelieu is very central and desirable, but the price (150 francs) rather beyond what I wished to go in the present state of my purse; but I shall take the apartment myself or find some other tenant."

He adds that he wants a southern exposure, as his health requires "rooms free from chill and dampness because of old complaint in the ancles which obliges me to take baths daily." The letter concludes with an amusing touch: "Let there be a good sopha in the living room."

At sight of the apartment, however, Irving was completely won over. With Payne reserving a room for himself whenever he should want it, Irving accepted the place and sent this description to his brother:

I am just now moving to my new quarters at 89 Rue Richelieu. I am greatly pleased with them. My apartments consist of bedroom, sitting room and dining room and use of kitchen and appurtenances, and a cellar.

Payne has furnished them handsomely. They have a warm southern exposure and look into a very spacious and handsome court, and, being newly finished and fitted up, are very complete. I shall have a bed for you whenever you choose to pay Paris a visit. Shall live much at home, having an excellent *femme de menage* to cook, etc.[200]

Details later supplied by Irving for his sister, Mrs. Paris, gave the additional information that the apartment was in "one of the best private hotels in Paris . . . everything about the establishment particularly genteel and well-regulated." And to Thomas Moore he reported: "We manage to live very comfortably. Have our separate rooms, where we can occupy ourselves as we please, without interfering with each other, and need not meet except at meal time." [201]

For the "homeless" Payne, the Rue Richelieu apartment was the fourth Paris abode within three years, counting the country cottage. Though his stay at 89 Rue Richelieu was curtailed at the start—he and Irving being joint occupants not much more than a fortnight— the apartment would remain Paris headquarters for Payne or some of the Irvings for several years. Before the end of the winter the dining room was converted into a bedroom for Peter Irving, who had come to live with his brother, and accommodations were made for their nephews at various times. It was from this address that Irving conducted his brief experiment in dramatic writing—mostly a kind of long-distance collaboration with Payne, after he had left for London.

The collaboration of Payne and Irving has been represented by some writers to Payne's disparagement. It has been stated that Payne "pestered Irving about writing for the stage" and that Irving was "farming out his precious time to Payne." There is not the least justification, however, for the belief that Irving entered upon the joint effort unwillingly; the evidence, in fact, is quite to the contrary.

Irving had reached a turning in the road. Both his *Sketch Book* and *Bracebridge Hall* being completed and published, he had to have a new literary project. A lifelong devotee of the theater, he had lately begun to suspect dramatic tendencies in himself, and wanted to try them out, if not on the stage, then in writing for it.

The idea of branching out into the dramatic field seems first to have occurred to him the previous summer during a visit to Germany, where he had taken part in drawing room theatricals. From Dresden he wrote to Charles Leslie expressing pleased surprise on discovering "the fund of dramatic talents within me." There also Irving began, in collaboration with a dramatic amateur, one Colonel Barham Livius,[202] a translation of the German opera *Der Freischütz*, which, with the magnificent music of Carl Maria von Weber, was the sensation of all Europe in the early 1820's.

On returning from Germany to Paris and re-establishing contact with Payne, Irving either voluntarily or at Payne's request took on the task of retouching one of Payne's translated plays—"a slight literary job," he calls it in writing to Peter. The remark appears in the letter describing the new apartment, and Irving adds: "I am tempted to accept the invitation of Payne to assist in his literary pursuits and divide the profits."

Irving's essay of dramatic writing, therefore, as well as his informal collaboration with Payne, had begun before their sharing of the Rue Richelieu apartment. Indeed, in the letter detailing his needs in living quarters, written while Payne was still living at the Palais Royal, Irving had mentioned several plays: "I want you to send me the ms. of Married and Single. . . . I shall do the needful with Richelieu in a day or two. . . . I hope you are getting on with Azendai."

As for Payne's fitness as a collaborator, Irving had long believed in his friend's ability, and as much as two years earlier had written praising "the ease and gracefulness" of his style. Also, in the belief that Payne could succeed at original writing if he would, Irving had offered a stimulating suggestion: "I want to see you swimming without corks, throwing away translations and reconstructions and writing something out of your own brain."[203]

Furthermore the value of Payne's practical experience in the theater, though perhaps not fully appreciated by Irving, was not greatly underestimated by him. He knew that in any experiment in writing for the stage he could not have a more capable associate than his old friend.

"Payne determines to go to London," Irving's journal recorded on October 18, about two weeks after the joint tenancy began.

On the same date the two set out on what must have been a pleasant autumn day's excursion into the country. For Payne it was partly a business jaunt, since he was still responsible for his cottage, which later, with Irving's assistance, would be sublet to the American consul at London, Colonel Aspinwall.[204] "Fine morning. We go together to Versailles [continues the diary]. Go in cuckow to St. Cloud and set off to walk through the wood. Clouds up and threatens to rain, get in cuckow and ride. Visit Payne's house, return home by myself."

A few days later Irving wrote his brother: "Payne sets off *privately* for London to treat with Kemble about Richelieu and Belles and Bailiffs, another adaptation from the French, in which, under the title of Married and Single, he has altered some scenes. . . . I shall send with him the rough copy of Azendai that it may be shown to Bishop and the proper directions procured for the music." [205]

There was a very particular reason for Payne to "set off privately." In fact, it would seem that he ran quite a risk in going to London at all, for despite his continually paying off old debts there were still unsatisfied creditors in England. He therefore felt obliged to conceal his identity under the name of J. Heyward, at least to the extent of having mail addressed to that name, in care of the publisher John Miller, though only Irving and a few other intimates knew of the dual role. Indeed Payne himself found it difficult to enact, and it is doubtful if it helped matters greatly, for in London acquaintances were likely to bob up on all sides.

It was a bad time of year for a Channel crossing, and a severe storm caused a delay in communications that gave Irving some uneasiness. But Payne reached London eventually and reported in a letter of November 7: "Detained at Dieppe 10 days waiting for boat. At last got out in the storm—was in a gale all Monday night and part of Tuesday—16½ hours. . . . At Brighton had the happiness of finding that I had just missed 'Clari,' which had had a considerable run of some nights."

(Six months after the première, Payne had not seen *Clari* performed.)

> Got here Wednesday and having rode all the way in a terrible rain, was stiff, stupid and tired. . . . Packed off Richelieu and Married and Single instantly to Charles Kemble. . . . Dined with Leslie and Newton and got a lodging under the name of Heyward (which I am every minute forgetting), and, heartily weary, found my bed was over a livery stable, where the hackney coaches entered every hour and in which every horse had a violent cough. I feel as if I had not slept for a month.
>
> And now for business. I saw Charles [Kemble] today and was very well received. My description of Azendai and my confidential disclosure of your connection, seemed to excite him. Asked me to his box tonight and to dinner either today or tomorrow. . . . Shall hand him Azendai tonight. . . . Think I shall dine with Miller tonight and with Charles tomorrow.[206]

Payne remained in London nearly two years this time; and his correspondence with Irving—or rather Irving's side of it, for Payne kept Irving's letters and Irving apparently did not keep many of Payne's—tells the rest of the story of the collaboration.

In addition to the three plays that Payne carried with him—*Azendai, Richelieu,* and *Married and Single*—the two Americans within the next few months, worked on three other pieces: *Charles II, The Mother's Curse,* and *The Waggoners.* Of this total only two would reach the stage: *Charles II* the following season, and *Richelieu* later. The musical piece *Azendai,* on which Irving expended considerable work, was apparently never produced.

It is probable that Payne made the translations and that Irving revised, polished, and sometimes added verses for songs. His journal, however, speaks several times of "correcting" Payne's work, and there is also a letter to Peter which says: "Payne is making a literal translation of Azendai and I am looking it over and making notes, where there must be alterations, songs, choruses, etc." This division of labor has led some writers to conclude that Payne was capable of nothing but literal translations and was generally incompetent— an impression that Irving would have been prompt to deny.

By far the most successful of the collaborated pieces was *Charles II; or, the Merry Monarch, a comedy in three acts with some songs.*

This play had an odd history. It was based directly on a piece by the French dramatist Alexander Duval, *La Jeunesse de Henri V*, but because the legends of the youthful exploits of France's Henry V and England's Charles II had points of similarity, the American adapters applied the story to the English king. In this they were further justified by the fact that Duval's play in turn had been derived from an earlier one by Mercier, actually built about the pranks of the fun-loving Charles. It was a mischievous though mild Charles II that Payne and Irving imagined, compared with some later literary representations of that monarch.

Irving finished work on the play soon after Payne left for London, and wrote on November 22: "The Jeunesse is copying out and will be sent in a day or two to see if it is likely to find a market. I think it will make a most interesting piece. It will do for either theatre." [207]

After two months of negotiations Payne sold *Charles II*, together with *Richelieu*, to Covent Garden Theatre "for 200 guineas down, and copyright may double it." The adaptation of *Charles II* was dedicated to Charles Kemble and was first produced by him at Covent Garden on May 27, 1824, a year after the première of *Clari*. Kemble himself acted the part of King Charles; John Fawcett,[208] who had created the role of the father in *Clari*, was Captain Copp, the innkeeper; and Ann Maria Tree, famed as the singer who introduced "Home, Sweet Home" to the world, was Mary, the innkeeper's charming and vocally gifted niece. And still another old friend to contribute to the comedy's success was the composer Bishop, called in to supply the incidental music.

The play is neatly and carefully written and is really very funny. It had a strong appeal to English audiences, for the legendary exploits of the pleasure-loving Charles and his literary nobleman Rochester were still recalled by old inhabitants as tales told to them in childhood.

Here is the story of the play in outline: Young Charles and his courtier Rochester, both disguised as sailors, go to a public house in a suburb known as Wapping, where their excessive thirst and reckless merriment arouse the suspicions even of Captain Copp, who has seen jolly sailors before. As a very special prank Rochester picks the pocket of his royal companion, who, on leaving, finds himself without funds and obliged to offer his watch in payment. Since this is a rare jewel set with diamonds, Copp concludes that it has been stolen and goes to call police, leaving his niece and her suitor (a minor member of the royal household disguised as her singing teacher) to guard the thieving sailor. But Mary, at whom the masquerading monarch has made some pretty passes, relents and allows the prisoner to escape.

The following day, a jeweler having declared the watch undoubtedly the property of the King, Copp and Mary go to the palace to return the supposedly stolen trophy. There the resemblance of the King and Rochester to the disguised guests of the night before calls for ingenious explanations, and at the end to round off the play theatrically Mary is betrothed to her singing teacher with the blessing of the King.

Copp is a character not in the original French play, and his creation is generally and, it would seem, rightly attributed to Irving. Copp's song, repeated several times and always interrupted just as it reaches the verge of impropriety, was the hit of the piece. It was undoubtedly the work of Irving. He wrote Payne November 28 that "the scrap of a song was hastily done and does not suit me," so he sent "another scrap to substitute," and it was used:

> In the time of the Rump
> An old Admiral Trump
>   With his broom swept the chops of the Channel;
> And his crew of Big Breeches
> Those Dutch sons of ——

At this point Mary claps her hand over the Captain's mouth, exclaiming: "Oh, Uncle, Uncle, don't sing that horrible, rough old song!"

The "hiatus," as Charles Lamb called this interruption—Lamb declared he could not get Copp's song out of his head and that it "kept him awake o' nights"—we know was also Irving's idea for he had expressly suggested: "Let it be stopped short at the critical point by the daughter's placing her hand upon his mouth. Thereafter he need sing only one or two lines." [209]

Two other songs appear in printed copies of the play, and these were probably Payne's work, since it was Irving's opinion that "a few songs might be added but I should think it would do as it is." Indeed Payne, who never skimped on material, may have supplied even more songs that were cut out by the management. The sentiment of Mary's little song when she enters the palace and gazes on its grandeur certainly bears a family resemblance to "Sweet Home":

> Not in the pictured halls
> Not amid marble walls
>   Will young love dwell.
> Love's home's its heart alone
> That heart, too, all his own,
>   Else, Love farewell.

Irving journeyed to London and was present at the second performance of *Charles II*, of which he recorded: "It succeeds very well, though the critics attack the language." (Perhaps the critics did not like the word omitted from Copp's song!) But the press in the main was favorable, and one observer remarked especially of the costumes that they "were as if cut out of the frames of old pictures, down to the veriest trifle." This may well have reflected Payne's energy and peculiar flair for such details. The overworked actor-manager, Kemble, would have been only too glad to turn such a matter over to an author who was not only able but also eager to make a perfect job of it.

Whatever Irving's part in the authorship, he requested that it be not revealed that he had had anything to do with re-creating *Charles II*. This he repeated in several letters, telling Payne, "I wish you would present this piece, either in your own name, or, if you would prefer, fabricate a name . . . but at all events do not let my name be implicated in the thing." He suggested that Payne might "save his conscience" by saying that the play had been "revised and occasionally touched up by a literary friend." [210]

Concerning the other plays of the collaboration, Irving, cautiously determined not to risk his reputation in an unproved field, insisted that his name "be kept completely out of sight." He had no objection to "any bargain" Payne might make, begging him to "recollect only that I do not wish my name on any account to be connected with them. It would be quite disastrous to my plans."

Knowing that Charles Kemble had been told of the collaboration on *Azendai*, Irving wrote: "If Azendai should not be already accepted, I wish you to withdraw it definitely. It cannot, I fear, be represented without my name leaking out as author. Should it, however, be in the hands of the committee and beyond recovery, enjoin secrecy on Mr. Kemble in regard to my name." Especially he objected to having the play "debated upon by those skim-milk gentlemen they have as privy councilors."

To Irving's credit it must be recorded that, while he declined to risk being named as coauthor, he also repeatedly declared that he would share none of the profits. Nearly all his letters to Payne of the season of 1823–24 stress this point. On December 23 he wrote: "Act precisely in your own interest. If you can make anything by them, so much the better, I won't share a farthing." And on December 29: "I thank you for your liberal offer of sharing proceeds of both pieces, but I can only share on 'Married and Single.'"

On the last day of January 1824 Irving informed his partner that he had had enough of the playwriting effort: "I am sorry to say I cannot afford to write any more for the theatre . . . the experiment has satisfied me that I should never at any time be compensated for my trouble. I speak not with reference to my talents, but to the market price my productions will command in other departments of literature." [211]

He is "perfectly satisfied" that Payne has "done his best with the manuscripts" (*Charles II* and *Richelieu*) only regretting that "you did not find more liberality on the part of those you dealt with"; and repeating that he wants Payne to have "any material benefits from the experiment."

There is, it is true, one letter in which Irving deviates slightly from this stand about material benefits. In March 1824 he had begun to plan a trip to London, and wrote to Payne: "If you can get the money for me from the theatre I wish you would remit it, as it will assist me in meeting my traveling expenses, and my purse is running low. Of course take your proportion first."

Opera in English was the rule in London at the time, which meant that foreign operatic works as well as plays had to be translated for English audiences. Irving, who had translated the librettos of *Der Freischütz* and *Abu Hassan* with Colonel Livius, was quite as anxious to disclaim responsibility for his part in this work as for his play collaboration. About the two German pieces, he wrote to Payne: "I wish you to ascertain whether Kemble has received 'Der Freischütz' from Livius, and what he feels disposed to do in the matter . . . I wish 'Abu Hassan' to be offered to Elliston by Miller as from Livius." [212]

The Irving-Livius translation of *Freischütz* was finally brought out by Charles Kemble at Covent Garden on October 14, 1824. Later Elliston accepted *Abu Hassan* and produced it, with Weber's music, at Drury Lane.

London had gone wild over the music of Weber that year, and following the usual custom of competition to the strangulation point, four different theaters brought out *Der Freischütz* in as many different translations. [213] All had different subtitles. Irving's can be distinguished, and the Covent Garden production identified as his, by its secondary title, *Or, the Black Huntsman of Bohemia*. It is sometimes referred to as "Payne's *Freischütz*," but that is disproved by the correspondence.

Although the Covent Garden *Freischütz* was not the first of the London adaptations to be produced, it ranked high in public interest. The *Times* reported of the opening that "the house was thronged from pit to very ceiling." When it was performed the second time *Charles II* was used as the afterpiece, double bills being still in vogue; and from then on, Covent Garden presented either *Charles II* or *Clari* as the secondary item every time the Weber-Irving-Livius *Freischütz* was put on. [214] That at the start was on consecutive nights, but later no oftener than twice a week, for it was still unusual in London for a play to be repeated nightly, and even the genius of Weber could not justify long-continued consecutive performances of his opera.

When "by command of His Majesty" Covent Garden presented a special performance of *Der Freischütz, Charles II* was played also, and according to the *Morning Chronicle* the Royal Party "seemed highly entertained" by the afterpiece.

There were also that season many Covent Garden performances of *Charles II* and *Clari* in combination; and the celebrated Miss Tree, creator of Clari and Mary Copp, made her farewell to the theater in April, singing and acting both famous parts. At about the same time Payne commented in a letter to Irving:

> Charles and Clari are acted, one or both, regularly every Wednesday evening and often twice a week, without producing any difference whatever in the feelings or conduct of the managers toward me. They seem, even, to be rendered more reluctant to notice my pieces by attention exerted by these.[215]

Payne does not tell us, but the current newspapers do, that within the same season (1824–25) "the new song, 'Home, Sweet Home,' " without the play, was an advertised attraction at the leading theaters. When Mme. Catalani, one of the most celebrated of contemporary concert singers, "positively took leave of the British public for the season" she featured the song on her program, a fact particularly mentioned in advance advertisements.

Theatrical affairs were not the only matters touched upon by Irving in his letters from Paris. He took time to mention in one a few of the domestic happenings at 89 Rue Richelieu:

> The chimneys smoked and have all been devilled by the *fumiste,* so I suppose they will smoke worse than ever. Your room has been painted and papered under the direction of the indefatigable Marianne [the very capable *femme de menage* mentioned earlier by Irving]. . . . Your dog dirtied himself out of all toleration and I have sent him into exile. Marianne told me you were to give 15 francs a month to some dog landlord— enough to support a Christian soul and more than the dog is worth.

Here, as in several subsequent letters, Irving assumes the prerogative of a long-trusted friend, older in years, to admonish Payne on his extravagance and mismanagement and to give some advice on the technique of dealing with managers. As to money management Irving's ideas were sound and sadly needed. As to managers they were certainly worth listening to, though perhaps less practical. Irving had never had direct contact with the lords of the theater, whereas Payne, who had been treated abominably by most of them, knew them for the tribe they were. Nevertheless bits of Irving's letters bearing on this point may be quoted:

> Write to me whenever you please, or rather, when you are in good humor, but no croaking letters. Fabricate good news, if you please, but suppress all bad. . . . Don't get into pets with managers nor cut your fingers in cutting your bread.
>
> I am really concerned that you have so much vexation and difficulty, but hope all will clear up pleasantly and profitably. . . . Do not suffer yourself to be discouraged, or on any account get on ill terms with managers. Deal with them always coolly and good-humoredly—it is the most dignified, the most advantageous and the most comfortable way.

Then follows a line worthy to rank with the good old copybook maxims:

"Coolness and courtesy give a man a vast advantage, even in quarrelling."

Irving's January 1824 letter varies the usual theme with a note of praise: "Your play by Mr. Sinnett is cutting and putting in order. It has the materials within it to make a most beautiful and attractive piece. . . . I cannot tell you how much satisfaction I feel in seeing you turn such a good piece of work out of your hands. . . . It varies so much from the original that you may lay claim to absolute authorship." [216]

The play referred to here was *The Spanish Husband*, for which the outlines of the plot were supplied by J. H. W. Sinnett, a London friend of Payne's. Despite Irving's high opinion of this work, however, it would not find a producer for several years.

The financial advice contained in this letter is more urgent than usual:

> Let me again and again impress you with the importance of management in your expenses, that you may make your industry profitable. You have it in your power to make twice, three times, as much as you need to spend; but through mismanagement you are continually toiling to make up foregone and needless expenses. . . . I may bore you with iteration of this topic, but I trust you will properly understand the motive which dictates it—not a love of finding fault or a desire to wound your feelings, but a sincere wish for your welfare.

Two months later, the air is the same: "Have just received your two letters. I am sorry you are writing in dumpiest mood; don't let yourself be cast down. Gad, man, you've made a little lump of money since last autumn; and if it has been rather sopped up in old debts, what's to prevent your making more? . . . live prudently and don't give way to doubts and fears."

By May Payne evidently considered assuming again the risks of theatrical management, and Irving characteristically advised against it: "I am sure that with a little economy and management you can live independently and comfortably by the exercise of your pen. . . . So long as I could make bread and cheese my own way, I would not bother my mind with the miseries of theatrical management, even though it would enable me to eat truffles and ortolans." [217]

Payne was a spendthrift, certainly, but he was not a carefree defaulter. Surviving records show him almost continually concerned about or paying debts. Irving's letters yield such bits as these: November 22, 1823: "I have heard nothing of the duns you seem to apprehend, except our one-armed landlord, who called to know when you would return." December 29: "I have your letter enclosing draft on Lafitte [Paris bank] for 800 francs, which shall be appropriated as you wish." January 7, 1824: "I have paid all the bills you mention." January 17: "I have this morning received the draft on Lafitte, and will apply it as you request." January 31: "Have received bank notes of 50 pounds which shall be dispersed according to your wishes."

Irving's journal refers to other payments, and his letter of May 5 mentions another financial matter attended to for his friend: "I ought long since have acknowledged your letter enclosing the bill for 40 pounds. I sent the 100 pounds to Mr. Wheatley, according to your request."

But the payments made at that time were only sufficient to keep some creditors quiet. Others became insistent, and early in the following year a letter of Irving's remarked kindly: "I am glad you are likely to pay off your Paris debts soon, for some of your debtors have become rather troublesome."

After still another year had passed, with some of the same debts still unpaid, the situation had naturally become acute, and Irving complained that it was causing him great annoyance:

> I wish you could find some way to pay off these petty scores, as they continually threaten to seize the furniture and make my residence in the apartment very uncomfortable. I have never been placed in such a situation before. I am tenacious in money matters. I pay at once for everything and cannot bear to have an account standing against me, much less be dunned for one. . . . Since I have been in this apartment, however, I have been so beset and with such a degree of impertinence, that I actually begin to feel as if I were grossly in debt and balking my creditors.[218]

Payne replied directly the following month, and in the meantime he must have reached some understanding with those particular creditors: "Your letter about the *duns* I have answered the best way I could to stop their annoyance. Be assured I have suffered severely at not having had the means to prevent your being disturbed by creditors, who would have been paid off long ago, had I been dealt with as I wish to deal with others." [219]

He begs Irving to "consider everything as entirely yours until the whole sum between us is paid off." Three months later Irving's journal records: "Payne transfers the furniture of the apartment to me." [220]

The correspondence of Irving and Payne at this period, if only an engaging little footnote to American literary history, is important in what it reveals of the characters of the two.

Irving, unusually rational for a literary man—or indeed for a human being—was only eight years the older, but his attitude toward his younger friend was almost fatherly. For years he strove to save Payne from himself,[221] from that perversely self-destructive streak, which was less a moral fault than almost an aberration.

Payne, certainly highly intelligent, was of average reasonableness and adaptability about everything but the management of money. There he seemed to lack a sense of reality. This trait was his greatest misfortune. It inevitably subjected him to misunderstandings and misjudgments of motive and actually overshadowed his many finer qualities.

Notwithstanding that extreme characteristic, there is ample evidence that he was able to receive Irving's advice in good part; indeed, with an understanding of its motives and a recognition of its fairness. After the receipt of many admonitory letters Payne could write: "I am very grateful for the kind feeling which prompts your advice about economy and hope you will not find it thrown away upon me"; [222] and still later: "I shall always be grateful for the kindness you have shown."

And to these expressions of thanks Irving could reply, with a saving touch of humor: "Among the many important obligations I have conferred upon you perhaps you might have mentioned the vast treasury of advice, given freely and gratuitously."

Despite deep temperamental differences the friendship continued; [223] and circumstances would soon put Payne's appreciation of Irving to an extraordinary test.

[15]

GENTEEL TRIANGLE

IT IS ONE of the penalties of fame that those who achieve it may have no secrets. Posthumously, at least, their intimate experiences will be spread before the world in the most casual manner, often, indeed, acquiring commercial value.

Such observations are inescapable when one reads the catalogue of a Philadelphia book auction house, dated April 1904. Laconically it advertises the sale, among other items, of an unusual literary find:

"Lot No. 539. A love correspondence between Mary Wollstonecraft Shelley, wife of the poet, and John Howard Payne; in which Washington Irving is somewhat involved." [224]

The sale attracted a considerable number of collectors and dealers, with the letters probably reserved for the climax. "Lot number five hundred and thirty-nine. . . . *A love correspondence.* . . . What am I bid?"

The hammer fell at $860—"a price somewhat disappointing to the auctioneers," the press, next morning, reported.[225]

The Payne-Shelley letters had then only recently come to light after nearly eighty years in obscurity. "Complete lives" of Mary Shelley had been written without so much as mention of Payne. Biographers of Payne had embroidered the little that was known of his attachments to women, oblivious of what was certainly no minor incident in his life. That Irving's connection with the matter had never been known is less surprising, for he himself was unaware at the time of being "somewhat involved."

After the brief period of collaboration with Irving, who was still in Paris, Payne had remained in London. It was there, in 1825—and spring again, that fatal season—that a decorous intimacy began between him and the poet's widow, Mary Shelley. It was early in the summer that Payne definitely declared his love, and that Mary, half in jest but also in earnest, confessed herself as more than a little attracted by Irving.

Three years a widow, Mary Shelley was twenty-seven at the time; the still untethered Payne was thirty-four; Irving, reputedly bound by the memory of the dead sweetheart of his youth, was a much-sought bachelor of forty-two.

Mary Wollstonecraft Godwin Shelley was almost a genius in her own right. At the age of nineteen she had written that strange, prophetic horror tale, *Frankenstein*, story of the man-created monster that ruined his maker, through which, all unconsciously, she gave the world a word for certain sinister achievements of the coming machine age. Her literary powers, however, were very far outdistanced by those of Percy Bysshe Shelley, with whom she had eloped when she was seventeen and to whom she was married two years later, after the death of his first young wife.

Mary had come naturally by unconventional ways and exceptional mental equipment. Her parents were among England's leading social thinkers of the late Georgian period. Her father, William Godwin, author of *Political Justice*, was a philosopher whose idealistic theories of government, radical for their time, had gained him many starry-eyed followers, of whom the most distinguished was young

Shelley. Her mother, Mary Wollstonecraft, was a pioneer feminist whose book *A Vindication of the Rights of Woman* had shaken the complacency of the "man's world" long before the phrase "woman's movement" was invented. It is ironical that this prophet of woman's emancipation was destined herself to fall a sacrifice to the supreme physical function of her sex, and to die giving birth to a daughter.

That daughter, bearing her mother's name, had been brought up by an unsympathetic stepmother and, after some conventional schooling, chiefly educated in her father's study through omnivorous reading. She had emerged a highly intelligent and socially uninhibited young woman, one who asked for what she wanted. "Lady-like" in demeanor, for all that; attractive in appearance, with "light, supple figure, bright, animated expression and calm, gray eyes," lively in disposition—"witty and social with friends, mournful in solitude" [226] —she was altogether a person of great charm. Her elopement with Shelley while he still had a wife, though not inconsistent with certain theories of her father, had been disapproved by him and, according to some authorities, was not forgiven for years.

The Godwins had always been poor in a monetary sense.[227] So, during his earliest productive years, had been Shelley, all but disinherited by his wealthy and titled father. And so was Mary when, after Shelley's death by drowning in Italy, she had returned to England to attempt by writing to support herself and her infant son.[228] At the time of her friendship with Payne she was living in a London suburb, Kentish Town, in a retirement enforced by her financial situation. She belonged indubitably, however, to that higher aristocracy in which brains have a value above banknotes, and leading figures of the literary world were among her correspondents and intimates.

Payne may have met Mary at one of the Wednesday evening at-homes in the London apartment of Charles and Mary Lamb, where no financial ratings were required for admission and no favors expected in return for hospitality. Or he may first have known her through his devoted friend and her half brother, William Godwin Jr. Wherever they met, Payne was to tell her that summer that he had refrained for some time from seeking her society for fear of falling in love with her.

Since we have so vivid a word picture of Mary, it would be pleasant to know something about the physical appearance of the two others of the trio.

Unfortunately, there is no exact record of the way Payne looked when he first knew Mary Shelley. Diarist Crabb Robinson's terse non sequitur, "He is the author of 'Brutus' and has a good face," [229] tells a good deal but is hardly specific. However, we know that Payne, when younger, had been rated very handsome, and the charm of his personality was famous. Now, even after years of struggle, he was doubtless still personable. He still had the "fair and florid countenance, eyes large and blue and forehead high and white," [230] though the dark hair was thinning and the "rather stout, sprightly, compact figure" had begun to take on the contours of middle age. But in spite of gain in weight the statement, sometimes printed, that he had "had to leave the stage because of portliness" [231] is not accurate.

About Irving's appearance at the time there can be little question, for one of the most famous of his portraits, that by Gilbert Stuart Newton, though painted somewhat earlier, was "altered" in the summer of 1824, only a year before the Shelley episode. It was partly for the purpose of sitting again for Newton that Irving, when he came to London to see *Charles II* performed, had stayed on for a few weeks. And it is known that Mary Shelley, in a party with Thomas Moore, the Kenneys, and others, visited Newton's studio during these sittings.[232] It may have been there that Mary first saw Irving, and if he was as fine-looking as Newton makes him—large, wide-apart, and thoughtful eyes, mouth half smiling, genial yet firm —no wonder she was attracted.

Mary Shelley's first recorded reference to Washington Irving is a little in advance of her first letter to Payne. It occurs in a note to Louisa Holcroft (Mrs. James Kenney) in Paris: "Do you ever see W.I.? He talks of visiting England this autumn, but he has not, unfortunately, fulfilled his promise. Remember me to him and tell him I claim his promised visit when he does come." [233]

There is also an indirect reference to Irving in her first note to Payne, but one to which he probably attached no significance. It was written from 5 Bartholomew Place, Kentish Town, on April 14,

1825, and asked him to come "for a cup of hyson" and to meet a Mrs. Harwood, who "called to see me today and expressed a great desire to find some opportunity of conversing with you about your American friend."

In this first letter, as in several other early ones, Mary used the formal address of the day, "My dear Sir," and the equally formal subscription, "I am, my dear sir, your faithful servant." But Mary was not a formal person. Soon she would be addressing him quite as man to man, "My dear Payne." Payne, on his part, except when she was "excellent friend" or "dearest friend," never relaxed the formality: she was still, to him, "Mrs. Shelley." Neither ever became for the other "Howard" or "Mary."

The closer acquaintance of the two had a somewhat inauspicious beginning. The invitation to tea, which Payne was delighted to receive, had mentioned Sunday evening; but Mary's never too legible handwriting was here particularly hard to decipher, and instead of "Sunday" Payne read "Monday." Consequently, on Sunday evening Mary waited in vain for the expected guest, who arrived on Monday evening, only to find her gone out. In deep disappointment he walked back to town, reread the invitation, and clipped from it the illegible words, which he sent to her with this apology:

My dear Mrs. Shelley: I do not know when I have been more mortified than at the impression which my mistake in the day must have given you. . . .

I hurried back . . . certain of finding my acquittal in a mistake of yours, but to my infinite horror, after I knew you meant *Sunday* (a riddle is always so easy when we explain it), I perceived Sunday was the word. But who would ever have taken what you have written for Sunday, unless that explanation had been previously enforced by a walk from the Strand to Kentish Town? Here is the word. The equivocal letters are your M's and O's, to show that a clearer head than mine might have been perplexed. No other days *could* have done me this ill turn! Once assured I may hope for forgiveness, I shall take care to *make* an appointment for it to be conferred.

Mary's prompt reply is dated April 20:

My dear sir: If I had been at home on Monday evening we would have mocked the unkind god who introduced such confusion into my ill-formed pot-hooks. It was ill done, indeed, after causing me to form a thousand conjectures concerning your absence on Sunday, to lead you to the empty nest the day after. Will you tempt fortune again? . . . Will you walk over Saturday or Sunday, or another that may be convenient to you? . . .

> I am, my dear Sir,
>
> Yours faithfully, Mary Shelley.

To offer the apology in person, Payne was all too eager. He could not wait for Saturday or Sunday, but on Thursday evening took another walk to Kentish Town, only to subject himself to a second disappointment, for again Mary had gone out. Genuinely concerned, she immediately dispatched another note (this one addressed to J. Heyward, Esq.), and he must have found it extremely reassuring.

> April 22. My dear Sir: I was excessively annoyed to find that you had called fruitlessly yesterday. I had calculated that you would not receive a note in time for a visit, so did not include Thursday "in the bond."
>
> Will you drink tea with me tomorrow—as a cold of Percy's [her child] will detain me at home from my expected engagement.
>
> If you are in the Strand, you will find stages in St. James, Covent Garden, every hour—and if in Lancaster Street, attain the turnpike of Battle Bridge at 10 minutes exactly after any hour being struck, and soon one of our vehicles will pass—which, being directed, will set you down at my door.
>
> You see how diligently I try to repair an inconsequence which must not make you think me unpunctual, which I am not, and believe me, dear Sir,
>
> Very truly yours
>
> M. Shelley.

Tomorrow came, and the visit, belatedly realized, was doubly delightful. Part of the conversation concerned *Lionel Lincoln*, the newest novel by James Fenimore Cooper, whose previous work Mary had admired. She had read only the first volume of *Lionel*, but Payne promised to send the other two. Not all the talk was of literature, however. Mary had found a sympathetic listener, and she poured forth the story of her unhappy situation—her struggles to make ends meet, her devotion to her ailing father, now reconciled, and her attachment to her friend and neighbor Jane Williams, whose husband and Shelley had been drowned together—a circumstance forming a very strong bond.

Payne was deeply touched by this recital. With the books next day, he dispatched a letter, which, beginning properly enough with comments on Cooper, rapidly becomes more personal and is already almost a declaration of love.

"Your yesterday's conversation filled me so full of yourself that my poor pillow had but a small part of its due," he declares. In her, "a heroine in love and friendship and duty to a parent," he discovers the "rare union of superior intellectual endowment with simplicity, fervor, elevation and purity of character."

> To any ordinary woman I would not dare say this. It would certainly be interpreted to my disadvantage. But I think you would never have entered upon what related to yourself, with me, had you been utterly indifferent to my opinion.
>
> Be certain that I feel the limit I am bound to set to the compliment of your unreserve, and that I am incapable of presuming upon it, even in my wildest dreams. I am only just vain enough to think that I have no vanity. May I not, then, praise you and like you, and more, much more than like you, without a box on the ears, or frowns, or wonder that I should have been so impertinent as to tell you so?
>
> I can only be convinced by your honoring me with the preference of your commands, whenever there is anything in the world I can at any time or in any way do.

In her reply of April 30 Mary refrains from direct reference to the more personal passages of his letter, except to disclaim credit for some of the praise:

> You are very good to say all you do in your letter; but you put too high a praise upon what was the result of the instinct, as it were, of self-preservation, which led me to cultivate the only society which could alleviate unendurable sorrow. But while you disclaim vanity, you must not make me vain, or perhaps, worse, egotistical. . . .
>
> I was unable to go to the theatre yesterday evening, but if Virginius [234] should be acted, and you think practicable, I should like to see it. If I do not see you before, I will write concerning arrangements for the opera. By the bye, a box would be preferable, if it can be obtained.
>
> You are good and kind and therefore deserve nothing but kindness. But we must step lightly on the mosaic of circumstance, for if we press too hard the beauty and the charm is defaced.
>
> Adieu, I am truly yours,
Mary Shelley.

This is the first of the many letters that show Mary availing herself of Payne's offer, not only to "do anything in the world at any time," but in particular to use his professional connections to provide her and her family and friends with seats for the best theatrical offerings. Mary is generally blamed by readers of these letters for repeatedly accepting those favors and asking for more, especially after her rejection of Payne's suit. But apparently it did not occur to her that there was anything reprehensible in this, and she seems to have felt justified in that she was at least giving him the satisfaction of serving her. She was still young, and Payne's bounty was pulling her out of a lonely life. It was only a few months earlier that she had written to a friend:

> You may imagine I see few people, so far from the center of London; but in truth I found, even in town, poor, un-dinner-giving as I was, I could not dream of society. As to theatres, etc., how can a "lone woman" think of such things? [235]

Now her situation was suddenly changed. Payne, a poor man, was able to offer rich gifts. He answered Mary's request at once, enclosing orders for the next day's opera and four admissions to a comedy the following week at Drury Lane.

> If you like me to be with you, let me know by 3 o'clock of the appointed day; if more convenient to make up your party without me, do so. . . . I am reluctant to wear out my welcome. You are therefore safe from my persecutions except when you so far oblige me as to require my services, and then nothing shall stand in the way of your slightest wish.

Here, as several times later in their correspondence, Payne offers Mary the means of entertainment and at the same time suggests his own withdrawal should other company be more agreeable. Even allowing for the formal courtesy of the time, this was rather a strange attitude in a suitor—an attitude which, he should have known, never won fair lady. Independent mentally as Mary was, she must inevitably have been affected by Payne's valuation of himself; and that, in his letters to her, was all too low. It was not a pose on his part. His circumstances were still precarious; hard experience had apparently robbed him of the conceit he may once have had; and with Mary he wished to be entirely honest, feeling himself safe, with her, in so being.

Now, though "bound to the oar" with "a contract for 500 octavo pages" he found time to add:

I can have your company without oppressing you with mine. You are perpetually in my presence, and if I close my eyes you are still here, and if I cross my arms over them and try to wave you away, you will not be gone. This madness of my own imagination flatters me with the forlorn hope of a delightful vagueness in part of your note. From sheer perverseness, it sees imperfectly and calls it twilight, then plays fantastic gambols with the self-created obscurity.

Amen! If the *Fata Morgana* WILL fling these pretty pictures over the heart, are we to shut our eyes and not rejoice in them? They are as beautiful as reality while they last, and when reality itself fades, what becomes of the difference? I would not have you check my delusion.

Yet, for all your smiling, I know very well what that part of your letter means which I pretended just now not to understand. I am grateful, and care nothing about myself, so I may care for you, and tell you so without your being angry.

This time Mary graciously rewarded his humility and replied to the more personal touches with a charming lightness, though at the close she frankly gave evidence of sensing more than mere friendliness:

My dear Payne [the first time she has not said "My dear Sir"]: Your octavo pages admonish me not to trespass upon your time. . . . The engagement of Saturday I consider fixed as fate, if you will permit it, for we depend upon you as escort. . . . Come early, because we are musical enough to wish to hear the overture.

Although you deprecate the subject, I must thank you for all "favors received" and I include kind thoughts as well as kind actions, although I know how entirely your imagination creates the admired as well as the admiration. But do not, I entreat you, frighten me by any more interpretations, although be sure I am and always shall be your sincere friend.

Here Payne apparently felt that he had gone too far, and replied at once:

My excellent friend: You will find me punctual. I was frightened at myself after I had sent that last letter, for, though all true, it might have been kept to myself. It is considerate of you to take it in such good part, and more than considerate to think of reducing my extravagance to a diet of friendship. . . .

Never mind the octavo pages, but let me hear from you whenever you think of anything I can do; and be certain it is impossible I should ever again frighten you with my dreams, after the 8 and 40 hours ague I have suffered from apprehension of punishment.

Do you wish to go to the opera when "Così fan tutte" comes out? Have you any desire to see Kean during his nights, and if you have, in what character?

Believe me, my dear Mrs. Shelley, Yours very sincerely, JHP.

Had there been telephones in those days, most of these charming letters would not have been written. Payne would perhaps have imparted his more romantic sentiments in writing; but the appointments upon which so much of the correspondence hinges would have been made by more direct means. As it was, most social engagements had to be arranged by letter, and since the post was slow, notes within the city were often sent by messenger. We may judge by several references that Payne, elegant in all things, employed a private note carrier and general factotum.

Dropping in to call—another custom that would go out with the coming of swift communications—was still permissible. So Payne again walked to Kentish Town, only to find his inamorata absent. She had half expected him, however, and had left a note, but this the maid somehow failed to deliver.

Mary by this time certainly knew that Payne was in love with her, and had she been deliberately trying to ensare him further—it really seems that she was not, despite the boon of the theater tickets—she could not have employed a more effective technique. He was to suffer several more days of agonizing "ague" before he received the delayed message, together with another; but the two were of a kind to make the suspense seem worth while. Said the first, the message not delivered by the maid:

My dear Payne: We were altogether unlucky last night, since our opera was changed and we did not see you, and moreover, beheld Clari cruelly murdered—nothing ever was managed so ill—and parts, quite different from yours, in the worst possible taste. We quitted it on an incipient hiss, which threatened damnation.

What divine weather! I live now—Kentish Town is odorous with hay. Shall you be here today? I hope not, because I go out—but I leave this in case of a call.

And the second, enclosing the note delayed:

I am afraid we shall hardly have courage to make another visit to that desperate coquette, the opera—unless it were for something stupendous

and certain. We wish to see Così fan tutte, but do not wish to be disappointed—but before I decide, I must consult my gentle oracle [Jane
Williams].

Kean! Yes, truly—fire and water for him! What will he play?

Here Mary's remark was further proof of her unconventionality,
for Kean was then in deep disgrace, having been found guilty of improper conduct involving the wife of one of the theater's directors.[236]

The substance of these undated notes suggests that they were written at an early stage of the friendship, but Mary's "odorous with
hay" remark, which gives so quaintly poetical a picture of the Kentish Town of the period, may describe a later season, perhaps June
rather than May.

Whatever the month, the "something stupendous" in opera soon
arrived, when the great Italian soprano, Pasta, whom Mary especially admired, paid a visit to London.[237] Though Payne preferred
the French coloratura de Begnis, and the relative merits of the two
had apparently been discussed, he was zealous that Mary should hear
the singer of her choice, and despite the great demand for admissions he obtained Elliston's card for three of Pasta's performances
and "had other applications out, so that if you require more they
will be ready, and you may arrange for six, which shall be sent to
you whenever you like to appoint, and in good time."

In a somewhat later note Payne gives this humorous behind-the-
scenes picture of Mary's operatic favorite: "Think of your *elevated*
and *intellectual* Pasta! She was swearing in very vulgar French all
the other evening, whenever off the stage—frightening the servants
by mere arrogance and ill temper. My *gentle* and innocent de Begnis
could not have done that. No doubt you will say Pasta does many
other things de Begnis *could* not."

At this point Payne's too great modesty in effacing himself as escort seems to have been almost misinterpreted by Mary. In one note
she asks: "Are you, by the bye, tired of playing the *escudero* to us?"
And he replies: "Do not imagine I am weary of anything you may
require of me. I only wish you not to think yourself bound by politeness to ask me to be your escort, if you can supply my place more

agreeably to yourself and others, and I say this honestly and without affectation."

Mary is quick to repair the error. She writes on three successive days, each time about his obtaining admissions for her—once for tickets to Drury Lane, where she wishes to take her stepmother, once for "four admissions to Covent Garden, as I wish to accommodate Mrs. Williams's mother," and yet again to ask him to buy for her (with promise of reimbursement) tickets to Mme. Pasta's benefit —and in each note she expresses the wish of seeing him at the theater: "I trust you will do us the pleasure of joining us, as I want to see you and thank you in person for your kindness."

About the benefit tickets Payne writes: "Enclosed you have Pasta's four tickets. The number of the box makes me think it is too near Heaven, and I do not like to trust such good company so near to the angels. But I am certain the best has been done, as the places are in great demand. If you like to use all four, do so. I can get a ticket at the door as I go in. If not, will you reserve one for me? Ever most sincerely, JHP."

Mary expressed superlative gratitude by addressing him here, not as "my dear Payne," but as "Amabillissimo Cavaliere": "Will you be so kind as to tell me what you paid for our benefit tickets, that I may relieve my burthened conscience of a part of my debt to you, though the part I feel most, your more than polite kindness, your goodness in annoying yourself so much for me, must remain unpayable."

She was obliged to write again before Payne could be prevailed upon to state that the benefit tickets had cost half a guinea each.

It is not possible to decide upon the consecutive order of all of these notes, usually dated merely by the day of the week, nor is it necessary to do so. They show the friendship proceeding pleasantly, with those little jokes, banterings, misunderstandings, and explainings that are part of such situations.

To one note Payne subscribes himself, in playful reference to his farce *Grandpapa*, produced about this time, and to some jokes it had occasioned: "With the tenderest paternal solicitude, your affectionate Grandpapa."

In one Mary asks: "By the bye, next week I shall go to the Lambs'. How far do you feel inclined to accompany me thither or meet me there? Remember, this is my 'pleasure,' not my 'advantage,' so do not inconvenience yourself." And he replies: "If I should not have the pleasure of seeing you the day you select for the Lambs, pray apprise me by post. Believe me, I shall always be more than 'inclined' to accompany you just as 'far' as you may be 'inclined' to let me."

Later there is this reference in one of hers: "Your note looks as if you remembered all the nonsense I talked to you and Jane and the silent man in the Lambs' garden. But as you know, I am rather given to talk nonsense, and then, only half of it was nonsense, a make-believe, which means everything and nothing, if this is intelligible." Then his reply: "I have no recollection of any conversation in the Lambs' garden, but be certain of this—I am determined never to remember anything about you which may not be remembered with pleasure."

Payne, besides singing Irving's praises, had apparently supplied Mary with Irving's books, and in wholehearted loyalty to both friends had sometimes allowed her to read Irving's letters. She may even have seen the one about the furniture duns, for not only was Payne concealing nothing, he was actually at all times putting his worst foot foremost.

In one note Mary says: "Thank you for W.I."; and in another, after referring playfully to a Spanish gentleman seen the preceding night at the theater, "who caught the attention of the ladies in so marked a manner as to attract his," [238] she adds: "And yet I am still faithful to W.I.!!!"

Although the three exclamation points seem to label this a joke, Payne's reply suggests that for the first time he senses something out of the ordinary in her admiration for Irving: "I am glad that you return to Irving, for it is tantalizing to have one's heart in a state of miscellany . . ."

A note of Payne's that immediately follows contains references to a conversation of the previous Saturday and to "badinage," "plays upon words," and a "little reproof" administered by Mary.

All this is somewhat obscure to the reader, though we can judge the half playful, half personal import by Mary's instant reply:

> A bad conscience, you know, my dear Payne, is proverbially susceptible. And the feeling that what passed last Saturday was not quite *en règle* made me captious. I accused myself and so did not like to be accused (as I thought) by another. This explanation must be my apology for looking seriously upon badinage. I was annoyed at finding a picture turn into a man.

Was it a picture of Irving or a picture of Payne that had "turned into a man"? Whichever it was, Mary's apology and an ensuing note stating that she had presumed to make an engagement for him to dine with her at her father's house the following Sunday were sufficient to cause his next to begin "My dearest friend" and to proceed with the assurance: "You are always safe in promising for me, when the promise involves a chance of your society. I was about to have written to ask you whether you ever dined at Gower Place [home of the Godwins] on Sunday."

There was a long talk as they walked home after dinner that Sunday evening—the talk to which the letters had been inevitably leading. To Payne's avowal her reply, as he would later report it to Irving, was "that the high feeling she entertained for the memory of her husband forbade a future connection. 'Having once tasted Nepenthe,' she added, 'What is there left for me to hope for?' " [239] If Mary had said no more, we could forgive her; but when, seemingly for the sake of entire honesty, she continued that "if she ever made another alliance it must be with one whose character and mind should be worthy of him who had drawn her from obscurity, and that her selection must not dishonor his choice," she seems to have been unnecessarily cruel and unappreciative, not only of Payne's friendship, but actually of his character.

"She apologized for the remark," however, "and seemed considerably moved at the necessity she felt of giving pain by disclosing the truth." (This from the later report to Irving.) But Payne was not offended. "I told her I thought the better of her for all she said, and that I understood its bearing thoroughly."

After this conversation Mary was willing to go on as before, but it could never be the same again to Payne. He continued to send her books and theater tickets, and she paid him a somewhat overdue compliment by requesting tickets to *Brutus*, "a play I have long wanted to see."

The notes passed back and forth, and apparently Payne called again, for she remarked that she was sorry to have seen him "in such bad spirits lately," adding: "You are kind and good to all but yourself. If you took to being bounteously courteous to yourself, I think you would arrive at being, as all other objects of your kindness are, quite in good humor and grateful for your own society. . . . You made me expect another letter. [i.e., another of Irving's]. Is it indelicate of me to ask for this?"

Her renewal of the subject of Irving was apparently all that was necessary to bring forth Payne's decision to have done with the affair, though he obliged by enclosing Irving's latest—which, as it happened, contained encouragement and praise as well as the usual advice—with this explanation:

> I did not send this letter, because I thought I might find others which would answer your wishes as well and which contained less about my petty affairs. . . .
>
> [It] cannot strike you as it does me, but I send it lest circumstances give a false coloring to its being withheld. To understand it, it is necessary that you should know that Irving's advice has been of great service to me on literary points. He and his brother have been the only persons who have ever boldly and unhesitatingly encouraged me with the hope of ultimate [literary] success. . . .
>
> It is a very agreeable thing to be impelled by the enthusiasm of such a mind, to hear its praises and to know it is sincere. It cannot touch you so nearly as to justify what I taught you to expect of it. But here it is.

Payne's professional activities had been continuing, even during his greater absorption with more personal matters; and that explains the opening remark in this letter of Irving's, the last of his sent to Mary:

> I am sorry to find that you are still "among the brokers." Do not let the Covent Garden committee make a Jewish bargain of you. I distrust them mightily and have no high opinion of Charles Kemble's friendship or liberality. . . .
>
> Do not let them put you out of conceit of "The Spanish Husband." If

ten theatres were to send it back, it would only prove to me that they wanted discernment. It is a play which I am convinced will succeed and will give you both profit and reputation. . . .

I wish to God you could get ahead in your circumstances and then maintain yourself. I feel that I could then be of real service to you. At present, I am afraid, while you are laboring to pay off old scores, you are sometimes unnecessarily running up new ones. I speak only from what I have observed of your Paris affairs.[240]

To the brief comment on himself in Mary's most recent letter Payne replied at some length, apparently relieved to present his defense, even though the verdict had been pronounced.

You are mistaken in the kind of apprehension you express of my finding my own mind disagreeable society. On the contrary, I do not find any discomfort in it, but I know it is not the kind of mind likely to be understood, and still less to be valued, and therefore more at home out of the world. It is better than I am, if you can understand the paradox. . . .

I have given way to an absurdity and have only myself to blame. Indeed, I do not think my deep interest in you ought to permit me to wish that interest should be returned. Still, I must *feel*. . . . It is therefore better that I should not meet you until after this strange fever is over.

I am sure you will allow me to be your friend in a corner and let me see your handwriting whenever you can find any commission for me to execute, and that you will spare me anything beyond the matter of fact, as you are too kind not to speak kindly, and in this sort of delirium one cannot help perverting mere politeness by fancying what is not, until it becomes quite indifferent whether it is, or is not, if that time is ever good enough to arrive.

Then follows his resolution:

To return to the point at which our conversations began and have ended— Washington Irving—be assured that I shall act the hero in this matter; and shall feel quite reconciled to the penalty to which my folly has condemned me, if my friendship should prove the stepping stone to one in every way so much more gratifying and desirable.

Mary replies that she has "read with great pleasure Irvine's letter" —she repeatedly makes this quite inexplicable error in his name— "with pleasure greater because it dwells upon your circumstances."

You are wrong in thinking that any details of this kind ever annoyed me. I am familiar with difficulties and what you call petty cares. . . . I trust you will attend to his advice and be inspirited by his admonitions . . . and moreover, be a *little* economical.

Your letter gives me pain because you feel it and because it seems to place a barrier to any further meetings. Thus it is ever one's fate either to be deserted and neglected, or—which turns out the same thing—to be liked too well and so avoided. Few indeed have your kind generosity to offer (and I am sure sincerely do offer) to do services to one thus circumstanced with you—nor do I think I do other than please you when I receive your offers, not only with thanks, but with "acceptance bounteous."

I shall be glad to see Irvine's letters, and the handwriting, crabbed after your distinct syllables, will become as clear to me as Lord Byron's letterless scrawl.

More than the letters, however, she now says she cannot expect to have.

As to friendship with him, it cannot be, though everything I hear and know renders it more desirable. How can Irvine, surrounded by fashion and rank and splendid friendships, pilot his pleasure bark from its gay press into this sober, enshrouded nook?

But our conversations shall not end with W.I., if they began with him, which I do not remember. Why indeed should they end at all, but go on and grow sober as our years increase? Nor, if you desire to renew them, let a long interval elapse; for I mean to live only ten years longer and have 37 engraved on my tomb.

But you have taken the affair in hand so sagely, and methinks, may I say it without a charge of vanity, so disinterestedly, that I resign the rule to you.

In her immediately ensuing notes Mary brought matters back to earth by asking for orders for Drury Lane, a box for the opera, and tickets for Sadler's Wells, "if they can be procured without inconvenience." Payne complied on all points and then wrote to inform her that he was going back to Paris and enclosed a letter from "Irvine" that explained the departure.

This return to Paris involved a prospect which we may believe was none too pleasing to Payne. Stephen Price, once manager of the Park Theatre in New York, a man with whom Payne many years before had disagreed, had come to try his hand at theatrical management in Europe, and Irving, having strongly recommended Payne for a position in any establishment that Price might set up, had arranged for the two to renew acquaintance in Paris.

Mary's suggestion about seeing Payne again had apparently almost broken down his decision to avoid another meeting to judge by a remark in his next note to her: "I mean to see you if I can before my departure, though I have a sort of despairing hope that I cannot. It would be painful to me—infinitely so—not to see you, if possible, but I shall not be sorry to have the impossibility to regret."

He had sent her Dunlap's life of Charles Brockden Brown, which she wished particularly to see, and she commented: "Poor, dear Brown, what a delightful person he seems to have been!" And through that she made occasion to refer again to Irving, though in a manner she was quickly to regret:

> As to my favorite, I.—methinks our acquaintance proceeds at the rate of the Antediluvians, who, I have read somewhere, thought nothing of an interval of a year or two between visits. Alack, I fear that at this rate, if ever the Church should make us one, it would be announced in the consolatory phrase that the Bride and Bridegroom's age amounted to the discreet number of 145 years and 3 months.

She tried to repair this in a note the next day:

> Now, my dear Payne, though I am a little fool, do not make me appear so in Rue Richelieu by repeating tales out of school, nor mention the Antediluvians. But I am not afraid; I am sure you love me well enough not to be accessory in making me appear ridiculous to one whom I like and esteem, though I am sure the time and space between us will never be shortened. . . . But again, be not a tell-tale, so God bless you. Give my love, of course platonic, to I.

"If Antediluvian modes are to be revived," Payne replied, "I will not be an accessory, but will do my best to promote customs more compatible with the terms to which you have limited your stay in this only world in which wedlock is tolerated." Before departing he wrote once more to "My dearest friend," sending "A thousand and a thousand wishes and prayers for your happiness. May God forever bless you. Most faithfully yours."

Business required Payne's first attention on returning to Paris, and it was some days before he was able to carry out the course by which he had determined to "play the hero" in the matter of Mary Shelley. It was a perplexing situation. The woman he loved was ready, he knew, to fall desperately in love with the friend he valued above all others. What should he have done? There is room, of course, for difference of opinion.

We are chiefly concerned with reporting what he did do. He made a package of Mary's letters—in his haste or confusion including the one about the Antediluvians!—and added to them copies of his own. (There was nothing extraordinary about his having these, as it had long been his habit to keep copies of letters of his writing, especially important ones.) The double bundle he handed to Irving with a note, dated merely "Tuesday evening":

> My dear Irving: I have reflected a long time before I determined to show you this correspondence, because from its nature it might appear indelicate to expose the letters, especially to you, as you are more involved than you even appear to be. It was some time before I discovered that I was only sought as a source of introduction to you.

After this one touch of bitterness he goes on:

> I think you will, on reading the letters, feel that I might have mistaken the nature of my acquaintance with the writer without any gratuitous vanity. At the same time, you must admit that she is a woman of the most amiable qualities, and one whose wish for friendship it would be doing yourself an injustice not to meet. Of course it must be a perfect secret between us that I have shown the letters. They are at present not known to anyone. You must not look upon the affair in a ridiculous light, as if you should, I shall never forgive myself for having exposed so fine a mind to so injurious a construction.
>
> I have felt myself in honor bound to withhold nothing from you, and you must judge of what I do now, not from your own disinterested views of the subject, but from those by which I have been guided and the strong feelings I have sacrificed.

Then follows the brief report of the conversation on the walk home from the Godwins', and the note ends with a statement of his decision to turn the prize over to Irving:

> I wish you would see and know Mrs. Shelley whenever you go to London. . . . No doubt it will cost you some reflection fully to appreciate the trouble I am taking to make you well acquainted with one whom I have known so well—to transfer an intimacy of which any one might be proud. I do not ask you to fall in love, but I should even feel a little proud of myself if you thought the lady worthy of that distinction.

For Irving the letters must have provided a diverting "nightcap," though his only reference to them, an entry in his journal for August 15, 1825, is brief and noncommittal in the extreme: "Read Mrs. Shelley's correspondence before going to bed." [241] If he ever made a further comment on the subject, it is not recorded; and certain it is that Payne's efforts were of no avail in promoting a friendship between Mary and "W.I."

Mary did not keep Payne's letters, and it is perhaps significant that in her published journals the year 1825 is left blank.[242] Did she neglect the usual record of daily happenings that year, or did she write and destroy what she had written? Whichever it was, we, the greedy public, are cheated after all. We shall never know the really private thoughts of Mary Shelley about the suitor she did not want and the one she could not have.

[16]

LOOKING AT LONDON FROM PARIS

"I HAVE broken my contract with Price by sending him eleven plays when I only stipulated to send four."

It was four months after his return to Paris to attempt to work for Stephen Price, then in London, that Payne sent this report to Irving.[243] According to the arrangement, engineered entirely by Irving, Payne was to provide for Price within a year fifteen French plays translated and adapted for London performance and was to be paid 150 pounds in periodical installments.

Irving had been unstinting in his praise of Payne to Price, and to Price's remark that he thought Payne would be useful "if I could place confidence in him," Irving, so he wrote Payne, had replied:

I told him that the very theatrical people who might have prejudiced him against you had caused or increased your embarrassments by their want of faith in acting up to their promises. . . .

I told him that from all I had known of you and your affairs . . . I was convinced that you were a man whose principles were fully to be relied upon. That you had been embarrassed and distressed by a variety of circumstances, and imposed upon in your pecuniary arrangements, but that you were eternally struggling and making all kinds of sacrifices to pay off old debts and fulfill old engagements with scrupulous correctness.[244]

The Payne-Price combination lasted less than a year. It should not have been expected to succeed, notwithstanding Payne's wish to "rip off old scores and be friends again," [245] for the two were temperamentally incompatible, and neither could entirely erase from his mind the memory of earlier disagreements. Though Payne, continuing in his quixotic course, had submitted more plays at the end of eight months than the full year's agreement called for, there was a lack of understanding of business details. Furthermore, Payne's usual financial embarrassment caused him to draw on Price for one 50-pound payment before Price considered it due. Irving interceded, urging Price to honor the draft and reminding Payne that it was his own mismanagement that caused him to be "hampered for the want of 50 pounds," adding: "My dear Payne, it will always be your lot, even if the Bank of England were emptied into your pockets, so long as you will not take care to mend the bottoms of them." [246]

This note, dated May 25, 1826, was written from Madrid, where Irving, soon after, would become attached to the American Embassy. One of his earlier letters had commented: "If Price does not live up to the mark, you will certainly have done your part and will have got a stock of ms. hurried out of you which you would not otherwise have produced, and which will surely bring you something in the market."

When the bargain he had made for his friend collapsed, Irving accepted the outcome calmly: "You have done your duty bravely by Price, and if he is not content with you, you may be with yourself, and that is something." But later Irving was disapproving when Payne wrote:

I told the story of Stephen Price to Mrs. Shelley, and will transcribe to you what she replied:
"I smiled, but the smile was somewhat a mournful one, over your account of how you mean to treat your haggling, huckster manager. There are persons with whom it never does to do other than keep to the letter of

the bond. . . . Keep to your rights and they sympathize in sordid feeling; but if you enter into the pale of liberality, the ideas of their claim become gigantic in the extreme.

"But there are sensitive persons like yourself who cannot encounter these machines— It is the china and brass vase of the fable—the more delicate the one, the more rough the other." [247]

"(I am blushing at the compliment, but you are too far off to see it)," Payne added, in parentheses, so it must have been something of a damper when the usually good-natured Irving replied: "I am sorry you wrote to Mrs. Shelley about your dealings with Price. When there are any jealousies or misunderstandings in business, much mischief is sometimes done by complaining to a third person." [248]

Though the arrangement with Price was what had brought Payne back to Paris, it was on the whole a good deal of fuss about very little. Of much greater consequence was the London production in his absence of three of his adapted plays, negotiated quite independently of Price. All were plays that attracted attention.

The lightest and slightest of the three—*'Twas I; or, the Truth a Lie*, a two-act farce produced as a musical afterpiece at Covent Garden, December 3, 1825, with the celebrated Mme. Vestris acting and singing the leading role—was the most successful. Though the *Times* at first denounced it as "mawkish, insipid nonsense," it undoubtedly was one of Payne's hits with the public. It seems also to have been highly regarded by the leading lady, for the authorized sketch of her life in the British Dictionary of Biography mentions the role of Georgette Clairville in *'Twas I* as one of her outstanding parts. (Incidentally, the piece had been rejected by Price.)

Young William Godwin, writing to Payne of the première, reported: "I saw your first night. It went off triumphantly. Not one single hiss and two encores . . . its fourth performance tomorrow and two next week." And theatrical advertisements in the London press prove not only that *'Twas I* was in continual demand the first season, but also that its popularity lasted for several years.

The other two plays produced with their adapter *in absentia* were both brought out at Covent Garden Theatre in the same week of February 1826. The first, *Norah; or, the Maid of Erin*, was fairly successful, but it was quickly overshadowed in interest by the second, *The French Libertine*—a considerably altered version of Payne's and Irving's *Richelieu*—which was to cause a violent teapot tempest in London's theatrical circles.

Payne in his Paris exile, with no dependable means of learning what was going on in London, lacked direct knowledge of matters of vital concern to him. To what extent he regarded this as a handicap we can judge by the February 2, 1826 item in his diary, which records his having just discovered secondhand news of the forthcoming production of *Norah:* "Last evening I dropped into Galignani's [office of an English-language newspaper published in Paris] and with great astonishment saw 'Norah' advertised in Tuesday's papers for performance Wednesday." His entry a few days later was a speculation on the première:

> Well, I suppose today I shall know about Norah. What a singular situation is that of a playwright whose fate is decided so long before he can know the decision. . . . I really think that if I were to fail, I should not sleep any the less soundly for it . . . my interest is so used to blows that on that head I am grown callous.

A week later his diary records his feelings as he imagines the opening performance of the other play, *Richelieu.*

> Sat. Feb. 11, 20 minutes before 8: Here am I all alone . . . copying the fourth act of Richelieu [this probably was the copy later sent to America for publication] while the actors and actresses at Covent Garden are just in the midst of it! To them this is a moment of excitement. To me, who have looked to this hour with so much anxiety for three years, it seems as though there were no such hour. I feel no immediate eagerness or deep emotion. I chiefly think of the attacks to which it will afford a pretext and the sufferings of which in this case I may peculiarly be made a victim.
>
> Meanwhile, I am still copying . . . and even the cat has sought some other corner, not to disturb my solitude. The rattling coaches under my windows shake as I write, and seem to press upon me the, at this moment, awful truth, "the play is ended."

Richelieu was the delayed fruit of Payne's and Irving's collaboration, and was the most carefully prepared of all their joint undertakings. Aside from the original translation it was considerably more the work of Irving than of Payne.

This play was adapted from *La Jeunesse de Richelieu,* by the French playwright, Duval, author also of the play on which *Charles II* was based. Payne had put it into English while still quartered in the remodeled structure built by the real Richelieu, the Palais Royal. Irving had begun his work of revision shortly before he and Payne took up residence in the street named for the profligate churchman-statesman whose reputed amours formed the subject.

A letter of Irving's written soon before moving to 89 Rue Richelieu had said: "I will do the needful with Richelieu in a day or two." Later he would find that many more revisions would be "needful," but at the time Payne went to London in 1825, *Richelieu* was considered in good enough shape to be taken along and offered to Charles Kemble, by whom it was accepted after a brief delay.

All this was more than a year before the beginning of the Mary Shelley episode, but even after that odd little romance had ended and Payne had returned to Paris for the conference with Price, *Richelieu* was still undergoing alterations by Irving. In fact, over a period of three years Irving's letters and diaries refer again and again to his work on this play.

How nearly the dramatic story adhered to established facts of Cardinal Richelieu's life it would require much study to decide. The adapters perforce accepted the French playwright's defamatory characterization of the man. On this account, perhaps, before its performance in London (with Payne in Paris and Irving in Madrid), the play was considerably altered by the theatrical management as to details of plot, though most of Irving's carefully polished dialogue was probably retained.

In deference to the French minister to England, a kinsman of Richelieu, the villainous hero was renamed Duke de Rougemont. He is shown as a man of many loves who "betrays a virtuous and indiscreet wife" by obtaining admittance to her house "disguised as a valet to her husband, a reputable citizen in reduced circumstances." The play opens "just as the Duke has possessed himself half of the lady's affections and entirely of her person" and closes after the wife, detected, "has died under the struggle." These the *Times* declared the main incidents, though stating that the Duke's other intrigues filled in a good deal of the background, with "one scene in which there is a large table literally covered with love letters, all sent to the Duke since the night before."

There was a considerable delay between the play's acceptance and the première, one cause of which was Charles Kemble's wish to have rewritten the role of the Duke's mistress (a character of sufficient prominence to have a name part). This rewriting Irving undertook, and in October 1825, wrote to Payne: "I have rewrote the character of Mme. Fleury. . . . You will find that I have made her a countess and elevated her character. It heightens the piece, makes the character worthy of good acting. . . . Altogether I think the play much improved, and as it was a suggestion of Charles Kemble, I think it will please him." [249]

Kemble was not the only one to be pleased, however. Before a play could be licensed it had to have the approval of the official arbiter of plays, one George Colman, a man described as "squeamish beyond precedent." Though himself a former playwright whose work had been notoriously coarse, Colman, when he became the authorized play examiner, veered to the opposite extreme. His ultra-conservatism, indeed, led to the report that he "cut out all references to the deity, every form of prayer or hymn, such modified apostrophe as 'O Lord' and 'demme,' objected to such words as 'heaven' and 'Providence,' and would not allow a lover to address his mistress as 'an angel.'" [250]

This worthy had been in office about two years when Payne's and Irving's *Richelieu* provided him with a rare opportunity to wield the censor's authority, and he at first refused it a license.[251] Payne had undergone every other trial known to the world of the London theater, but this was his first brush with the censor. He relayed the news to Irving, who wrote: "You do not mention what is the objection to licensing Richelieu. The moral is certainly unexceptionable and the indelicacies of the original plot I thought had been completely eradicated."

The license was finally granted, but only after Kemble had written "a spirited letter to the Lord Chancellor"; and then Irving felt that "all this fuss about it will excite curiosity and benefit the copyright." As to the renaming of the piece, he remarked: "Kemble talked of entitling it 'Richelieu or the French Libertine.' That would look like an illiberal reflection. He might call it the French Lovelace, as a companion to the English character of that name."

Payne was not wrong in anticipating attacks on *The French Libertine,* as the play was injudiciously renamed. In fact, when it finally appeared it moved some London theatrical reviewers to such hypercritical expressions of horror as recall nothing so much as the furor aroused by Payne's first ill-fated venture in dramatic writing, when he was but fourteen years old.

The *Times,* though it declared the adaptation "not worth ten lines of notice were it not an attempt to introduce a style of entertainment which we are not to see endured in this country," pronounced it dull and "the kind of vulgar ribaldry which will not do for England," while the *New Monthly Magazine* "condemned on principle such an experiment on the English stage." [252]

Had this been one of Payne's own hastily projected ventures, its unfavorable reception would not have been so surprising; but that it should have involved the discreet and decorous Irving, who, for all his chuckling humor, never offended the prevailing taste, is remarkable. Here the American collaborators had strayed into something not only too sophisticated but also perhaps too subtle to be generally understood in the London of 1826. The satire, humor, and exaggerations were not plainly enough labeled to keep them from being taken seriously by many playgoers, as well as by a large section of the influential press, and after six performances *The French Libertine* was withdrawn from the London stage.

As Payne had said, he was "used to blows," and he does not seem to have been felled by this one administered on the other side of the Channel. He finished making the copy of the play to be sent to America, in the form in which it stood after Irving's final painstaking revisions, using the title that he and Irving had given it, with *A Domestic Tragedy* added as subtitle.

Though he had thus far consented to take both credit and blame for plays prepared with Irving's assistance, Payne felt he could no longer fail to acknowledge indebtedness to his collaborator, and that he proposed to do in the case of *Richelieu*. "Something to prevent my appearing to pass off another person's work as my own, is necessary," he told Irving.

Long before the production of *Richelieu*, Payne had suggested dedicating the American edition to Irving and Irving had consented, though the dedication would reveal—what was already known in London's theatrical circles—that he was largely responsible for this unsuccessful work. They had discussed the dedication after Payne returned to Paris to confer with Price, and later Irving had written from Bordeaux: "Do not send the dedication without letting me see it. I want it to be as simple as possible and free from all puffing and praising."

When Payne apparently felt somewhat piqued by that request, as seeming to imply a lack of confidence in his judgment, Irving wrote: "I do not see how you could conjure out of my letter anything like disapprobation of your dedication. It is simply an expression of your own friendly feelings, about which there can be no cavil."

The dedication agreed upon took the form of a letter, and it appears as a preface to the printed version of the play. Although it had Irving's entire approval, some writers, once more considering only half the evidence, have referred to Payne's prefatory tribute as "fulsome." A mere reading would have proved that it was not.[253]

Though a dramatic dose too strong for London would naturally be doubly so for the New York of the early nineteenth century, *Richelieu* was nevertheless forwarded to Irving's New York brother Ebenezer, who obtained publication "at publisher's own expense" of 1000 copies, 700 of which were left on Ebenezer's hands.

None too well pleased, Ebenezer, apparently without reading the dedication, wrote to his brother Washington: "I have been unable to get anything out of your friend Payne's drama of 'Richelieu.' The publisher tried hard to get it performed at one of our theatres but could not succeed; the managers were afraid to attempt it, alleging that it was deficient in *incident*, particularly in the latter scenes."

Eventually, through pirating, *Richelieu* was acquired by some New York playwright who altered it, probably removing the subtleties while retaining part of the plot, and brought it out as *The Bank-*

rupt's Wife. Under that title it was acted in American theaters for years. As late as 1860, however, Irving's nephew Pierre still regarded the play as something of a scandal, "better suited to the closet than the stage."

Read today, *Richelieu,* so shocking to the London of its period, seems first of all so old-fashioned as to reflect the very moral standards that it then offended. Nevertheless it is impressive in parts for its sparkling dialogue, especially the speeches in which with sinister adroitness the ignoble cardinal meets any and every compromising situation. Irving must have had great fun with those lines. But that so broadly satirical a piece should have had so tragic an ending makes for confusion as to the play's main intent. Humor and pathos (or tragedy) can of course be effectively used in alternation, but satire and tragedy combine strangely. This fault in dramatic method was probably chargeable to the original author, but apparently neither adapter was impressed by it.

Irving certainly thought well of this piece, but not well enough to sign his name to it. It stands today as Payne's work, as does also *Charles II*, though the earlier play, which Payne actually had more part in creating, does more credit to his name.

When Irving went to Madrid, Payne was left alone in the Rue Richelieu apartment and he enjoyed being able to play host to friends from abroad, "having a comfortable habitation in which to bid you welcome," as he wrote to one. There is evidence that by his hospitality various literary and theatrical persons from London were saved hotel expenses while in Paris.

"Coles slept here," says the January 3, 1826 diary. And on January 4: "Bowes spent the night. When one has a spare room for friends, it must be open to more than one." Bowes and Coles are not identified, except as men who brought news of the London theater.

Somewhat earlier there had been another visitor, not recorded as a house guest though he may well have been one, whose coming gave Payne "infinite satisfaction." That was John Gorham Palfrey, who years later would write: "In 1825 I arrived in Paris. . . . Sought Howard out. . . . Found him sharing lodgings with Washington Irving (then in Spain)."

Palfrey, once a boarding pupil at the old Berry Street Academy in Boston and practically brought up by William and Sarah Payne, was now twenty-nine, a writer of some distinction, and an ordained Unitarian minister. Payne found in him "less of the pride of the pulpit than we are apt to find among the rigid professors of the principles of puritanism"; and the man himself "the same kind and circumspect creature he always was." [254]

Palfrey, likewise, discovered Payne little changed after more than thirteen years, and was "delighted that . . . he retained all the freshness and simplicity he had carried away . . . as gentle, unhackneyed, sincere and sanguine as a boy."

Mutually cordial, this reunion was to the expatriate "like a glimpse of home."

To Irving in faraway Spain Payne's continued residence in the Paris apartment, now that he was the only regular occupant, seemed both unnecessary and extravagant, especially for one who, whatever his earnings, was never able to make ends meet.

"I can tell you how you can make out after January," wrote Irving some months after his departure. "Let out your apartment. You may hire a neat room sufficient for your purposes, for a fraction of the rent you are now paying, and may almost live on the remainder."

Irving recounts the economies he himself has practiced and urges Payne to do likewise: "The moment I found my resources interrupted and that there was not a pittance I could call my own, I left the hotel in which I was living, took an apartment at a small rent and put myself upon a rigid course of economy. I shall continue this until I see my way clear. I have a pride and satisfaction in so doing. Excuse my harping upon this old theme, but it is not often that a preacher has a chance of mounting, as it were, upon his text and holding forth from his own example."

A specific economy recommended by him was in domestic service: "For ten francs a month you may procure all the attendance you require and may get rid of a woman who is an expense, a cause of expense and a nuisance into the bargain."

Here Irving referred to Marianne, the *femme de ménage,* of whom later he would speak in even stronger terms: "If you have not yet discharged your lodgings and that blood-sucker, Marianne, I advise you to do so at once. Why should you be working to pay for rooms you do not occupy and to feed a mouth that does nothing but chatter?" [255]

This characterization of Marianne may imply that Irving knew of the line the housekeeper was trying to take with Monsieur Payne, about whom she had grown sentimental. Payne's diary records her having demanded a kiss on New Year's day and later complains of her "damnable affectation of sentimentality, endeavoring to take advantage and establish claims." [256]

As no further mention of Marianne has ever come to light, we have only these brief comments to suggest one amusing detail of Payne's trials as a householder.

Whether because of the expense of the apartment, the importunities of Marianne, the difficulties of living in one city and operating chiefly in another, or a combination of the three, Payne did finally give up the Paris place and return to London. The late summer of 1826 found him back in his old London haunts; and the historic Rue Richelieu chapter was definitely ended.

[17]

LONDON: FINAL YEARS

AFTER quitting Paris, in 1826, Payne spent six more years in London before returning to his native New York. This is a period less fully documented than any other of his career; but, thanks largely to the London press and a publication of his own, some of its important events have been established.

It was immediately upon his return that he made another brief essay of independent editorship by bringing out a small weekly publication called *The Opera Glass for Peeping into the Microcosm of the Fine Arts, and more especially the Drama.* It first appeared on October 2, 1826 and continued for twenty-four weeks.

Despite its ponderous full name, the *Opera Glass* was a modest little pamphlet of but eight pages of three columns each. It differed from the half dozen other theatrical weeklies then appearing in London by including, besides comment on current plays—not neglecting the editor's own—bits of dramatic biography, anecdotes, greenroom gossip, and some news of theaters in foreign cities (Paris, New York, and even Buenos Aires).

The *Weekly Examiner* remarked upon the literary quality of the *Opera Glass* as compared with "several inferior publications of the same stamp," and the *Times* paid Payne's little review the compliment of reprinting, within the brief six months of its life, several items from its "Behind the Curtain" section. An early issue, that of October 23, is heavily bordered in black signaling the demise of the eminent French tragedian, Talma.[257]

We have previously seen signs that Payne was potentially a serious music lover. Had he lived a century later, he doubtless would have collected recordings of fine music as throughout his life he collected rare books. The *Opera Glass* gives evidence of his increasing regard for the tonal art. There are appreciative comments on the overture to *Oberon,* the new Weber opera just brought out at Covent Garden; and notices of oratorio and other sacred music. Under "Notes on the Philharmonic Society" appears a brief but noteworthy mention of a very great contemporary:

> The associates of this Society have just distinguished themselves greatly. They have voted 100 pounds to Beethoven in his discomfort and disease.[258]

The last issue of the *Opera Glass* appeared in March 1827. Early abandonment of the venture may have been caused by a severe illness from which Payne suffered in the spring or early summer of that year. We know nothing of this beyond a brief reference in a letter to his sister Anna, written the last day of July, to "a serious illness of several weeks—*twice* expected to die." Characteristically he had waited until months after the event to tell the family of this near disaster and then supplied no details.

Payne had put forth the *Opera Glass* as a side line. His first play after returning to London was *Peter Smink; or, Which Is the Miller?* a one-act adapted comedy first performed at the Haymarket. Although both Price and Elliston had refused this piece, it had a very good initial run and was repeated in London and elsewhere for several years. Here again, as in an earlier success, *'Twas I*, much of Payne's triumph was due to the singing and acting of the brilliant Mme. Vestris, who proved a particular hit as the miller's daughter.

Martha Lucia Elizabeth Vestris, London-born, but "Madame" by virtue of her marriage at the age of fifteen to a Frenchman, was a favorite singing actress. Her "great sprightliness and vivacity, baby face and almost faultless figure" were combined with "one of the most luscious of low voices." [259] She often assumed men's parts with songs written for high male voice, as well as roles with songs composed for female voice in low key.

Payne had not always admired Mme. Vestris, and a few years earlier had referred in his diary to her "coarse, pouting lips, indecent dress and castrata voice." But the very qualities that he then found unattractive may have been what enabled her to give the right fillip to certain light French pieces to which he seemed able to give the effective touch in translation. She was to contribute materially to at least two of his subsequent productions.

One of these was the French opera by Boieldieu, *La Dame Blanche*, in the English adaptation called *The White Maid*. Here Mme. Vestris acted and sang the role of George Brown, son of the house of Avenel, on whose estate a sacred statue ("La Dame Blanche") becomes the supernatural agency which determines the family's fate.

The original French libretto was by the eminent author Eugène Scribe, who had based his story upon a combination of two novels of Sir Walter Scott, *Guy Mannering* and *The Monastery*. In the middle 1820's the opera was having a great run in Paris.

The adaptation of this opera proved one of the most difficult undertakings of Payne's entire career. Sir George Smart, Covent Garden's ambitious musical director, wanted a text exactly fitted to the music; hence he directed that the English version be made "so as to preserve every note of the original music, with English equivalents for every particular word in which it was conveyed in French." [260] And Payne tried to carry out the assignment, which other translators are said to have refused.

There were also difficulties on the production side. Originally announced for September 1826, *The White Maid* was not performed until January 1827. Several postponements were necessary because the leading soprano, Miss Mary Ann Paton, the Spirit, had withdrawn from the cast and a substitute had to be found to take over an exacting role.

Payne considered Miss Paton's withdrawal capricious, and in the *Opera Glass* reproved her in terms that could hardly have increased her liking for him. [261] This stricture was one of the items from his paper that the *Times* saw fit to copy. Thus unpleasantness was piled on top of agonizing effort; and both would be capped, when the piece was finally produced, by an unfavorable press reception.

Most adverse of all was the London *Times,* though even the usually friendly *Examiner,* while praising the music, was severely critical of the libretto: "We regret to say that nothing could be more undramatic and absurd than the development of this silly plot. The notion of a spirit, or pretended spirit, singing ten minutes at a time, in the midst of a multitude of people, is ludicrous."

This of course was no more ludicrous than many other operatic situations, and the same paper, in more reasonable vein, did concede that "in justice to Mr. Howard Payne it is necessary to say that all this inconsistency was forced upon him by the original." Further it was admitted that "the musical sale of the estates" (an operatic auction, apparently) was "a most elaborate exhibition of skill and artistry."

Nevertheless *The White Maid,* later a great favorite in America, had no more than twenty London performances, [262] though it was well liked by audiences and at the première it was "announced for repetition without a dissenting voice." [263] Its unpopularity with the British critics, to judge by the comments of some of them, partly reflected their resentment of the mixture of character and incident in this compound of the two Scott novels. [264] Others may have sought to punish Payne for his criticism of Miss Paton.

Begun with this noble failure, the year 1827 ended for Payne with a small but sparkling success: a one-act farce, *The Lancers,* another adaptation, first performed at Drury Lane December first.

This was one of the few pieces that Price had accepted from Payne, and the manager thought highly enough of it to use it in celebration of the first anniversary of his direction. Its story of two officers who have but one coat between them was declared "an amusing bagatelle of much drollery and equivoque"; "the situations whimsical, the dialogue neat and piquant." [265] *The Lancers* played for many consecutive nights at Drury Lane and remained in the repertory for years.

Payne by this time was a thoroughly seasoned playwright—or adapter, to state the case more exactly. His successes could no longer be regarded as lucky accidents, and even his failures had a certain professional dignity. In retrospect it would seem that, although he no longer brought out six to a dozen plays a year, he was fairly launched on what might have become an increasingly worth-while career of writing for the stage. Actually he was nearing the end of his efforts in that direction.

So far as is recorded, the year 1828 saw no new play by Payne. His old ones, however, were being repeated with great regularity. Even under Price, *Brutus* had occasional revivals at Drury Lane. *Clari* and *Charles II* continued as stand-bys at Covent Garden and were also frequently performed at the minor theaters. Replacing Miss Tree as Covent Garden's Clari was Mary Ann Paton of the *White Maid* unpleasantness; while Molly Glover, third daughter of Payne's friend J., was that theater's new and very youthful Mary Copp.[266]

Payne's single new product of 1829 was a three-act comedy, *Procrastination; or, the Late Mr. M.* (Haymarket, September 29). It is regrettable that this play seems to have been lost, for its story, unusually engaging, has a touch of originality which most of the plays adapted lacked. "The avowed work of Mr. Howard Payne, *Procrastination,* in these degenerate days of drama, may rank as a work of rare merit, merely on the score of its including some attempt at character." This was the gratifying comment of a new publication, impressively named the *Court Journal.* Another paper, remarking upon the play's pleasing freshness, also found that it had "a decided moral purpose," an observation which might give an erroneous idea had not the dependable *Examiner* provided a summary:

> We anticipated that the plot would turn on Mr. M's being late for dinner. Mr. Payne, however, has done better—he has made him procrastinate till he is too late for everything, all but marrying the woman best calculated for him, and her he has never thought of, or the fate of both would have shared the result of all his other resolutions.
>
> One is kept in suspense to the last as to what the author will do to bring his hero off safely and avoid a suit for breach of promise. It was a merry thought to make him discover at Coventry, on his progress to town to fulfill his engagement of marrying a rich widow, that he had left his purse at home; then, instead of returning for it post haste, to wait and see the procession of Lady Godiva.

And now the *Examiner* asks: "Was it a sly and two-edged sarcasm of Mr. Payne's to make his hero forget his appointment with the widow, through being engrossed with a sketch of Mr. Geoffrey Crayon's?"

Surely there was no sarcasm here, but introduction of the name "Geoffrey Crayon," an early pseudonym of Irving's, was of course for Payne a bit of fun within the fun of adapting (or possibly writing) this play.

How much more of *Procrastination* may have been his own there is no way of knowing. Although it was stated that most of the material was from various French sources, search thus far has failed to reveal a hint as to any other author.[267]

In August 1831 the Haymarket brought out two new plays, *Du Barry* and *Fricandeau.* Both were generally attributed to Payne, but it is doubtful if both were by him, for an advertisement in the *Theatrical Observer* names Poole as author of *Du Barry.* But for the definiteness of the announcement, we might think this another instance of London's well-known custom of bringing out simultaneously two or more versions of the same play.[268] Were there an error here, neither author would have cause to feel cheated, for both plays were soundly denounced by the press, *Du Barry* on moral grounds.

And the same year, 1831, brought Payne one plaudit from a high official source. It was then that the Lord Chancellor Brougham—a mighty man in the theater and incidentally the personage for whom a fashionable vehicle had been named—in a discussion of the merits and shortcomings of the British stage, propounded a question: "Has there been produced in the years since 1804 any play, a rational comedy or tragedy fit for the amusement of men or women?"

The eminent jurist answered his own question by naming half a dozen, among which "Mr. Howard Payne's 'Brutus' stood near the top of the list." [269]

Payne's outstanding achievement of 1832, the year of his departure for America, was a swift-moving and very successful three-act burletta called *Woman's Revenge.*

Its production at the Royal Olympic Theatre connects this play directly with an interesting development in the London theater: emergence of the woman manager. It was the versatile Mme. Vestris who had lately taken over management of this little theater, thus earning the name of being London's first female lessee. Actually, however, Mme. Vestris was the second, for a year earlier Fanny Kelly had undertaken to manage another minor theater, the Strand. But whereas Miss Kelly had been sued by Drury Lane and Covent Garden for daring to infringe upon the patent rights of the "great legitimates" and could only continue as a producer by building a theater of her own,[270] Mme. Vestris succeeded in carrying out her project. And of her early productions, none was more brilliantly successful than Payne's *Woman's Revenge.*

The manageress did not take part in this little comedy in which, for a welcome change, the protagonists were English gentry. The largest role, that of a well-to-do spinster of tart tongue but golden heart, fell to the sprightly Mrs. Glover. "You be loike a great artichoke, me lady—rum rhind but rare eating," says a rustic beneficiary of this heroine's disguised goodness; and the characterization is borne out by her own parting line: "The right revenge is woman's —to forgive." [271]

For all its benignant overtones, *Woman's Revenge* was broadly humorous. It opened on February 27 and was repeated nightly until the theater closed for the season, six weeks later.

Payne sailed for New York from Portsmouth on the steamship *President,* June 11, 1832. The surprise here is not that he finally gave up the fight, but that he had held out so long in the face of conditions which had defeated many men seemingly made of sterner stuff.

A month earlier two important London publications had commented on the state of the theaters. Said one, the *New Monthly Magazine:* "The condition and prospects of the great houses are steadily growing worse. . . . Old enterprises on the brink of destruction; new ones catching at a straw." And the other, the *Court Journal,* "Such is the state of theatricals in this country that only ⅓ the number are open today that were open before the war; and salaries of performers are only half what they used to be."

But now as the departing American gazed out upon that "mighty monster" the ocean, day after day for six long weeks, it may be that he thought less of what he was leaving behind than of what might lie ahead. For years, he knew, the theaters of New York and other American cities had been performing his plays, often with great profit to managements, but without a cent of recompense to himself. On the strength of this consideration friends had long urged his return, but, Harrison says, "he was hesitant to show himself not quite so well off as when he went away."

Actually, was he less well off? He had fought against terrific odds and had done what no American had ever done before. His achievements abroad, by any fair reckoning considerable, had won for him a unique place in the theatrical history of his own country. Of that remotely realized result he had, of course, no anticipation.

Although it held great hopes, the future seemed unplanned. Only one thing was certain: he had turned his face toward home.

Part Three

1832 TO 1852 AND LATER

[1]

BENEFITS REMEMBERED *

NEW YORK in 1832 was a thriving, bustling city more than twice as large as it had been two decades earlier: a husky adolescent growing too fast for its clothes. To one long accustomed to the urban maturity of European cities the American metropolis might have seemed a little crude and unfinished. To Payne, however, the striking difference was not between New York and London or New York and Paris—perhaps that was too obvious—but between the city he had left and the one he found on returning.

He was prepared for certain changes. As much as three years earlier his sister Lucy had written: "The city has enlarged well on toward Bloomingdale. The Village of Greenwich is in the city— more than a mile beyond is city also. . . . The section we called Corlaer's Hook is greatly changed, by removing those mighty hills, which appeared as eternal as the earth. In place of them are wide streets, handsomely built up." [1]

Lucy had not reported, however, the new stores of "jewellers and mercers" in Broadway, the wholesale merchants in South Street, the "four manufactories of steam engines" and "ship yards in a constant state of activity," or the transformation of Wall Street from a residence section into a "far-famed mart [with] all intent on one purpose—gain." [2] Nor could she know of the innovation that 1832 would bring: completion of the New York and Harlem Railroad, "beginning at Pearl Street in the Bowery and extending northward 7½ miles—single cars drawn by 2 fine horses at the rate of 10 or 12 miles an hour; or 2 beautiful cars, attached, drawn by 4 horses with great apparent ease." [3]

* The notes to Part Three begin on p. 406.

Payne's ship, the *President*, after a six weeks' crossing, was piloted into New York Harbor on July 25 and docked in the late afternoon.[4] Having told no one of his coming, he could not be surprised that there was no familiar face searching for his as he walked down the gangplank. He set forth on foot up Broadway, bound for his brother's residence, then at 67 Varick Street, near the corner of Varick and Canal—site a hundred years later of the Holland Tunnel approaches.

"I soon got to the end of the part of town I remembered and pushed along a mile and a half through streets undreamed of when I departed," says a memorandum of this homecoming. "Everything looked strange: bright vermilion brick houses were interspersed with houses painted yellow, blue or straw-color, stone color and all other colors, and none of them without green blinds, everywhere closed."

Why were the blinds all closed? Why, despite so many signs of growth and progress, was the city so strangely silent?

No doubt the returning native soon learned the cause. He had arrived in the midst of the great cholera epidemic. The dread disease, which for a year had been raging in Europe, had now reached New York, and was at its peak near the end of this July. No wonder most families had fled to the country, many shops were closed and business almost suspended. The scourge would take 3,500 lives in this city of a quarter million inhabitants, before it ran its course.[5]

If the home town had changed in the traveler's absence, that traveler, in turn, bore little resemblance to the boy who had sailed away nearly twenty years before. According to a candid description of him, soon to be printed in the New York *Mirror*, he was now a "short, thick-set, plump, full-whiskered, middle-aged, English-looking man, briskly whirling around a corner." [6]

Probably he did not move very briskly this warm afternoon, for it had become nearly dark by the time he reached the Varick Street address. He rang the bell, and a woman's face appeared at an upper window. It was his sister Anna to ask what the stranger wanted.

"Is Mr. Payne at home?"

"No."

"Is Mrs. Osborn at home?" (He knew it was not Lucy at the window.)

"No, I believe Mrs. Osborn has gone out. Is it anything particular?"

"I merely wished to see some of the family. Is Miss Payne in town?"

"I am Miss Payne."

"I suppose you have no recollection of me?"

"I can't say that I have, sir."

"What—have you forgotten your brother?"

With that Anna "jumped and ran to let me in and it was some time before she said a word more than 'Is it possible?' "

At length Lucy and Thatcher arrived. Howard was introduced to each in turn as "an English gentleman," and was not at first recognized by either.[7]

It was a sad time in New York, that summer of 1832. Though the happily reunited middle-aged group—two sisters and two brothers, in the Varick Street house—escaped the epidemic, each day brought news of fresh cholera victims. In August, however, the number of cases appreciably lessened, and by fall the danger had passed.

Normal life suddenly revived. Shops and business houses reopened. The theaters—there were now three of them—sprang into life. In September the Park, where Payne had made his debut so many years before, acquired a brilliant new attraction, for it was then that the Kembles, Charles and his daughter Fanny, arrived from England for their first American engagements. Almost simultaneously, at the Richmond Hill, Italian opera was first heard and definitely launched in this country. And at the theater called the Bowery a young American actor named Edwin Forrest was rapidly rising to stardom.[8]

Social activities too were soon flourishing, and the home town boy lately returned from abroad received a number of pleasant invitations. This we know by several items recorded by New York's former mayor Philip Hone in his famous diary. Hone's entry of October 31, 1832, has this to say: "Dined with Bucknow—a large party and a fine dinner. After which I went to Henry Hone's, where a pleasant party was assembled. . . . Here I met for the first time John Howard Payne, the author of Brutus and several popular dramatic translations, who has been in Europe for twenty years and upwards. . . . He is now 38 years of age, a handsome man, of gentlemanly manners and very agreeable at a dinner table. He recited for us and read Shakespeare, and, being something new, I was much pleased to make his acquaintance." [9]

Hone, famed for his hospitality, was a competent judge of dinner companions, though he underestimated Payne's age, which was actually forty-one. His characterization of this guest as "handsome" we might think flattering, in view of the *Mirror* description; but no doubt Howard's once-famed good looks returned under the stimulus of hospitality and friendly attention.

There were three of the Hones, Philip, Isaac, and Henry, and apparently they were brothers. Philip, to whose administration as mayor was credited much of the city's recent improvement, was the famous one. He was evidently well impressed by Payne, for we find John Howard listed among the guests at the next two dinner parties at the former mayor's home.

This was a presidential election year, and as usual partisan feeling ran high. A great issue was the tariff, and the press was divided. William Cullen Bryant's *Evening Post* supported Jackson and free trade. Other New York papers came out strongly for Henry Clay and protection. But after the sixth of November, or the tenth or the twelfth—for returns came in slowly in pretelegraph days—both sides accepted the result, Jackson's re-election, in typical American fashion. It was then that a new topic was to be noted in most of the papers: "our amiable and gifted countryman, Mr. Payne." [10] And for the next few months Payne was almost to relive the most praised period of his boyhood. Though no longer the wonder boy, he was now hailed with an enthusiasm and a warmth that must have been not only heartening, but almost bewildering.

The New York *Mirror* took the lead in honoring him. That paper was a weekly devoted to literature, the drama, and the fine arts generally. Not only did the *Mirror* come out in two lengthy installments (November 24 and December 1) with a comprehensive account of Payne's life and work to date, it was also the first to propose a testimonial benefit in his honor.

"It is known that our theatres and our actors have for many years enjoyed the advantage of the exertions of Mr. Payne without acknowledgment to him in any shape whatever," said an editorial.[11] The public conceded the justice of this observation, and a committee of seventy leading citizens was formed to sponsor the project. November 29 was the date set for the benefit, to be held at the Park— "America's Old Drury," it was sometimes called, although America, even then, was impatient of aging buildings, and during Payne's absence in Europe the Park, damaged by fire, had been torn down and rebuilt from the ground.

The custom of benefit nights for prominent stage persons—actors and sometimes playwrights—had been accepted as a matter of course in the United States and Britain for as long as anybody could remember. With stage stars the practice was invariable. It was expected that toward the close of a season or an engagement every leading actor would announce in the press a performance whose proceeds would be wholly or chiefly his own. The services of the rest of the company presumably were donated, and the management sometimes claimed no share. Thus the Kembles, by appearing in a series of several brief engagements in New York, were able to profit by no fewer than eight benefits for themselves in the 1832–33 season alone.[12]

The welcoming benefit arranged for Payne by his fellow townsmen was planned as something different. It was called a dramatic festival and had features which made it a social as well as a theatrical affair. The house was gaily decorated; the pit, usually occupied only by men, was "opened to the ladies"; and a striking, almost official, touch was given by attendance in a body of the city's militia officers in dress uniform. Over Payne's protest the price of tickets was raised to $5 (regarded as excessive) for all parts of the house except the gallery, from which the underprivileged were permitted to view both stage and audience for a dollar.[13]

The program by "volunteer talent," according to the original plan, was to have consisted entirely of Payne productions. It was confidently expected that Charles Kemble would appear in *Charles II*, for Irving and Payne had dedicated that play to him and he had performed it innumerable times in London. Some consternation was therefore caused by Kemble's refusal to appear as King Charles, stating that he wanted to reserve this play for his own benefit.[14] He proposed instead that he and his daughter perform a number of their own choosing; and since the Kembles were the current sensation, the committee was obliged to consent. Other extraneous features were then introduced, with the result that the program became what today seems a strange hodgepodge, of unconscionable length.

The five-act *Brutus* in its entirety opened the proceedings, with Edwin Forrest in the title role. Musical numbers followed: "Home, Sweet Home," of course and the finale of *Clari*. Then came the poetic address to the guest of honor—something without which no testimonial of the time would have been complete. That also had been especially prepared, and its author was Theodore S. Fay. This was singularly appropriate, since Fay's late father had composed the prologue for Payne's stage debut, and the son's tribute began with a reminiscence of that event:

> One snowy night in time of yore
> At least some twenty years ago—or more—
> Upon the stage a radiant boy appeared
> Whom heavenly smiles and grateful thunders cheered;
> Then through the throng, delighted murmurs ran,
> "The boy enacts more wonders than the man." [15]

The Kembles came on in "Shakespeare's Katherine and Petruchio" (whether or not the entire *Taming of the Shrew* is not stated). And the evening—which by this time must have been morning, though the performance had begun at half past six—ended with *Charles II*. Here local actors were assisted by James Wallack, who played Captain Copp, "having put off an engagement at a great loss and traveled from Philadelphia under severe indisposition, to show his kind feeling for our countryman."

We say that the evening ended with this number, but it did not, quite. For at the close of the stage performance "there was a loud and general cry for Mr. Payne," who, the *Evening Post* reported, "was at first embarrassed but presently recovered, and the grace of his manner, the sweetness of his voice and the clearness of his enunciation affected the audience with a kind of surprise."

Payne, who never failed in gracious acknowledgment, here found himself "dazzled, dizzied, surprised and overwhelmed . . . incompetent to acknowledge the kindness as I ought . . . your own goodness paralyzes the power to thank you." Mercifully brief, his response concluded: "To all Americans who devote themselves to literature and the arts [such an occasion] will give a glorious lesson. It will . . . show them that they belong to a country which is incapable of forgetting her sons . . . a country of which I was ever proud, and now, since I have seen other countries, yet more proud than ever." [16]

According to most accounts the dramatic festival realized for Payne $4,200, but he himself stated in a letter a few days later that the proceeds were "overestimated in the papers, and will yield between 2 and 3 thousand dollars." [17] Whatever the amount, the money was presented to him at a dinner in his honor arranged by "a few friends of literature and the drama" at the City Hotel only two days after the benefit.

Testimonial dinners for distinguished citizens had become customary, and earlier in the year three eminent New Yorkers had been so honored: Daniel Webster, Gulian Verplanck, and Washington Irving. The dinner for Irving had been given soon after his return from Europe in April; though by the time of Payne's homecoming Irving was on a tour of the American West, and that accounts for the absence of his name from lists of those honoring his old friend.

Payne certainly had not expected a testimonial dinner ("by no means a distinction to which my humble labors can give me any claim"), much less a dinner on top of a benefit. The unprecedented double compliment he could only accept as "the welcome of personal friendship." [18] Of the names signed to the testimonial presented to Payne on this occasion nearly all were of persons whose importance would still be recognized a century later: William Cullen Bryant, poet and editor; Gulian Verplanck, Congressman, writer, and influential citizen; Philip and Isaac Hone; John Trumbull, the artist, always Payne's loyal friend; George Pope Morris, the poet; Prosper M. Wetmore, a prominent citizen; and Archibald Gracie. [19]

The fame of the dramatic festival soon spread. Even London papers commented on it; [20] and those in Boston, Philadelphia, and other cities which had enjoyed the American playwright's unrewarded offerings suggested local efforts to even the balance. In Boston on April 3, 1833 the second testimonial benefit for Payne was given.

It was ever Payne's fate to be overpraised or overblamed. Though he went to Boston by invitation and was warmly received in the highest circles, [21] an almost unaccountable animosity sprang up in circles less distinguished. There were those who felt that he was receiving too much attention; and a sort of whispering campaign grew into what a later generation would call "a smear."

This combined with other circumstances to make the Tremont Theatre festival less successful than that at the Park had been. Though there was no one here to object to an all-Payne program, there were no stars, either, to give particular attraction to the plays selected. [22] Furthermore the Kembles had been announced to appear shortly in Boston, and that served as an anticipated counter attraction. Consequently the festival audience, though "unprecedentedly brilliant—a galaxy of beauty and fashion exceeding anything ever before witnessed in the city"—was "unexpectedly thin" in numbers, and the "pecuniary result" was disappointing. [23]

Openly the opposition to Payne had been confined to one minor newspaper—the Boston *Atlas,* and vigorously combated by the powerful and respectable *Transcript* as well as by the *Globe, Gazette,* and *Sentinel.* But the invidious *Atlas* had whispered the word "charity"—surely the first time that word had ever been applied to a theatrical benefit—and the charge had quickly spread. The *Transcript* took up cudgels for Payne:

> For shame! Charity, forsooth! Here is an early townsman of our own—himself and his family well known and highly respected here for years—produces a vast number of plays which are uniformly successful, caught at avidly by our managers, for 16 years the stock pieces of our stage.
>
> What is done for Mr. Payne all this time? Do the managers show *him* any attention? They do. They *allow* his friends to take the theatre on paying a much greater sum than could be brought into it by any other means, and to give a benefit as some remuneration for what his country-

men have enjoyed in gratification, and the theatre in profit, from 16 years of his labors. . . . What follows? Mr. Payne is represented as a supplicator for charity and an undeserving one! We have scarcely patience to repeat an imputation so disgraceful to the maker!

The *Evening Gazette* interestingly estimated: "Averaging the [different] plays of Mr. Payne at twenty performed in Boston each season, it would take more than one year, acting every night, Sundays not excepted, to have got through the number of actual representations we have had of his pieces. For all this, the author has been but inadequately paid abroad, and not at all here." [24]

Yet the unpleasant gossip went on. Some of the persons who whispered loudest were at the very time making capital out of Payne's Boston visit. The town was placarded with bills announcing a revival of *Brutus*. (This, the *Transcript* said, would be its 150th Boston performance, with never a cent to Payne.) Furthermore, over the protests of Payne himself the opera *The White Maid*, with his libretto, suddenly appeared on the Boston boards. This had never been published, and the manuscript had been "obtained clandestinely from London."

The charity charge of course reached New York, and the *Mirror* of April 10, 1833 protested: "In regard to the pecuniary profit of the benefits to Mr. Payne, they are just as much charitable donations as the sums paid to Walter Scott by his publishers, the subscription money received by an editor, the fee handed a lawyer, or the reward allowed to any artist or artisan who receives a *quid pro quo.*"

Despite the justice of his position and his many loyal defenders, Payne found the imputation of charity very humiliating. He was inured to indignities, but being unfairly discredited by his own countrymen was harder to bear than being cheated by the London managers. He returned to his brother's home in New York, where invitations came from other cities which sought to honor and belatedly to repay him. He was understandably chary of accepting them.

The testimonial benefit for Payne had set a precedent in New York. Other claimants for like honors were suggested, and within a year three more of the town's celebrities were similarly feted and aided: William Dunlap at the Park on February 1 (1833), Lorenzo

Da Ponte at the Richmond Hill, July 1, and Thomas Apthorpe Cooper at the Bowery, November 7.

It was almost before the curtain fell on Payne's New York benefit that a similar one for Dunlap was suggested. Here was a man of acknowledged talents—a playwright, an author, a portrait painter, now approaching seventy without ever having been sufficiently rewarded for his labors. Once the proposal was made, the public readily conceded its fairness, and the press co-operated heartily.

Dunlap himself had felt for some time that the honor was due him rather than Payne and had remarked in his diary on the night of Payne's benefit: "I know that if payment is due the American dramatist, one who translated by contract for a foreign stage is not the man." That, of course, was before the wave of hostile sentiment had been set going in Boston; but even after Dunlap's benefit had become a reality he continued in his diary to belabor Payne, and on February 28 recorded the report that Payne was "much annoyed by notices in the *Evening Post* respecting Dunlap's benefit." [25]

It seems extremely unlikely that this was true except in Dunlap's imagination. Payne had always known and respected Dunlap and even as far back as *Thespian Mirror* days had spoken highly of his work. From London he had written Dunlap in the most friendly fashion, and on returning to New York had called on his old friend, as Dunlap's diary tells us. Payne, we know, had also provided the "Rules and Regulations of the French Theatre," a gift to him from Talma, which is incorporated in Dunlap's *History of the American Theatre:* a contribution of great value which Dunlap could not have obtained from any other source.

But Dunlap was growing old, and "his last years were marked by continued poverty and much illness." [26] No doubt he felt that life had cheated him and that a younger man was getting all the rewards. The unfortunate thing about his criticisms of Payne, published later, is that they have all too often been accepted at face value by writers who may not have realized that the justice of the allegations might be questioned.

The next beneficiary of a New York dramatic festival was the veteran poet and teacher Lorenzo Da Ponte, who, long before he became a citizen of the New World, had distinguished himself in the Old as Mozart's librettist (*Don Giovanni, The Marriage of Figaro,* and *Così fan tutte* have texts by Da Ponte). For these achievements his fame has greatly increased with the years, but in the New York of the 1830's he was an unassuming and probably underestimated citizen, by his own statement "an octogenarian soon to be a nonagenerian." [27] After an unsuccessful attempt to keep a grocery store in New Jersey Da Ponte had become the first professor of Italian at Columbia College. He was also responsible for the beginnings of Italian opera in America.

Payne, through his brilliant brother Thatcher, had a legitimate contact with Da Ponte, for Thatcher Payne had been one of the old master's favorite language pupils; indeed, for a time some years earlier, Thatcher apparently had made his home at Da Ponte's house, 343 Greenwich Street.[28] It is not suggested, however, that the Brothers Payne had anything to do with the testimonial for Signor Da Ponte, first suggested by the *Evening Post,* even though Thatcher and the *Post*'s distinguished editor, Bryant, were extremely good friends. The movement to honor and assist Da Ponte seems to have been an almost spontaneous one; for here again it was widely realized, once it was pointed out, that a worthy individual had been denied his just due.

For all these brilliant special events, New York's theatrical mores were little changed. There continued to be the useful number of regular benefit nights, maneuvered by leading actors for themselves; and Payne had the satisfaction of seeing several of his plays used on these occasions in the theaters of his home town. Forrest appeared for his own benefit in *Brutus* and *Thérèse,* both the same night.[29] And the Kembles, for *their* benefit, finally did put on *Charles II,* Fanny as Mary Copp and her father in that role peculiarly his own, King Charles.

Lucy and Anna Payne attended this performance, and (so Thatcher wrote to Howard, then in Boston) "were in ecstasies," sisterly pride here doubtless adding to their lifelong enjoyment of a good play.

To Payne the most important of the later benefits were a few

performances of his *Virginius* at the Park, apparently the only productions this work ever received. Here we find him in the double
role of playwright and patron; the *Mirror* reporting that "he de-
votes his stock of material to promote the interests of unpatronized
talent."

The talent here was the American actor C. B. Parsons, to whom
Payne granted the privilege of performing *Virginius* for Parsons'
benefit.[30] The actor appeared in this play "several times . . . to
thin but delighted audiences." Samuel Woodworth, Payne's childhood friend, wrote the *Mirror's* appreciative critique of these performances and of the play itself declared that he found "no point
of resemblance between Mr. Payne's 'Virginius' and that of Mr.
Knowles. It will even be a matter of surprise that the same subject
could have been treated in a way so entirely unlike, by any two
authors."

By the following year the special benefit habit was apparently
becoming established in New York, for even the author of that other
Virginius, John Sheridan Knowles, was honored by a "dramatic festival" at the Park. The reason for the Knowles festival is not known,
as this beneficiary was British, and he had certainly not been neglected, either in England or America.

Payne had long thought highly of Knowles, but apparently
Knowles had only recently made Payne's acquaintance. There is a
letter of Knowles to Payne, written shortly before his departure
from England, regretting "that our intimacy has been so brief." [31]

By the time of the Knowles benefit, however, Payne was far away
from New York and from things theatrical. He was traveling West
and South in an effort to launch an entirely new project—one by
which he hoped to re-establish himself and to obtain proper recognition abroad for his native country.

[2]

JAM JEHAN NIMA

"NOTHING overcomes mere prejudice more effectually than acquaintanceship, and there is a sort of remorse, mixed up with the sense of having been unjust through ignorance, which always changes those who were once embittered by want of knowledge of each other, into the most earnest friends."

This is Payne speaking, through his "Prospectus of a New Periodical," issued in New York in the summer of 1833, just a year after his return from Europe. The proposed periodical, given in advance the strange name *Jam Jehan Nima*, was planned to be an international weekly published in England, with the idealistic aim of furthering Anglo-American friendship through making the two countries better acquainted. "Supported by the united talent of both countries," it was to contain "the most accurate information from both upon every subject—except politics—which can have interest or importance either in America or Europe." Above all, it was to make the United States better known and hence more respected in England.[32]

The proposal was timely, for the country was then freshly smarting from the attacks of that discourteous English visitor, Mrs. Trollope.[33] Hence a plan to improve America's standing abroad was welcomed at home, especially as it was promised that the publication would "enable misrepresentations of our country to be answered ere they have time to take root."

Theaters and benefits had not been Payne's only interest or occupation during his first year back in America. Literary work of various kinds had also engaged him. He had made efforts to form a connection with a New York publication, "but found every place in the enterprises then existing, not only filled but capably filled."

He had considered trying again to start a journal in New York, "but found that the country contained as many dailies, weeklies, monthlies and annuals as it seemed to require." [34]

Though his planning for himself might be impractical, his mind was discerning, and while engaged in fruitless job hunting he had been constantly noting signs of his native country's place and growing importance in the world, and these observations found expression not only in his new plan. Some of them were embodied in a review of a new American novel, James Paulding's *Westward Ho!* which Payne contributed to the New York *Mirror* soon after returning from Europe. Here he speaks with a voice almost prophetic:

> It may be that the minds of the New World are destined to extraordinary influence over those of the Old. We have seen their effects in politics. We may yet see them in morals and even in the *belles lettres*.
>
> The peculiar circumstances under which our country came into being have favored the best sort of originality in her character. . . . We had made ourselves a nation, and a noble nation, by scorning to be anything but American, long before we ventured to be American in our letters. . . . For everything superior which America has achieved, she is indebted to that primitive mental independence.
>
> . . . When we say national, we do not mean a 4th of July nationality, which is satisfied with an oration and Hail Columbia, but a nationality which thinks and judges for itself, which does not blindly take its cue from a different order of society . . . but which studies to reach right principles of its own, and to those steadily adheres.[35]

Such sentiments were highly approved, but the exotic name chosen for a publication designed to further them came in for criticism. Though it was explained that the words "Jam Jehan Nima" were of the Persian language and, freely translated, meant "The World from Inside the Bowl," many felt that the name was visionary and obscure.

The only objection the *Mirror* had heard to "Mr. Payne's gigantic project" was the name. "We hope he does not alter it. It has both novelty and appropriateness; and it is nothing against a name that everybody has not always been familiar with it. We remember what complaints there were against 'Der Freischütz,' when it first came out. People are generally inclined to laugh at what they do not immediately comprehend." [36]

On the whole it was agreed that Payne had an excellent idea and a brilliant plan. He could hardly have thought of one, however, more difficult to finance or, from a practical point of view, to execute; the editorial or literary task, ambitious as that was, being, of course, the simplest part. It was the kind of undertaking that, to be prosecuted successfully, would have required an "angel" of the kind destined to appear in the coming era of American millionaires, some half century later. Lacking that, such a project, even to exist, would have needed either a capable advertising manager or some marked concession to popular taste; but there is no indication that either figured in Payne's plans.

To be sure, he had learned from experience that a publication must be financed somehow. He was not going to start again without advance backing, and he seemed to believe that this could be supplied by subscription. At the rate of $10 a year—high for the time—he calculated that "5000 effective subscribers" would be sufficient to set the project going.

About four months after announcing the plan he published a list of the New York subscribers to date—some 400 names, including those of many prominent and some distinguished persons. "The Hon. Martin Van Buren, vice-president of the United States" heads the list, "His Excellency, W. L. Marcy, governor, and Hon. Gideon Lee, mayor" follow, and most of the other names are grouped under professional classifications.

General Winfield Scott, 5 Bond Street, leads off for the military. Colonel John Trumbull, American Academy of Fine Arts, heads the artists' group, and Washington Irving the writers'. Da Ponte is first on a list of Columbia College professors, and Colonel Aaron Burr, 23 Nassau Street, leads the prominent members of the bar. The three Hones are also included, Payne's special friend Isaac Hone, 87 Chambers Street, being down for two subscriptions and each of the other brothers for one. The Honorable Henry Hone, 1 Bowling Green, is designated as "New York representative in the state legislature"; and after the name Philip Hone, "former mayor of New York" (address here given as 235 Broadway), is an impressive list of titles.[37]

Outside New York, one distinguished man whose subscription

was solicited considered the plan impractical, although he endorsed its aims. That was John Quincy Adams, once President and a President's son, then living in retirement on the family estate. His letter to Payne, with its courteous, constructive criticism, now seems almost more valuable than a subscription would have been:

John Howard Payne, Esq.
New York

Sir:

Your letter of the 9th instant, enclosing the Prospectus of a new periodical work projected by you, has remained so long unanswered, from an instability of sentiment regarding it, fluctuating between a warm appreciation of the design and an involuntary hesitation of doubt with regard to the probable, or perhaps possible, success of the undertaking which you propose. That the success cannot correspond with the merit which the talent engaged on it necessarily presupposes or with the burdensome expense with which it might be charged, is the prevailing impression upon my mind.

It would require a long and tedious dissertation to set forth all the considerations upon which I should deem a periodical publication in *London,* upon American topics, of impractical execution. To suit English taste, everything American must be satirical or censorious, and for American Palates, a Periodical without Politics is like a French Tragedy without Love. Should you nevertheless conclude to make the attempt, my best wishes for its prosperity will be with you, and of the creditable execution of anything that you may undertake I cannot entertain a doubt.

I am with much Respect, Sir, your obedt. Servt.

J. Q. Adams.[38]

Apparently undeterred by this sound and friendly suggestion, Payne late in 1834 set forth to carry out his stated purpose "personally to visit each of the 4 and 20 states in the interests of the enterprise." [39] In so doing his aim was not only to lengthen the subscription list, but also to find suitable material for publication in his journal.

His travel experiences were extremely varied. He began with Boston, where, despite some detractors, he still had warm and loyal friends. One of these was W. W. Clapp, editor of the *Evening Gazette;* another was S. H. Jenks, a son of an editor of the *Transcript.* The younger Jenks, who had been a member of Payne's little militia when both were boys, happened to be in Nantucket in 1834, and Payne addressed a felicitous note to him:

> Pray oblige me by saying whether I could do anything by a trip to Nantucket of two or three days. Would the land of whales assist me with oil for the enlightenment of two hemispheres? . . . Old association will lead you to forgive me for thus troubling you, and I can only add, trouble me in the same way as much and as often as you like.[40]

After Boston, Baltimore; then Charleston and Louisville. The farther the tour progressed the more the traveler was "surprised and delighted" by society on the far side of the Alleghenies. In November he is known to have been in Cincinnati and by the end of December in the considerably more frontierlike town of St. Louis.

From there early in January 1835 Payne wrote his sister Anna of being "imprisoned by ice" and suffering from "bad cold and rheumatism in my wretched and patched-up chamber . . . the rooms of all taverns wretched and badly furnished." Nevertheless, on his arrival December 30 he had been impressed by "the great kindness of my welcome" (the famous Western spirit, no doubt). He was "visited by the mayor and several gentlemen, civil and military, who sat on the bed. . . . Judge Peck, one of the great men of the law, comes and sits with me for hours and has given me a new sort of physic—silk weed, full of virtue." [41]

In spite of illness he had been "perpetually in society," invited to "a grand ball on the 8th, 600 ladies invited and all St. Louis to be amazed." He had also attended a party "at Monsieur Pierre Chocteau's, director of American Fur Co.," and there had "met all the belles and received a message from Gov. Clark, the companion of Lewis in travels among the Indians, years ago." He was to go next to Natchez and New Orleans, the letter adds.

New Orleans was to prove one of the adventure spots of this tour. For here another theatrical benefit was given for Payne, and here he became the victim of press attacks even more virulent than those made in Boston two years earlier.

New Orleans not only was famous for its French opera and theater: it also had a thriving American theater, which, until shortly before Payne's current visit, had been managed by an old friend of

his barnstorming days, J. H. Caldwell. Caldwell was among those
who had appreciated Payne's unrewarded contributions to the American stage, and some months earlier had written suggesting a benefit.
Now the invitation was renewed, although in the interim the New
Orleans theater had passed out of Caldwell's and into less friendly
hands.

Difficulties began with the city's French language newspaper, *La
Abeille*, better known by its English name, the New Orleans *Bee*.
This paper, which had originally joined the Louisiana *Advertiser* in
welcoming the northern visitor, suddenly reversed its attitude and
opposed him on every possible ground.[42]

The first objection was that the proposed benefit would be unfair
to the actors, who "must forego the nightly salary of from 5 to 10
dollars, for one they do not know except by name and fame." On
the actors' denial of unwillingness to contribute, the *Bee* then pleaded
the cause of the management, "asked to contribute facilities gratis."
This apparently had been requested, but when it was refused, the
theater was paid $350 for the benefit night.

Mostly, however, the *Bee* concentrated on Payne himself, alleging
his motives to be mercenary and his works somehow "foreign in
spirit," and repeatedly deriding him as "the translator of ballets."
Whether or not this loose wording derived from the fact that Payne's
adaptation of *Clari* had consisted of transforming the silent miming
of dancers into original dialogue and song is not important. For
when the *Advertiser* replied to the attacks the writer for the *Bee*,
first accusing Payne of having written the reply, then revealed what
lay behind the accuser's steadily increasing animus. Payne had been
caught in the middle of an old private feud between the two papers,
and the *Bee's* English language editor, once discharged and *arrested*
(so he stated) by the *Advertiser*, was now pouring out his smoldering
hate on a convenient bystander who happened to be Payne.

Somewhat insane on the whole, the attacks were none the less
deadly; and before he finished, the assailant threw in the charity
charge and also attacked Payne's nobly conceived journalistic project, calling it, with a complete lack of justice or even of information, the selfish and somehow unpatriotic scheme of "one who knows
little about us and cares less."[43]

After such a barrage it would have been surprising if the New Orleans benefit—its program consisting of *Thérèse* and *Charles II*, with the usual welcoming poem—had been very profitable, and compared to New York's, it was not. It did, however, put into Payne's pocket $1006.50,[44] of which by this time he doubtless was considerably in need.

The phrase "character assassination" had not been invented in 1835, but it accurately describes the treatment here accorded Payne. His only reference to it, in an open letter to the New Orleans committee immediately after the benefit, seems a model of restraint: "Various arts were put in action by the envious and disaffected to disgust me from accepting the invitation proffered, and to disgust others with me for not having repelled it. . . . The subject involves my character as a citizen and a gentleman."

But Payne took no superficial view of what had happened. He had begun to realize that beneath such a position as he found himself in lay inequities inherent in "the deplorable state of patronage of the literary portion of the drama." This was a subject which up to that time had had little if any attention in America. Payne's thank-you letter to the benefit committee deals with the subject of authors' rights in a manner that shows him to have been, here also, a pioneer:

> Dramatic authorship in the English language . . . has always been the least protected by the laws of both America and England. . . . In England, until very lately, dramatic writers were sustained by no law but the law of custom, and custom only entitled them to claim the profits of the third, sixth, 9th, 20th and 40th performance; and no sooner had a play appeared in London than prompters . . . made vast perquisites by supplying copies to all the provincial theatres of England and forwarding them to managers in this country.
>
> At length the subject was brought before Parliament by Mr. Bulwer. A law was very recently passed, securing to the author of any play appearing in the English language the right to enforce compensation during 5 and 20 years, for every performance of that play . . . within the jurisdiction of the British government.
>
> What are our laws on the subject? We have none. Dramatists are at the mercy of managers. The now obsolete law of custom in England remains feebly imitated by us, not in four benefits for a success, but in one alone.
>
> My countrymen were disposed to atone to me for the want of a pro-

tective law by what they deemed an act of voluntary justice. . . . I could not but feel that acceptance, under title of a benefit, of the profits of one night, after performance in a theatre of many [of my] plays innumerable times during 19 years—could be less than a simple recompense. . . . How could I, unless . . . payment long deferred must necessarily be construed as alms bestowed? [45]

Writing again to Anna, this time from New Orleans, Payne mentioned "all the turmoil of the benefit," but it is doubtful if the family ever knew how distressing it had been.

Yet the southern trip was bringing some rewards. From New Orleans there were side trips to "Pensacola, Alabama, Georgia and the Carolinas." The *Jam Jehan Nima* subscription list was growing, though slowly. Mobile "yielded 100 subscribers," says a letter from Alabama, and the Pensacola Railroad Company "subscribed for 25 and deposited the money in the bank, requesting me to draw without regard to my prospects, whenever I might wish, and the sooner the better. However, I do not wish to touch any of my paper funds until I can touch them all."

Here Payne was complying with the promise of his prospectus that no subscriptions would be collected until the list should have reached 5,000. Furthermore, he knew that the railroad was not yet a reality and that even the new additions to the old city of Pensacola had not passed the blueprint stage.

"Everybody is speculation mad and the fortunes suddenly gathered by cotton lands—especially those stolen from the Indians—make money-getting seem a matter of enchantment."

You rub an old lamp, like Aladdin, and you find rich plantations and horses and negroes all around you. The only lamp they seem to require here is the one which lights them to some way of taking in the natives.

The first notion of a New Englander in building a town is a meeting house, a school house, a tavern, a blacksmith shop. But here they think only of a Bank, an Insurance Company, a Railroad and a *Bar*. The church and the teaching follow, when the town begins to grow.

In such boom times one found "expenses enormous—$2 a day the current charge for living." (Verily, the old order changeth!) There was also a Wild West aspect to it all: "You scarcely see a shop of any sort without a plentiful supply of dirks and pistols.

Everyone wears them. I have myself been induced to put on armor, but no one has molested me, so I cut my nails with my dirk and never load my pistols." [46]

The wild spirit must have been infectious, which perhaps accounts for Payne's acquiring a most unusual souvenir—nothing other than a live rattlesnake! [47] Before sending this prize home to the family— surely as unwelcome a gift as could well be imagined—he referred to it jokingly in a letter to a New York friend, written seemingly in devil-may-care spirit, and thus describing himself: "With a lady under one arm and a basket of magnolia and a bucket and tin cup and two tumblers hanging to the other, the rattlesnake trailing be- hind, and a party of ladies and gentlemen pretty well soaked from a sudden squall and fierce breeze, a picture might be formed of my honorable associates and myself, well worthy of a Hogarth." [48]

In the new country friends were easily made. Among them Payne mentions Colonel Maunsel White of New Orleans, "who has invited me to his plantation to stay all summer, and offered me a gift of land, which I did not accept." He also records "valuable engage- ments with Catlin, the artist and traveler among the Indians."

The acquaintance last named seems, in view of subsequent events, to have been the most important of them all. Catlin's accounts of Indian customs, made doubly vivid by his drawings, doubtless sug- gested to Payne a vital and distinctively American topic for discus- sion in his periodical. And it was this new interest that led him to the next step, a truly momentous one in his career.

[3]

INDIAN SUITE: CONTRASTING MOVEMENTS

THOUGH Payne had resolved to bar politics from his pro- posed international weekly, his effort to launch that publication led him to involvement in a political struggle of large proportions— namely the difficulties existing between the State of Georgia and the

Cherokee Indians, with the federal government powerfully aiding the former.

From Florida he continued his journey into Alabama and Georgia for the double purpose of obtaining subscriptions to his magazine and gathering material for its pages. By late summer he had reached the Great Smoky Mountains, abode of the Creeks and Cherokees. Here his adventure with the Indians was in two parts. It began peacefully enough with his witnessing an aboriginal religious rite, the Green Corn Dance of the Creeks. It ended three months later with his seizure and incarceration by Georgia militiamen on suspicion of abetting the insubordination of the Cherokees.

On his journeyings West and South, Payne had been able to travel part of the way by train. The "iron horse," however, was then only half a dozen years old, and rails had not been laid extensively. Most traveling was still by horse-drawn coach, and on the regular stage lines one proceeded in what for those days was travel comfort. But in the less settled regions there was no way of getting about except on horseback. He bought a horse, "with saddlebags and border accoutrements," and hired a guide. To the family at home he sent an account of the adventure.

> I cannot describe my feelings when I first found myself in the Indian country. We rode mile after mile in the native forest, neither habitation nor inhabitant to disturb the solitude and majesty of the wilderness.
>
> At length we met an Indian in his native land. He was galloping on horseback. His air was Oriental. He had a turban, a robe of fringed and gaudily figured calico, scarlet leggings and beaded belt and garters and pouch. We asked him how far it was to the square. He held up a finger and we understood him to mean one mile. Next [we passed] two Indian women on horseback, loaded with watermelons. We bought some. . . . Passed groups of Indian horses, tied in the shade, with cords long enough to let them graze. . . . Passed groups of visitors, with horses and carriages and servants. . . . Saw the American flag (gift of the government) floating over the hut-tops of the square.[49]

This emblem was a reminder of facts impossible to avoid:

> The United States have in vain attempted to force the Creeks to volunteer a surrender of their soil for compensation. A famous chief among

them made a treaty to that effect a few years ago [which] took effect in part, if at all. Perpetual discontents have ensued.

The United States have assumed a sort of jurisdiction over the territory, leaving the Creeks unmolested in their natural habits and property—with this exception in their favor: beyond any tribe except the Cherokees they have the right, if they wish, to sell to individuals at their own prices, but are bound to treat with the republic at a settled rate (which last mode of doing business they rather properly looked upon as giving them the appearance of a vanquished race and subject to the dictation of conquerors).

So what the diplomats could not achieve, was forthwith attempted by speculators, and among them the everlasting Yankee began to appear, and Indian independence began to disappear.[50]

But now, in August 1835, visitors from miles around, and at least one from faraway New York, had come to see the Creeks' most famous festival. "When the green corn ripens the Creeks begin their year. Until after certain religious rites, it is considered infamy to touch the corn. . . . Every fire in the towns is extinguished, every house newly swept and washed, enmities are forgotten."

Lighting the new fires of the year, brewing the ceremonial black drink, and performing the war dance—"constant firing and war-whooping, music of chanting and the pebbled gourd . . . boys with corn-stalks for guns"—these were features of the first day. The second, Payne regretfully was obliged to miss, for the sake of accompanying some white friends on an excursion to Toccoa, Amicalola, and Tullulah Falls. Well liked by the Indians, he was allowed, however, to spend a night among them, sharing their "field bed," where "I spread out my buffalo robe, pulled off my boots and slept delightfully."

The festival's final day included the event of greatest appeal to outsiders: the dance of the women. Payne, always with an eye for feminine pulchritude, admitted that "the assemblage of the females I was rather solicitous to see, so was at my post early."

A long line of females entered, all dressed in long gowns with gay colors and bright shawls of various hues, and beads innumerable . . . tortoise-shell combs in their hair, ears bored all around from top to bottom, and from each bore, a massive ear-drop, very long and generally of silver.
They slowly proceeded round and round, only turning at a given signal

to face the men. . . . Every eye among the women was planted on the ground. I never beheld such an air of universal modesty. It seemed a part of the old men's privilege to make comments aloud, in order to surprise the women into a laugh. These must often have been droll and also personal, I understood, and not always the most delicate.

Conspicuous among the dancers were the two daughters of the chief, Apotheola, "both very elegant girls." [51]

The eldest delighted me exceedingly. She seemed about 17 or 18, tall, of a fine carriage, graceful and elegant and quite European. She had a white muslin gown, a small black scarf embroidered with flowers in brilliant colors, gold chain, coral beads, gold and jewelled earrings (single ones), hair beautifully dressed in European style.

The elder princess, I am happy to say, looked only at me. Some one must have told her I meant to run away with her. . . . A very frolicksome, quizzical look in her eye, but excepting her look at me (which only proved her taste), her eyes dwelt on the ground, and nothing could be more interestingly reserved than her whole deportment.

Seriously, Payne found it "a great satisfaction to have seen this festival, so precious to them, probably performing for the last time in the land of their fathers"; and he added the thoughtful comment:

It was strange to behold in the new world customs perhaps older than in the old, and a melancholy reflection to know that these people are rapidly becoming extinct, and that, too, without a proper investigation of their hidden past, which would perhaps unfold to man the most remarkable of all human histories.

The stranger from the North had not only witnessed a ceremony. He had become interested in a subject that appealed to his sense of justice: the claim of the original Americans to territory which had been theirs from time immemorial. Probably he had not done much political thinking about the "rights of minorities," but later generations would have reason to applaud him for being on what here was fundamentally the right side.

The festival only aroused his wish to look further. Next door to the Creeks lived the Cherokees, who at that very time were resisting efforts of the federal government to remove them from their native soil. Here was a current topic of vital interest; and it was to learn more about it, as well as to investigate the possibility of writing a history of the Cherokees,[52] that he called on John Ross, their principal chief. With this the great Indian adventure began.

Had Payne not lived abroad for twenty years, he might have had more knowledge of the background of the struggle in which he was soon to become involved; though probably few Americans other than special students of Indian affairs could then have traced that struggle back to its beginnings.[53]

Before the Revolution it is said, the Cherokees had held sway in much of the land that later comprised Georgia, Alabama, Tennessee, and parts of North Carolina, though the outer boundaries were not fully defined. By the nineteenth century they had long since accepted their new neighbor, the white man, and had definitely "forsworn the warpath against the Whites" at about the time the far more numerous whites began to crowd more and more into the Indians' land. Several cessions of land had been made before the famous peace treaty of 1785; more treaties followed that, and with each of them the Indians surrendered more of their land. In addition the United States, in return for certain territorial concessions, had a long-standing agreement with Georgia for expulsion of the Indians from that state.[54]

During the years of the steady reduction of their holdings the Cherokees, long noted for their progressive ways, their well-kept farms, and orderly communities, were greatly advancing in culture. One of their number, Sequoyah, invented the Cherokee syllabary, which made literacy easily and quickly possible to those, old or young, who had missed attending the English-language mission schools. A Bible, a hymnbook, and textbooks were printed in Cherokee, as well as an informative weekly newspaper. All these advances occurred soon after the tribe had organized a regular government, to which, a few years later, they would give the name Cherokee Nation. This name was soon to be used against them, since it was argued that a nation within a nation could not exist.

In 1820 two signal misfortunes befell the new nation. One was the discovery of gold in the Georgia section of Cherokee country, which increased the avidity of the whites to own more Indian land.[55] The other was the passage by Congress of the famous Removal Bill, which authorized, for compensation, the removal of the Cherokees and several other southern tribes to territory provided for them west of the Mississippi.[56] And inasmuch as President Andrew Jackson considered removal the only practicable solution of an extremely difficult problem and feared that this sectional disturbance would lead to civil war, the influence of Washington was enlisted in favor of transplanting the Indians.

All this might have settled matters had not a majority of the Cherokees, led by John Ross, refused to leave their native soil. Ross continued the fight for several years. He made numerous trips to Washington and took the matter to the Supreme Court of the United States, whose decision in favor of the Cherokees [57] was simply disregarded by those bent on the tribe's removal. By 1835, the year of Payne's visit, the resisting Cherokees had reluctantly agreed to discuss a new treaty, and some had already left for the West. Three years later, the fight entirely lost, those remaining began their tragic exodus, hundreds dying on the way to the new country. With the last detachment would go John Ross.

In advance of his visit to Ross, Payne had been told that the chief was "selfish, sordid and violent," but found instead a man "mild, intelligent, entirely unaffected, of about five and forty years of age." [58]

Mainly of Scotch descent and only one-eighth Cherokee, Ross was one of several educated half-breeds who preferred allegiance to their Indian ancestry. For some twenty years a member of the national Council, he had been principal chief since before the tribe declared itself a nation. In his dealings with the whites he strictly adhered to a policy of nonviolence and had thoroughly schooled his followers in it.

When sought out by Payne, Ross was domiciled in "a log hut of but a single room, scarcely proof against the wind and rain," which was situated in Tennessee, just across the Georgia line. His former beautiful Georgia plantation, "on a rising ground . . . with rivers running through it, and in the distance a noble mountain," [59] had been stolen under the infamous lottery system, devised by Georgia speculators and permitted by local law, to enrich themselves and get rid of the Indians.[60] Ross, returning from a trip to Washington, had found his place occupied by the strangers who had drawn it in the lottery. All the best Indian homes, with their lands and buildings and all furnishings and improvements, were thus appropriated: of its kind perhaps the most disgraceful little chapters in American history.

Arriving late in September, Payne had intended to stay only one day with Ross,[61] but, being "received with unlooked-for cordiality and unreserve" and given access to many papers, prolonged the visit. He decided, at Ross's urging, to stay for the Council, which would convene October 12, and in the meantime busied himself with transcribing treaty documents, writing a paper descriptive of conditions —in which he inadvertently characterized the Georgia state militia, known as the Guard, as "a troop of border cavalry whose appearance reminds one more of banditti than of soldiers"—and, finally, with preparing "an address for the Cherokees to the people of the United States," which, if approved, was to be "sent around by runners for the signature of every Cherokee in the country." [62]

The Council, a regular annual event, was a general meeting of all tribesmen who wished to attend. That of October 1835 was held at Red Clay, Tennessee, the Cherokees' emergency capital, since they were no longer allowed to convene on Georgia soil. Because of concern over the threat of removal, this was a large gathering of some 1500 or 2000 persons, and was in session more than two weeks.

Payne, by this time thoroughly convinced of the injustice of removal, declared: "The Cherokee nation now stands alone, moneyless, helpless and almost hopeless, but without a dream of yielding. With these clouds around them, in their little corner of Tennessee, the nation holds its annual meeting. I cannot imagine a spectacle of more moral grandeur than the assembly of such a people under such circumstances."

Impressed, as well, by the picturesque outward appearance of this great legislature in a forest, Payne provided a brief description of the arrival of the assistant chiefs, warriors, headmen, Going Snake the Council speaker, and all the rest, which is one of the few existing accounts of such an assemblage:

This morning offered a foretaste of what the next week is to present. The woods echoed to the tramping of many feet. A long and orderly procession emerged from the trees, the gorgeous autumnal tints of whose departing foliage seemed in sad harmony with the noble spirit now beaming in this departing race. Most of the train was afoot. There were a few old men and some women on horseback.

The train halted at the humble gate of the Principal Chief; he stood ready to receive them. Everything was noiseless. The party, entering, loosened the blankets which were rolled and flung over their bodies, and hung them with their tincups and other paraphernalia on the fence. The chief approached them. They formed diagonally in two lines, and each in silence drew near to give his hand.

Their dress was neat and picturesque. All wore turbans, except four or five, with hats; many of them wore tunics with sashes, many long robes, and nearly all some drapery, so that they had the oriental air of the old Scriptural pictures of patriarchal processions.

The salutations over, the old men remained near the chief and the rest withdrew to various parts of the enclosure; some sitting Turk fashion against the trees, others on logs and others upon the fence, but with the eyes of all fixed upon the chief. They had walked 60 miles since yesterday, and had encamped last night in the woods. They sought their way to the Council ground. It was explained to them.

Parties varying from 30 to 50 have been passing in the main road . . . all day. All seem to contemplate the approaching meeting as one of vital import.[63]

Among the few white men at the meeting Payne was surprised to find a friend of his youth—one John Schermerhorn, "who was an upper classman at Union College when I entered; we had been intimate then." Now he was the Reverend Mr. Schermerhorn and a commissioner appointed by the President "to discuss with the Indians the subject of removal." Going well beyond the line of duty, Schermerhorn with great zeal set about to force upon the unwilling Cherokees a treaty on the basis of a five-million-dollar offer made by the government for the remainder of their land. Ross had declared the gold mines alone worth more than that, and the whole worth twenty millions.

When first apprised of the presence of an old acquaintance at the Indian Council, Payne "felt happy to recognize in the wilderness one whom I had known so early in life," but he soon found that Schermerhorn was prejudiced against Ross.

"I was urged to read some papers being prepared against Mr. Ross and the Cherokees. I did read them, since I wanted the entire evidence. . . . I entered into no discussion, but assured Schermerhorn, with the freedom of an associate in boyhood, that I considered his course a mistaken one."

Before this meeting there had been two Cherokee factions, one of which—the smaller, anti-Ross group—had favored removal. A very important achievement of this Council was the temporary uniting of the two in favor of Ross's ideas and the appointment of representatives of both groups to take the case again to Washington. Hence Schermerhorn's effort to gain the Cherokees' acceptance of a treaty at this gathering was defeated. Later he averred, probably with some truth, that the encouragement given the Indians by Payne's presence and known sympathy had had much to do with the result.

"The Council adjourned, Mr. Ross pressed me to return to his house." Payne assented and resumed his work.

It was Saturday evening, November 7th, and I had determined on Monday morning to depart. Mr. Ross and I were engaged the whole evening in writing, my papers piled upon the table, ready to be packed.

Suddenly there was a loud barking of dogs, then the quick galloping of horses, then the rush of many feet, and a hoarse voice shouted, "Ross, Ross!" . . . The door burst open. Armed men appeared. . . .[64]

The room was filled with the Georgia Guard, their bayonets fixed, and some if not all with their pistols and dirks. An exceedingly long, lank man who proved to be Sergeant Young [the leader] planted himself by my side, his pistol resting against my breast. . . . "Give up your papers and prepare to go with us," he said to Ross. . . . "Have your horse caught and be off with us. We can't stay."

It was useless to reply. . . . We set away. The greater number of their horses had been left at a distance in the road. When we were all mounted our cavalcade consisted, I believe, of 6 and 20. Mr. Ross and myself . . . were permitted generally to ride together, the Guard being equally divided in front and rear of us.

The earlier part of the night was bright and beautiful but presently a wild storm arose and the rain poured in torrents. The movements of our escort were exceedingly capricious; sometimes whooping and galloping and singing obscene songs, sometimes walking in sullen silence.

During one of the pauses Payne was startled to hear the air of "Home, Sweet Home" sung by one of the Guard. He could "scarcely believe his senses." [65] "What song was that I heard you humming?" he asked.

"That? 'Sweet Home,' they call it. Why do you ask?"

"Merely because it's a song of my writing, and the circumstances under which I now hear it strike me as rather singular."

My partner simply grumbled that he was not aware that I had written the song; but added knowingly that it was in the Western Songster, and the verses generally had the author's name annexed.

We halted at Young's [a tavern]. It happened, curiously enough, that the Western Songster was the first object that caught my view, standing open at "Sweet Home," and, fortunately for my character, "with the author's name annexed."

After another 24-mile ride through the forest, the soaked and muddy cavalcade crossed the line into Georgia, where the Guard discharged their muskets in triumph . . . and we were directed to dismount.

Our prison was a small log hut with no windows and one door. At one end was what they called a bunk, a wide case of rough boards filled with straw. In one corner sat an Indian, chained to a table by the leg, his arms tightly pinioned . . . charged with refusing to give his name to the census taker, and his denial unheeded. . . . They removed him and left us the only prisoners, but not alone. The door was always open and the place a rendezvous for the Guard and all their friends. We were shown the largest bunk and tried to sleep. . . . The time dragged on most drearily.

Payne asked permission to send a letter to an officer of the Federal troops at the Agency, "which might bring a reply that would set our affairs straight." This was refused; so were his requests to write to the President, to the governor of Georgia, the governor of Tennessee, and even his own family. He managed, however, to scribble a note to the governor of Tennessee and to smuggle it out, though he does not explain how the Guard was eluded.

Sergeant Young, at whose place "Sweet Home" had been found, arrived after a day or two. He "seemed in better humor," brought books for Payne and clothes for Ross, "said he had my pistols and I could take them when I liked," and "told me he wanted to subscribe to my publication."

Payne urged the sergeant to state on what grounds the arrest had been made. This plea brought the astonishing statement, instantly denied, that Ross had tried to impede the census—the same crime as that charged against the poor chained Indian. As for Payne, "I can tell you one thing they've got agin' you—they say you're an abolitionist."

Though he "could not help laughing at the absurdity of this," he later came to realize that in the South at this time, some twenty-five years before the Civil War, being an abolitionist was a serious offense; it had become, in fact, "the mad-dog cry of the time." But an even more heinous charge was named by Young: "We've got a letter where you say we look like banditti."

On the ninth day of their imprisonment, Ross, the great leader of the resisting Cherokees, was called into conference with the officers—and suddenly released. Payne, the outsider, amazingly, was held.

In the presence of the officers Ross could only tell the friend left behind to "make himself easy—everything will come out all right." "Then my companion mounted his horse and left me alone, with feelings, and under a suspense and doubt by no means to be envied."

Four days after the release of Ross "Sergeant Young told me he was going to his home. He had several times bantered me about 'when I expected my furlough' and 'why didn't I get on my horse and ride off.' He repeated his jeers this morning."

Soon Payne observed preparations for something unusual. The men were all summoned to be made ready at the roll of the drum. His horse was brought and he was ordered to mount. His clothes, including an overcoat, were heaped in a loose pile on the horse. Remonstrances that the saddle was not tied and the bridle not his own only brought roars from a senior officer, lately arrived.

This "Captain-Colonel" stood in front of his men and addressed Payne: "Hold your horse there, sir, and beware how you speak a word. . . . Look upon them men. Them's the men that you in your writings have called banditti! . . . You're a damned incendiary, sir! You've come into this country to rise up the Cherokees against the whites. You've wrote agin' these worthy men. You've wrote agin' the State of Georgia. You've wrote agin' the gineral government of the United States. Above all, you've wrote agin' me. . . . With your foul attacks you've filled the Georgia papers."

Astonished by this complete falsity, Payne attempted a denial.

"Hold your tongue, sir! . . . Take your papers and cut out of Georgia . . . and I order you never while you exist to be seen in this state of ours. . . . Let this be a lesson to you, and thank my sympathy for a stranger that you've been treated with such extraordinary kindness. And now, sir, clear out of this state forever, and go to John Ross, God damn you!"

Moving slowly, because of the load piled on the horse, Payne had not gone many yards before a stranger offered to help adjust his baggage, and another quickly and silently appeared to hand him a note, which proved to be from Ross. Before he could read it the irate colonel of the Guard and another officer "dashed up like fiends . . . cursed and threatened me. . . . I went on, and for the last time had the honor of hearing the Colonel's eloquence in a volley of oaths, threatening my life if ever he caught me daring to speak to another man in Georgia.

"I turned abruptly, entirely ignorant of the way, into a little wood. Before me was a muddy streamlet across from which arose a hill with a hut at the top. I determined to walk up to that hut and seek assistance in adjusting my things for a journey. . . . But I could scarcely drag my horse through the stream. He was ravenous for water and kept me standing in the middle of it while he drank. The woman of the house was much agitated by my presence. She asked, trembling and in tears, if the Guard would not hurt her for speaking to me."

Some fifteen miles farther on, having crossed the line into Tennessee, Payne was received with great kindness by an Indian family, who "looked upon me as one risen from the dead. . . . I was for the first time apprised of the dangers which had beset me. I found that during my 13-days captivity the most industrious efforts had been made to excite the country against me as an abolitionist and a foreign emissary. The minds of the country had been familiarized with the expectation of my being hanged. Those best acquainted with the spirit prevailing looked upon my situation from the first as the more perilous of the two, and when I was found to have been detained after Ross, it was considered altogether desperate."

A newspaper friendly to the Georgians had carried the report of an alleged plot of Ross and Payne "to arouse the Cherokees and Negroes to the commission of hostilities against the whites," averring that "papers found in their possession will go far to prove the hostility of their designs" and adding, amazingly: "Their communications had in large measure been carried on in the French language; for want of knowledge of that language the Guard was unable fully to comprehend their designs." [66]

At first greatly puzzled as to "what could have created the French part of the charge," Payne at length concluded that a few harmless documents in Cherokee, which he carried, had been mistaken for French. . . . He also recalled that the Guard had one day brought a stranger to the prison, who inquired of him: "Parlez vous français?" and, receiving an affirmative reply, had straightway disappeared, "having reached the end of his French vocabulary," Payne opined.

"These then were the French letters! This was the French plot! And I have reason to believe that the wiseacres who kidnapped us sent far across the country for a learned Theban to translate the *French* out of the original Cherokee."

It was only by lucky chance, as he afterwards realized, that he had not picked up and preserved, "as a curiosity and an illustration of our time," one of the Abolition pamphlets that were then circulating in the South. "Had the slightest document of such a nature been found in my possession, no explanation could have saved me." [67]

Reaching the Agency, Payne was hailed by the United States army officers "with the cordiality of compatriots and gentlemen." Ross was on hand to welcome him, and also Dr. Elizur Butler, a missionary long active among the Indians, who had undergone similar persecutions, having for some time been confined in the Georgia penitentiary for the crime of befriending the original Americans. This man—a physician—had written Payne's family of his plight, "in order that the result apprehended [the death penalty, apparently] might not come upon their knowledge too suddenly." [68]

As it turned out, this intended kindness was of course unduly alarming. Greatly perturbed, Thatcher Payne wrote to Lewis Cass, Secretary of War, to the Department of State, to the Attorney General and members of Congress; but "because of the government

policy on Indians," these officials "did not feel themselves authorized to interfere." [69] Thatcher was "preparing a memorial to the
governor of Georgia" when word came of his brother's release.

That information may first have reached New York through the
newspapers, following Payne's own account of his arrest and detention published in the Knoxville *Register* December 2, 1835. This
paper devoted ten columns to the detailed statement, in which Payne
boldly named names, denounced his outrageous treatment as "of
deeper interest than the mere insult and inconvenience to an individual," and appealed to the people of Tennessee, the people of
Georgia, and finally to Americans generally to be warned by his
experience against conditions permitting "insulting inquisitions . . .
midnight intrusions into the sanctuary of homes, imprisonment of
citizens without disclosure of charges, contempt of the boundaries
of states, mockery of the privileges of the Constitution."

This stirring appeal brought one remarkable result, "altogether
unasked for and unlooked for." Two weeks after its publication both
houses of the Georgia legislature—the same body which, less than
two years earlier, had passed the odious lottery act—adopted a
resolution of "firm, decided and unequivocal disapprobation of the
conduct of the Georgia Guard in the recent arrest and confinement
of John Howard Payne," enumerating the legal offenses and declaring: "the Guard have violated the character and reputation of the
State of Georgia by their act of wanton and uncalled-for vandal-
ism." [70]

Citizens of Knoxville proffered Payne a public dinner, but he declined. A week after publication of his letter he wrote his brother
that he was "leaving in the mail stage to get trunks and go by rail
to Charlotte. Mr. Ross was here today, on the way to Washington
with a delegation, and advised the stage. My horse being known is
exposed to those scamps, and besides, I can travel faster in a stage.
Ross's son will take the horse to Washington."

On the way north he ventured to enter Georgia, and on Christmas
day, "incognito, from Augusta," he wrote to Colonel Mordecai
Myers of Savannah: "The horse you bought for me is the most
amiable of horses, spirited yet gentle. I am indebted to him for a
change in jailers. [Have obtained] Ross's son to ride him to the

seat of government and he is now my representative at the court of General Jackson." [71]

Payne's published statement, so gratifyingly endorsed by the Georgia lawmakers, may have done much to discourage the use of highhanded methods by ruffianly whites against the Indians, but the problem of removal was by no means settled.

After Ross and his delegation had left for Washington in the hope of negotiating a treaty satisfactory to both factions, Schermerhorn took advantage of the leader's absence to bring about what was of course an entirely unauthorized Council. Though this was but scantily attended, Schermerhorn succeeded in pushing through it a treaty and obtaining the signatures of seventy-nine Cherokees, many of them of the group that had long favored removal. Despite the spurious character of this document, it was believed by many to provide for a fair settlement, and later Schermerhorn was able to obtain for it the President's approval [72] and ratification by both houses of Congress.

Righteously angered, Ross continued the fight two years longer, but without avail. He remained on cordial terms with Payne, whose belief in the justice of the Cherokee cause was only heightened by the outcome. Though the cause was lost, principle was not, and Ross addressed eloquent memorials and protests to the Senate and House of Representatives.[73] These, probably without exception, were written for him by Payne. They are of a quality to do lasting credit to his name.

[4]

HOME THEME, WITH VARIATIONS

CHRISTMAS of 1835 was not a very merry one in New York, for the town was still enshrouded, if not by actual clouds of smoke, at least by the shock and aftereffects of what still remains the greatest fire in the city's history.

On the night of December 15 a blaze that started in Merchant Street had quickly spread through the busy industrial section near the water front. Drygoods stores, shops of jewelers and watchmakers, importing houses, banks and brokerage offices, two newspapers with their presses—in all, 20 square blocks from Conties Slip to Hanover Square—were largely wiped out. Near zero temperatures froze hydrants; a fierce north wind spread the flames; Philadelphia sent firemen and apparatus. The property loss was so great that the press hardly noticed a considerable loss in human lives.

It was quite Howard Payne's luck to return from the South in the freshness of the devastation. The home folks, thank heaven, were safe, though his brother had suffered financially from the calamity.[74]

Thatcher, who had pursued the study of law throughout a brilliant but arduous teaching career, was now well established as a lawyer.[75] He had married—"a wealthy alliance," Howard recorded —and with his wife and baby daughter Eloise was living at 30 Bond Street. This little street, only two blocks long, near what would later become the heart of the business district, has disappeared from many maps; but in the 1830's the houses of the Bond Street row were regarded as among the finest in the city.[76] Here Howard was warmly welcomed; here Lucy, Anna, and Aunt Esther hastened to greet him; and little Eloise became at once Uncle Howard's delight.

He was soon to find, however, that the Indian adventure had allied him with what in New York was a little understood and generally unpopular cause. Ironically, although he had started out to gather evidences of his country's virtues and advancement with the ultimate aim of presenting them fairly abroad, he had stumbled into and personally suffered by one important condition in American life which he himself felt had fairly deserved the censure of Europeans.

But the fundamental justice of the issue did not seem important in a Northern city ravaged by recent disaster and beginning to line up for another presidential campaign. Some New Yorkers admitted that it was too bad about the Indians, but most of them felt that removal was the only practicable way to save the unfortunate people.

Payne was either ignored by the home town press or more than mildly chided for having got mixed up in the Indian affair. The

Evening Post carried a few notices of his misadventure, but otherwise paid no attention to the matter. The *Morning Courier*, conceding
that "personal security is a mere mockery if such offenses can be
committed with impunity," yet blamed Payne for "writing inflammatory documents for the Indians" and dismissed him with the silly
gibe that "if 'Brutus' had staid at 'Home, Sweet Home,' all this
would not have happened." The town's newest sheet, the *Herald*,
whose editor would become notorious for his poisonous pen, delivered the most outrageous comment: "It is supposed he will be
hung to the next tree. Let us get up another benefit for him before
he crosses the Styx. No time to be lost." [77]

Doubtless many New Yorkers resented these small, atrocious
attacks; but such fair-minded persons had no way of making their
sentiments publicly known. The one publication to come to the defense of "this amiable, gifted and deserving man" was the *North
American Quarterly Magazine*, which naturally was much less widely
read than the daily papers. The quarterly's editor, Sumner Lincoln
Fairfield, not only reprinted the entire Knoxville *Register* statement,
but also declared of Payne that, "assailed by native sycophants and
foreign miscreants," he "retains more Christian gentleness and ex-
hibits more forbearance under continual oppression than any of his
unworthy foes could feel or manifest. . . . A milder and more
amiable spirit breathes not beneath the heavens. His are the manners
of a gentleman, the thoughts of a poet and the knowledge of a
scholar." [78]

Again Payne had to seek some kind of breadwinning occupation.
His plan for an international weekly now seemed more difficult than
ever, and he wrote his valued friend Jonathan Meredith of Baltimore
that he was "disgusted from seeking further patrons" and felt "the
necessity of some new exertion to make the close of my career less
stormy than its previous course has been."

Over the next few years the new exertions were many, though not
all his industry contributed to his practical advancement. He wrote
to Payne Todd, son of Dolly Payne Madison, to suggest employment
in arranging the Madison papers—work that Payne could have done
well. He prepared for the National Institute a paper suggesting a

plan for a library and model gallery for New York University. He wrote at length to Senator Henry Clay on the subject of the copyright bill then before Congress:

> I am persuaded that such a law will be quite as serviceable to our litera-ture as just to that of England. . . . *The interests of the author should be paramount.* The law should be so framed as to prevent its being turned into a mere job law for the publisher. Carelessness upon this head nearly defeated the British bill to protect writers. . . . I do not despair of even yet witnessing the time when a little of our embarrassment from a super-abundance of money may be relieved by expenditures for the purpose of bringing our heads up to the prosperity of our pocketbooks.[79]

Turning to the theater, he offered the actor-manager James Hackett "a dozen full dramas a year," including "three original ones upon American history"—a suggestion apparently not taken up, perhaps because Payne set the price of $2500 on his proposed services. He also offered to provide James Wallack with "an Ameri-can historical play" for the opening of the National Theatre. He sent the rising young American star Charlotte Cushman several plays, including *The Banished Son*, "making Texas the scene of refuge."

"The new republic of Texas" had, indeed, become of very great interest to Payne, and he wrote numerous letters "seeking some ar-rangement for a commission with the Texas government," preferably one that might send him abroad. "A long novel with a Texas setting" also engaged much of his time. Though the novel was never pub-lished, several of his efforts in the field of magazine writing, made at this time, were successful.

As the year 1832 had brought the great pestilence to New York and 1835 had ended with the disastrous fire, so 1837 was marked by "a general panic in stocks" and resultant business depression, when "men who thought themselves wealthy became bankrupts" and "sales of rich furniture were one of the signs of the times." Specie currency was introduced, and "around Wall Street, New York never saw such a time." [80]

In the late summer of '37 Payne memorialized the panic in a long piece called *The Uses of Adversity*, a sort of combined light satire and ponderous morality play, studded with Biblical allusions and bits of seventeenth-century verse, which appeared in a small weekly magazine called *The Ladies' Companion,* published in New York by W. W. Snowden.

In the three years of its life this publication had had occasional contributions by such writers as Bryant and Irving as well as many lesser ones; but its pace had always been quite pedestrian. It remained for Payne, not previously represented in its pages, to give the little sheet a suddenly quickened tempo by his unusual contributions to the August 1837 number. He appears not only to have written the bulk of the paper that month, but also to have supplied what would prove the most noteworthy of all this magazine's contents. That was a modest sketch whereby the world was given four previously unpublished poems of John Keats.

It was more than two years earlier, during his tour in the interests of the proposed international weekly and previous to the Indian adventure, that Payne had made this extraordinary literary find. Had his *Jam Jehan Nima* materialized, he would doubtless have made the Keats poems and his discovery of them the subject of an article for that publication—indeed, he seems to have been saving the material for that use. That he now put it forth in *The Ladies' Companion* suggests that his earlier project had been abandoned.

On his Western journey Payne, a perceptive traveler, "had ceased to be astonished by the multitudes of fine minds and remarkable courtliness of manners . . . often met with in regions we are taught to regard as demi-savage, when [in Louisville] a new wonder burst upon me. I had been introduced to a gentleman by name of Keats: a merchant, thriving and much respected, a resident there for many years—by birth an Englishman." The new acquaintance "exerted himself strenuously to seek patrons" for Payne's publication; and at length "and through a third person" Payne learned that this man was a brother of the poet John Keats.

"There was no ostentation of literature, no attempt at conversational parade," about the American Keats. "He was manly but modest; and rather disclaimed the least pretension to regard, excepting as a man of business, a person devoted to the best interests of his adopted country. . . . When I conversed with him upon the subject of his famous brother, I found him ardently attached to the memory of that gifted but ill-starred enthusiast. . . . I do not know when I have enjoyed a greater treat than I did one evening at the home of George Keats, when he indulged me with a glance at the private correspondence, including much of the unpublished poetry, of that distinguished brother."

The four unpublished poems, which George Keats gave to Payne include two sonnets, "As Hermes Once Took to His Feathers Light" and "Fame Like a Wayward Girl"; a lyric, "Hither, Hither, Love"; and a poem of greater length, not easily classifiable, that might be called a prophecy in verse. This had been sent to George Keats in a letter from his brother with the remark: "If I had a prayer to make it would be that one of your children should be the first American poet." John Keats, Payne says, was, remarkably, "not aware that we had ever possessed a poet."

Of the poetic gems by the great Keats here discovered by Payne, he remarks that they "seem to have been brought forth without an effort, as if, in the rapid scribbling of a letter, the writer's mind had unconsciously and involuntarily flowed into poetry . . . not in the least aware that he had just given forth treasures which might last as long as 'his hand's language.' " The lyric, "Hither, Hither, Love" Payne calls "a specimen of one of these unpublished effusions in the handwriting of John Keats, just scribbled as if playing with his pen, in lines sometimes crooked, sometimes straight, sometimes with a few words blurred out by his finger before the ink was dry." [81]

Payne sent copies of the August *Ladies' Companion* to friends far and near, and as a result of his contributions, new subscriptions came pouring in. The publisher and his new associate editor, however, had already become mutually dissatisfied. Payne wrote a friend that he was paid nothing after the first four weeks. [82] The September issue contained considerably less of his work, and on the cover of the October number appeared a notice by Snowden: "Mr. Payne never held the slightest control over the pages of this work."

Obviously, whatever his other grievances may have been, the publisher resented the industry of a contributing editor who so completely stole the show. Snowden could not realize, of course, that through the Keats piece alone Payne had made a collectors' item of at least one number of a periodical, whose other early issues had little to distinguish them.

About the time of the *Ladies' Companion* incident a new monthly, the *Democratic Review,* was being launched in Washington. The editor, John Louis O'Sullivan, had offered Payne $960 for his *Jam Jehan Nima* subscription list; and although this was refused, Payne accepted an incidental offer to become a contributor. The February and March 1838 issues of this magazine contain his two-part essay commemorating the life and achievements of William Martin Johnson, an American poet, whose writings were never elsewhere published or recognized.

The subject of this piece, though poor materially, was richly endowed mentally, and in him Payne felt that he had discovered an authentic poet. The excerpts from Johnson's writing, incorporated in the article, have not only aesthetic merit but also a tang and sophistication that might even appeal to modern readers.[83] In this "slight but tardy attempt to rescue from oblivion one entitled to remembrance by the double right of genius and misfortune" Payne revealed his own intellectual independence and natural gift for expression. As Johnson, when he first came to Payne's attention, had been living in East Hampton, the second half of the essay is in the main a leisurely and gently humorous tribute to that village and its folkways, which makes it a work that either of Payne's famous friends, Lamb or Irving, might well have been willing to own.

This engaging piece was intended as the first of a series entitled *Our Neglected Poets.* The second was to have been on G. Blauvelt, Payne's early New York friend, long since deceased, of whose poetic work little was ever published. The Blauvelt article and several others were written and submitted as agreed, but they were never printed. Apparently the magazine was not able to meet Payne's moderate suggestion for payment: "16 pages a month at $50 a month for half a year." [84]

Inspirited no doubt by rediscovery of his largely latent literary powers, Payne during 1838 revived efforts to bring out in book form his *Life of Jesus*, apparently written some ten years earlier in Paris. There is this line in his New York diary of September 30, 1838: "Called at Hingston's, spoke of my Life of the Savior." [85]

Evidence that this work had been a product of that energetic Paris period which brought forth *Clari* and a dozen adapted plays is contained in a letter from Irving in Paris to Payne in London, dated November 1823: "As to your Life of Christ, you have chosen the wrong market for it. Murray is one of the best and worst of publishers. When you bring him a name that will command a market, he is prompt and liberal in his dealings, but he is otherwise apt to hold manuscripts in hand without giving any reply, for weeks and months, and to treat authors with neglect and almost rudeness." [86]

Irving's reference here is to the influential and ruthless John Murray of London, publisher not only of books, but also of the *Quarterly Review* (incidentally the magazine credited with having caused the death of Keats by the malevolence of its criticism of *Endymion*).

From Irving's comment we may assume that Murray had rejected Payne's book on the life of Jesus as early as 1823. Two years later Payne probably had the manuscript in Paris when he was visited there by his American friend, John Gorham Palfrey. Since Palfrey was a minister, the work may have been shown to him then. At all events, it was Palfrey who recorded years later that Payne's *Life of Jesus* was "beautifully executed on the common theory of the three years' duration of the ministry of Jesus." [87] As Palfrey, later editor of the *North American Review*, was a man of exacting literary standards, his comment makes it regrettable that this work seems to have been lost.

Of general interests and activities, and the personal side of Payne's life in this New York period, we have a few glimpses through letters and the pages of his diary. We learn that for him this was a time of soul-searching. Often attending services at Trinity Church with his sister Lucy, he considered "taking the Sacrament," but hesitated.

> I felt a degree of uneasiness at my conduct in relation to the Sacrament . . . reflected upon my waywardness and inconsistency . . . pondered my

moral escapes and the glimpses of a New Heaven and a New Earth which now and then have broken in on me through the clouds in which my soul so long has dwelt . . . prayed that this might be the last time I should turn my back on the Holy Sacrament.

Then there were friends and social activities. With his sisters he went to an evening reception at the Palmer home, 15 Waverly Place —"the street crammed with carriages and houses magnificent with lights." "Anna and Lucy looked well," but Howard felt out of place, being "the only one with a white stock."

On a Broadway bus he met his old friend Henry Brevoort. "At last his eye rested on me, with the peculiar chuckle of the Irving knot, found especially in Irving, Paulding and Brevoort—a sort of sputtering way of speaking in a chuckle, preceded by a roguish lighting up of the eye."

At the Paynes' in Bond Street, Bryant called to see Thatcher, and Howard observed the poet's hat "filled with papers, in the passageway." Bryant "lolled back in his chair with his head thrown back and his eyes looking up" and Thatcher "sprawled full-length in his 3-cornered chair, listening to Bryant's stories of Italy."[88]

Little Eloise was now five years old—a lovely child, "with a disposition to match her sunny hair." When she went with her mother to Newport, Uncle Howard wrote his small but appreciative relative about an interesting new acquisition at 30 Bond:

> We've a frisky gray kitten come to live here. She runs around such a while after her tail, and when she catches the end of it in her mouth, she flings herself down and rolls over and over, coiled up like a ball, then springs into the air and lifting her back to a high crook, gallops off sideways, laughing.
>
> She dashes so merrily into the breakfast room when breakfast, dinner or teatime comes! Pussy! Why are you staring at me now and saying "Mew-mew-meauew"? Yes—I understand. In Cat, that means, give my love to your little niece and tell her I'd love to have a frolic with her.[89]

Yes, Payne had recovered his equanimity after the disturbing Cherokee adventure: that is evident. But he had by no means lost interest in the Cherokee cause, even after that cause, for all practical ends, had been lost. During those years back in New York, while engaged in so many other matters, he was constantly building up and enlarging his plan for an extensive history of the tribe. Although apparently only the first section of the history was completed —and that, perhaps a tentative draft, has not been preserved—we have today many volumes of his manuscript notes for this work: further impressive proof of his industry.

[5]

CHEROKEES EAST AND WEST

SUMMONED by John Ross early in 1838, Payne, for the first time since returning from the South, journeyed to the nation's capital.

Thanks to new steam and rail transportation, the trip from New York to Washington could now be accomplished with a speed heretofore unheard of. It was a complicated process, however, and concerning it Payne provided data that could hardly have been more precise had he been consciously contributing to a history of travel for the period:

> Washington City, Fuller's Hotel
> February 27, 1838

Dear Thatcher:

Left New York at 5:20 by steamer from foot of Broad Street. . . . Reached Philadelphia before 2 . . . rested till 7:30 a.m., when omnibus took me to Market Street for tickets and another omnibus to R.R. depot, where cars started at 9 and reached Baltimore at 3. . . .

New York to Philadelphia, 8 hours and 20 minutes; Philadelphia to Baltimore, 7 hours and 30 minutes; Baltimore to Washington, 2 hours, 55 minutes. 18 hours, 45 minutes traveling, after getting train tickets. Numbered tins are placed on every piece of baggage and also tins in your pocket, corresponding. . . . The express mail to Philadelphia, $5. Omnibus to Market Street, 50 cents. Fare to Baltimore, $4; from Baltimore to Washington, $2.50. Tea, supper, a night's lodging and dinner besides.

The administration of Martin Van Buren as President was then completing its first year, and at the White House the anniversary of the Father of His Country was duly celebrated with "a birth-night ball on the 22nd," which Payne briefly described:

> Luckily I went provided with my purse, for much to my surprise, found I had $5 to pay, notwithstanding I went by invitation.
>
> Mr. Webster was in high spirits, his daughter with him. I was introduced to Mr. Clay. . . . Presently there was a flourish of trumpets and folding doors flew open, and Mr. Van Buren entered, and passed to the center of the room to triumphal march, bowing. He stood for a while elevated upon a platform at the upper end of the room, and subsequently came down and flirted with the ladies.

Outside official circles there was interesting activity in the capital:

> Morse is here and has been showing his telegraph with great success. The government is paying the expense of a large experiment. Also a young man with a vast improvement in application of the electro-magnetic principle to the propulsion of boats, machinery, etc.; another inventor with a flying machine. . . . Forrest is announced to play a few nights.

All such interesting contemporary matters, however, were secondary to the still unsettled affairs of the Cherokees. He had come to help Ross prepare statements that would enable the tribe to accept removal to the West, now that removal was inevitable, but without acceptance of the false treaty; also "to place the management of emigration and the location of future residence under the direction and control of the Cherokees themselves."

To obtain Payne's aid, Ross had written: "If it will not seriously interfere with your literary engagements in New York by coming to Washington, I hope to have the pleasure of seeing you. . . . As to your expenses in coming, staying and returning . . . I will cheerfully defray them, and consider it but a feather in the scale of importance of your being here. . . . You will please accept a small check herewith enclosed and apply it to your own benefit." [90]

The small check was for $100—an amount not so small in those days. Payne remained in Washington throughout the spring and early summer and aided Ross by writing numerous letters to the press and preparing various papers for the Cherokees' official use. [91] The most famous Cherokee document presented to Congress that year, the memorial dated February 22, 1838, and signed by 15,656 members of the tribe, was probably composed largely by Payne. This eloquent plea, opening with the line "Our only fortress is the justice of our cause, our only appeal on earth is to your tribunal," was "laid on the table in the Senate and referred to the Committee on Indian Affairs of the House"; but the question of Indian removal became a hotly debated one in that Congressional session.

Of his other contributions to the cause Howard wrote his brother in April:

> I have drawn up a treaty which is to be submitted as one which they [the Cherokees] are ready to sign at once, ceding the territory forever and arranging for removal, but not likely to be accepted by Van Buren. . . . I am keeping up with the Cherokee question in Boston, New York and Philadelphia, besides managing most of the official correspondence here. Indeed, I believe I write nearly all that appears upon the subject, either diplomatic, epistolary or editorial.

A few months later (on July 1) Howard reported to Thatcher on "termination of the Cherokee matter. . . . Mr. Ross and delegation left last evening, he satisfied with the prospects created by the position he had contrived to create."

Although he had "worked pretty hard and that without expectation of more than expenses," Howard was able to report to his brother that Ross, on departing, had stated that "they would leave me what they could spare just now, and put ten $100 bills on the table, saying that my time ought to be paid for." Thus Payne, for his past work for the Cherokees and a good deal that he would do in the future, received payment which he declared "munificent considering immense claims on means comparatively small."

The last communication which he prepared for the Cherokees that year, Payne told his brother, was "sealed with the seal given me by Aunt Esther—her father's seal. I told Ross my grandfather was a Jew, and if they [the American Indians] were part of the Ten Tribes [a theory of some ethnologists] the stamp would be part of the family arms—an omen of our all coming together at last." [92]

Back in New York, Payne devoted a year or more to the literary labors already described, but the spring of 1840 found him again in "Washington City" [93] on business even more serious than that of the earlier visit. Again he had come at the urging of Ross, who since their last meeting had made a trip to the Western country. It had been a saddening experience. Cholera and the exposures of the journey had made awful inroads on the emigrants. The once proud and prosperous tribe were now not only decimated, but, robbed of their possessions and driven from their homes, had to some degree deteriorated.

The time had passed for appeals and petitions. Now Ross felt that the need was for "the protection of the rights of the Cherokees from illegal encroachments and destruction." On New Year's day 1840 he had written Payne: "The Cherokees greatly need your aid. I am fully persuaded that you could render essential service at this time, therefore I should be happy to have your talented pen employed." [94]

Payne was fully aware of the changed situation. Though realizing the futility of contending "against the power arrayed to crush the Cherokees," he wrote:

> I hold it a duty to let the world know all the circumstances of their removal. That such acts can pass unreproved by Providence, at some time, the entire history of the world forbids us to expect, and posterity ought to be possessed of the means of seeing *why* the heavy blow falls on them.[95]

Under Van Buren there was a new Secretary of War, Joel R. Poinsett, traveler and statesman now chiefly remembered for the red, white, and green Christmas plant discovered by and named for him. Poinsett, though a humane and kindly man, was adamant in enforcing Indian removal. Hence important communications from Ross to Poinsett about the further conditions of removal, had to be written; and Payne's "talented pen" was kept busy.

In August of 1840 we hear again of Poinsett, when "under hand and seal of the War Department," his name is signed to a brief but interesting document:

> John Howard Payne, having signified to the Department, his desire to visit the Indian Territory west of the Mississippi for the purpose of acquiring information respecting the history of the Indian tribes, and requested the permission required to enable him to do so, such permission is hereby granted, and he is commended to the friendly attention of civil and military agents, officers and citizens.[96]

Except for missionaries and soldiers, Payne was perhaps the earliest white visitor to the new homeland of the Indians. On this journey to the Cherokee Nation West he accompanied Ross and a group of tribal leaders; and oddly enough, the trip to what is now Oklahoma was made by way of New Orleans.[97]

Payne returned briefly to New York to prepare for the new adventure. It was now four years since the press of his home town had pilloried him, and in the interval public sentiment regarding him apparently had undergone a change. He reported that "everyone seemed delighted to see me, and so many came to see me depart that it almost made me apprehend some misfortune yet 'hanging in the stars.' "

Leaving New York on September 1, he journeyed, again by boat, to Philadelphia, and had as traveling companion another American celebrity. "An extremely agreeable time all the way with Audubon," he reported to his brother, and, in more detail, to George Watterston, the man lately appointed to the newly created post of Librarian of Congress:

> I had a very agreeable companion from New York today in Audubon, who came hither to look after his reduced copy of the Ornithology. He tells me he employs 50 persons here, young men and women, to color his prints, and pays $240 a week for the work, but he adds that he finds the enterprise growing profitable notwithstanding the vast expense.[98]

The rest of the Western journey, even the trip to New Orleans, was strenuous. The party "traveled most uncomfortably day and night by railroads and their connecting stages and omnibusses to Wilmington, North Carolina, then Charleston, then Augusta." From New Orleans, on September 15, Payne wrote: "Here we *begin* our journey West, having been delayed 2½ days and 2 nights on way. Travelling very oppressive, bad roads, bad appointments of every sort, but have met old friends, who made my time pass most agreeably. Here I have not had a moment to myself. . . . Off in 2 hours on board steamboat, Flying Dutchman, which leaves at the mouth of Arkansas." [99]

Ross and his party reached the new Cherokee homeland the middle of October, and Payne, the observer, was at once obliged to admit that although this country was unlike the old, the Indians, from the standpoint of naturally beautiful surroundings, had not been cheated. The whole new territory he found "beautifully varied and picturesque, the country elevated and undulating."

> Here appears a small forest, there a wide prairie, swelling into numerous knolls, which are often surmounted by trees, grouped as gracefully as if set there by a landscape gardener for effect. These lovely prairies sometimes . . . are hemmed around by timber, descending to the vales below; sometimes the ring of wildwood ascends gently to a great height and so shuts in the prospect with an amphitheatre of leafy eminences, and sometimes the eye may wander over an extent apparently boundless, with nothing before it but a grassy surface of treeless levels and mounds and hills, of every shape and size.
>
> The region seems like one which has just been richly peopled, but, by some witchcraft, despoiled of a sudden of the tasteful abodes and population. It has nowhere that I have been, the aspect of a land yet untouched by plough or human footstep . . . yet mostly it is.[100]

Now the people were assembling for the first Cherokee Council in the Indian Territory, "an ever-moving multitude of men, women and children, of all complexions and costumes, and of Indians from various tribes."

Three rude edifices had been constructed: a dwarf log house for the National Council or Senate, a larger one for the Representatives, and the largest, a simple roofed area "with logs laid for benches and an ample pulpit of rough boards," which was the general meeting hall. Nearby, at tables "laid under sheds of boughs," the people were fed "at public cost," and "the highest sat with the lowest" in "the perfect republicanism of the Council Grounds."

In one respect a forerunner of the United Nations, this large general assembly was conducted bilingually. John Ross addressed the crowd in English, pausing at the end of every sentence for translation into Cherokee by an interpreter. Ross "might have been his own interpreter," but chose this method "to avoid suspicion of change or concealment."

Payne remained about three months at the new home of the Cherokees; and though he later declared, "the main object of my mission thither, to obtain historical material, has not been much advanced," [101] his observations would provide colorful material for any history of the tribe.

The people were as yet unsettled: "everyone engrossed by personal affairs—putting up cabins, fencing, farming and so on. Perhaps under any circumstances," he further remarked, "few among them would feel the value of 'that second life in others' breath,' which atones, in some minds, for the infelicities of the first life in our own." [102]

Ross, long a widower, had left his daughter in school in the East,[103] but had his youngest child, a boy, with him. It seems fortunate that there was no wifely order to be disturbed by the peculiar kind of home life in the wild, new country, where the chief was not only director and adviser, but host at all times to his uprooted tribesmen. His house, Park Hill, which, for all its poetic name, was nearly as humble as his Tennessee cabin had been, was a free tavern, open to any and all comers day and night. "No door is fastened. Every apartment is open to everyone indifferently. There is no lack of dirt anywhere, but those who are particular can choose the cleanest. Mr. Ross and I occupy as our sleeping room and study the demi-floor of the log house, up to which there stalks every now and then, a silent Indian, stands a while and then stalks down again." [104]

Though Ross had been "joyfully received" on his return, there were those among the people who blamed his long resistance to removal for the impoverished condition in which they now found themselves. Furthermore some of the spirit of the old anti-Ross faction was still alive, and among the inhabitants of the new Nation were most of the men who, from various motives, had signed the false treaty. Payne observed:

> With some reprobates about, sometimes an extra gun is set quietly in the bedroom, and Mr. Ross . . . hints occasionally in the softest accents imaginable that perhaps the charges in the pistol may as well be looked at . . . and as the door stands open for any to enter at any hour, there is no knowing who may be coming up the pasageway.
>
> Then he will lay a chair across the top of the stairway and add, "At any rate, there's a stumbling block if anyone mounts this way in the dark." When suspicious noises, like the tramp of a horse, are heard in the night, he gets up and looks out and watches. I do not apprehend that we are in any danger, however, unless from a shot in traveling through places where persons could hide behind logs or bushes.[105]

In a letter to his sister-in-law Payne, in some amusement, re-marked "much in the manners and morals of the people to make a staid East Hamptoner, such as I am, stare."

Downstairs, there are two 4-post beds in each of the two main rooms; and at night they are always occupied. If these are insufficient for the guests, beds are spread in the center, or those who have blankets spread them; and the rooms once fitted, an open passage between the 2 is blanketed over by the remaining visitors. . . .

Men, women and children thus lodge indiscriminately; and as I gather myself in my own bed I hear them laughing and talking themselves to sleep, and in the morning the bass and treble tongues tune up again, and some one seems by common consent to be the joker for the rest, and a grave voice cackles on a while, then all the listeners laugh and the grave voice resumes and is again succeeded by the laugh.

Food, as well as sleeping room, was free at Park Hill.

At meals as many as the table can accommodate sit down indiscrimi-nately; and outside the door, which always stands open, 2 or 3 dogs are intently eyeing the table . . . and Indians in their blankets, as earnestly watching in silence and waiting their turn to be invited in. Thus set after set is summoned until all are satisfied. The housekeeper never knows whether she has to lodge and keep 25 or 50, or double the number; but the guests seldom fall below 5 and 20.[106]

Next to the annual Council the most notable event of the tribe's first year in the Indian Territory was the trial of a prominent Cherokee for the murder of a fellow tribesman.[107] Archilla Smith, the man accused, convicted, and eventually hanged, Payne described as "tall, reckless and violent; expert with rifle and ready with toma-hawk and knife."

As the transplanted Nation had not yet had time or money to build a courthouse, the trial was held in a log hut eighteen feet square, with bare dirt floor. Though it was conducted with extreme infor-mality—the jurors, their guns ever ready, playing cards with the prisoner and sometimes asking to borrow his pipe—Payne found that the case was tried "according to the rules of evidence" and that "the principles of justice and reason, borrowed from the white man's body of laws were scrupulously applied." Jail was lacking as well as courthouse, and Archilla Smith, both before and after his conviction, rode his horse, apparently at liberty, but actually always accompanied by a guard.

Though a signer of the false treaty and hence an enemy of Ross, the prisoner came twice to Park Hill and both times sat at the crowded board with the other guests. Once he brought his three young sons with him; they were "treated affectionately," and one of them "went out to play with the Principal Chief's son."

After the trial and conviction, John Ross was "surprised just before dinner time one day to see a whole cavalcade, with Archilla at its head, ride up to the gate." He had come this time to beg the chief's intervention to prevent the carrying out of the death penalty. Though Ross declared that he "had no discretionary power whatever," the condemned man "determined to stay to dinner." After looking over some pages of the New Testament in Cherokee, he sat down with the rest, and "no man ate more heartily or unconcernedly than he." After dinner he "shook hands all around and departed." [108]

Payne regarded as the high point of his sojourn with the Cherokees the visit to Park Hill of George Guess, or Sequoyah, as he was more commonly called—the famed inventor of the Cherokee syllabary.[109]

On the first visit to Ross, Payne had obtained what information he could about Sequoyah. There, in the Tennessee cabin one evening during the October 1835 Council, "with the place full of Indians," the main events of Sequoyah's life had been related to Payne, and "many who knew the facts, confirmed them as the interpreters proceeded." [110]

Now Sequoyah was an old man. He had gone West several years ahead of the rest of the tribe, and here Payne looked forward to seeing the celebrity himself and probably adding materially to the somewhat meager information obtained from others five years earlier. When Sequoyah arrived at Park Hill he was accompanied by an interpreter, and with that man's help Payne gleaned a few more facts. "Then he told me there were some ancient memories of the past which I ought by all means to gather. I begged him to communicate them and he said he would.

"We were all in the cock-loft of Mr. Ross's story and a half house. . . . Guess [Sequoyah] sat in one corner by the fireplace

and I on the opposite side at a desk, and the two others in between."
The interpreter "was equally anxious with myself to hear, for the
Cherokees know little about their own annals."

> Sequoya's air was what we picture to ourselves as that of an old Greek
> philosopher. He talked and gesticulated gracefully, his voice alternately
> swelling and then sinking into a whisper, and his eye firing up and then
> its wild flashes subsiding into a gentle and benignant smile.
>
> He had a turban of roses and posies upon a white ground, girding his
> venerable gray hairs; a long, dark robe, bordered around the lower edge
> and cuffs with black; a blue and white minutely-checked calico tunic,
> beaded belt, large wooden-handled knife in tough leather case, a long,
> dusky-white bag of sumac, and long Indian pipe, which he replenished
> and smoked incessantly. . . . One of his legs is lame and shrunken, and
> he wore plain buckskin leggings, one of deeper hue than the other.

The interpreter, or "linkster"—the more usual Amerindian term
of the time—was "a short, thin, long-visaged, deep-voiced personage,
covered with what had once been a 'whity-brown' overcoat, with
vast bone buttons, some of which remained, while the fragments of
the coat draped him . . . in fantastic shapes innumerable."

Payne had ample time to observe these details, for it was deemed
best not to break the old man's train of thought by interruption.
There would be a long series of sounds something like "Okee tester-
ragy tertemirgy ooshahler chucking o-ooo-o-ogby."

"Three-fourths of an hour passed, then half an hour, but no translation." At last, "after a whole evening of fidgeting," Payne was
told by the interpreter that "it was all about the sending of some
wampum belts to various tribes." Exasperated, he asked to have the
story amplified next day. Sequoyah agreed, but when morning came
he had sunk into a reserve that Payne found characteristic of the
Indians. Here the great man was typical, and nothing more could
be coaxed out of him.[111]

Late in December 1840 Payne left the Cherokee country and made
on the return trip a brief stop at the home of some missionaries.
They were better sources of historical and tribal information than
the Cherokees themselves.[112]

As to this journey of exploration, he felt that its "best objects

[were] imperfectly realized." Even so, he had succeeded in gleaning some rare information never before recorded. His brief and, to him, most disappointing sketch of Sequoyah adds much to the all too scanty knowledge of that man, himself almost illiterate, whose unaided invention of a workable system for reducing a spoken language to a written one has been ranked with "the great intellectual feats of all time."

Payne's two long letters descriptive of the murder trial, later published in the New York *Journal of Commerce* and in book form, contain unique and valuable information. And his observations and comments on Cherokee customs and costumes, like his account of the Green Corn Dance of the Creeks, are regarded as important by ethnologists and historians.

All this ranks among his major achievements. But it fell so far short of his expectations at the time that he "felt something like one who has traveled a couple of thousand miles to plant and plough 5000 acres, and reap one single ear of corn." [113]

[6]

ENTR'ACTE: WASHINGTON AND NEW YORK

"I AM GLAD you like President Harrison," Payne, from Washington, wrote his six-year-old niece on March 29, 1841. "If ever I get a chance, I will tell him and know he will be pleased. He is very good and kind. I traveled with him . . . when he came on to be made President, and he did not remember that he knew me; but since he has got to be President, he has heard that I was myself and sent for me to come and receive his apologies for not having been aware of that when he saw me in the railroad car."

The message of little Eloise to the new executive, however, was never to be delivered, for less than a week after Uncle Howard's letter was written, President William Henry Harrison died. He had been in office just one month. [114]

Harrison, the ninth President, was the first to die in office. There was some dispute over the question of succession, but it was soon decided that the Constitution was clear on that point. Vice-President John Tyler, the Virginian who had been given second place on the ticket "to placate the Southern Whigs," [115] became President; and thus was established the system ever since taken for granted.

What may have been Payne's acquaintance with Harrison is not further recorded. But he had first known John Tyler when they both were boys in their late teens. At the time the eighteen-year-old Payne made his first Southern tour John Tyler, then nineteen, was a law student in the Richmond office of the distinguished Edmund Randolph, who had been Attorney General under Washington. Tyler's father, then governor of Virginia, was so pleased with "Young Roscius" as to "extend to him an invitation to dine at the gubernatorial mansion, with a distinguished company, especially invited to meet him." [116]

Whether or not his acquaintance with the Tyler family had continued through the years, it was revived in Washington, as witness a friendly note of Payne to President Tyler's son nearly a year after the beginning of the new administration:

John Tyler, Jr., Esq.
  at the President's, Washington

My dear Sir: You said the other night at the Assembly that you would come over and sit with me, if I would tell you when I was sure to be at home. I am at home this evening and wish particularly to have a chat. Can you drop in? I am in F Street, opposite Gen. Hunter's (the District Marshal), and next to Gen. Towsen's—the first of two entrances to a wooden White House. Do come.

Yours ever,
J. H. P.[117]

At the time of Tyler's accession in April 1841 Payne had but lately returned from the Indian Territory. His articles in the *Journal of Commerce* and *National Intelligencer* had established him as an authority on Indian matters, and his activities for the next few months continued to be centered about the Cherokees.

The War Department needed a man "to study the former treaties made with the Cherokee Indians, with reference to their rights under the treaty of 1835 and the liability of the United States in case of the claim of the Indians arising under it." [118] Payne easily qualified and was appointed to the post at a salary of $1600 a year—a fairly good salary for the day.

Here, however, his experience was such that he soon worked himself out of a job. "When he made his report the next year he was informed that his work had been so well done that the business could be managed by the regular force of the Indian Bureau." The Commissioner of Indian Affairs was "directed to communicate freely with Mr. Payne and make himself familiar with all details on which he had been employed." Once more he found himself without settled employment, but as regular jobs are irksome to those of his temperament, he probably felt no very great regret except for withdrawal of the pay check.

Even in those days Congressional committees investigated many matters of public concern, and Payne is known to have been called to testify before the House Committee on Indian Affairs. He was asked among other things if he had been paid by the government while in the employ of John Ross; and of course replied that he had not.[119]

In New York in the meantime Payne's family was sharing the excitement caused by the first American visit of Charles Dickens. Though Dickens was then only thirty years old and the greater part of his creative work lay ahead of him, he had published *Sketches by Boz, Pickwick Papers* and *Oliver Twist*, and they had made him so celebrated abroad that Americans vied for the honor of entertaining him. A great "Boz ball" at the Park Theatre, with "gorgeous" appointments and twelve *tableaux vivants* representing Dickens characters and works, led off the New York festivities.[120] This was followed by a public dinner; and later Lucy wrote Howard that "Thatcher and Elizabeth were invited to an evening party at the Bryants', where they were introduced to Mr. and Mrs. Dickens."

Payne had known Dickens in England. The distinguished young writer, also something of an actor, had put on amateur performances of *Clari* in which he himself played a leading part. Although at the time of his American visit Dickens required no introduction, Payne had written tendering his good offices [121] and had received a cordial reply. And Thatcher, after meeting the great man at the Bryants' "small party," wrote his brother: "He told me he had received a letter from you while he was in Boston and expected to see you in Washington."

Howard would have had cause for gratification had he known that Dickens, during the American visit, "bought an accordion . . . and played 'Home, Sweet Home' on it every night, to himself and Kate [his wife] with great expression and a pleasant feeling of sadness." [122] This may have provided an antidote for the too great cordiality of his welcome.

Dickens, according to Thatcher, seemed "to have done all in his power to allay the fever excited by his presence; and I think has shown great good sense in withdrawing himself from public festivities since leaving here. The mania was at its highest here, and I should think would have been extremely tiresome to him, besides defeating all rational objects he may have in visiting us." The real object of the visit, in Thatcher's opinion, was "the copyright matter, a case of clear right, but as hopeless, I should think, as that of the African or Indian."

About the time of the Dickens visit New Yorkers were considerably worked up over another and less happy affair, the sensational trial of one John Caldwell Colt, bookseller and occasional author, for the murder of a local printer, Samuel Adams (apparently no connection of the eminent Bostonian of the same name).

Payne had a double interest in this trial. As an ardent bibliophile he had been a frequent customer at a bookstore that the accused had formerly kept in New York. And in both New York and Washington Payne, for some time, had known the defendant's younger brother, Samuel Colt,[123] inventor-to-be of the famous revolver. Samuel Colt, in addition to his work with firearms, had made experiments with laughing gas and was one of the pioneer inventors of the submarine. Through assisting him with introductions and publicity—and no doubt with money too, when he had any himself—Payne had acquired an interest in the various inventions,[124] though the great eventual success of the most productive one, the revolver, came too late to profit him.

The unfortunate John Caldwell Colt, like his brother, was of the ingenious sort, and besides dealing in rare books he had written and lectured on such disparate topics as chemistry and accounting. Aged thirty-two when tragedy overtook him, he had just completed a text-book on bookkeeping, and it was in a quarrel over money matters connected with this work that Adams was killed. John Colt eventually confessed to the murder, but declared that he had acted in self-defense.[125]

The trial was a sensational one, with "ladies barred from the courtroom" [126] when Colt's common-law wife, mother of their infant son, was called to the stand. In the absence of photography, which was just around the corner but had not yet arrived, the press had artists on hand to sketch the principals. Colt was of course convicted, but many persons urged commutation of the death sentence.

Payne had had a high opinion of this Colt brother, and had supplied him with many letters of introduction on his departure for New Orleans a few years earlier. These referred to him as "a valued friend" and "a perfectly just and honorable man." [127] Now Payne made a special trip from Washington to appear as a character wit-ness at Colt's trial [128] and also wrote a plea for his friend, which was published in the Alexandria *Index*. That extolled the man's pre-viously good conduct and described his respectable connections and excellent family background, with ancestry traceable to the Coult line, English peers.[129] But nothing could save the ruined Colt, who, on the eve of the day set for his execution, wrote a touching letter of thanks:

Mr. John Howard Payne, Esq.
My dear Friend:

I have long had a great deal to say for your kindness. But I have been expecting you from Washington for months back, and consequently neg-lected to write. Besides, I am a poor hand to write to those I esteem most. My dear friend, I owe you everything for the able history you gave of me. I have no means to make you conscious of it. . . . I hear you are in town, and fear you will not come to see me, so write this to say at parting, Good bye, God bless you, my dear friend, God bless you. We will meet in Heaven. From your unfortunate friend, J. C. Colt.[130]

As Colt supposed, Payne by that time had again returned to New York, and he did perform the dreadful duty of calling at the prison house the morning after receiving this letter. There he found himself involved in more than a farewell to the condemned. The *Evening Post* tells what happened:

Colt was visited by several persons during the forenoon, and about 12 o'clock Samuel Colt, accompanied by Caroline Henshaw, his [J. C. Colt's] mistress, went to his cell, and at his urgent request, the Rev. Mr. Anthon [131] united the ill-fated and wretched man with that female in the holy bonds of matrimony. Messrs. John Howard Payne, David Graham, Justice Merritt, the Sheriff, Robert Emmett [Colt's attorney] and his brother, Samuel Colt, being present to witness the ceremony.[132]

The sad ceremonial ended, Colt's request that he be left alone was granted. Four hours later, at the awful time appointed, the "vast assemblage of persons outside the prison" dispersed in disappointment. There was no execution for them to witness, for Colt had managed to cheat the hangman by stabbing himself through the heart.

It was not the climax of the terrible Colt matter that had brought Payne back to New York. He had come to complete arrangements for a new assignment. The question of what he should do next, which had agitated him since termination of the War Department job, had finally been answered by his appointment as United States consul to Tunis. This of course had been effected, perhaps easily, by his friend President Tyler, but because of technicalities it had been long pending.

On September 4, however, Howard was able to write to his sister Anna: "My confirmation occurred on the 23rd [of August, 1842]. Support came from both parties and the prevailing impression is that I am permanently provided for. The place is not exactly what I would have chosen, but as the only salaried consulate, and a diplomatic, not a commercial, appointment it is considered here as greatly desirable. It pays $2000 a year without outfit or perquisites. My commission is signed, sealed and countersigned, but not delivered."

Simultaneously with the appointment had come another honor, and this he described facetiously to Anna: "Do you know I am a

colonel? [I'm colonel] on the Staff of the 4th Division of Infantry
of the Militia of the State of New York, under command of General
Aaron Ward. . . . All officers and soldiers under my command
are required to be obedient to my orders and diligent in the exercise of their several duties!" Furthermore, he is "now authorized
to wear two epaulettes and to draw a sword and spear."

Though he might poke fun at himself as a military man, there
is evidence that Payne took his new governmental appointment seriously. He entered upon it with a sincere desire to serve his country
well.

Wishing also to "do the cause of the President some service," he
felt that this could be effected by writing an authentic article about
him—a thorough and factual article, as free as possible from gar-
bling and false emphasis. As a means to this end he wrote the President's daughter-in-law, Mrs. Robert Tyler, for "certain memoranda"
for which he had "teazed her husband and brother-in-law in vain." [138]

President Tyler's wife had died during his first year in office, and
the charming young wife of his eldest son had become hostess at
the White House. As she was Priscilla Cooper, a daughter of the
actor Thomas Abthorpe Cooper and the lamented Mary Fairlie, both
associates of Payne's boyhood, he may be said to have known Mrs.
Robert Tyler since before she was born. Nevertheless he addressed
her formally as "My dear Mrs. Tyler" and, promising before his
departure "to visit the mansion, where I owe all affection and allegiance," subscribed himself "faithfully and respectfully your obedient friend and servant." It is not known whether Priscilla supplied
the requested data or whether the article was ever written.

What may seem the most important aim on Payne's part at the
time of accepting the new post was expressed in his first official letter
to the Secretary of State. That was so to plan the necessary journey
as to investigate "the new sources of trade proposed to be opened
for the United States with the coast of Barbary, and especially
Tunis." For this he selected the brig *Glide*, "a vessel destined for
a voyage of experiment and inquiry." His luggage was put aboard
the brig, but after many weeks of waiting "litigation made it necessary to transfer the cargo" to the *Fidelia*, a ship sailing by way of

France and England. The new vessel was the smaller of the two, but contained "much better accommodations" and had "a high character for swift sailing." [134]

Again writing to Anna, who by this time had gone to Boston, Howard succinctly described this period of delay: "I really begin to feel ashamed to show my face in the street and hear the so often reiterated, 'What, not gone yet?'" In this same letter he recalled his sensations on seeing Anna depart by boat for Boston: "A rush of recollections of the past, bringing up the entire history of our lives and of our whole family, and all our vicissitudes, until I became wrought up almost into an agony."

It was on February 11, 1843 that Payne finally embarked on the Tunis adventure. He was fifty-one years old.

[7]

MISSION TO TUNIS

THE UNITED STATES had maintained a diplomatic representative in Tunis since the beginning of the nineteenth century.[135] The office, in fact, had been established before conclusion of the famous Tripolitan wars, in which ships of the young American republic defeated the ancient Barbary powers and thus helped to end the practice of piracy in the Mediterranean.

When Payne took it over, the United States consulate in the city and country of Tunis—the name Tunisia not yet adopted—had greatly deteriorated. Indeed, the position by that time might have been regarded—according to the inclinations of the incumbent—as a sinecure, an opportunity for graft, or, because of neglect of office and premises, an almost hopeless burden.

Of his two most recent predecessors, one had spent his time in Italy,[136] leaving affairs at the consulate in charge of a young clerk. The other had made the job financially worth while by lending money at high interest: a crime in Mohammedan countries but "one of the abuses of the consular power well understood in Tunis." [137]

Payne, throughout his term in office, would remain at his post. He would shun, and endeavor to eradicate, illegal practices; he would draft a plan for the extension of trade between his own and the North African countries; and he would expend great effort— involving differences with the native ruler, the Bey—on a remodeling of the consular residence, that it might be not only habitable, but also "worthy of the dignity of the United States."

Though travel time between the Old World and the New was constantly being lessened, Payne's ship the *Fidelia* touched Havre only after "four winter weeks at sea." From there side trips to London and Paris served to re-acclimate the wanderer to life in foreign lands.

It had been thirty years since, "all buoyant with hope and novelty," he first saw London. Now it all seemed "a strange dream." The city looked "old and changed"; and after the clear air of America "the odor of coal in the air and the dinginess of coal smoke everywhere" combined with "a multitude of recollections and apprehensions" to give him "a sense of uneasiness."

> Throngs of strangers where I used to meet familiar faces, altered streets and buildings. . . . Yet the greater part of London is just as I left it. The same old books seem to be standing in the same old second-hand book shops, with the dust and price marks of 20 years ago.
>
> In one lone street, a blind beggar, playing "Home, Sweet Home" on a flageolet, before a barber shop, where I went in for a shave. . . . At night, when I strolled like an unseen ghost into Drury Lane theatre . . . a full-length statue of Kean, whom, on quitting England, I had left alive. There was a skull in its hand, which pointed to an inscription, "To this complexion must we come at last." The dead, marbled eye of my old acquaintance seemed to rest upon me and his stony lips to direct on me their melancholy smile.

From London, Southampton, and thence to Paris, arriving early of a March morning. "Paris, ever praised for its beauty, is now still greater and more beautiful . . . mighty works set on foot by Napoleon having found their accomplishment." On land he travels by railroad, "all new since I went away," and on water by that other innovation called in America "the Robert Fulton," and in France the "Jean Papin."

And here the traveler pauses to philosophize: "After all, what matters that which we call fame? What matters it, even during life, to any one but the inventor, whether his invention bear his name? . . . The main point is assured when an obtuse world is persuaded to permit a great improvement, either mechanical or moral, to make it healthier or better." [138]

After several days on the Mediterranean, with a stop at Minorca "long enough to get acquainted with everybody," he comes at last to the crescent-shaped harbor of Tunis. On one side rise "wildly picturesque mountains" and on the other the hills of ancient Carthage: Carthage with its many reminiscences of Hannibal and Scipio, of Dido and Aeneas, "where one takes as much interest in verifying the truth of fiction as the truth of history, the poetical one perhaps even more intensely . . . because Virgil has laid the hearts of those he described open before us."

To the considerable amusement of the new consul, his arrival at Tunis was accompanied by military pomp. Twenty-one guns were fired from the harbor port known as the Goletta,[139] and the salute was returned from the consul's vessel, the United States sloop *Preble*.

"The captain and I, in full costume, descended, someone guarding my honorable heels as I let myself down by a rope to the edge of the capering boat. Just as we were clearing the vessel, 'Bang!' went a gun, once more, from the Preble. 'That is for you, sir,' said the captain; whereupon I stood up, as instructed, the captain steadying me on one side and a midshipman on the other." Sentries saluted from along the shore, and the new official finally "stepped on classic ground, rendered the more prosaically commonplace by ragged sailors and work people, and double lines of galley slaves, marching by in chains."

Large four-wheeled cabriolets were waiting to convey the consul and his party to the capital. A picturesque little man who turned out to be the dragoman (interpreter), "with a long, grisly beard and vast mustachios, tall red cap . . . broad sash and immense blue breeches, gathered below the knee, naked calves, Turkish slippers and a large sabre," mounted his charger and galloped on ahead. "We rode and we rode and we rode, two hours in the hot sun. So flat was the way, so silent, so lonely, so treeless, that I might have fancied myself on the American prairie, had there been more vegetation. . . . Two or three loaded camels, a carriage-load of carefully veiled Moorish ladies, beggars, children, must needs all scurry to get out of the way of the official carriage."

At last is seen "the American flag over a tall house . . . and over other houses, flags of European nations," and on the wall of Tunis the Tunisian flag, with the crescent and star—"all raised in honor of the new consul." Then through many gateways to "a high, vaulted place, like a huge cave, where stands a band of musicians. Is not that attempt at 'Hail Columbia'? It is. . . . All the musicians bow and play and play and bow."

A young man, the consul *ad interim,* rises to greet his new chief. "Mr. Gale, I believe?" "Yes, sir." These are the official premises.

But what premises! After the pomp of the entry, something palatial in the way of living quarters might have been expected. Instead —"Dreary indeed seemed everything—a YAHOO of a house! Large and awkwardly arranged. Long, dark passages between thick walls led up into a queer-looking hall, with a sort of skylight apartment opening on three sides, with uncouth doors, half glazed, and massy iron gratings . . . behind these, windows and shutters." The place was further uninviting in that there was "not a comfortable bed in it."

> Some hard wool-mattrasses [sic] and harder than wool-pillows were laid on boards, raised about two feet from the ground. On one of these I sought repose. . . . I looked up at the raftered ceiling . . . and just at the wall-top was a black, irregular blot. My imagination was full of scorpions. . . . After watching the spot till it seemed to move and crawl downward, at last I got to sleep, thinking how the bite of a scorpion might be cured.

After that first uneasy night Payne and his assistant, Mr. W. R. B. Gale, made an inventory of the mansion's furnishings:

1 old marble mantelpiece
1 old chandelier, incomplete

1 very small pier table to stand between windows

1 very old and broken looking-glass with the case of a small clock once belonging to it, but which has no hands nor glass and a broken dial

6 pictures and their frames

1 round mahogany stand

1 large ensign, old and torn

2 large consular seals

1 small do

1 spyglass, imperfect

6 swords and belts, all damaged [140]

This list Payne forwarded to Washington in his first dispatch from the new post, written May 14, the day after his arrival, and accompanied it with what might be called an understatement: "The American consular mansion here is very much out of repair and entirely destitute of furniture while those of all the other countries are in good condition and elegantly fitted up." Papers also had been found "in great confusion, and nothing to enlighten me regarding official forms and other requirements."

Of the importance of one duty, however, he had probably been instructed in advance. That was the call upon the Bey, the native official by whom Tunis was directly governed. His Highness held court in a palace known as the Bardo, "an irregular mass of edifices, enclosed by lofty walls, with cannon and watch towers, and surrounded by a deep, wide moat.

For the ceremonial call Payne of course donned the official costume worn by American consular representatives of that day. This uniform had once been very elaborate—"blue coat and cape . . . lined with white silk, embroidered with gold . . . white breeches and gold knee-buckles"—but some fifteen years before Payne's time it had been considerably simplified. The plainer outfit consisted of "a black coat with gold star on each side of the collar . . . the underclothes [probably meaning small-clothes, or knee breeches] to be black, blue or white, at the option of the wearer . . . a 3-cornered *chapeau-de-bras*, with black cockade and eagle, and a steel-mounted sword with white scabbard." [141]

Thus attired, preceded by the picturesque dragoman, and accompanied by Mr. Gale and Captain Wilson of the ship *Preble,* the new consul reached the palace entrance. Past grim throngs at the gateways, through long, dark passages, scrutinized by numerous ministers, saluting sentries and guards, across an open colonnade leading to apartments ("one of them the Hall of Justice, where a wave of the Bey's hand may mean great good—or Death"), Payne and his escort finally reached a carpeted drawing room.

"Fronting me as I entered sat a person in a tall red cap; at his left stood two others—young and plump—with similar caps. All had long, double-breasted, blue frock coats, descending to the heels, with yellow buttons stamped with the crescent and star. All had diamond orders, but the diamonds of the one seated were the richest and most numerous."

The dragoman kissed the royal hand. ("The manual exercise of courtesy is not expected of consuls, all kissing of high and mighties being done by dragomans," Payne explained.) "The minister interpreted Mr. Gale's Italian into Arabic, after my English to Mr. Gale."

"Peace be between us. Please to be seated," said the Bey.

The conversation was brief and formal. "His Highness hoped I would find my new residence comfortable and happy and assured me that nothing should be wanting to make it so." Of a large squadron of American ships at that time cruising in the Mediterranean, Payne observed that he "hoped our vessels would visit Tunis more frequently in future." And the Bey replied that he was "always happy to welcome the ships of *friends*—dwelling on the word friends."

"A black now entered with little cups of coffee on a silver tray. We all partook. . . . I felt considerably annoyed that, from the combined effects of standing so long in the sun and the unsettledness arising from my recent voyage and the novel situation, my hand trembled so that my cup went tap, tap, tap against the saucer as I set it down. . . . You may know how glad I was when, my bow being made, I found myself once more through the guards, out of the palace gates and on my way back to Tunis."

Soon followed visits from all the consuls and their respective suites, "glittering in gold and silver, and uttering hollow, diplomatic civilities." Since there were as yet no chairs in the American establishment, these calls were probably brief. All assured the newcomer that he "would find Tunis a most unendearing place."

There was "little beyond merely ceremonious visiting" among "the foreign aristocracy of Tunis [the consuls], no society, no parties," Payne wrote his sister Anna. Yet in respect to gossip the capital city, with its more than a hundred thousand inhabitants,[142] was "worse than a village. . . . There is a superabundance of small talk about everybody." He noted what at first has seemed "one of the oddest things: When I asked 'Where is Mr. So-and-So?' 'Oh, he's gone to Carthage to breakfast, he'll be back for dinner.' "

With its endlessly hilly terrain and oddly varied architecture, the ancient city was exceedingly picturesque. Payne described to Anna the view from his terrace:

> In the foreground scarcely anything but housetops, giving the impression of a fine city of pigmies, every terrace being crowned with little structures of different shapes, some round, some conical . . . and amid them tall chimneys that you might take for dwarf obelisks, and here and there the summit of a minaret.

In the distance lay the harbor, "with all the anchoring, arriving and departing ships; and beyond, high hills "receding more and more, till they complete the shores of the bay fronting ancient Carthage, and then stretch farther and farther into the sea. Within this range is comprehended every point wherein Virgil imagined the events of Aeneas's shipwreck and adventures with that celebrated widow, Mrs. Eliza Dido."

The American official residence was "connected with a long range of consular and ministerial and aristocratic mansions on either side, whereto it forms the apex of an angle." As for the house itself, "if it were cut away from the others, it would resemble in shape an old-fashioned grand pianoforte, large enough for a belle of Brobdingnag to play upon."

A terrace a hundred feet long and half to a quarter as wide surrounded the house and faced part of the city wall. Outside the wall ran "the common, open sewer of Tunis. . . . For a nose new to Tunis [this had] less attraction than for the inhabitants, who say it is a charm against the plague, which is afraid to venture near it."

By Gabriel Harrison's account one would think that Payne's re-modeling of the consular residence was his only important work in Tunis. This was far from so, but work on the house was a major occupation from beginning to end of his term. Together with the shock of learning that the three-hundred-dollar rental had to come out of his own meager salary and was a year in arrears on his arrival, came the discovery that the owner of this "mass of filth and degradation" was none other than the Bey himself. Payne recalled that official's expressed concern for his comfort, and also observed that at that very time the Bey was spending a large sum on the mansion assigned to Queen Victoria's representative. It therefore seemed opportune to ask the royal landlord to improve another piece of his property.

"The honor of our republic requires that it [the consular establishment] be enabled to wear an appearance, if not equal to that made by the greatest European nations, at least not entirely inferior to that made by the least," Payne wrote the State Department. "Each of the others has a house elegantly furnished. At each a liberal table is kept. Each is provided with one or two carriages and a supply of carriage as well as saddle horses."

A first note from consul to Bey brought a prompt reply but no results. A second brought a few workmen, "who fooled around and each time only took something away." Work was finally begun "in the severest heat of August." The tenant was "dislodged from the only comfortable sleeping room by removal of the roof," which was not replaced. Then the roof was removed from the central patio, which for months was left open to the sky, "while the heavy December rains flooded the entire establishment."

By the end of the year Payne decided that there was nothing to do but pay another visit to the Bey. Again accompanied by vice-consul and interpreter, he set off to the palace. This time he carried a list, translated into Arabic, of all the repairs required at the residence.

The second siege was more formidable than the first. "A dense crowd in white Burnooses blocked the entrance. . . . A row of officers like images lined the room at the right hand of the Bey." Nevertheless the business of the Hall of Justice was suspended for the reception of the unexpected visitors. The Bey seemed impressed by the list in Arabic and promised immediate attention.

But promises were one thing in Tunis, performance was another. A week of bitter weather ensued and nothing done. More prodding seemed necessary. The consul did not deign to go again to see the Bey, but sent Mr. Gale and the dragoman with a note to His Highness. It stated that the United States consul, to save His Highness further trouble, "would take matters into his own hands and charge expenditures against the rent."

This brought an immediate and somewhat alarmed reply:

Glory to the one only God! From the slave of all-powerful God, the Mouchir Achmed Pacha, Bey, Emir of the Tunisian armies:

To our Ally, Sidi John Howard Payne, Consul General of the American Government at Tunis:

We acquaint you that we have received your letter regarding the affair at the consul's residence. We had even previously ordered our L'oukil [architect] in relation to it. We now come from dispatching the Bach Bouche [chief of the guards] to compel that everything shall be done as desired.

May God be your holy guardian!

Written this 9th day of the month of El Hadja in the year 1259 [January 9, 1844].[143]

Next morning appeared "a swarm of workmen and a giant of a guard, covered with tunics and jackets and cloaks, all brilliant with gold here and there: the same man who stands before the Bey on presentation days and grasps by the shoulders each of His Highness's loving subjects who come up to kiss the royal hand, the aforesaid grasp to prevent the loving subject from sticking a knife into the Bey."

The handsome and wealthy young Moor who was the Bey's *oukil* came too, but Payne by this time had found an architect whom he greatly preferred, "a German of great taste and talent"—John Baptist Honegger of the Grand Duchy of Baden, who had directed repairs at the residence of the British consul. This man was also noted as an archeologist and had "excavated some important treasures in Carthage, among them a vast gymnasium and temple." [144] "Poor in everything but health and worth and genius and wisdom," Honegger found the remodeling of Payne's residence a task sufficiently challenging to enlist his earnest effort. "As an attention due to me as the representative of a government which he enthusiastically respects," he devoted two years to the work "without a thought of recompense." [145]

The house was found in worse condition than expected. When Honegger declared that the foundations would have fallen soon, the Bey ordered it almost rebuilt. Payne "caused walls to be cut away, windows to be enlarged, old things made new and new made somewhat resembling civilization." For the "massy iron gates" of the patio he substituted "recesses which will contain plaister casts of statuary when I can get them." Honegger provided for everything essential to comfort, and as a special feature "added a long closet for documents, parallel with the library, with a large window at one end opening upon the main entrance, whence everybody who comes to the entrance door can be seen, unperceived, from the writing table withinside."

Efforts to interest the government in assuming the cost of the remodeling had been fruitless, but now Payne could inform Washington that he would have a house "equal to the best in Tunis without expense to the United States. . . . The Bey's outlay will be 11,000 to 12,000 piastres." [146]

But the Moorish workmen moved slowly "unless urged onwards by presents from day to day . . . the Bey and his underlings [were] extremely tardy in payment," and Payne found himself "giving from 8 to 16 men each, from one to five piastres daily." He also assumed the expense of papering and other minor matters, as well as that of furnishing. He had brought some furniture and many books from America.

It is too bad to spoil another fine legend, which has it that the remodeling was an unalloyed success.[147] Actually the job was never quite finished; and the landlord became sadly in arrears to the tenant. One year after his second call on the Bey Payne wrote his young niece that the house was still "in terrible disorder—all doors and windows out for nearly a year—music of hammering, but little done." He then drew an amusing word picture of his domestic state at the time:

"I live like Robinson Crusoe. Had the present of a dog, which I named Flora. She has had three sets of children, of which there remain nine, of different sizes and colors, some very little and some very big. Also a particular friend of Flora's—a small, ugly, drab-colored dog, but very sensible, belonging to my vice-consul, and named Sultan, which has taken a fancy to spend all days and nights with me."

> All this goodly company assembles around my table to partake of my meals besides devouring their own. You would laugh to see this canine convocation around the table, some with their forelegs up at its sides, some sitting gravely upon chairs, and when impatient, pawing at my arm to attract notice; some supporting the head wheedlingly upon my knees and every now and then talking to me in their dog talk, and each receiving a bit of bread, or whatever happens to be dispensable.
>
> Mrs. Flora and her oldest son, Pet, have, in addition to their share of breakfast and tea, all that is left of the meal after I have done, and the instant I set down my second cup, they habitually make a pounce and lap away most eagerly, and then the congregation breaks up.

At night the greedy crew was an efficient watch: "The entire party sleep in and about my bedroom floor, and if they hear the slightest stir in the night, set up a yelping enough to startle a regiment of evildoers. I have given names to all the 13, but the 6 last. There is, besides Flora and Sultan and Pet—Florette, Freckle, Watch and Sly. Will you send me word what I am to call the other six?" [148]

The master of this strange household must have been able to speed up the remodeling soon after writing his niece, for we have a very different picture of the mansion as it appeared to a visitor a few months later. This is supplied by an American, Francis Schroeder, secretary to the Commodore on the United States frigate *Cumberland*, part of the squadron that paid a two days' call at Tunis in August 1845.

Payne rowed out into the harbor to greet his fellow Americans "in a boat well-manned by Moors, and accompanied by a German friend and one janizary." In conversation with the Commodore over the ship's side, the consul extended an invitation to "as many men as could be spared" to be his guests at the consulate. The consul was "immediately recognized by his brilliant uniform," and at least one of the ship's officers, Schroeder, had "rarely been so prepossessed" as by the man who wore it—"his countenance expressive of the kindest impulses as well as of a high degree of intellect."

The guests from the ship found the consular mansion, although unfinished, "a very comfortable establishment . . . topped by an American flag of tremendous proportions and of the silkiest texture." They mounted a marble stairway to "an enclosed court, paved with checkered marble, and communicating with . . . handsome apartments, of the same cool construction and paving. Ottomans and lounges were divided among the rooms," and the library was "a charming room . . . with deep morocco chairs . . . and a thousand or 1200 books in handsome cases."

About 2 o'clock, "after some agreeable commotion among three or four fancy-dressed blackamoors, under an Italian chief servant, a *déjeuner à la fourchette* was served." The guests at this repast included, besides the ship's officers, Sir Thomas Reade, the British consul, "an elegant old man of seventy"; a "very talented and agreeable German architect"; "the nuncio of the Pope—a newly-created bishop in rich robes, tall, magnificent, . . . who sipped his champagne with praiseworthy gusto, laughing and delighted with everything"; and "an Illyrian merchant . . . the drollest gentleman in Tunis . . . who had learned to look upon Mr. Payne as the very particular salt of the earth."

Some of the men from the ship were asked to spend the night, including the cruise historian, who, alas, must have been lodged on the wrong side of the house, for "the evening exhalation" from the nearby sewer gave him "a perfectly sleepless night." That, however, was forgotten in the next day's excursion to Carthage, ending at a particularly sightly spot on the beach. There, "imagine our surprise to find the magic of a white-spread table, cold fowl, pillau, ham, melons, grapes, figs, peaches, champagne, rheinwine and brandy. . . . The consul expected every man to do his duty. . . . We had expected a luncheon, but such sacrifices to Ceres and Bacchus in the site of their ancient orgies, we had not dreamed of.

"The scene was enchanting . . . the grand picture of the opposite shore, with the masts of ships, and the surf casting silver at our feet. . . . The breeze came deliciously from the sea and the evening sun threw shadows refreshingly over the table. . . . A toast to the health of the author of 'Home, Sweet Home' brought the neatest reply in the world. . . . Never was there such a picnic!" [149]

The dispatches that Payne sent to Washington during his first term in Tunis were addressed to three Secretaries of State: A. P. Upshur, John C. Calhoun, and James Buchanan. Calhoun succeeded to the office upon Secretary Upshur's death in an explosion on board the ship *Princeton* in Washington, February 1844—an accident in which several other prominent persons lost their lives and President Tyler narrowly escaped with his.[150] Tyler did not seek re-election, and with the new president, James K. Polk, the following year, Buchanan came in as Secretary of State.

In addition to domestic matters and expenses Payne's dispatches covered a variety of subjects. The political situation in Tunis, unsettled when he arrived, soon became "more complicated and critical." The ancient land of Tunis, older than Carthage, which through the centuries had been fought over by Romans, Arabs, and Turks, had become by the nineteenth century a pawn of the modern European powers. "Many suppose France would not be reluctant to annex Tunis and Algiers," Payne reported, and added: "All history proves how readily a powerful and ambitious protectorate can create a plausible excuse for seizing what it came to succor." [151]

There were, besides, difficulties with Sardinia over trade, and other disturbing situations. The Turkish fleet was seen in the Mediterranean; an Austrian admiral came to Tunis for an appraising look around; and the murder of the British consul's chief dragoman was thought to have political implications. These scattered events might not have seemed menacing had not the Bey, "a small-scale Napoleon, with a military mania," long been making warlike preparations.

"Everything around me threatens war," Payne wrote his brother, "but I hardly think difficulties will have results so serious."

Other matters from time to time merited report to the State Department. He wrote to the Secretary of State concerning valuable but neglected trade opportunities. "A very profitable trade," the American consul observed, "might be created in this region which would open unknown springs of wealth to the New World, which the European nations have overlooked." For the "oils, olives, soap and wool" produced in Tunis the United States "might supply lumber, stoves, cotton, candles, rum and tobacco." Creation of "a traveling agency of some sort to explore conditions in Rhodes, Cyprus, Beirut, Salonika and Alexandria," he suggested as a means of promoting such trade.[152]

Then, too, he was obliged to report to the Secretary, that "refugees are regularly fed and lodged in the consular mansion at my own cost [described as "trifling"] except when Mussulman ordinances prevent their partaking of Christian fare." Here we might think that Payne was taking a leaf from John Ross's book, had he not explained that "a foreign consulate here is always considered a sanctuary, whither slaves and debtors, even criminals, of their country, cannot be followed by the laws for a certain time." [153]

So much new life at the lately moribund United States consulate could not but attract attention throughout Tunis. The natives began to look upon the new consul as a man who might right some of the wrongs under which they had long suffered.

Amid the confusion of the remodeling and the threats of war without, Payne began to receive complaints against one of his predecessors. That was Dr. Samuel D. Heap, who, until his transference to Constantinople a year before Payne's arrival, had been United States representative in Tunis for eighteen years, and considered "any other person's coming a usurpation." [154]

A brother-in-law of Commodore Porter [155] and otherwise highly connected, Dr. Heap was a former surgeon in the Navy, and during his residence in Tunis had acted as the Bey's physician. Yet it was reported that Heap had made a practice of lending money at interest to the natives.

Soon Payne learned that since he arrived in Tunis one unfortunate debtor, a Moor, had been imprisoned "for debts to the American consul." Astonished, Payne ordered the prisoner released and sent a report of the case to the Bey. The Bey replied that "the man was imprisoned for debts to Dr. Heap." [156] The prisoner, "in a sad state," was sent before Payne, who "had him consider himself on parole, and not to depart from under the consular roof without my permission." Payne "demanded of the Bey a promise that the man might not be punished for having sought refuge under the American flag," and the Bey promised that "no harm would come to Hadj Khil."

Now, much less ceremoniously than before, Payne went again to call on the Bey, who "refused to see others" but sent for the American consul to enter. "For the first time I did not find him seated in state, but standing." [157] . . . "He shook hands and laughed heartily." [158]

Later Hadj Khil was set entirely free, and "many respectable Tunisians called at the consulate and thanked me for having shown justice and mercy to one of their brother Mussulmans." Payne reported the whole matter to Calhoun and concluded with this recommendation: "I have considered any use of the consul's name without his knowledge as requiring to be emphatically discontinued."

But the case of Hadj Khil had a momentous sequel. Dr. Heap, who had resigned his Constantinople post and returned to Tunis, now decided on a trip to America. He "called at the consulate for a passport to quit Tunis," Payne wrote his sister Anna, and "peremptorily demanded that Hadj Khil be sent back to prison," although admitting that the man "had always paid his debts."

Apparently there was some altercation over this, but "after the first storm, Dr. Heap left for America and his sons treated me with civility and often came to see me and dine with me."

For some time, however, Payne had been hearing that the Heaps were representing him as "only a strolling player, thrust into momentary consequence by an accidental President." And simultaneously his difficulties with the Bey over the expense of rebuilding the house were mounting. "Week after week, month after month, neither material nor funds were forthcoming." He had to provide them both. His threat to retain the current rent to meet the advances drew no objection though the Bey did complain that the house was costing too much. [159]

It was when these perplexities were at their height that the United States ships in command of Commodore Morgan arrived, giving occasion for Payne's elaborate entertainment of some of the officers. The Commodore himself did not come ashore, and it was afterwards reported that he had been "visited on board by some of the Heap family." [160]

Payne "implied to the Bey" that the American ships had come "to see that the work on the consulate was done." Alarmed, the Bey "sent inspectors who promised more than was asked for"; and Payne took advantage of the situation to ask the Bey for the return of about 7000 piasters of the sum that he had advanced. When the Commodore set sail after only two days in the harbor, it was rumored that the shortness of his stay "expressed disapproval" of the consul's demands.

Apparently Payne felt justified in his attempt to bluff the Bey. He reported the incident fully to Washington with the suggestion: "The ships of the Mediterranean Squadron do not visit the Barbary coast often enough, or stay long enough," and recommended "the importance [of appearance] of our ships of war, whenever difficulties, however trifling, arise with the Barbary rulers." [161]

But here, as often before, lavish expenditures were creating great complexities for Payne and distorting a situation in which he was otherwise right. Furthermore his health had begun to be "seriously affected," and on a physician's advice he decided on a vacation in Malta. Somewhat earlier he had written to his friend James Buchanan congratulating him on his appointment as Secretary of State. Now, suddenly, through the workmen, the tradespeople, the servants, came rumors that the new administration in Washington had brought another change: that Dr. Heap had been reappointed consul to Tunis and Payne had been removed!

Having made plans for a brief vacation, Payne now began to prepare for a long one, should the rumors prove correct. The "collateral supervision of affairs with the Bey" he entrusted to that "well-disposed individual of superior intelligence," Sir Thomas Reade. The sum due him from the Bey Payne now estimated as 8,399 piasters,[162] and of that he directed that "500 Spanish dollars" be paid to Mr. Honegger, the incomparable architect.

Payne left the Chevalier Gaspary to represent him in his absence should that happen to be temporary. Gaspary was "a French gentleman, born in Tunis, who acts as our representative at the Goletta." He was another extraordinary person, to whom, as to Honegger, material considerations apparently were secondary, and Payne had previously reported: "I have never witnessed more promptitude in office, without fee or expectation of fee."

That same remarkable trait—indifference to monetary reward— was to be found in still another Tunis resident, Ambrose Allegro, who ever since 1801 had served the United States consulate as chancellor, secretary, and interpreter under eight incumbents, without pay. Although this faithful servant had finally been transferred to the Netherlands consulate, Payne, whose preparations for departure had some of the characteristics of a last testament, remembered Allegro also by writing the Department of State that it would be fitting if the veteran's "old age could be comforted and his poverty relieved." [163]

Payne's friends in Tunis, "indignant over reports of my removal, urged me . . . never to be seen in Tunis except as what they protested I ought to be, the United States consul general. They gave me the most hearty and attentive aid in packing my library, making my inventories and in short fully closing my business." In mid-October, leaving "all ensigns flying, according to the rule," Payne departed for Malta and thence to Palermo. There, near the end of November, he received official notice of his recall. It was "politely worded, contained no complaint," and included "permission to draw $500 to pay expenses home." [164]

[8]

MATTERS OFFICIAL AND UNOFFICIAL

PAYNE made a leisurely trip home, spending nearly two years on the way. This was partly due to "compelled delay," involving his effort to collect his financial claim against the Bey.

Having left that matter in the capable hands of Sir Thomas Reade, the British consul, Payne, after a brief rest at Malta, had gone on to Palermo "to help myself to some literary material." Palermo he found "very gay from the visit of the Emperor and Empress of Russia and their daughter." [165] The American visitor jokingly wrote his sister that he was "flourishing around among Sicilian princes and princesses." He was also cordially received in the home of Palermo's United States consul. Altogether, despite his recent ouster, the situation held some cheer, and this was increased by a letter from a friend "of 23 years residence in Tunis" informing him that Sir Thomas "had succeeded in his amicable application to His Highness, the Bey, for settlement of all expenses made in repairs to the United States consulate." [166]

But here again promise proved unreliable. Months passed, and, "still waiting for settlement of the Tunis matter," he spent some time at Rome and Naples, and later went on to Paris. At length, doubting that settlement would ever be made "unless our government takes the claim in hand," he finally set sail for home and arrived in New York in July of 1847.

The government did take the claim in hand. It was presented to the President's cabinet, with the result that the State Department demanded of the Bey that it be paid. In August 1849, nearly four years after Payne left Tunis, a letter which his Tunis successor, Consul Heap—most reluctantly, no doubt—had been obliged to write to the Secretary of State, reached Washington. It enclosed news of the Bey's capitulation in the matter of "expenses incurred by Mr. Payne on the consular house here," together with a formal statement of that dignitary:

Praise be to God!

   To our Ally, Mr. Heap, consul general of the American government at Tunis. . . .

   Mr. Payne asked for repairs and improvements to be made at the consulate. We ordered the director of the works on our estates to execute the repairs. . . . The oukil, having expended a considerable sum . . . was at length obliged to discontinue executing the further demands made by Mr. Payne because they were unnecessary.

   Mr. Payne declared that he had discharged from his own hands a sum of piastres 12,149¾, on said repairs, from which he had deducted the rent of the consulate house for two years, thus reducing the claim to 8,399¾ piastres.

Though he regarded "the sum not due by us," the monarch had ordered it paid, "in consideration of the feelings of friendship which unite our two governments" and "to give further testimony of our friendly sentiments toward the government of the United States." Dated July 9, 1849, the message ended with the courteous Mohammedan benediction: "May you remain under the safeguard of God!" [167]

Translated into Western terms, the amount of the claim came to about $1500, but Payne probably did not receive as much as that. From Washington he sent his brother a copy of the Bey's letter with the comment:

> The piastre is rated at 4 to the dollar, sometimes 7½. I always took the middle sum and made it 6. I suppose Heap intends to pay me according to his rule in accounting with the government. In that case I get only $1100. The money, however, is sure enough, be the sum what it may. . . . The entire amount I am to receive will set me about, if not altogether, free from debt.[168]

For Thatcher Payne, temperamentally very different from his brother, satisfaction in the news of Howard's final triumph was somewhat tempered by that last sentence. He wrote: "Your suggestion that the entire amount of the claim when received may fall short of the amount of your present indebtedness is entirely new to me, and no friend of yours could hear it without concern." [169]

It is doubtful if this affair would ever have been satisfactorily terminated if Payne had not acquired a new friend, one influential in Washington: William L. Marcy, former governor of New York, who at the time of Payne's return to America was Secretary of War. The contact with Marcy was originally personal, and had come about without any effort on Payne's part. It grew out of his visit to Palermo, where at the house of the American consul he had met a Miss Knower who was Marcy's sister-in-law. Through her, when he went on to Italy, Payne made the acquaintance of other Marcy relatives.

About his sojourn in Italy he had remarked in a letter to his brother upon the presence of numerous "invalid countrymen, who swarm to Sicily and Italy, it would almost seem, merely for the sake of dying under discomforts scarcely to be found elsewhere by such sufferers—certainly never in their own land." [170] One such invalid, actually a dying man, was a brother-in-law of Marcy. Payne "helped close the eyes" of this man and performed such useful service to the widow as greatly to endear himself and earn the gratitude of the entire clan.

On November 16, 1846, Marcy from Washington wrote Payne, who was still abroad, a warm letter of thanks "for your kindness and assistance to our deceased brother, and to our sister in her truly forlorn condition—a stranger in a strange land. . . . Our eyes will follow you wherever your destiny may lead, and our hearts will devoutly wish for your welfare."

Marcy was as good as his word—very fortunately, for Payne greatly needed assistance, not only in the matter of the Bey's indebtedness, but also in an effort to reinstate himself in a breadwinning occupation. Immediately on his return from abroad, he paid a visit to Marcy at his Washington home and began at once the quest for new government work. Though he stated no preference for foreign service, he seems to have been slated almost from the first for another foreign post. The appointment, however, was long in coming.

Not to depend entirely on the chance of public employment, Payne put numerous lines out in both New York and Washington. He made an effort to publish the first volume of his Cherokee history, which in the summer of 1848 he declared "ready for the press." [171] He also applied for the open position of librarian of the New York Historical Society at a salary of $1500 to $2000 a year.[172] He even entertained some thought—as few did not—of joining the California gold rush. The government still seemed to offer the most dependable opportunities, however, and he decided after March 1849 to make his headquarters in the capital.[173]

This was a period of short-term presidencies. The election of 1848 had brought a new administration, and again a temporary one. For it was then that Polk, after a single term in the White House, was succeeded by General Zachary Taylor, swept into office as the hero of the lately concluded Mexican War—an episode which Payne, in Tunis, had missed. Taylor would die after one year as President and would be succeeded by Millard Fillmore.

Both Taylor and Fillmore were Whigs, but Polk had belonged to the Democratic-Republicans, forerunners of the Democratic party. It was reported in Washington that Polk had removed Payne for political reasons, but Payne felt little party preference and had friends as well as enemies in both camps. Tyler, who had originally appointed Payne, though nominally a Whig, was a lukewarm party man, whereas Marcy, who served in two cabinets, was a Democrat. With the arrival of the Taylor administration Marcy was out, but before he went back to Albany he called on the new Secretary of State, John Clayton, with a plea for Payne, and also wrote an excellent letter in his behalf:

My acquaintance with Mr. Payne is of recent date, and my desire to serve him is coeval with it. Had I known him earlier as I do now, I would have done my utmost to retain him. . . . He has, in my opinion, eminent qualifications for diplomatic service. He has spent many years in Europe, is familiar with many of the languages spoken there, is a ripe scholar, has a wide-spread fame in the literary world and is also an accomplished gentleman.[174]

"I am vegetating here in that state of stupid torpor which is known as 'waiting patiently,'" Payne, in Washington, wrote his niece in May 1849. And to a friend three months later: "I am entirely in the dark as to plans regarding me. Only I hear obscure hints that if I am not sent back to Tunis, I shall otherwise be taken care of, and must hold on. This holding on without anything to hold to is mighty dull work."[175]

At Marcy's farewell party, however, the applicant had acquired another valuable acquaintance: Senator Tom Corwin of Ohio, through whom an appointment with Secretary Clayton was arranged. "I could not be heard long and was tolerably flurried," Payne reported of that interview.[176] Corwin, who "advised Tunis for vindication, definitely stipulating a transfer to Rome," also suggested getting strong letters. He wrote one himself:

I feel a deep solicitude on account of the unworthy treatment under which Mr. Payne has suffered so much and so long. His fate seems peculiar. . . . Some years ago he was reviled and persecuted for no other reason than being found at the residence of John Ross. . . . In Tunis, his clear sense of justice was promptly exerted in favor of a persecuted Moor . . . for this he is again ostracized. . . . Of all the diplomatic corps now abroad, on my conscience, I do not believe there is one so well adapted to such service as Payne.[177]

This from a new friend. An old one, Washington Irving, was quite as willing to supply a testimonial:

His life has been one of vicissitudes, but I have had opportunities of witnessing his upright and honorable conduct in the midst of difficulties and perplexities. He appeared to me capable and industrious in the despatch of business. His residence abroad makes him well acquainted with foreign languages, and in his own language he has ever commanded one of the most graceful, flowing and perspicuous styles I am acquainted with.[178]

The summer of 1849 dragged along: another year followed, with action still pending. Payne had a job of some kind in Washington, for in May of 1850 he wrote of being "vexed by my employer for not paying me punctually, though I only get enough to live on temporarily. . . . I am entering up my old writings, methodizing my papers [179] and getting ready to make my will . . . also trying to sell wild lands" (apparently some acquired in the West).

The strain was telling on his health. A doctor advised his having all his upper teeth removed, so he wrote the family, adding with grim humor: "I do not see why people should keep teeth in a world where it is so hard to earn employment for them." [180]

Though the death of President Taylor had probably contributed to the delay involving Payne, it had also brought a cabinet change very favorable to him. As Secretary of State, Clayton had been replaced by Daniel Webster, who, it happened, had held the same post in the Tyler cabinet at the time of Payne's original appointment, and was familiar with his case.

Shortly before the reappearance of this powerful friend, Payne had also acquired a formidable enemy. That was Thomas Hart Benton, long a senator from the frontier state of Missouri—a man capable and resolute, but notably irascible, relentless, and a terrific fighter. And Benton, it developed, was a friend of Payne's Tunis rival, Dr. Heap. Now, at least the boredom of waiting was over. A bitter fight ensued. Benton began by opposing Payne's renomination for foreign service, but he was named, regardless, by President Fillmore.

"I know you heard of my nomination to Tunis. . . . I suppose you have since heard that it was not acted upon," Payne wrote Marcy in October 1850. "Benton . . . will try to defeat me on political grounds. . . . It is necessary that every true friend I have should be on the alert. I know you are one and therefore appeal to you."

Benton's special contribution as a statesman lay in his advocacy of measures essential to development of the West: cheap land, homesteading, transportation. On such points as these he was doubtless right. It is quite as certain, however, that his opposition to Payne's reappointment was based upon a sadly garbled version of the facts.

Payne's prediction to Marcy of being opposed on political grounds proved correct, though Benton's attack, when openly made, took an oddly nonpartisan turn. He discharged a battery at Payne at St. Louis in November 1850, in a fiery speech that began with a lengthy "eulogium to the late General Taylor [not of Benton's party], for his refusal to remove a public official on political grounds or for opinion's sake." The official referred to was Heap; but the oblique approach was confusing, because the real intent was to discredit Payne.

The *Evening Post* of New York published all of Benton's speech, a very long one covering many topics; and though the attack on Payne was but one of them, it occupied three quarters of a column. It is easily boiled down, however, to four main statements, three of them charges against Payne and wholly erroneous. A week later the *Post* also published Payne's denial. Read side by side, the charges and the refutation constitute a fair history of the case.[181]

Said Benton: "Dr. Heap was removed by Tyler to make room for Mr. Payne." This of course was inaccurate. The fact was that a year before Payne's appointment Heap had been transferred to Constantinople and W. B. Hodgson appointed to fill what had been Heap's place in Tunis, and that it was not until Hodgson's resignation that Payne was named. "The office was spontaneously and to my surprise conferred upon me by Mr. Tyler," said Payne, in rebuttal.

Said Benton: "When Polk came into office, he replaced the two gentlemen as they were—Dr. Heap in Tunis and Mr. Payne in New York." This statement was correct, and Payne added: "Without any charges or suggestions or pretense of unfaithfulness or unfitness, I was removed to make room for Dr. Heap."

Benton: "But as soon as Mr. Polk was out and General Taylor in, then Mr. Payne concluded that his chance had come again and immediately applied for the removal of Dr. Heap and the reappointment of himself." This statement was subtly misleading. Payne explained: "I applied immediately upon my return, to the administration of Mr. Polk, for public employment. . . . I afterwards acquiesced in a suggestion officially made to me of renomination to the office [in Tunis] . . . and continued the application until Mr. Fillmore nominated me." Payne could have added that he had had little desire to go back to Tunis and had only applied for reinstatement there after other posts, "more coveted," proved unavailable.[182]

Benton: "To make sure, he [Payne] filed charges against Dr. Heap." Payne: "What are termed my charges are simply the journal of my consular acts, made in my official capacity, long before my successor was appointed: before I dreamed of my own removal."

Read a century after it was written, Payne's refutation seems more elaborate and wordy than necessary, but its factual accuracy is attested by State Department records. He accepted Benton's representation of Heap versus Payne as political, though, viewed with detachment, it seems to have been at the start entirely personal. It was simply that Heap had decided he wanted his old job back, and had applied for it when a change of administration brought a change of party also.

Benton in the St. Louis speech had also taken occasion to refer to Payne as "the composer of a good song and some poor plays, written not with Shakespeare pen." To this Payne, disclaiming delusions of literary grandeur, retorted in kind: "Will the learned Senator admit that his own philippics, numerous and long as they are, are not such as Webster, Clay or Demosthenes would have spoken?"

In the midst of all this unpleasantness, and before the case of Benton versus Payne could be resolved, there occurred in Washington a tension-relieving incident that must have given the displaced consul some feeling of moral if not material satisfaction.

The great Jenny Lind, after her historic New York triumphs, had arrived for her first visit to the capital. On December 17 (1850), she was booked for a gala concert at the newly reconstructed National Hall—"burnt-out shell of an old theatre converted into one of the finest concert halls in the United States." [183]

Eager to hear the singer who had been so enthusiastically acclaimed in New York, official Washington turned out en masse that December evening. Seats were reserved for the President and his family as well as for the cabinet members. General Lewis Cass, lately a defeated candidate for President, General Winfield Scott, and many other dignitaries were present, and not far from them sat a plain, untitled job hunter by the name of Payne.

There were the usual coloratura numbers—"Flute Song," "Bird Song," "Casta Diva"—these followed by a song entitled "Greetings to America," written by Bayard Taylor especially for Mlle. Lind. Then, according to several newspaper accounts, came the program's culminating moment.

"The matchless singer had entranced the throng with her operatic arias and exquisite melodies, but the great feature of the occasion seemed to be an inspiration. She suddenly turned her face to the part of the audience where Payne was sitting and sang 'Home, Sweet Home' with such pathos that a whirlwind of excitement swept over the vast audience. Daniel Webster almost lost his self-control, while all eyes were turned upon a small-sized, elegantly-molded, gray-haired gentleman, who blushed violently on finding himself the attention of so many glances."

Well might one reporter observe that "We can easily imagine Payne thrilled with rapture at this unexpected and magnificent rendering of his immortal lyric"; and another, that "No common poet ever received a more enviable compliment." [184]

Could this incident have influenced the outcome of Payne's quest? Conceivably it did. Nevertheless decision was further delayed, and after the Christmas recess of Congress "the same miserable state of suspense began all over." Payne wrote the folks at home: "Mr. Marcy consulted with the President and Mr. Webster. Some allusion was made to the nomination as having been on political grounds. . . . Mr. Fillmore smiled and said he did not think I had enough politics to hurt, either way. . . . The Governor [Marcy] might have replied, 'Just enough to hurt in every way and not enough to help in any.' My active supporters are all democrats, and they do not like to begin a stand which may remove a democrat." (Heap was nominally of that party.)

Later Howard reported to the family: "Marcy met Webster at a dinner party . . . Mr. Corwin on the other side [of the table], the Governor [Marcy] speaking across the width: 'Why, he has been nominated and his nomination is before the Senate. It needs to be brought up.' 'I'll *have* it brought up,' said Webster." [185]

This letter was written the last day of January 1851. Senate confirmation of Payne's second Tunis appointment soon followed, and on March 17 he wrote to Daniel Webster asking permission to call at the Secretary's office "to thank you personally for your kindness and support under circumstances of much difficulty."

Difficult circumstances he himself expected to encounter in Tunis, and, wishing to be prepared, he asked in this letter how he should act "should cases be brought before me at Tunis of proved usury. By the law of the Koran all payment of interest is usury among Mohammedans. The Bey once informed me that for him even to look upon the word interest was a sin."

As further preparation for efficient service Payne asked Webster for a copy of the Statutes at Large; and to complete his vindication, requested that on his expected re-entry he might be landed "from a national ship." [186]

In the midst of all the public activities during Payne's four years back in America, personal events also had crowded upon one another. At home, within two years, the family lost two of its valued members. Aunt Esther died at eighty-six the year after Howard's return; and in the following year occurred the death of his sister Anna, who being still in the fifties, might reasonably have expected a longer stay on earth. Now, of the nine Payne children, only Lucy, Howard, and Thatcher were left, though the family circle had been increased and hopefully renewed by Thatcher's wife and daughter.

Anna, who probably had never recovered from the shock of losing her sister Eloise, had been in failing health for some years. In the summer of 1849 she had gone to the home of friends near Portsmouth, Rhode Island, and there she died in October. Shortly before the end she had written to Lucy of the brother then in Washington: "If Howard comes, give him my love. I shall expect to see him on my return." She was never to return, however, and Howard traveled from Washington for her burial.

Anna was nearest Howard in age, and in early childhood they had been much together. His letters to her had become increasingly warm and appreciative through the years. In a New Year's letter some years earlier he had written:

A thousand thoughts and introspections have come upon me as I have looked back upon the days of our infancy, when we were more closely associated than we have ever been since, and I have looked forward to the hour, which is growing closer and closer, when we shall be better known to each other; and have felt a delight in fancying that with those of our kindred who have finished their career before us, we shall . . . feel a degree of pity for our former selves, that we should ever have recoiled at the idea of a change, which will so clear our mental vision.[187]

Howard had also written feelingly to Anna of Aunt Esther, for whom he had always felt a special sympathy:

Our excellent Aunt Esther, who has been faithful to me through evil report and good . . . who has invariably believed, if I was abused to her, that things would wear a very different face when both sides were known, and if I was praised to her, that I was not praised half as much as I ought to be. . . . The hour cannot be far distant when our aunt will fade from us into a delightful and grateful recollection.

And now that hour had come, and Howard, returning to New York from Washington, wrote to his cousin Thomas Isaacs: "I am more than ever sensible of her loss, now that I have got back to the place where I have been in the habit of visiting her daily, and where I find her no more in her chamber, her bed or her chair. . . . There was a benignity and a delicacy, united with deep feeling and sound sense and perfect religious faith and principle, in her character." [188]

In New York the winter between those two sad family events, that of 1848–49, had been a particularly bitter one, with continuous ice and snow. "Two degrees colder than the night of the great fire," Howard recorded in his diary for January 10. And another entry described his return a few evenings earlier from his brother's new home in Brooklyn Heights, whence "the coachman, nearly frozen," had driven him to the ferry:

Overslept in sleigh after crossing. Left and took another. Broadway nearly empty. Driver remarked that he never saw Broadway so thin, or, to use his own phrase, "empty of so few people." . . . Came direct home. Crossing Washington Square, cold bitter indeed. Suffered intensely. . . . Right ear frost-bitten.[189]

The reason Howard was hurrying across Washington Square that frigid night is that he was then living at 40 West Washington Place. This, by the old numbering, was about a block west of the Square [190] and may have been immediately adjacent to St. Joseph's church, still standing.

During the late 1840's, especially after the Thatcher Paynes gave up their Bond Street house, Howard, during his sojourns in New York, occupied various bachelor quarters. A few of his letters are from 119 Leonard Street, others from 84 Broadway, and at least one mentions "a handsome suite of rooms at 673 Broadway." But these lodgings he did not keep long.

From the Washington Place address there are several letters dated 1849; and from there he must often have crossed to the east side of the Square, where, in a building owned by New York University, he kept a room for his books and papers. He had written to the Reverend I. M. Matthews, then the University's chancellor, in May of 1848: "I have observed that rooms are let in the University to persons not employed there. I am desirous of obtaining a study where my books and papers may be safe if I am called away. Could one be afforded on any terms suitable to a literary person?" [191]

It was apparently as a result of this letter that the quarters there were obtained. Eventually these became an abiding place, not only for his books, but for Payne himself when he was in New York. Just a month before his second sailing for Tunis he wrote to Eliza Watterston, a daughter of his esteemed Washington friend: "I have housed myself ever since my arrival [from Washington] in a room at the University, where my books have so long resided."

And so it appears that Payne was one of the earliest of the literati to lend glamour to New York's famous Washington Square. His room at the University was to be his last "home" in New York.

[9]

INEVITABLE HOUR

BY THE YEAR 1851 steam navigation had advanced greatly. The fastest ships now crossed the Atlantic in ten days. On one of them, the *Humboldt,* Payne left New York the ninth of May and landed at Havre the nineteenth.[192]

He had embarked in broken health, and as implied in a parting message to the family, with distinct forebodings: "Give me your prayers and accept my benediction . . . my gratitude and affection. Be sure that I shall bear them in my heart through this world and I hope a much better one, perhaps the only one in which we shall ever meet again."

Fortunately the voyage proved healing as well as incredibly swift. Arriving in Paris May 21, less than two weeks after leaving New York, he could only exclaim: "How strange it seems!"

Payne's request to the State Department that he be landed at Tunis from a national ship involved a month's stay in Paris: a delay that caused him some misgiving. For the Mediterranean fleet was still in command of Commodore Morgan, who, Payne could not forget, had been friendly to Heap. Payne wrote the Commodore immediately on reaching Paris and waited anxiously for a reply.

"The lack of a letter from Morgan gives me concern. So does the omission of the consul at Marseilles to acknowledge mine. Can there be any unfriendly movements in these quarters? Morgan certainly sided with Heap concerning the settlement with the Bey. Yet certainly he could not think of slighting the orders of government. . . . I apprehend that difficulties will be created with the Bey to thwart my reception, or at any rate cast a shadow over it."

The ninth of June rolled round, Payne's birthday, and he confided to his diary:

A strange feeling comes over me as I open this new account with time. This is my—what a chill comes over me at the thought—my sixtieth birthday. But ten years of man's allotted time remains to me—and what certainty is there that I may be permitted to continue even one-half that term in the world?

I am weary of the self-reproaches and unfulfilled resolutions, which are already recorded upon similar anniversaries in previous notebooks. It is of no use remonstrating with myself thus on paper. Let me earnestly pray that the record of the future will speak less discouragingly than the experience of the past.

"Nervous, fidgety and apprehensive," he put in the time as he could. He shopped around for a watchcase, a lamp, and books, looking for bargains and haggling with the French shopkeepers, who "pretended that they lost on all they sold." He had his consular uniform "regenerated—the embroidery cut off—$50." [193] He considered buying an ice machine which merely "formed a thin coat of ice in two places after being worked for about twice fifteen minutes . . . it would be a very agreeable luxury in Tunis, if really manageable."

The long delay was expensive, of course. He was "obliged to draw on the Barings, and received a supply of money and a kind note from Mrs. Bates." [194]

And after all, the worry and delay proved to have been unnecessary. For he finally learned that "the Frigate *Mississippi* had twice been for me at Marseilles, the third call was waiting for me. I posted at once, reached Marseilles the 24th and on the 26th was en route to Tunis. Voyage 60 hours. Before breakfast, at anchor off Carthage. Salutes were fired, I was visited from shore, put on my fine clothes and landed under salute."

A fortnight later *Galignani's Messenger* of Paris, an important English-language paper, added to Payne's own account: "He was received with marked respect, every head that wore a hat being uncovered as he passed by a long line of spectators, extending from the landing place to the quarters of the government."

Not until he entered the consular residence did Payne discover that Heap had taken his revenge in a manner unforeseen:

"Oh, such a place as I found it! The mansion had been shorn of more than ⅔ of its improvements—some wrenched away with great trouble and most wantonly." [195] Heap, furthermore, had "emptied the place of furniture, leaving not even a chair or a bed." A week later Payne exclaimed in a letter to a Washington friend:

> Behold me installed in my old abode at last—but how? Never would I have believed that anyone claiming to be an American, and especially the representative of America for so many years abroad, would have had the littleness to expose even the most worthless of his countrymen to such annoyance.
>
> When I entered, with every consular flag displayed in honor of my arrival, and a band of music at my portal, fiddling and drumming a welcome in its queer way, I did not find even a broken old chair to sit on . . . and repairs and embellishments I had taken unwearied pains to establish were gone, and difficult indeed must have been their removal.
>
> Tomorrow [July 4] is our National Fête. I have scraped together 6 chairs and a table, and luckily enough, brought some champagne and glasses with me for the occasion from Marseilles. If I have more visitors at any one time than I can seat, I must ply them with potations until they find a seat for themselves. [196]

A few days later he recorded: "My reception here has been most respectful. All the consuls have called in full uniform . . . but have not yet seen the Bey. Heap alone looks on me with an evil eye."

Dr. Heap was nevertheless a stickler for diplomatic etiquette. He volunteered to go to the palace to re-present Payne to the Bey.

"I took with me the Chevalier Gaspary, our vice-consul at the Goletta. Heap went by himself in another carriage and met me at the palace. Thus, separated and surly, we seemed like two parties going to fight a duel," Payne wrote the family. The rest he reported briefly to the State Department:

"Dr. Heap presented me to the Bey.

" 'Welcome be his arrival,' said the Bey."

Payne: "I derive the most gratifying encouragement to believe that politically and personally we shall always be friends."

The Bey: "It is not the first time we have known Mr. Payne. . . . We trust we shall be friends, not only as formerly, but better friends in future than ever." [197]

The Bey's attitude as revealed in this brief colloquy was regarded by *Galignani's Messenger* (July 30, 1851) as "particularly credit-able" to the Tunis ruler. Perhaps the Bey looked upon Payne's re-turn as a good omen. Matters had been going badly in Tunis. A cholera epidemic had "carried off vast multitudes." The govern-ment was discouraged, business was at a standstill, and agriculture and commerce were languishing. It was a time, the Bey may have reasoned, when friends should be cultivated.

At all events, Payne was surprised not long after his return to receive from His Highness "a flourishing letter" to be forwarded to the President. It was in a beautiful silk bag embroidered with gold, and with gold cord and tassels, the envelope bearing the great seal, and addressed to "His 'Ally,' 'Miller Fillmore,' telling 'Mil-ler' how well His Highness had received 'the respected John Howard Payne, the envoy of a great and powerful nation.'" [198]

The Bey was not the only one pleased to have Payne back. Another was Ambrose Allegro, the aged Tunisian who for so many decades had served the United States consulate for little or no pay. Payne had succeeded in having some money set aside for Allegro by the government; and as a consequence "the great and good President Fillmore" received another letter sent through "the warmly wel-comed and dearly valued consul of your country." Altogether Payne seems to have been justified in reporting to his brother: "My return has created a sensation. The Moors call it a special intervention of Providence to do justice," while in the official colony Heap's mis-behavior "has created . . . an interest in my favor."

That summer was hot, even for Tunis.

The Bey was induced to have some of Heap's worst depredations to the consular house repaired. The apartment which Payne had planned exclusively for official business, Heap had converted into a pantry! That was "restored to its original distinction." The ter-race, found in very bad shape, was somewhat patched up, though "the workmen withdrew, Moorish fashion, without touching ⅔ of it." On the whole the mansion had "very much the appearance of a gen-tleman who would be in full dress but for the want of a shirt and vest and shoes and stockings." [199]

By July Payne was able to report the bedroom nearly refurnished;

but most unfortunately "the change of climate, heat and long worry" had combined to wear him down. He suffered from diarrhea, which he "tried to conquer by diet. Mighty dull work being sick in a big, empty house with servants who have great difficulty making out what I mean and nearly as much in executing it, when they do." (Several servants trained for duty at the consulate had died of the cholera.)

Later, in somewhat better health, Payne referred to "that operation [extraction of upper teeth] to which my upper jaw was so mercilessly subjected just before leaving"; and with wry humor reported the miraculous appearance of a new tooth, "blooming alone . . . just as I was beginning to consider the moment to be on the approach when all such ivory adornments would prove no longer useful."

The "tedious delay of my goods and chattels from America" caused some anxiety, but in October the shipment finally arrived. Then how cheering was the sight of the old desk: and with what pleasurable anticipation did he begin the unpacking of the books— those almost human friends!

But—what was this? Was there some conspiracy, shared even by the inanimate, to shock and disappoint him? "Monstrous nails, the largest and fattest of their race," used to secure the hoops around the packing cases, had been driven so deep that "numbers of valuable volumes and engravings were pierced through and through. Thick quartos pierced, one entirely through and another half way, so as to render it necessary to tear them asunder by main force. Some of my picture frames spoiled and all glasses broken." [200]

After the torrid summer the wintry rains came on early.

"One accustomed to American provisions against the dismal season feels it infinitely more here, though less severe," Payne observed. The dampness of the house gave him a severe attack of inflammatory rheumatism,[201] affecting particularly his right arm, so that the preparation of dispatches was agonizing. "Got a receipt out of a book—Dr. James, inventor of James' powder—since when, can write without trouble for a while," he reported.

Added to everything else the mails were delayed. "I have scarcely seen a paper from America since I arrived and am without a line even from any of my relations for the last three months," he wrote to Eliza Watterston in December. He had been wanting to send Miss Watterston's father, the Congressional librarian, "a decision about the Carthage marble which I was trying to obtain from the Bey for the Washington Monument, but His Highness has not sent me any word."

As the winter progressed Payne was sick—very sick—often suffering from oppression in the chest. "I cannot rid myself of the idea of being jammed between walls in a deep well-top, and not being able to breathe. . . . For two or three nights, almost in a state of suffocation—noise in throat as of a dying person." [202]

Again "all the doctor books" were examined; and apparently a Sicilian physician was called. "Spasmodic disease of nerves coupled with catarrh . . . affair altogether neuralgic," seems to have been the diagnosis; whether his own or the doctor's is not clear. By "living altogether on rice, a powdered valerian and other things, can go to bed without great oppression." The diet was interrupted, however, when a large box of gingerbread arrived from home. He devoured it eagerly—"the most comforting treat in a long time."

The weather continued severe for that climate, and "on Washington's birthday there were 24 hours of sleet and hail and a downright fall of snow—the terraces and distant hills covered with a white mantle, to the exulting wonderment of the natives . . . no similar marvel since 1826." [203]

Much milder days came early in March, and Payne found himself "a little better, though not particularly strong. Can walk slowly on a level without losing breath, but on slight ascent, panting and laboring inescapable." Nevertheless, though "almost led to forgetting his way into the air by the winter's indisposition," he determined to go out in order "to show the sights to three Americans, all from Kentucky. A real American here is the rarest. . . . Must go to Carthage with them tomorrow. The excitement of American society doubtless will be a great help to me."

For whatever stimulation it afforded, the trip to Carthage was too costly. Payne would never venture forth again. A month and a few days later, on April 9, 1852, this dispatch was on its way to Washington:

To the President and Government of the United States: I hasten to bring to your knowledge the decease of John Howard Payne, our consul, who died this morning at 6 o'clock.

Gaspary.[204]

We have few details of Payne's last illness beyond those that he himself supplied. A friend who saw him frequently that last winter described him as "sitting in an armchair by a red-hot stove, drinking brandy and water and looking very sad." [205] Another stated briefly that his illness was "very long and painful."

But apparently he was not neglected. His Moorish dragoman was devoted to him to the last. And, thanks perhaps to the friendship of the Catholic bishop in Tunis, four Sisters of Charity—their names given as Rosalie, Josephine, Marie, and Celeste [206]—nursed him in his final hours, "closed his eyes and saw his spirit pass." Years later one of them, Sister Rosalie, would "compliment Mr. Payne's patience and gentleness," adding that he "exhibited the instincts and refinement of a gentleman." [207]

Payne had long anticipated "the inevitable hour," and had remarked not long before to a friend: "On the subject of Death, I have lived on this globe of ours through so many vicissitudes that I no longer see in it much to make me reluctant to resign it." [208] The philosophy and religious faith with which he was prepared to meet the end are voiced in his letter of early March, to Lucy, apparently the last he ever wrote:

It would be hard to reconcile ourselves to the adversities which seem to overcome through life every effort and aspiration of some persons, were there not sound, convincing reasons for regarding all similar trials as a mere preparation for . . . a better and nobler field hereafter.

Happy are such as can see and feel in all that presses heavily against them, mere education for a yet superior state of being, and who are conscious that there is no evil but despair of good, either for themselves or others.

Payne was buried in the Protestant cemetery of St. George's, on a hill overlooking Tunis Harbor and the ruins of Carthage. A Greek priest said prayers at the grave. Of the persons present at the funeral—and it seems likely that there were many—we have the names of only three: Moses Santillano, described as the English interpreter at the British consulate, who had become a devoted friend; M. Pisani, the British subconsul; and A. Chapelie, a French official.[209]

A flowering pepper tree planted by Chapelie was for some years the grave's only marker. When attention was called to that fact, the government at Washington had placed above the grave a white marble slab, bearing the arms of the United States, the time and place of Payne's birth (both erroneously stated), and the date of his death. There was also carved on the stone a quatrain composed by R. S. Chilton, a young clerk attached to the State Department:

> Lo, when thy gentle spirit fled
>   To realms beyond the azure zone
> With arms outstretched, God's angels said,
>   "Welcome to Heaven's Home, Sweet Home." [210]

Later, friendly persons planted flowers, and Payne's tomb became one of the tourist attractions of Tunis, particularly for English and American visitors. A kindly man who succeeded to the consulate some years later, Amos Perry, though he had had no knowledge of Payne until he arrived in Tunis, "plucked and pressed flowers, growing luxuriantly around the grave . . . and in writing to friends across the ocean, frequently enclosed the flowers with a copy of the inscription on the stone, and learned that these memorials were greatly prized." [211]

Payne's immediate successor at the consulate, Joseph Gaspary, did not live long himself. Dr. Heap, by that time well past the age of seventy, was then reappointed to the coveted post, but he soon followed his rival to the cemetery. Then came W. P. Chandler, the consul who interested himself in Payne's letters and on some of them made and initialed marginal comments. Chandler was followed by Perry.

To Perry fell the task of salvaging what was left of Payne's effects and sending them to his relatives in America. This, after a lapse of time, was no simple matter; indeed, it would not have been easy even directly after Payne's death, for illness and the work on the house had kept him from getting really settled.

To pay his Tunis debts, amounting to about a thousand dollars—though it was stated that $700 would have settled them [212]—his furniture was sold on the order of his brother, who asked that everything else be shipped to him at his expense. Apparently, however, there was no one on the ground of sufficient responsibility to see that this order was carried out.

It was at the request of that old-time friend of the Payne family, "the venerable poet-scholar-journalist, William Cullen Bryant, and under instructions of the Department of State," that Perry "instituted careful inquiries" about such effects as remained. Not many were recovered. Perry found that the private papers had been read and scattered and some of them pilfered. It is not clear what had become of the books.

> A few manuscripts, some of them diaries, and numerous packages of letters were found mixed up with moldy newspapers and decaying rubbish in a dozen or more boxes and bags, stored in a damp cellar in the Goletta. The most valuable volumes of manuscript and choice mementoes of friends . . . a quaint old seal ring with a Hebrew inscription (that used to belong to Payne's grandfather), a cane given him by Washington Irving, were sought in vain.

Word of Payne's death apparently did not reach America with the greatest possible celerity. It was not until more than a month after the event that some newspapers printed reports of it.[213] When the news did become known it brought forth besides a few brief press notices, two tributes that were distinctive and memorable. One of them was offered by Jenny Lind, then completing her two years of American triumphs. In New York on May 21, 1852, she gave a particularly brilliant concert. Tripler Hall was "filled to utmost capacity," and on the program that evening "Home, Sweet Home" was honored, not as an encore, but as a regularly announced number.[214] "A meaning and a sentiment never before conveyed by her" were noted in her singing of the ballad—"a priceless gem of a song, as it fell from the lips of the world's best singer at the time news of [Payne's] death was received." [215]

A few days later came a noteworthy journalistic tribute, that of Payne's lifelong friend John Gorham Palfrey in the Boston *Evening*

Gazette. Palfrey, who, it will be remembered, had grown up with the Paynes in their father's school and their home, was indeed almost a brother, and there was brotherly affection in his letter to Thatcher Payne: "The intelligence of Howard's death had touched me. So lovable a person one shall seldom see. I have scarcely loved any one as in other days I did him."

Palfrey had written "an impromptu notice—I don't know whether you will altogether like it." [216] Actually, the notice was a brief essay, almost a classic of its kind, with at least two paragraphs that might form an appropriate epitaph:

> Many mourn him. The fascination of his early brilliance has left its record on many minds. . . . Always buoyant, full of resource and rich in the stores of a varied and peculiar experience, his society had a singular attraction. Always busy about something, he kept his mind cheerful and wide awake. . . . His grace of expression, from boyhood to age, combining remarkably the exactness of art with the ease of nature, had a singular charm; and I presume a collection of his letters might be made which would take a high rank in that department of composition.
>
> But what I like most to think of is, that a life begun in some respects so inauspiciously should have passed to its end so blamelessly. . . . To be the spoiled child of public enthusiasm and not be a ruined man—to lose the huzzas that have cheered one on the threshold of life and not become blasé or a misanthrope, to be made drunk with admiration in the feebleness of one's teens and not awake to a chronic imbecility or spleen, bespeaks the presence of elements of a noble nature.[217]

[10]

PRECIOUS DUST

With the placing of the white stone above his grave, the final chapter in the life of John Howard Payne would seem to have been written.

In his homeland far across the sea, not many years later, the United States would fight its great Civil War. New generations would be born. American inventors and engineers would launch their country, and to some extent the world, upon constantly changing ways of life.

And through the years and all the changes, "Home, Sweet Home" would go marching on. The great public still loved it, believed in its sentiment, gladly heard it again and again. Long past the stage of novelty, it had not grown stale; with added age, its attraction was in its familiarity.

There was a very famous singer in those times whose devotion to the old song was extraordinary. That was Adelina Patti.

> To hear Patti at any stage of her long career in "Home, Sweet Home" was an experience of which [even] the most blasé . . . never seemed to tire. That simple act brought the public of two continents to her feet. . . . At the Albert Hall it was an experience absolutely unique merely to watch the breathless and expectant audience with heads bent forward, hanging on every note.[218]

Patti had sung "Home, Sweet Home" from earliest childhood. Her use of it on concert programs is said to have dated from an occasion early in her career when she was invited to the White House to sing for President Lincoln and his family. It was a sad time. The war was still raging, and the Lincolns had lately suffered the loss of their youngest son. "As Patti sang, the President sat with his head resting on his hands. When she completed her final number, he rose from his seat, went quickly to a small stand at the foot of the piano, took from it a book with a green cover and placed it on the piano rack, opened to 'Home, Sweet Home.' Then he returned to his seat and resumed his former posture without a word." [219]

From that time on, no Patti program was complete without "Home, Sweet Home." At the concert celebrating her return to America after twenty years of European triumphs—and New York had seen "nothing so exciting since Jenny Lind"—the press reported "her 'Home, Sweet Home' beautifully sung." [220] She even sang it when she was presented with the Beethoven Gold Medal at Queen's Hall, London, more than a decade later.[221] And a decade after that at Windsor Castle on command of Queen Victoria, when " 'Home, Sweet Home' brought tears to the Queen's eyes." [222] Patti's last appearance, at the age of seventy-two, she made, dramatically, at a concert for the

London Red Cross in 1914, after the First World War had begun; and "her voice was . . . still beautiful, as it faded into silence for the last time in 'Home, Sweet Home.' " [223]

In retrospect, the half century between the end of our Civil War and the start of the First World War seems, by comparison with subsequent decades, almost an age of innocence—a time when our customs were taken for granted and our troubles ended at the water front.

It was midway of that relatively tranquil period that William Wilson Corcoran, a Washington financier and philanthropist, conceived the idea of removing Payne's "precious dust" from Tunis to "a more appropriate sepulchre in the bosom of his native land."

The inspiration came to Corcoran as a result of hearing "Home, Sweet Home" played by the Marine Band. That of course was the air without the words, and Corcoran's response to the instrumental rendition suggests the question: Would that air to any other words have sounded as sweet? The answer must be that after more than half a century of association, the air and the words had become inseparable; the sentiment of the words had given the air its meaning.

Corcoran was a man of ideas and action. As early as 1859, long before recognition of native art became fashionable in our country, he had taken the first steps toward founding the Washington gallery that bears his name, dedicated to the interests of American art and artists. Nearly a quarter century later, at the age of eighty-four, he was still capable of initiating large projects and carrying them through to completion. Remembering how, when a boy, he had thrilled to Payne's youthful achievements as an actor, Corcoran suddenly saw the way to honor America's first native stage idol and the author of the world-famous song.

On October 14, 1882 he wrote to the Secretary of State, Frederick Frelinghuysen, "because you seem to be the natural custodian of Mr. Payne's grave in Tunis," suggesting that "one who sang so sweetly in praise of Home should not rest in any soil less dear to him than the land which gave him birth. . . . When favored with official permission, I will charge myself with the duty of providing for the removal of the remains and giving them a new and suitable resting place." [224]

Frelinghuysen's reply was one of "warm approbation."

This was the first step in official negotiations, which, oddly enough, derived added importance from the circumstance that the United States no longer maintained a representative in Tunis. Therefore it was necessary for the Secretary of State to "instruct Mr. Lowell [James Russell Lowell, the distinguished poet, then United States minister to England] to request the kindly assistance of the British government in obtaining from the Regency of Tunis permission to exhume Mr. Payne's remains." In December Mr. Corcoran was informed that the British government, "through Earl Granville, Her Majesty's Minister of Foreign Affairs, has instructed the representative at Tunis to afford all necessary assistance."

Corcoran's project had by this time achieved wide publicity in both the United States and England. It had come to the notice of one American who was deeply and exceptionally interested, and that was Payne's niece, his darling "little Eloise," by that time Mrs. Lea Luquer and the mother of three children. Her letter of inquiry to Mr. Corcoran brought the statement that he had not consulted her because he had "believed Mr. Payne had no descendants or collateral kindred." She granted her consent to the proceeding.

One cannot but feel that could Payne's own preference have been asked, he would have elected to stay where he was. It seems certain that he would have considered the disposal of the body—of any body—a matter of no great importance. No two members of his immediate family had been interred in the same burying ground. [225] The Paynes, it might be said, had been buried where they fell—his mother in Boston "in the old churchyard of Tremont Street, near the Common"; his father in the Old Friends' Cemetery, New York; his sister Eloise in Lancaster, Massachusetts; Anna in South Portsmouth, Rhode Island. Thatcher, who survived his brother by nine years, is buried in Brooklyn's Greenwood Cemetery. Lucy, who was the oldest of the children and outlived them all, died two years after Thatcher; her grave in East Hampton's main cemetery is next to that of Grandfather Isaacs, but no other members of the family are buried there.

To Howard, however, no choice could be given, and the plan for redisposal of his long-lifeless body went on apace.

In Tunis the British consul in the 1880's was Thomas Fellowes Reade, who may have been a son or grandson of Sir Thomas Reade, Her Majesty's representative during Payne's first term there. The elder Reade had been cordial to Payne in his life; and Reade the younger held the memory of the departed American consul in respectful, even affectionate, regard.

The exhumation took place on January 5, 1883 "with all the formalities required by law." [226] Besides Mr. Reade, the laborers, and a few native citizens, the witnesses included two Tunisian doctors and a lawyer, a commander in the British Royal Navy, and two persons who had attended Payne's funeral—M. Pisani, the former British subconsul, and Payne's ever faithful dragoman, Mohammed —as well as the United States consul at Malta, John Worthington, and his wife.

Believing that "probably no American would be present," Worthington, as he wrote to Sevallon Brown of the State Department at Washington, had "resolved to take a run over to Tunis and if possible get there in time to witness the disinterment . . . not in an official capacity but simply as an American citizen, who could not bear the idea that the body of the author should be taken from its grave . . . and not one of his countrymen present."

Apparently, however, there was one other American among the witnesses: an "occasional correspondent" of the New York *Tribune*, who sent to that paper a report which excellently complements Worthington's, especially in a description of the "not unattractive and decidedly neat Protestant Cemetery of St. George's," that had so long been Payne's resting place.

I was agreeably disappointed in this God's acre, as I had read in American newspapers that Payne's grave was neglected. On the contrary, the grounds were planted with flourishing and fragrant rose bushes, splendid clumps of heliotropes, and hedges of pinks and geraniums, while the walks were clean and smooth, and the stones and monuments snowy white in the morning sun. . . . Almost in the center of the enclosure was the grave of Payne . . . at its head a large and beautiful pepper tree, branches of which bent tenderly and droopingly over the tomb.[227]

This anonymous correspondent also noted in the Tunis cemetery "several Arab gentlemen, in their rich robes and picturesque dress," and especially "a certain (now old) Arab dragoman, whose attraction for the poet was deep and sincere. I saw this honest man, wearing his Arab costume and believing in the Mohametan religion, but full of Christ-like humanity."

Weird indeed had been the turn of fate! How often in the churchyard scene of *Hamlet* had Payne as the erratic prince confronted the gravedigger with the grim query, "How long will a man lie i' the ground ere he rot?" And now the American Hamlet's own remains were providing a partial answer to that question.

The condition as found here was briefly described by Consul Worthington in the letter to his State Department confrère:

> The coffin was badly decayed, and when raised was with some difficulty kept from falling apart; but everything relating to the remains was scrupulously and reverently preserved and handled. There was little else than the blackened skeleton left. Traces of the colonel's uniform [probably Payne's consul's uniform] were distinguished, some gold lace and a few buttons. I asked for a button, which was given me, and which I enclose to you. Mr. Reade also retains a button. I likewise enclose a twig from the pepper tree, this having fallen on the coffin. . . . Give Mr. Corcoran the pepper twig and thank him for his patriotic deed.
>
> . . . At 3 o'clock, after the body had been put into its lead coffin and soldered, and then into its hard wood coffin, and then into its outer box, it was brought to the little Protestant church, where it will rest tonight, and tomorrow will be taken to a vessel leaving for Marseilles.
>
> I tried unsuccessfully to procure a band to play "Home, Sweet Home," as the remains should leave the *marina* of Tunis. . . . However, as the body was brought into the chapel, an English captain played a dirge on the little American organ there, after which Mrs. Worthington sang "Home, Sweet Home" very sweetly, and then we all came away, leaving the poor body lying under the memorial window in the chancel, which a few large-hearted Englishmen had put there in tender and loving memory of one they loved and honored, not alone for the authorship of the most touching of all songs, but for the half melancholy and wholly beautiful character of the man himself.[228]

According to what the nameless *Tribune* writer added to this account, the little informal ceremony in the chapel must have been like a second funeral for Payne, sadder, perhaps, than the first: "Tongue cannot tell, nor pen describe, the effect of that song, sung under all the circumstances. . . . As the tender words floated tremulously through the holy place, hearts swelled, eyes were diffused, and a charm from the skies seemed to hallow us there."

On March 22, 1883 the three strong boxes containing Payne's remains reached New York from Marseilles on the steamer *Burgundia* of the Fabre line.[229] At one stage of the voyage the valued cargo had been threatened with indignities comparable to those that had often harassed Payne in his life.

From Tunis the caskets had been shipped to Horace A. Taylor, United States consul at Marseilles, on the French steamer *Charles Quint*. To that point the passage was undisturbed, but soon trouble began. Mr. Taylor reported:

> When the casket containing the body arrived I was informed by the agent of the steamship company that unless I made some arrangement to take care of all requirements, the health authorities would seize the remains and bury them again.
>
> I hired a barge, had the caskets put upon it and anchored it out in the bay, a long distance from shore. Notwithstanding this precaution, some days later, while waiting for the ship to sail for New York, the health authorities in some way learned that I had caskets containing human remains, anchored out in the bay, and they proposed to seize them and have them properly interred. I had the caskets opened and found that the body had absolutely "returned to dust." After numerous conferences and many and very emphatic expostulations, I prevailed upon the authorities to allow the remains to stay where they were until I could get them shipped.
>
> Another delay. The day before the vesesl was to sail I received notice from the company that the contract for shipment would have to be cancelled, owing to current rumors that the ship was to transport "a corpse"; that several passengers had cancelled their passage and quite a number of the crew had deserted.

Taylor's best efforts were of no avail. The company would not accept the shipment, despite the fact that charge for transport had been 1000 francs, or double first-class fare. Taylor managed to make a contract with the company owning another ship that was sailing in a few days. Nevertheless, to avoid a repetition of difficulties, "the box containing the casket had to be taken on board at night and stored in the hold." [230] And thus poor Payne, or what remained of what had once been Payne, returned to his native land. It was years, however, before any of these details were told.

In New York every honor was paid the oblong box containing Payne's "precious dust." Draped in the flag he had loved and guarded by a squad of policemen, the casket lay a day and a night in the Governor's Room of City Hall, whose windows look out over the former site of the old Park Theatre, scene of his youthful triumphs, and, farther to the south, face the Broadway end of Pearl Street, where he was born.

Flags of all public buildings as well as those on many hotels and business houses flew at half mast. The newspapers carried long editorials—nearly a column each in the *Times* and *Tribune*—praising the man and the one achievement for which he was generally known. "It may be questioned if there has ever been prepared for the remains of a celebrated man a home-coming so unique and so dramatic," said the *Times,* which also averred that in honoring Payne the nation was honoring itself.

> The eternal fitness of things demands that the mortal part of John Howard Payne should be resolved to earth again in his native land. . . . To Payne, thirty years dead, the reverential ceremony avails nothing. He has long since passed beyond the influence of the world's praise or criticism, adulation or fickle favor. But it is much to the living that the bones of an American author, beloved for his heart-touching song, should finally rest in the bosom of the continent that gave him birth.

The honors had only begun. The following day the stately corridors of City Hall echoed to "Home, Sweet Home" played by "Gilmore's entire band." The casket was placed in a hearse drawn by four white horses. Mayor Franklin Edson and the city aldermen, in several carriages, formed a procession, which, as the band played a dirge, moved slowly up Broadway to Canal Street, then by the Desbrosses Street Ferry to Jersey City. There a special car of the Pennsylvania Railroad was waiting to convey the casket to Washington. [231]

From its arrival in Washington, late in March, the coffin lay in a small cemetery chapel until the ninth of June, ninety-second anniversary of Payne's birth, when it was taken to the Corcoran Gallery to begin the great military parade that would be its final journey to the grave.

In 1883 the President of the United States was Chester A. Arthur, who, it happened, was a graduate of Union College, where Payne's name had long been a part of school tradition. By lending hearty support to Corcoran's undertaking, President Arthur doubtless did much to give the reinterment of Payne in Washington's Oak Hill Cemetery "almost the character of a national demonstration." [232]

For it is no disparagement of Payne or his work to say that the ceremonies of this day and the reverent spirit in which they were carried out were truly astonishing. Nor is this to assert that such tributes were his due. Probably few persons, other than presidents, monarchs, and military heroes have ever been so honored.

"The procession moved slowly up Pennsylvania Avenue, over to Georgetown, and up to the prettily shaded hillside to the cemetery," reported the New York *Times* in a front-page news story next day. "The spot was a charming one, in a grove of fine old trees, whose branches interlaced overhead. . . . It is an interesting fact that those trees were a part of Parrot's Woods, when Payne was a temporary resident of Washington 41 years ago, and that he frequently visited them and spoke of the beauty of the sylvan retreat and its surroundings."

In attendance, besides the President, his cabinet, and high officials, were many other dignitaries, conspicuous among them General William T. Sherman, the Civil War hero; James G. Blaine, soon to become a presidential candidate, and Robert Lincoln, the late President's son, himself a former Secretary of War. These, with the "robed priests, filed slowly across the open space to the platform. Two or three thousand invited guests—'the select of the capital'— sat facing a grassy square, where stood a veiled monument and a grave covered with a mat of evergreens. Opposite the President . . . a dense throng which could not be provided with seats, was so orderly that the police had little or nothing to do. . . . The turn-out of carriages was amazingly large, filling up all neighboring streets.

Arrangements for the press were particularly good, the places for correspondents being protected, in spite of appeals of prominent persons to be admitted to them." [233]

Though the *Times* declared that "the service was not long or tiresome," there must have been quite enough of it. The dynamic John Philip Sousa and his great Marine Band opened the ceremonies with, oddly enough, "A Lohengrin Mosaic." A Scriptural reading was given, an ode to Payne was read by its author, Robert Chilton, that young man of the State Department, now thirty years older, who had composed the quatrain for the Tunis headstone. [234] A choral group, known as the Philharmonic Society, sang Spohr's "Blest Are the Departed" and "Home, Sweet Home," the latter to "a somewhat new arrangement, which unfortunately was strange, and struck the great body of listeners unpleasantly, the differences from the ordinary version being principally in changes of time." The monument was unveiled, the oration followed, and "Bishop Pinkney read the Recommittal as the coffin was lowered to its grave and rolled into a cell beneath the monument."

The afternoon was marred by two mischances: one a brisk shower just as the funeral oration began, so that the crowd was "screened by hundreds of umbrellas"; and the other, the oration itself. It is to be hoped the rain distracted attention from the speaker's remarks, or drowned them out completely, for they were monumentally inappropriate.

The orator, one Leigh Robinson "of the Washington bar," had probably been chosen for his mastery of the pungent phrase. That he possessed, and by distortion and innuendo he turned it against the helpless and involuntarily resurrected Payne, with just enough sweet words to heighten the poisonous effect of the whole. Yes, "every home had been blessed" by his song; but beyond that and the precocious boyhood nothing about Payne was presented as admirable or even genuine.

A life nowise proportioned to its boyish promise and precocity. . . . Advantages, spoiling. . . . In the heyday of youth, as in the corruption of the grave, philanthropy has loved him. . . . Impatient of restraints and admonition, even of his benefactors. . . . His native land grew insufficient for him. . . . Perhaps it had been well if adversity had been stirred more freely in his cup. It happened otherwise. Life betrayed him with its kiss. . . . His life was in ashes before he was forty. . . . The double-flowering of the tree, fruitful of promise, devoid of fruit.

And more and still more, though this is enough. Possibly the speaker thought that he was but doing justice. He had come to bury, not to praise. But actually he knew very little about Payne's life or career and nothing whatever about the quality of his mind. His representations were based on hearsay, prejudice, and his own biased opinions, and he had made no effort to ascertain the truth. This is proved, if not by the falseness of the assertions themselves, if not by the suggestion that Payne's life had lacked adversity, then by two of the speaker's illustrations: "Wandering one night in London sick at heart, he sank down on the steps of a nobleman's mansion, and between the entrance lamps, wrote 'Home, Sweet Home.' "

That is so foolish as to be harmless; but the other is insidious: "With no undue diffidence he flung himself against Kemble and Kean in the arena of those triumphs which had made each 'a stately hiero-glyph of humanity.' " [235] Despite its complete and utter falsity as to both fact and insinuation, this sentence has an impressive sound that has made it all too attractive as a quotation.

The tragedy of this astoundingly perverted eulogy is in what it has done to Payne's memory and reputation. It contains the substance, and may actually be the source, of much later sophisticated opinion of him, resisted only by those who have carefully studied the facts or who possess rare independence of judgment. At the time little was known of Payne's life and achievements abroad or, indeed, of his activities in America, and few persons were able to dispute either the appraisal or the alleged facts. And Corcoran's careful provision for press coverage doubtless carried the speech around the world!

It is a relief to turn from the oration and take a look at the marble bust of Payne dedicated at this great American funeral. Although in photographs that include the base and lofty shaft, the whole monument may not seem impressive, the bust itself rewards close inspection, for the face is finely expressive of spirituality in both subject and artist. Corcoran was more fortunate in his choice of sculptor than of orator. The man he chose to execute this marble was Alexander Doyle of New Orleans. He wanted no pay for his work.

There have been two other efforts to perpetuate the memory of Payne in materials deemed less perishable than the air waves that carry a song. The earlier of them had resulted in a bronze bust, in Brooklyn's Prospect Park, in 1873, ten years before the Oak Hill Cemetery monument; the later would find expression in the memorial gates at Union College, dedicated in 1911.

The Union College gateway, planned to commemorate the one hundredth anniversary of Payne's student days, was erected at the suggestion of Hamilton Wright Mabie, long editor of *The Outlook*. Standing at the head of the main driveway from the college library, this gateway consists of a central pylon and a shaft on either side. "Home, Sweet Home," with two added stanzas, said to have been originally written by Payne although they are never sung, is carved on the stone in the center; and there is room for a bust. At the ceremony dedicating this memorial Payne's grand-nephew, Colonel Luquer, made a historical address, and the song was sung by Alma Gluck.

The moving spirit behind the Prospect Park memorial was Gabriel Harrison, Payne's first biographer, and the actors, artists, and writers who made up the Faust Club of Brooklyn were the sponsors and donors.[236] The bronze head of Payne was modeled by Henry Baerer, a German sculptor who had previously designed the Beethoven bust for New York's Central Park. Both Baerer's and Doyle's Payne sculptures were based on the familiar Brady daguerreotype, done when the subject was about fifty years old.

At the unveiling in the Brooklyn park, on a beautiful September day, the fresh voices of a thousand school children gave new beauty to "Home, Sweet Home" and there was an oration, vastly superior to the one which a decade later would mar a greater and more conspicuous ceremony. Here Payne was thoughtfully described:

A pioneer in the uncultivated field of intellectual labor in America, when our country was in its infancy. We had produced great statesmen, good lawyers, tolerable generals . . . but Payne was the first American who honored our country abroad in dramatic art. . . . In usefulness to dramatic art and literature he is not easily matched. It will not do to consider him as actor or author alone. All through his life the two pursuits ran together. He has earned an honest fame by the utility of his talents and the abundant fruit of his patient and useful life. . . . When it is remembered that in the presence of the wealth and greatness of the old world, he gave our country an honored name and fame in England, what gratitude can be too magnanimous? [237]

These were the words of a noted lawyer, William C. DeWitt, corporation counsel for Brooklyn, who would later draft the charter for Greater New York. It has taken Payne's countrymen the better part of a century to catch up with DeWitt's appraisal.

Adelina Patti's singing of "Home, Sweet Home" in the epochal year 1914 may have marked the end of the song's prodigious popularity. If this be so, it had had a vogue of just nine years under a century when it slipped out of almost constant use and took its place with the ballad classics.

The song's author may be judged more fairly with the passage of the years. We now can see that his work in three fields was impressively useful. In the theater, striving primarily to earn a living, he achieved important pioneering results. Among the Cherokees and again at Tunis, unhesitatingly aligning himself on the side of justice, he performed humane and valuable service.

His theatrical work is of course paramount; and in estimating it, what is important is not that he did not emerge another Shakespeare, or even another Edmund Kean: it is rather that an American of his period, untrained, single-handed, and powerfully opposed, became and for some years remained distinctly a part of the theatrical life of London. That he contributed materially to the useful stage literature of his time is undeniable. Drury Lane and Covent Garden are high courts of the dramatic art whose names have come down through three centuries. Even today it is no mean achievement for an American actor or playwright to form a connection with them. Yet there still exist numerous playbills of the 1820's that reveal both of these mighty institutions performing or announcing Payne plays the same night. There is also ample evidence that productions of this lone

American more than once helped to save England's two greatest theaters from imminent financial disaster.

Our knowledge of Payne is still increasing. The last word concerning him may not yet have been said. But in the light of what we know today he is no longer overshadowed by a single work which, for all its just renown, was but a by-product of his total achievement.

NOTES

IN THESE footnotes credit is given for most of the material directly quoted in this book, whether from letters, diaries, and other documents now in manuscript and here first published, or from printed sources. Authorities are named for many statements of fact.

These abbreviations are used:

DAB Dictionary of American Biography
DNB Dictionary of National Biography (British)
L Luquer collection
NA National Archives
NYHS New York Historical Society
NYPL New York Public Library
UC Union College

PART ONE, pp. 19–105

1. No official record of the birthplace of Payne has been found, but two century-old, hand-written documents (L) state that he was born in New York. The statement is also found in the New York *Commercial Advertiser*, February 28, 1809; *Evening Post*, March 18, 1809; New York *Mirror*, November 24, 1832; *Morning Courier*, December 8, 1832. See also discussion by Dr. Clarence Ashton Wood in *Long Island Forum* for September 1938.

2. Facts about Aaron Isaacs from *A History of the Family* (manuscript, 1861), by Lucy Payne Osborn (L).

3. East Hampton Library.

4. Harrison, *Life and Writings of John Howard Payne*, tells the story of Experience Talmadge in this way: "Her Uncle Talmadge was the Earl of Dysart, English nobleman of wealth. The earl died unmarried. . . . An agent was sent to this country to notify his brother, but after a long voyage it was found that the brother had died but a few weeks after the earl. . . . Having left a family of daughters only, the estate reverted to the crown."

5. Facts about William Payne from family records (L).

6. John 1: 47, "Jesus saw Nathanael coming to him and saith of him, 'Behold an Israelite, indeed, in whom is no guile.'"

7. (L).

8. Henry P. Hedges, *History of the Town of East Hampton, New York* (1897).

9. Esther Singleton in *The Antiquarian*, November 1924.

10. Certificate of baptism, signed by John McKnight, April 21, 1800 (L).

11. Stokes, *Iconography of Manhattan Island* (1928).

12. In addition to Great Dock Street (1791), addresses given for "Payne, William, schoolmaster," are "5 Dye Street and school, 7 Little Queen, do" (1792 and '93); "academic school, 23 Cedar Street" (1794–

389

95); "academy and house, 29 Ann Street" (1795) (NYHS).

13. John W. Francis, *Old New York* (1857).

14. Lucy's *History of the Family*.

15. T. T. P. Luquer, *An Unconscious Autobiography, William Osborn Payne's Diary and Letters, 1796–1804* (1938).

16. Lucy's *History*. The two Boston citizens were Thomas Handashyd Perkins, merchant and philanthropist, "generally known as Colonel," and Stephen Higginson, a member of the Continental Congress and great-grandfather of Henry Lee Higginson, founder of the Boston Symphony Orchestra (DAB).

17. John Gorham Palfrey in Boston *Evening Gazette*, May 29, 1852. The Boston city directory for 1807 lists "William Payne, schoolmaster, Berry Street; house, Atkinson Street" (Massachusetts Historical Society).

18. Samuel Adams Drake, *Old Landmarks and Historic Personages of Boston* (1900).

19. William Payne writing to John Howard (February 23, 1812), says: "For the use of that old stable seven years and eight months I paid $2092" (L).

20. Among pupils named as taking part in Berry Street Academy entertainments are William Endicott, A. Fessenden, D. Sargent, and Theophilus Parson. Parson eventually became a distinguished judge. Another pupil was Maria Theresa Gold, daughter of a prominent resident of Pittsfield. She later became the wife of Nathan Appleton and mother-in-law of the poet Longfellow. One of Payne's earliest letters (February 1, 1804), is addressed to her and says: "We miss you very much this winter, but your pleasing letters are some compensation for your absence. . . . My father says that for the benefit of our seminary he values them more than . . . a whole pocketful of recommendations" (L).

A reference to Maria Theresa after her marriage, is found in a letter of Eloise Payne (Boston, June 20, 1806), to her cousin, Harriet Isaacs, which contains a brief but interesting account of a visit to the studio of Gilbert Stuart: "I left off abruptly to accompany Mrs. Appleton to Stuart's Painting Room, where she is sitting for her picture, and certainly I have never passed three hours more pleasantly.

He is a very anecdotal man and he exerted himself today, I thought, to be agreeable. He is a vain man and a great egotist, so we had an opportunity of paying him many fine compliments without offending his delicacy. We availed ourselves of this circumstance and put him in a wonderful good humor" (L).

21. Drake, *Old Landmarks*. A plaque on a business house in Federal Street now marks the site of the Robert Treat Paine residence.

22. Palfrey, Boston *Evening Gazette*.

23. In October 1774 (see Congressional Record of that year) the Continental Congress adopted a resolution "to discourage and discountenance horse racing and all kinds of gaming, cock-fighting, exhibitions of shews, plays and other expensive diversions and entertainments. Congress urged similar action upon the states . . . Massachusetts repealed its anti-theatre act in 1806." Seilhamer, *History of the American Theatre During the Revolution and After* (1889).

24. Letters of William Osborn Payne from Luquer, *An Unconscious Autobiography*.

25. Harrison.

26. Palfrey.

27. "The Old Oaken Bucket," one of some 300 poems by Woodworth, was written in 1817, when its author was thirty-two years old.

28. Family record (L).

29. Statement published in New York *Evening Post*, January 24, 1806. It may be that Payne's lifelong extravagance resulted from his parents' indulgence of him during this period of childhood illness. There is some indication of the beginning of such a tendency in the earliest preserved letter of Payne, written when he was not quite eleven and had gone from his Boston home on a visit:

"I promised Anne Maria [identity not known] that I would give her the Children's Friend, 4 vols—handsomely bound, Price 4 Dollars to be had at Mr. Blake's Cornhill & if you will be so kind as to send them . . . you will oblige your dutiful Son, John H. Payne" (L).

30. *Old New York* (Francis).

31. Ralph Bennet Forbes. A letter by his son Robert Bennet Forbes (*The Critic*, December 1882) says: "Payne was in my

father's counting house early in the century."

32. Stokes.

33. *Longworth's Directory and Almanac for 1805.*

34. Park Theatre advertisements, contemporary newspapers.

35. Letters of Payne and Coleman from Hanson's *Early Life of John Howard Payne* or from Luquer or Union College collection.

36. Longworth.

37. *American Literature*, June 1933.

38. Ireland's *Records of the New York Stage* (1866) says that Mrs. Jones was "a daughter of a very respectable English physician, one Dr. Granger," and an older half sister of the Wallacks. It was as Sir Edward Bloomly in *Cheap Living* that Mrs. Jones appeared in Boston in men's clothes. Letters of Robert Treat Paine Jr. to John Howard Payne (December 1805 and February 1806) warmly defend her against "unmerited calumny" (L).

39. William Dunlap (1766–1839), playwright, actor, manager, portrait painter, author of several historical books, and once president of the American Academy of Design.

40. Of the three young men in the office, one may have been Clairborne Chew, later a Forbes partner; and another Joseph Osborn, a relative of Payne's, who later turned to publishing.

41. (L). Henry Brevoort was a descendant of Elias Brevoort, one of the early Dutch land proprietors of New York. There is evidence that the "young lady" referred to by Brevoort was Mary Fairlie, a local belle, of whom Payne later was considerably enamored.

42. Compare this description of Payne (1806) with Palfrey's nearly half a century later (Boston *Evening Gazette*, 1852), in which the boy Payne is declared as having been "A perfect Cupid in his beauty, and his sweet voice, self-possessed yet modest manners, wit, vivacity and premature wisdom made him a most engaging prodigy." Another description is that of John W. Francis, quoted in Duyckinck, *Cyclopedia of American Literature* (1855): "At the age of thirteen a more engaging youth could not be imagined; he won all hearts by the beauty of his person . . . the premature richness of his mind and his chaste and flowing utterances."

43. (L).

44. Of other offers of patronage Payne wrote his father: "It has been mentioned to me, but not directly . . . that the professors of Columbia College have had a meeting at which it has been agreed to give me a college education, gratis, except for the expense of books, which is estimated at $35 for the entire time."

45. Wemyss, "Chronology of the American Stage" (1852).

46. The Hallam Family, a company of players from London, gave what is believed to have been the first professional theatrical performance in the New World, at Williamsburg, Va., September 1752 (DAB).

47. From copies of *Julia; or, the Wanderer* (NYPL).

48. "Thespis," in his admission of error, concludes: "It *may* be, but I *know* at least that he saw and approved it [the "Theatricus" piece] before it appeared." This statement is probably false. It is unbelievable that Payne would approve adverse criticism of the actors, especially Mrs. Jones, of whom he had said in the *Thespian Mirror*: "She cannot be otherwise than excellent."

49. Press comments on *Julia* from New York *Evening Post*, February 8 and 13; *Morning Chronicle*, February 8; *American Citizen*, February 10; *Commercial Advertiser*, February 11 and 12, 1806.

50. Hanson.

51. John S. Curtis, "The Sloops of the Hudson," *Quarterly Journal of the New York Historical Association*, January 1933.

52. Colonel Willett, the hero of Fort Stanwix, was a grandson of New York's first mayor and would himself become mayor of the city in 1808.

53. Payne to his father, June 18, 1806 (L).

54. Charles Brockden Brown to Payne, August 25, 1806, quoted in Dunlap's life of Brown.

55. Young Payne's state of mind at the time is expressed in the poem, which begins: "On the deck of the slow-moving vessel alone." (See Appendix)

56. Seaman to William Payne, February 1, 1806 (L).

57. To James Lewis, June 27, 1806 (L).

58. Hanson.

59. *Memoirs of Eliphalet Nott* by C. Van Santvoord (1875). Dr. Nott was not only an educator and a minister, but also inventor

of the first base-burner stove made in this country.

60. Hanson.

61. August 2, 1806 (L). In those days single beds were almost unknown, and in inns and taverns total strangers were often obliged to sleep together. According to one account (perhaps legendary) Dr. Nott slept on the outside to keep his temperamental pupil from escaping (UC).

62. To Eloise, October 9, 1806.

63. *Union College Centennial Anniversary, 1795–1895.*

64. January 14, 1807 (Harvard).

65. For the poem, "Home, Dear Home," see Appendix.

66. Payne's correspondence with R. T. Paine Jr., apparently began with a letter from New York, December 28, 1805, in which Paine is addressed as "Honored Sir." The poet in his replies is less ceremonious, addressing John Howard as "My dear, ingenious Cousin," "My little truant Coz," and "Dear Coz" (L).

67. Nott to Sedgwick and Bleecker, November 17, 1807; to Harmanus Bleecker, December 4, 1808; to William Payne, November 8, 1807 (UC).

68. To Seaman, February 9, 1807. "Believe me, sir," this letter adds, "no object is nearer my heart than that of regaining the confidence my imprudencies has suspended." It was in connection with the Seaman matter that William Payne had written his son (August 24, 1806): "Experience will teach you that the sense of property is in many persons extremely delicate. . . . Few have that indifference . . . which makes them undervalue what they bestow from mere Good Nature, and fewer still, if any, confer a favor upon a principle so disinterested as not to anticipate a sense of obligation in the object of their liberality."

69. To James Lewis, April 25, 1807.

70. Payne biography by Rosa Pendleton Chiles. Payne's letter to his mother, May 10, 1807 (Harvard).

71. Published in *Lispings of the Muse* (London, 1815).

72. New York *Mirror*, November 24, 1832.

73. Boston *Evening Gazette*, 1852.

74. About the death of Mrs. Jones, in November 1806, Payne, from Union College, stated in letters to friends that he had written a poem on the sad event and quoted this stanza from it:

Death, with reluctant wing, half ling'ring flies
    And, armed with terror, pitying, shakes his spear;
He strikes—and as the lovely victim dies,
    Relenting, mourns her with a silent tear.

75. Advertisements in contemporary newspapers.

76. This, the original Park Theatre, was destroyed by fire in 1820, eleven years after Payne's debut. The building then erected on the site was what is usually called the Old Park, though actually it was the new. This was used until 1848, when another fire accomplished its end.

77. *Douglas* was founded on an old Scotch ballad, and the Reverend Mr. Home spent five years writing, revising, and polishing his play; but as penalty for engaging in so worldly an occupation he was condemned by the church to be unfrocked. In 1950 *Douglas* was revived in Edinburgh with Dame Sibyl Thorndike as Lady Randolph.

78. *American Citizen*, February 25, 1809. The *Commercial Advertiser* merely recorded: "On Friday evening the house was well attended to witness the first essay of Master Payne as a theatrical performer."

79. Joseph D. Fay, a humane and somewhat sentimental man, noted for his oration on the laying of the cornerstone for the first monument to the prison ship martyrs, April 6, 1808. His fondness for Payne is expressed in a letter dated November 25, 1808:

"You are very young. I know your heart is amiable and affectionate, and though your temper is 'as powder,' I am sure you are generous, noble and forgiving. But what makes me take a more than common interest in your welfare is the peculiar cruelty of your fate. . . . Other boys have to answer for little—you for everything. Others may give their days to pleasure and their nights to rest, without receiving censure. You must toil all day and night—and yet perhaps fall short of expectation" (L).

80. *American Citizen*, February 25, 1806.

81. Cooper and Price, "men of wealth and fashion, occupied adjoining houses on Broadway, at the corner of Leonard Street, and lived in extravagant luxury" (Longworth's *Almanac and New York Registry*).

For a time they ruled the New York theatrical world, though eventually the actor, William Twaits, attempted to break the Cooper-Price monopoly by setting up what he called the Opposition Theatre. That effort failed, however.

82. (DAB).

83. *American Citizen*, March 6, 1809.

84. Hanson.

85. Quoted in Duyckinck, *Cyclopedia of American Literature* (1855).

86. For the Roman actor, Gallus Quintus Roscius, 126–62 B.C. Hamlet refers to Roscius when the players arrive at Elsinore, Act II, Sc. 2.

87. New York *Mirror*, November 24, 1832; also Harrison.

88. Harrison.

89. *A Boston Dramatic Critic of a Century Ago* by Philip Hale (Massachusetts Historical Society Proceedings, 1935–36). The best-known works of R. T. Paine Jr. are two long philosophical poems, "The Invention of Letters" and "The Ruling Passion."

90. The Baltimore *Federal Republican*, October 20, 1809, explains that the "humble weed" poem is "an allusion to the origin of the Corinthian order in architecture." Paine the poet would write to Payne the actor that the Boston prologue, as it appeared in a Baltimore paper, was "grossly misprinted—'chapter' for 'chapiter.'"

91. *Actors and Actresses of Great Britain and the United States* by Brander Matthews and Laurence Hutton (New York, 1885).

92. Boston *Patriot*, April 19, 1809.

93. David Poe had a brother, Sam Poe, a sea captain, lost overboard on a voyage to the West Indies, who was "a better actor than his brother . . . a very eccentric and entertaining person . . . the best mimic our country has produced. A theater within himself—author, actor, scene-painter, could even be the music between the acts—all mother's wit" (Payne, in *The Ladies' Companion*, August 1837).

94. Advertisement in Boston *Mirror*, April 17, 1809.

95. The *Dramatic Censor* of Philadelphia said of Payne's *Lovers' Vows* that "by a union of both antecedent translations he has made a better acting play than either."

96. Reprinted in New York *American Citizen*, April 22, 1809.

97. To R. T. Paine Jr., June 11, 1809 (Hanson).

98. To R. T. Paine Jr., October 6, 1810 (Hanson).

99. William Stanley Hoole, *South Atlantic Quarterly*, July 1937.

100. Hanson.

101. Providence *American*, September 8; *Phenix and Patriot*, September 9, 1809.

102. *Ladies' Companion*, August 1837.

103. *John A. Latrobe and His Times* by John Semmes (Baltimore, 1917). This was the original Holliday Street Theatre, finished in 1794. The second to bear the name was erected in 1813 (Maryland Historical Society).

104. Irving to Payne, November 2, 1809 (*Life of Washington Irving* by Stanley T. Williams, 1935). Some tributes to Payne from Baltimore papers: "Such acting has never been surpassed on the American stage" (*Federal Republican*). "A maturity of intellect and a knowledge of the human heart . . . rarely found among old and experienced actors" (*American*). "Of Master Payne as an individual no encomium may be considered squandered praise" (*Federal Gazette*).

105. *Mirror of Taste and Dramatic Censor*, January 1810.

106. Thomas C. Pollock, "The Philadelphia Theatre in the Eigtheenth Century" (New York, 1932).

107. *Dramatic Censor*, January 1810.

108. Hanson.

109. Richmond newspapers of January 1810 (Valentine Museum).

110. To R. T. Paine Jr., October 6, 1810 (L).

111. To Benjamin Pollard of Richmond, November 13, 1810 (Harvard).

112. "Old Charleston Theatre," by William Stanley Hoole, *Southwest Review* (1940).

113. W. W. Corcoran, later a man of wealth and a patron of the arts in Washington, D. C.

114. To T. Beaumont, an actor, September 25, 1811 (Harvard).

115. To Caroline Crafts, July 11, 1810 (Harvard).

116. To Major Gibbons of Richmond, October 6, 1810. This letter states that the verses were written "as a jeu d'esprit, prompted by the remark that the name Mayo is in no way susceptible to a pun." For young gentlemen to address verses to

young ladies was quite the fashion of the period, and Payne was adept at it. In these addressed to Miss Mayo he conjures up a vision of the "twelve sister months" of the year and manages the pun, as well as the necessary flattery, by concluding:

From all the rest I gladly sever,
And in perennial joy with thee,
Dear May O, could abide forever.

117. It is often said that Dolly Payne Madison was related to John Howard, and although this cannot be fully verified, it may have some basis. Mrs. Madison's ancestors are known to have been Virginians, and Lucy's *History of the Family* refers to one of the original Paine (Payne) brothers who migrated to Virginia. A letter to John Howard from W. L. Marcy, written in 1846 (many years after this White House levee), refers to "old Mrs. Madison [who] claims relationship [to you] and is proud of it" (L).

118. Payne's account of White House levee (L).

119. Rebecca Power was the daughter of Nicholas Power, a prominent merchant of Providence. She married, first, Charles James Air, October 23, 1810; and second, Joseph Leonard Tillinghast, November 3, 1815 (Providence Athenaeum).

120. To Mrs. Air, March 12, 1812 (L).

121. To R. T. Paine Jr., October 6, 1810 (Hanson).

122. *A Particular Account of the Dreadful Fire at Richmond Va., December 26, 1811* (Baltimore, 1812).

123. Stokes's *Iconography* refers to Jacob (not Antony) Van Corlaer, "who in 1640, executed a lease to his plantations on the East River, with the contiguous hook."

124. To Jonathan Meredith, December 10, 1810 (Pennsylvania Historical Society).

125. Anna and Eloise Payne first set up a school in Newport, but later moved their headquarters to Providence. June 19, 1810 Eloise wrote her father of having received a loan from Howard to buy furniture for the new establishment, where, "besides thirty day scholars I have charge of eight in the house." George Channing's *Early Recollections of Newport* called this institution "one of the most noticeable Schools in America." William Ellery Channing also took a lively interest in the school and wrote the Payne sisters a long letter of "sincere affection" filled with advice to

"young ladies who live alone without parent, guardian or brother."

126. Lucy's *History*.

127. *History of New York* by Martha J. Lamb (1877).

128. *Apology for the Life of James Fennell, Written by Himself* (Philadelphia, 1812).

129. Hanson.

130. Dunlap, *Memoirs of the Life of George Frederick Cooke* (New York, 1813).

131. "The $800 which he was able to collect was barely adequate for fitting out the institution" (Hanson).

132. To Eloise (Hanson).

133. Hanson.

134. This statement is found in a letter of Lucy to Howard and in one from Howard to Dr. Channing, both of March 1812 (L).

135. (L).

136. To Mrs. Air, March 12, 1812 (L).

137. Among the Baltimore citizens who financed Payne's first trip abroad were William Gwynn, Alexander Contee Hanson, and Jonathan Meredith.

PART TWO, pp. 109–274

1. The London banking firm of Baring Brothers, with which Payne's funds were probably deposited. A director of the firm was Joshua Bates, whose American-born wife became Payne's friend and benefactor.

2. To the family at home, February 28, 1813 (L).

3. *Annals of Covent Garden Theatre* by Henry S. Wyndham (London, 1900); also *The London Stage, Its History and Traditions* by H. Barton Baker (London, 1904).

4. Mary Lamb to Dorothy Wordsworth, November 21, 1817 (Lucas, *Letters of Charles and Mary Lamb*, London, 1935).

5. To Whitbread, April 5, 1813 (NYHS).

6. (L).

7. Harrison. Mrs. Farmer-Powell-Renaud, celebrated actress, "sometimes known by the names of her three husbands" (DNB). Harrison says that Payne sent a letter of appreciation to Mrs. Powell, and she, not to be outdone in graciousness, replied: "If you saw any merit in my performance of the part it was entirely owing to a son I felt proud of."

8. To J. N. D'Arcy, December 2, 1813 (Huntington Library).

9. Doran, *Annals of the English Stage* (New York, 1865). Also Charles Hastings, *The Theatre, Its Development in France and England* (New York, 1901). Allardyce Nicoll, *Development of the Theatre* (London, 1927) states that previous to 1770, although certain conventions of costuming and scenery were observed, little attention was paid to historical accuracy. The movement toward realism in costuming and settings became more important in the early decades of the nineteenth century.

10. This comment of the London *Day* republished in the Boston *Polyanthos*, 1813. Other London press comments on Payne here quoted are from the *Morning Herald, Dispatch,* and *Sun* of June 5, 1813.

11. Dunlap, *History of the American Theatre.*

12. To William Dunlap, from London, April 4, 1814. With this letter was sent "Byron's latest work, 'The Corsair,'" as well as copies of the *Universal Magazine and Literary Panorama* (Harvard).

13. Allston and Morse had gone to London together in 1811. Mrs. Allston, a sister of William Ellery Channing, died there in 1815, and the only persons present at her funeral were Allston, Leslie, Morse, and Payne.

14. Dunlap.

15. Doran's *Annals*. Elliston's posthumous fame has been greatly enhanced by Charles Lamb's memorial tribute, which begins:

Joyousest of once-embodied spirits,
Whither hast thou flown?

16. Payne's scrapbook, which he humorously entitled "Egotisms, Playbills, Tickets, Scraps and Correspondence" (Harvard).

17. Violet A. Wilson, *Coaching Era* (London, 1922); also Charles G. Harper, *Stage Coach and Mail Coach in Days of Yore* (London, 1903).

18. Although no trace of a Trumbull portrait of Payne can be found in New York, and Liverpool and London galleries have no record of it, there are letters which prove that it was painted. Payne, from Buxton, August 18, 1813, wrote to Trumbull: "Mr Holbrouke" (the Reverend Theophilus Holbrouke, of Liverpool) "has placed your portrait of me in the Liverpool exhibition of pictures . . . I have thought it my duty to let you know this and hope it will not displease you" (NYHS).

19. To J. N. D'Arcy, 1813. A letter of Roscoe to John Philip Kemble, has this sentence: "Mr. Payne has certainly raised for himself an interest beyond that of his profession." (Harvard).

20. (DNB).

21. Harrison.

22. Manchester *Herald*, March 12, 1814.

23. The story of Payne and Emelia, except for a few details credited to other sources, is taken from the manuscript, in Payne's handwriting, in possession of the Henry E. Huntington Library of San Marino, California. It includes the copies made by Payne of his own and Emelia's letters and an explanatory summary, the first part of which, prepared by him in London for J. N. D'Arcy, is dated December 2, 3, and 10, 1813; and the concluding portion, dated May 1850 (Washington, D. C.). The manuscript was apparently found among Payne's letters by one of his successors in the Tunis consulate, W. P. Chandler, and has marginal comments in Chandler's handwriting, signed with his initials. Reproduction here is by permission of the Huntington Library.

24. Biggs, once "a member of Miranda's Expedition, of which he wrote the published history, and later attorney general of the British colony of Sierra Leone," Payne describes as "some ten or twenty years my senior—a highly cultivated and amiable person, but eccentric and nearly always in pecuniary trouble."

25. The red morocco box is the subject of this notation by Chandler: "This box was sold at the third and final sale of Col. Payne's effects at Tunis, August 1858. Bought by a Maltese or Jew or possibly a Moor. W. P. C., Philadelphia, November 21, 1859." Chandler adds: "I little knew the story of this box at the time. Had I known it, it would not have gone to the heathen hand it did."

26. Harvard.

27. Sarah Booth later appeared with Macready, Junius Brutus Booth (to whom she was not related), and other leading tragedians.

28. To Von Harten's offer of assistance, Payne replied: "To hang heavily upon anyone as a dependent will only, I fear, be the means of creating a thousand imaginary sources of disquiet in my mind and end in my doing something from wounded

pride to irritate and produce a break between us."

29. From the summary of Von Harten adventure.

30. The American patron was J. N. D'Arcy of Baltimore, then in London. On December 1 Payne wrote Emelia: "D'Arcy has proved himself a true friend. He unostentatiously enabled me to pay Miss H." (the dressmaker). Emelia had written on July 16: "Miss H. is greatly surprised that you did not get the Turkish dress, it went off on the 10th; the Rolla dress went the 12th, and your Hamlet dress will leave for Liverpool on the 19th."

31. The marriage record is cited as No. 400, page 164, of the parish book.

32. The London *Courier* of Saturday, December 7, 1816 carried this item: "Died on Sunday last, at No. 4 Windsor-terrace, City-road, Emelia, wife of Mr. G. Von Harten, in the 28th year of her age" (NYPL, newspaper room).

33. The only authority for this statement is a marginal note by Chandler. One letter of Payne to Von Harten (February 19, 1818) has been found, asking for financial assistance. It may have been in reply to this that Von Harten wrote an undated letter declaring himself "still hampered for resources . . . debts of honor still pending since death of my good Emelia" and referring to the expense of educating the girls (Harvard).

34. Payne's scrapbook (Harvard).

35. About Miss O'Neill: *On and Off Stage* by Sir Squire and Lady Bancroft (London, 1888) and *New Monthly Magazine*, 1834. Of her family it is recorded: "Her father fitted up barns to be used as theatres, divided receipts among performers . . . supported family in honest and virtuous indigence."

36. *Notable Irishwomen* by C. J. Hamilton (1904).

37. Notes on appearances in Ireland, scrapbook (Harvard).

38. Diary, February 23, 1821 (L). Here Payne records having seen Miss O'Neill (by that time wife of a wealthy member of Parliament), in the Drury Lane greenroom, and adds: "Time has changed my impression of her, fortunately for myself, though she still has my entire respect; yet had I known her before, I would not have committed myself so far as to fall desperately in love with her" (L).

39. Eloise and Thatcher to Howard, February 2 and 20, 1815 (L).

40. Thatcher adds: "If there is any foundation for it, we are wretched indeed. There is too deep a shade over the character of actresses in general to allow of individual respectability among them." Further comments in the same letter suggest that it may have been Howard's brother, rather than his father, who was deeply opposed to the stage. The next year, however, Thatcher writes: "I speak not of what the stage might be . . . were *all* its professors what *some* have been."

41. Payne's 1846 Diary, Berg Collection (NYPL).

42. O'Connell statement, London, January 1815.

43. "An Account of the Visit of His Royal Highness, the Prince Regent, to the City of London, June 1814" (London, 1815).

44. Eloise to Howard, September–October 1814 (NYHS). All quotations are verbatim, but because of the necessity of cutting, a few passages have been transposed.

45. Early accounts of the burning of Washington may have reported the White House totally destroyed.

46. The reference is to Howard's famous verses addressed to Maria Mayo. Maria's marriage to General Winfield Scott occurred three years after this letter was written.

47. The engagement of Eloise to Thomas Warner is mentioned in several letters to Howard: from Lucy, 1813; from Thatcher, 1816; from Anna, 1819 (L).

48. In later years the Warner family would attain distinction through the writings of Henry's daughter Susan, author of *The Wide, Wide World* and other fictional successes—literary museum pieces today, though best sellers in their time. (*Letters and Memories of Susan and Anna Warner*, by Olivia E. Phelps Stokes, New York, 1925).

49. The Treaty of Ghent was signed December 24, 1814; the Battle of New Orleans was fought January 8, 1815. The peace treaty did not reach the United States until February.

50. *The Hundred Days* by Philip Guedalla (London, 1934); *Napoleon* by Emil Ludwig (New York, 1948), and other authorities. Napoleon returned to Paris from Elba March 20, 1815. Payne wrote his

brother in May: "The emperor came to France a week after me" (L).

51. Brander Matthews, *Theatres of Paris* (1888), makes this distinction in names: "The association of actors, founded by Molière and made a national institution in 1680, was officially called the Comédie Française; the building in which this association later performed was the Théâtre Français."

52. Payne's translation of the rules and regulations of the Théâtre de la République, apparently the only such record in English, is printed as an appendix to Dunlap's *History of the American Theatre* (1832). On page 351 Dunlap states: "To the work on the French theatre, presented to Mr. Payne by Talma, and communicated to us, we are indebted for the 'laws, regulations and police' of the French theatres, which we give as a model for all countries."

53. Harrison. Also article in *Mercure de France* (1815) that says: "The different theatres have largely vied in offering him the freedom of their various establishments."

54. Payne's letter to the Théâtre de la République (as printed by Harrison) is dated March 27, 1815, a week after Napoleon's return to Paris.

55. Talma to Payne, June 17, 1815 (New York *Mirror*, November 24, 1832). Payne's faulty walk may have resulted from the nervous disorder of his childhood.

56. To J. N. D'Arcy, December 31, 1819 (Harvard).

57. Payne's introduction to *Accusation* (1817).

58. *Letters and Journals of Lord Byron*, edited by Thomas Moore (London, 1832).

59. Payne to Drury Lane Committee, April 26, 1816.

60. New York *Mirror*, 1832.

61. Payne's introduction to the magpie play, in *Trial Without Jury and Other Plays*, edited by Codman Hislop and W. R. Richardson (Princeton, 1941). A manuscript copy of *The Magpie and the Maid*, beautifully written in Payne's hand, is in the Harvard Theatre Collection.

62. Moore's *Letters and Journals of Lord Byron*. Byron thus distinctly identifies the Drury Lane adapter: "Mr. Concannon (the translator)" (the parentheses are Byron's).

63. About the magpie piece: *Theatrical Inquisitor*, Brooklyn Public Library; letter

to Meredith, Pennsylvania Historical Society; Thatcher's and J. D. Fay's letters, dated July 3 and July 11, 1816 (L).

64. William Wood's *Personal Recollections of the Stage.*

65. London *Times* advertisements indicate that only a few London performances of *Accusation* were given. Payne to his brother (May 1816) states: "Accusation was really acted five times with great success at Drury Lane." The *New Monthly Magazine* (London, March 1816) says: "The play has been repeated to considerable houses and without dissent, but its career seems at an end."

66. Harrison. That the *Accusation* manuscript was received in London, January 23, and performed February 1 is confirmed by both the *European Magazine* and the *Theatrical Inquisitor.*

67. Fanny Kelly, long one of London's favorite actresses, was a niece of Michael Kelly, famous Irish singer and friend of Mozart. In *Accusation,* according to the *New Monthly Magazine,* she was "as usual, all excellence, nature and feeling."

68. Allardyce Nicoll, *The English Theatre, A Short History* (New York, 1936), also "Early English Stage and Theatre Lighting" by W. J. Laurence in *Stage Door Year Book* (London, 1927).

69. *Reminiscences of Thomas Dibdin* (London, 1827).

70. Harrison (quotation traced to *Theatrical Inquisitor,* October 1817). The phrase, "some excellent productions" suggests that in London at the time Payne was credited as adapter of the Covent Garden magpie play.

71. Thatcher to Howard, July 1816, says that *Accusation,* as well as *The Magpie* had often been played in New York. Howard had written Thatcher in May of that year: "Price got it [*Accusation*] when he came to London and took it to America." A month later Payne wrote the Drury Lane management, "I understand the manuscript of D'Anglade [*Accusation*] was sold to the New York theatre for 13 pounds."

72. Payne to his brother, May 6, 1816: "An acquaintance began between the Honorable Douglas Kinnaird and myself, and the Honorable and I became very intimate . . . later I was reduced to quarrel with the Honorable" (L). Payne to O'Connell, October 16, 1816: "In France I prepared five plays by direction of Mr. Kinnaird, in-

curred expenses and lost the profit. . . . A quarrel ensued between Douglas Kinnaird and myself." (*Irish Monthly,* October 1889). Payne's 1821 diary also mentions "a quarrel with Kinnaird" (L).

73. On April 29, 1916 Payne wrote to William Ward of the office staff of Drury Lane, asking what had become of the items sent to Kinnaird some time earlier. This letter and the other Payne-Kinnaird correspondence are from Payne's first *Statement to the Sub-Committee of Drury Lane Theatre,* April 16, 1816 (Harvard).

74. Talma to Kinnaird, September 8, 1815 (Harvard).

75. Payne's "Notes on the Arms and Costumes of Mohammed" are several pages in length and painstakingly detailed.

76. Letter to Kinnaird, accompanying more items picked up in Paris, March 14, 1816.

77. Report to Sub-Committee of breakfast interview (Harvard).

78. Payne's second letter to Sub-Committee, May 13, 1816 (Harvard).

79. Report of Harris's offer to Payne, New York *Mirror,* November 24, 1832.

80. Payne to Harris, September 26, 1818 (UC).

81. Harrison. The *Theatrical Inquisitor* of February 1817 stated: "The tragedy of Adelgitha is in preparation at Covent Garden to introduce Mr. Howard Payne, the American Roscius." Payne's scrapbook contains advance announcements of this play for February 20, 21, 22, 24, 25, 27, 28 and March 1 and 3 (Harvard).

82. Scrapbook (Harvard).

83. To Harris, September 26, October 18, 1818 (UC).

84. Harris to Payne, November 2, 1818 (UC).

85. To Eloise June 19, 1817 (L). The entire letter is printed in *Actors and Actresses of Great Britain and the United States* by Brander Matthews and Laurence Hutton (1888).

86. Doran, *Annals of the English Stage.*

87. Hawkins's biography of Kean. The *Encyclopaedia Britannica* says that Kean's father was Edmund Kean, an architect's clerk.

88. *Letters of Washington Irving to Henry Brevoort,* edited by George S. Hellman (1914).

89. Doran's *Annals.*

90. Quinn's *History of the American Drama from the Beginning to the Civil War* (1923).

91. Payne was praised by the *European Magazine* for "a judicious softening of the awful plot." "Mr. DeVoltaire's 'Brutus,' according to Duncombe, one of the early adapters, was 'shockingly severe, without any softening of tenderness or humanity.'"

92. This part of the dialogue was entirely original with Payne. None of the earlier Brutus plays has an ending at all like Payne's.

93. To Kean, December 3, 1818 (UC).

94. Harrison says that *Brutus* was played twenty-three consecutive times between December 3 and the Christmas holidays, revived January 13 and continued up to fifty-three times the first season. *Brutus* is advertised in the London *Times* of January 25, 26, 27, 28, 29, February 1, 2, 3, 4, 6, 8, 10, 12, 18, 20, March 23 and 31 and May 7 and 12, 1819.

95. Cooper first appeared as Brutus in New York November 1, 1819. Henry Wallack had acted the part in New York two months earlier. Joseph D. Fay wrote Payne of an even earlier performance which he declared "miserable, worse got up than anything you can imagine. . . . The scene in Rome displayed Niblo's coffee house on one side and a part of the English bank with a steeple and clock on the other. The Forum looked like a country pig pen with the front side taken off, painted white with whitewash. The tomb of Tullius had a large mirror in it, and the priestess of Rhea looked like a good, fat landlady." O'Dell states that Kean, brought over by Price, played Brutus in New York December 4, 1820 and March 1, 1821.

96. Payne's suggestions for scenery, costuming, etc. are included in the edition of *Brutus* found in (John) Chamberlain's *British Theatre,* No. 71.

97. To J. N. D'Arcy, December 1819 (UC).

98. Harrison.

99. Payne's letter about *Brutus* to Drury Lane Sub-Committee, January 26, 1819 (UC).

100. Boston *Evening Gazette,* March 2, 1833.

101. (UC).

102. New York *Mirror,* November 24, 1832; Boston *Evening Gazette,* March 2, 1833.

103. (L).

104. Correspondence of Sir William Scott and Payne (UC).

105. Payne's handwritten copy of this letter to the Sub-Committee is at Union College; Harvard has the printed copy.

106. Genest's comment was published in 1832. In 1819 Payne had written to Sir William Scott: "I consider Livy's relation of the fall of the Tarquin as affording five incidents for a tragedy" (UC).

107. William Winter, *The Prompt Book*, Vol. 6 (1878).

108. Quinn, *History of American Drama.*

109. Letters to David Parish of Bath, November 7; to Samuel Williams of London, July 25; to J. N. D'Arcy of Baltimore, December 31, 1819 (UC).

110. Other applications are for managements in Glasgow and of two minor London theaters, Royal Coburg and Sans Pareil (UC).

111. Kean to Birmingham managers, February 1819 (UC).

112. Thatcher to Howard, December 24, 1814; Eloise to Howard, May 20, 1815; Thatcher to Howard, May 24 and July 2, 1816 (L).

113. Howard to Eloise, June 19, 1817 (L).

114. According to records at the New York Historical Society, plots No. 1248 and 1249 in Trinity churchyard are the graves of the infant sons of John Cheever Osborn and Lucy Payne Osborn; burial dates, 1817 and 1819.

115. To an American, Samuel Williams, Counting House, Tinsbury Square, London, Payne wrote July 25, 1819 asking for a loan of 50 pounds and pledging "a library in America—200 or 300 volumes, all elegantly and uniformly bound . . . bindings alone cost upwards of 70 pounds." The loan was made apparently without attachment of the library, and Payne declared it "impossible to express the feelings inspired by your kindness and especially by the manner in which it is made. The grace of the obligation gives it an importance beyond its pecuniary value."

116. Howard to Anna, December 30, 1819 (L).

117. New York *Times*, September 25, 1949. The Sadler's Wells Ballet originated in 1931 at Sadler's Wells Theatre. In 1946 it was transferred to the Royal Opera House, Covent Garden.

118. H. Barton Baker, *The London Stage* (1904); also W. Courthope Foreman in *Notes and Queries*, April 1925.

119. Clement Scott in *English Illustrated Magazine*, December 1898.

120. Foreman and Baker give the date of Sadler's discovery as 1684. Allardyce Nicoll, *The English Theatre, A Short History*, mentions no date earlier than 1740 for Sadler's Wells.

121. *Repository of Arts, Literature and Fashions* (London, 1832) says: "After the decease of Sadler, one Francis Forcer . . . became occupier of the well and music room; was succeeded by his son, who first exhibited rope dancing and tumbling."

122. *London Magazine*, May 1820; *Theatrical Inquisitor*, July 1820; *Literary Gazette*, August 1820.

123. Scott.

124. Baker.

125. "Charles II in 1660 granted letters of patent to Thomas Killigrew and Sir William Davenant, making them the sole guardians of theatrical amusements in the metropolis. The monopoly thus created for Drury Lane and Covent Garden lasted until the middle of the nineteenth century." Among many authorities for this statement are Watson Nicholson, *Struggle for a Free Stage in London* (Boston and New York, 1906), and "On the Monopolies of Drury Lane and Covent Garden," by Patmore Aymer, *Knight's Quarterly Magazine*, 1823.

126. Of the efforts of the minor theaters to circumvent legal restrictions *The Stage Censor, an Historical Sketch, 1544–1904*, by "G.M.G." (London, 1907) records: "Cibber renamed his theatre his 'Academy.' Macklin gave performances under the guise of lessons in dramatic art. Foote invited his friends to 'drink a cup of chocolate' with him."

127. London *Times*, April 9, 1820.

128. (DNB).

129. Scott. Also "Joseph Grimaldi," edited by Boz (Charles Dickens), London, 1846.

130. Playbills, scrapbook (Harvard).

131. *Theatrical Inquisitor*, December 1819.

132. *Theatrical Inquisitor*, September 1820. About Schiller's play, the *Inquisitor* adds the information that "altered by Holman, it was produced many years ago without success at Drury Lane. Since then the Lord Chamberlain has refused to license it

for Covent Garden . . . Mr. Payne has . . . retained all the most striking incidents and situations . . . and retrenched the verbosity of the German poet."

133. (L).

134. The London papers devoted countless columns to the trial of the Queen.

135. Boston *Evening Gazette*, March 2, 1833; also Harrison.

136. Harrison.

137. Scott, *English Illustrated Magazine*, May 1898.

138. Baker, *The London Stage.*

139. London *Times*, May 7, 1820.

140. New York *Mirror*, November 24, 1832.

141. Theodore S. Fay in the New York *Mirror* (1832) and Harrison's biography both state that an analysis of Payne's *Virginius* appeared in the *London Magazine*. The publication correctly so called, however, does not contain the analysis, but it does appear in the December 1820 issue of *Gold's London Magazine and Theatrical Inquisitor* (Newberry Library).

142. (L).

143. New York *Mirror*, July 10, 1834.

144. Payne-Irving letters of January 27 and 28, 1820 (L).

145. This paraphrased description of Fleet Prison and of the regulations is from "Writing a Play in Debtor's Prison" by T. T. P. Luquer, *Scribner's Magazine*, January and February 1921.

146. (L).

147. In 1815 John Miller, also something of a publisher, had brought out Payne's *Lispings of the Muse,* a booklet of verse. Miller also published the familiar engraving of Payne as Young Norval, after Leslie's portrait; and in 1823 and later Miller would reap a small fortune as the first publisher of "Home, Sweet Home."

148. DNB says of Mrs. Glover: "She was England's first comic actress and had a wonderful memory."

149. "One of the most popular and brilliant actresses of her time" (*Fanny Kelly of Drury Lane,* by Basil Francis, London, 1950). It was the summer before her appearance as Thérèse that she received the strangely beautiful marriage proposal of Charles Lamb.

150. The London *Times* of January 30, 1821 advertises "This evening, under Sir G. Smart, selections from Handel's sacred oratorio, 'The Messiah' and from Bee-

thoven's 'The Mount of Olives.' " These were the "fine strains" that Payne "heard through the wall."

151. Harrison. The *London Magazine* (March 1821) called *Thérèse* "almost one of the best melodramas we have seen."

152. London *Times*, March 2, 1821.

153. O'Dell's *Annals.*

154. Kemble's letter, dated June 1816, says: "Having but little legal information, I consulted my lawyer to know whether bail would be accepted or not. I am sorry to inform you that it would not, as I am not a householder and do not pay the King's Taxes" (L).

155. The first landlady to hold Payne's trunks was a Mrs. Sargeant of 4 Southampton Street, where he had lodged for years. The second was a Mrs. Potez, whose "intelligent but raw-boned" daughter Jane had been of a good deal of help to Payne as a copyist. The diary for February 21 mentions having sent some orders "to Mrs. Potez for Jane's birthday. . . . Mrs. P. and Jane called at the prison. Mrs. P. very kind and civil and said I *knew* they would always be glad to see me. So that breach is healed." March 9: "Went to Mrs. Potez; arranged to open my trunks tomorrow."

156. On February 24 Payne records calling on J. and her family at the new quarters. "Found them all helter-skelter. . . . They were obliged to sleep all in one bed and a sofa. Georgina [one of the children] said, 'Here we are, seven of us, in two beds and one nightgown, newly discovered at the North Pole.' She was in high spirits."

157. Payne to the family, December 31, 1822. A comment in this Palais Royal letter: "Living among kings gives one a respect for countries where a man governs only because a whole nation deems him worthy. It is a prodigy to see a sensible man on the throne of a great power, which seldom falls in the chance of succession. The highest numbers on the dice *will* sometimes come up, though, for nations as well as individuals."

158. To Talma, January 1, 1822 (L).

159. To Irving, March 30, 1822. The letter adds: "My valuable library and many other things, altogether having cost 6 or 7 hundred pounds, are in pawn in London . . . afraid all lost irretrievably. Elliston

was to have paid me 20 pounds which would have paid the interest" (L).

160. To Count de Roure, a fellow lodger at 29 Arundel Street, London (L).

161. *Life and Letters of Washington Irving*, edited by P. M. Irving (1862).

162. Irving to Payne, March 17, 1822. In Payne's behalf Irving called on William Hazlitt, then starting a new publication, and remained in London longer than intended. Payne wrote March 22, regretting "that your kind disposition towards me should have been a cause of any derangement of plans" (L).

163. Payne had written Elliston about *Adeline; or, the Victim of Seduction:* "a truly pathetic drama. Dresses modern but very elegant. Have kept Miss Kelly in mind in every syllable. Am certain you would do yourself harm in declining it. However, *de gustibus*, etc." (Harvard).

164. Mary Lamb to Mrs. James Kenney, October 1822 (Lucas). *Crabb Robinson's Diary*, vol. 1, p. 477, says of Mary Lamb's visit to Paris: "Her only male friend is a Mr. Payne, whom she praises exceedingly for his kindness to Charles."

165. Shortly after returning to London Lamb inquired of Payne, about the "Blue Silk Girl," "Where is she now?" And Payne replied (October 22, 1821): " 'The Blue Silk Girl' has never been seen since. She disappeared in despair at not discovering your name" (Lucas).

166. The Kenneys took a house at Versailles and it was there that Mary Lamb stayed while convalescing (Lucas). On October 28 Payne wrote Lamb: "Mrs. Kenney is jealous of your having written to me and not to them. She says she would be jealous of her cat if it purred more loudly for another. Her jealousy is worth having" (L).

167. Bishop recorded in his diary (August 9–12, 1821): "This week at the Académie Royale de Musique, saw a ballet called 'Clari' by Milon, music by Kreutzer" (Northcott, *Life of Bishop*).

168. Northcott; also Luquer, *Scribner's Magazine.*

169. To Bishop, November 9, 1822 (L).

170. Lamb to Payne about *Clari*, November 13 and 22, 1822.

171. Payne to Burroughs, August 5, 1822. To Bishop, October 22, Payne wrote: "I shall have one or two musical pieces out

in the rough in about a fortnight. I am now finishing a 5-act drama."

172. To Irving, June 6, 1822 (Harvard).

173. Chiles. Also "Pictures of Paris," from *Galignani's Guide Book* (1816).

174. *Journal of Washington Irving* edited by Stanley T. Williams (1931).

175. London *Courier*, May 9, 1823.

176. Story of play and quoted lines from editions of *Clari* in New York Public Library and Union College library.

177. Composers before Bishop had used the leitmotif, but it would remain for Wagner to give special distinction to this operatic device.

178. In the party with Kenney at the opening were Fanny Kelly, the actress; Richard Peake, a playwright; and Mrs. George Lamb, wife of a Drury Lane director.

179. Grove, *Dictionary of Music and Musicians.* The *Literary Magnet* (1825) said of Miss Tree: "The lower tones of her voice have a finer spirituality than anything we have ever heard." Ann Maria was a sister of Ellen Tree, later a famous actress who married Charles Kean, a son of Edmund Kean.

180. Payne's stage direction. F. Lauiston Bullard (*The Musician*, April 1913) says that in the audience that first night was James Bradshaw "a gentleman of wealth and fashion and a member of Parliament," who was so attracted by Miss Tree that he quickly made her acquaintance and later made her his wife.

181. All press comments here quoted are taken direct from London publications of May or June 1823 (NYPL and NYHS).

182. Of the play's continuing popularity, the *Weekly Dramatic Register* (February 10, 1825) remarked: "Clari remains an extraordinary favorite . . . as we have fifty times observed and could state with pleasure fifty times again." Of *Clari's* principal solo it observed: "We never remember a song which has completely permeated English society so rapidly."

183. *Quarterly Musical Magazine and Review*, 1824.

184. Northcott, *Life of Sir Henry R. Bishop* (London, 1920).

185. Kenney to Payne, May 10 and 12 and June 10, 1823. The May 12 letter disproves the statement that it was Charles Kemble who sold the *Clari* copyright to Miller. Another common misstatement,

that Goulding, D'Almaine were the first publishers of *Clari*, seems to confuse the little opera with some of Bishop's other works, notably "Melodies of Various Nations."

186. *The Theatrical Observer and Daily Bills of the Play* (official publication of the royal theaters), May 15, 1823, listed these as the songs in *Clari:*

1. Trio—Claudio, Giulio, Vespina and chorus, "This way, this way, place it here."
2. Duetto—Vespina and Jocoso, "For shame, get you gone, sir!"
3. Solo—Jocoso, "Ne'er shall I forget the day."
4. Solo—Clari, " 'Mid pleasures and palaces" (enc.).
5. Solo—Clari, "Oh, light bounds my heart!"
6. Duetto—Page and Vespina, "Yes, yes, I read it in those eyes."
7. Solo—Jocoso, "From flowers which we trim for the temple of love."
8. Serenade—Jocoso, Pietro, Claudio and Giulio, "Sleep, gentle lady."
9. Solo—Vespina, "Little love's a mischievous boy" (enc.).
10. Solo—Clari, "In the promise of pleassure the silly believer."

187. Vespina's solo:

Little love's a mischievous boy,
And uses the heart like a toy!
Full of rapture when first he takes it,
Then he pouts, throws it down and breaks it!

His smile has such witchery in it,
That all the world wants to win it;
But when in his cross moods they hear him,
All wish they had never come near him!

188. Northcott.
189. Bullard (*The Musician,* April 1913).
190. October 5, 1822. Bishop some years later brought out a Faust opera, but Payne did not supply the libretto.
191. J. Cuthbert Haddon (*The Metronome,* February 1920) gives this account of Bishop's "Sicilian Air": "Bishop, engaged by the London publishing house of Goulding, D'Almaine Co., to edit a collection of national melodies . . . found that he had no melody to represent Sicily . . . decided to make one himself. The re-

sult was the air three years later set to Payne's words. When the collection of national airs was published, several firms, believing it to be a real Sicilian air and therefore noncopyright, reissued it at a cheaper rate. . . . The result was a series of actions for piracy and breach of copyright. Bishop was called as a witness and deposed on oath to these facts" (i.e. that he himself had composed the air).

192. Harrison, one of the chief disseminators of this legend, says that Payne told the peasant girl story to James Reese in New Orleans in 1835.

193. William Pearman, who had sung Jocoso in the London première was advertised in the New York papers to sing four songs in *Clari:* "The Picture of a Playhouse," "A Garden Formed by Nature Wild," "Love Has Eyes," and "When My Bosom Heaves a Sigh." This brings up to a possible fourteen the song lyrics provided by Payne for the work, besides the three he said he had written for the Duke.

194. Rosa Pendleton Chiles says the first American Clari was "Susan Johnston, wife of the elder Wallack"; and Northcott says she was Mrs. Holman. O'Dell and the New York papers, however, provide convincing evidence that it was Ellen Johnson who first sang Clari in the United States.

195. Grove.

196. Bullard, *The Musician,* April 1913.

197. Two brief letters (L) refer to Payne's *Clari* manuscript (the words without the music). One, to Payne from Charles Kemble (November 28, 1824), says: "I have no knowledge whatever of the manuscript of Clari as sent by you from Paris, but I believe Mr. Bishop had it last." The other, to Payne from Bishop (40 King Street, London, November 23, 1826) : "My dear Sir: At length I have been able to find your manuscript of Clari. It had got amongst a multitude of papers in consequence of my moving here from my house in Gower Street. I regret that you have been inconvenienced by the want of it."

198. The original score of *Clari* was long part of the collection of Mrs. Julian Marshall in England. It came to America in 1884 and was acquired by Mrs. Luther Livingston of Cambridge, Massachusetts, and remained in her possession until her death in 1923. On March 6 of that year, at an auction at the Anderson Galleries in New York, it was bought by James F.

Drake acting for the trustees of the Eastman School of Music. "Other bidders for the desirable item were the Library of Congress, the New York Public Library and Amelita Galli-Curci, who sang the ballad with telling effect on her programs" (Barbara Duncan, in University of Rochester Library Bulletin, Winter, 1949).

199. To Anna, May 28, 1823. This letter begins: "Your last letter was just a month in coming. The first direct answer I have got from America since I left. It seems so social . . . like stretching out our arms and shaking hands across the Atlantic" (L).

200. Irving to his brother, October 3, 1823. (*Scribner's Magazine*, December 1910).

201. Irving to his sister, October 10, 1823. To Thomas Moore, *Life and Letters of Washington Irving*, edited by P. M. Irving (1062).

202. *Journal of Washington Irving*, edited by William P. Trent and George S. Hellman (1919).

203. January 8, 1823 (L). A similar sentiment had been expressed as early as 1817 by the *Theatrical Inquisitor:* "We wish to see him [Payne] better occupied than in translating even such pieces as 'Accusation.' The style and alterations are such as to make him worthy of something better. . . . Though we must admit his title to first rank among translators, we should prefer to see him aspire to a loftier and more difficult distinction."

204. In August 1823 Irving wrote to Payne: "Col. Aspinwall is looking at your house," and on October 4, "Col. Aspinwall took possession of your cottage September 15" (L). According to State Department records now in National Archives, Thomas Aspinwall was consul at London from 1815 to 1853.

205. P. M. Irving.

206. (L).

207. November 25, 1823 Irving wrote Payne: "Yesterday forwarded the manuscript of 'La Jeunesse.' Alter the title to 'Charles and Rochester' or 'Waggeries at Wapping.' "

208. DNB says of Fawcett: "One of his later creations was that of the father in Howard Payne's *Clari;* and in May of 1830 he took his farewell to the stage as Capt. Copp in *Charles II* by Howard Payne."

209. The words of Copp's song are in Irving's letter to Payne of November 28, 1823 (L). P. M. Irving says that Payne wrote Washington Irving: "Charles Lamb tells me he can't get Copp's song out of his head and is anxious for the rest of it. He says it keeps him awake o' nights."

210. In his preface to the first edition of *Charles II*, dated June 5, 1824, Payne says that he has never seen any of the previous translations of the play, but "must advert to material advantages from other sources, and regret that I am restrained from acknowledging them. . . . My manuscript has been revised by a literary friend . . . and the songs were supplied . . . by, I am informed, 'a very accomplished young lady.' " The "young lady" was fictitious. In the considerable correspondence of Irving and Payne about *Charles II,* covering the entire period of work on the play, there is absolutely no mention of assistance from any other person of either sex.

211. (L). Earlier Irving had written: "I do not feel that I could put pen to paper again for the theatre. I feel convinced that I have dramatic stuff within me, but I see I should never be paid for the bringing of it forth" (L).

212. For detailed discussion of Irving's work on the German librettos see George S. Hellman's introduction to *The Wild Huntsman* (Boston, 1924); also articles in *Music and Letters* (London), by George R. Price (October 1948) and Percival R. Kirby (April 1950).

213. Four different adaptations of *Der Freischütz* are advertised in the London *Times* of 1824–25.

214. Advertisements in London *Times,* October 1824.

215. To Irving, April 4, 1825 (East Hampton Library).

216. The praise was greatly appreciated by Payne, who wrote to Irving on January 26, 1824: "If I could give you any idea of the pleasure the encouragement contained in your letter gave me, you would be much obliged to yourself for having written it . . . I really feel as if the years to come, should they come before I go, will make some atonement for those which are past. . . . Once more let me thank you heartily for the cheering assurances of your letter. It quite gave me wings" (East Hampton Library).

217. May 5, 1824 (L).

218. January 28, 1825. Also Irving's other letters about Payne's creditors and payments, and about conditions at the Paris apartment (L).

219. February 1825 (East Hampton Library).

220. Irving's Journal (Williams), May 18, 1824.

221. Irving's letters of financial advice to Payne go back almost to the beginning of their acquaintance. There is one, written in 1809 when Payne, only nineteen, was at the successful stage of his American touring: "And now, John, take care of your money and don't squander it like a mere boy. Your sunshine may be short, yet . . . you may lay up a little competence that shall place you out of the reach of bad weather the rest of your life" (Williams, *Life of Washington Irving*).

A letter to Irving from Payne (1810) mentions a report (which he hopes is "embellished") of Irving's having "reprehended my profligacy with great force. . . . I have not mentioned this to anyone and do not . . . appeal from the justice of the censure," though the report "checked for a moment the impetuous current of my friendship. . . . Your opinion is like a casting stone, with many it will turn the scale at once." Payne adds that had he "secretly cherished this little pique, it would have destroyed everything like frankness" between them, but "now that I have imparted it the pique no longer exists. My feelings toward you are the same as ever; and I never wish to hear the subject spoken of" (L).

222. East Hampton Library.

223. In view of the long and intimate association of Irving and Payne, it is most ironical that in the 6-volume "extra-illustrated" edition of *The Life and Letters of Washington Irving* by his nephew, Pierre M. Irving, no likeness of Payne is included. Since many of the illustrations are "extra" indeed, including monarchs, statesmen, and literary and theatrical people, with whom Irving had little or no connection, the omission of any picture of Payne is conspicuous. It probably would not have happened had Irving been alive when the book was issued.

224. The Payne-Shelley letters were found among Payne's effects by W. P. Chandler, one of his successors in the Tunis consulate, and kept in the Chandler family for years. In 1904 the collection, consisting of twenty-nine letters signed by Mary Shelley and twenty-eight with the initials JHP, were sold at auction. They were edited with notes by F. B. Sanborn under the title *Romance* and were first published in 1907 by the Bibliophile Society of Boston. In 1907 the letters were owned by William K. Bixby. They are now the property of the Huntington Library, San Marino, California.

Unless otherwise credited, the letters of Payne and Mary Shelley quoted in this book are from *Romance*.

225. New York *Times*, April 27, 1904.

226. *Recollections of the Last Days of Shelley and Byron*, by E. J. Trelawney (Boston, 1858); also *Mary Wollstonecraft Shelley*, by Helen Moore (Philadelphia, 1886).

227. Godwin and his wife tried various means of earning a living, among them keeping a bookshop and publishing. They were the original publishers of *The Tales from Shakespeare* by Charles and Mary Lamb.

228. Percy Florence Shelley (1819–1889), of the three children Mary had borne to Shelley, was the only one to survive.

229. *Diary of Henry Crabb Robinson*, 1822 (Boston, 1869).

230. Hedges, *History of East Hampton*. This writer further describes Payne as a little under medium height. Later pictures show him bald of brow.

231. Pierre M. Irving's statement that "Payne speaks with bitter jocularity, since he grew too portly for the stage" is responsible for what is probably an erroneous belief. Though there are references in his letters to his having grown fat, it is doubtful if gain in weight had anything to do with his leaving the stage. And two years before the Shelley episode, in a letter to Elliston (requesting overdue payment for work), Payne says: "I have become quite thin and wish for *de quoi manger*" (L).

232. Irving's journal for July 17, 1824 (Williams) says: "Sat for Newton to alter my portrait. Moore, Kenney, Miss Holcroft and Mrs. Shelley came in."

233. *Letters of Mary Shelley*, edited by Frederick L. Jones (Norman, Oklahoma, 1944).

234. Knowles's *Virginius*. Payne's play of the same name was never performed in London.

235. Mary Shelley to Amelia Curran, April 1825 (Jones).

236. Kean's return to the stage after a sensational trial caused rude, mob-like demonstrations, but the excitement soon subsided (London papers of May and June 1825).

237. This London visit of Mme. Pasta was two years after "Home, Sweet Home" was written, and it was five years after that that she persuaded Donizetti to use the air in the opera he wrote for her.

238. An explanatory note added by Payne to the correspondence that he handed to Irving.

239. Payne's letter to Irving accompanying the correspondence.

240. Irving to Payne, from Havre, June 22, 1825 (L).

241. Irving's Journal (Trent and Hellman).

242. Frederick L. Jones, *Mary Shelley's Journal* (1947). The same author's collection of Mary's letters contains most of her correspondence with Payne.

243. To Irving, January 4, 1826. There is more to this letter: "I have made up my mind about Mr. Price. He shall have twice his number of plays in the course of the year. . . . I shall do this, not in the expectation of conciliating him, for he is not to be conciliated. . . . He endeavored to crush me when I was a child. I made my way without him. He wishes to injure me now that I am a man. . . . I have lived for years . . . in the face of his illwill; and if I did not hope God would take care of me without waiting for leave from King Stephen, I would go hang myself forthwith.

"P.S. Friday morning. I had written thus far last night and confess I have been in a little of a passion, but allowing for exaggerations . . . the feeling . . . is substantially true. . . . Really, now that I have had my say against poor Price on paper, I feel my rage quite cooled and could shake hands with him and forget all" (L, copy in letter book).

244. Irving to Payne, July 2, 1825 (L).

245. In June 1822 Payne had written Irving: "If Price really comes to Paris, it might be a good opportunity to rip off old scores and be friends. We might be mutually useful" (Harvard).

246. Irving to Payne, May 25, 1826, adds: "I feel that I have been unintentionally instrumental in creating this misunderstanding by suggesting the draft."

247. Mary Shelley to Payne (L, copy in letter book).

248. Irving to Payne, February 20, 1826 (L).

249. Irving to Payne about details of Richelieu: October 3, 22, 23, 1825; other letters concerning the play are dated January 27, February 7, April 12, 1826 (L).

250. DNB; also Tallis's *Dramatic Magazine* and *Censorship in England* by Frank Fowell and F. Palmer (1926).

251. Payne's diary, January 6, 1826: "A letter from Fawcett, very kind and feeling, mentions that the licenser has refused a license to Richelieu" (L).

252. London *Times*, February 12; *New Monthly Magazine*, March 1826.

253. *Richelieu* dedication, Berg Collection (NYPL).

254. Howard to Anna, July 31, 1826 (L).

255. Irving, about expense of apartment: December 22, 1825, February 7 and April 14, 1826 (L).

256. Payne's diary, January 2 and February 4, 1826 (L).

257. A few weeks before Talma's death he wrote Payne, promising to provide a Paris performance of *La Jeunesse* (*Charles II*), and adding: "I am sick to death and I play tonight" (L).

258. *Opera Class*, March 14, 1827 (East Hampton Library).

259. (DNB).

260. New York *Mirror*, December 1, 1832, adds that Payne's work in adapting *The White Maid* was "a herculean and thankless task, because all rhythm must be sacrificed in such a transaction . . . Sir George Smart and Mr. Fawcett called on Payne to say that . . . his duty had been done and gallantly."

261. Payne's criticism of Miss Paton's "perplexing conduct" (*Opera Glass*, December 5, 1826) referred to her as "a highly gifted individual" but compared her to "the spoiled children of popularity" and asked: "Are the many interests involved to be sacrificed to the vagaries of mere vanity?" Miss Paton replied in the *Times* (December 9) that she had given up the part "not from caprice but in-

capacity." It would have forced her to sing a song "in a tremulous voice like an old woman." The *Theatrical Observer* (January 2, 1827) commented sarcastically on Payne's attitude.

262. New York *Mirror*, December 1, 1832. This statement of the number of performances of *The White Maid* was probably supplied by Payne himself and may be regarded as accurate.

263. *Literary Gazette*, February 1827.

264. The London *Times* in its review (January 3, 1827) was plainly resentful of what it considered misuse of the Scott novels, declaring that "the author or adapter would seem to have selected a single incident from every one of the Waverley novels and jumbled them all together." The same critic then proceeded to devote a column to choice vituperation. But the *Theatrical Observer* (January 6) printed the protest of a correspondent who was "not a little amazed at the unmeasured abuse and impudent misrepresentation by the theatrical reporter of the Times newspaper."

265. *Weekly Examiner* and London *Times*, December 1827.

266. Of Molly Glover's debut as Mary Copp, the *Times* (September 26, 1826) reported: "The house crowded in all parts, and a crush in the one-shilling gallery. . . . Some persons in the pit, attempting to restore order, only made the tumult greater."

267. Press comments on *Procrastination* from *Court Journal*, September 26; *New Monthly Magazine*, October 1; *Examiner*, September 30; London *Times*, *Literary Gazette*, September 20, 1829 (NYPL).

268. There is also confusion concerning two other plays associated with Payne's name, *The Fall of Algiers* and *Mazeppa*. *The Fall of Algiers*, a comic opera "with poetry by E. C. Walker," was produced at Drury Lane in 1825 and played for several years. There exists a printed version of the same play that definitely names Payne as author (NYPL, Music Room).

Mazeppa, half drama, half equestrian exhibition, was produced at two of London's amphitheaters in 1831. Neither production apparently was Payne's, although Harvard has a manuscript in Payne's own hand, dated 1825, of a play called *Mazeppa, the Wild Horse of Tartary*, with explicit directions and diagrams, and water-color drawings of sets. The story is of a Tartar nobleman punished for intrigue by being tied to the back of a wild horse. In 1812, seven years before the appearance of Byron's poem "Mazeppa," Payne had written to Alexis Eustaphieve, Russian consul to the United States: "Returning Mazepa [sic]. . . . Sorry to relinquish all prospects of appearing in Mazepa" (L).

269. "The Court of Chancery on Theatricals," *New Monthly Magazine*, May 1831. The New York *Mirror*, December 1, 1832, states that Payne's name was "one of the first quoted in the high court of chancery, and several of his works were enumerated as among the stock drama of England."

270. *Fanny Kelly of Drury Lane* (Francis).

271. See Hislop's collections of Payne's plays.

PART THREE, pp. 277–387

1. Lucy to Howard, March 29, 1829 (L).

2. New York *Mirror*, June 20, 1832, also Stokes, *Iconography*.

3. Contemporary newspapers, quoted by Stokes.

4. New York *Evening Post*, July 26, 1832.

5. Stokes.

6. *Mirror*, November 24, 1832.

7. This statement and the quoted conversation, here somewhat abridged, are taken directly from Payne's memorandum of his homecoming (L).

8. Advertisements in New York newspapers.

9. Hone's Diary (manuscript), (this entry never before published) (NYHS).

10. New York *Mirror*, November 18, 1832. The *Commercial Advertiser* (November 22) called Payne "a modest, quiet and courteous gentleman and a true patriot at heart."

11. New York *Advocate*, November 22, 1832. That paper's editor, Major Mordecai Noah, two years earlier, had first called attention to the pleasure and profit that Payne's plays were giving Americans without any reward to him.

12. Park Theatre advertisements, contemporary papers.

13. "The gallery was a dollar and was packed. . . . There never was an assembly so thoroughly intellectual at the Park as that which graced it last evening." (*Evening Post*, November 30, 1832.)

14. Payne from New Orleans to his brother, June 2, 1835 (L).

15. Program details from festival playbill (Harrison).

16. Account of festival from New York *Evening Post*, November 30, 1832.

17. To Jonathan Meredith, December 6, 1832 (Harvard).

18. Payne's letter to dinner committee (L).

19. There was a succession of Archibald Gracies, and it cannot be known for a certainty which one this was. But it seems likely that he was a son of the original American bearing the name—the great merchant, shipowner, and famous host, who built the Gracie Mansion, now the official residence of New York's mayors, and there entertained poets, presidents, and at least one king (NYHS).

20. London *United Kingdom*, February 20, 1833. The *Court Journal* also noted the dramatic festival approvingly.

21. Payne to George Pope Morris from Boston, February 23, 1833: "I have scarcely a moment to myself—average three parties a day! I dined yesterday with the Governor, Lieutenant Governor, Attorney General, and leading law and legislative dignitaries, and was, in the evening, at a ball where I met many of the same grandees—with 'metal more attractive' in beautiful ladies, disposed of and in the market. H. G. Otis has called on me and I have met . . . in short, everybody of any standing" (Yale).

22. Four Payne plays were performed at the Boston benefit: *Thérèse, Charles II, The Lancers,* and *Love in Humble Life.* The "occasional address" for this benefit was written by Park Benjamin (the first), then prominent as editor and poet.

23. Harrison. Payne, in his February letter to Morris, had referred to the Boston benefit prospect as somewhat doubtful.

24. Most of these Boston newspaper comments are found reprinted in the *Evening Gazette* of April 6, 1833, including the editorials, which the *Gazette* attributes to the *Transcript* (Library of Congress). The Boston *Daily Advertiser and Patriot,* April 8, 1833 contained this communication: "The Committee on Arrangements of the Payne festival . . . cannot allow the article in the Atlas to pass without a comment. As the friends of Mr. Payne never admitted the word or feeling of charity,

we cannot allow that one paper, among so many, to be an evidence of the feeling of the community at large." The *Gazette* on March 2, 1833 had reprinted "a compression" of the New York *Mirror* articles on Payne, with important additions (Library of Congress) also (Massachusetts Historical Society).

25. Dunlap (NYHS).

26. (DAB).

27. Letter of Da Ponte in New York *Evening Post,* November 18, 1832.

28. Several family letters of 1821 and 1822 are addressed to "Mr. T. T. Payne at Mr. Da Ponte's, 343 Greenwich Street." Howard, writing from the South in 1835, tells of having met a man who had known Thatcher "at Da Ponte's."

29. O'Dell, *Annals of the New York Stage.*

30. Payne is known to have offered *Virginius* to Forrest for his benefit. "If Forrest likes to give it a chance, there will be no need of mentioning me in the business at all." (Payne to Prosper M. Wetmore, undated) (UC).

31. Knowles (London) to Payne, June 13, 1832: "Dear Sir: In the hope that you have not sailed, I hasten to say that any pleasure I could do you, you would be heartily welcome to. I cordially wish you health and happiness in your native land and regret that our intimacy has been so brief" (L).

32. "Prospectus of a New Periodical" (1833). This document observes: "The close intercourse of England and this country by means of literature and the arts has done more to wear away bad spirit than all the negotiations of our political ambassadors. . . . Our mutual influences exceed those of other nations because we not only think upon the same topics, but . . . our understanding of each other never suffers from those distortions, often inevitable in . . . any language not our own" (NYPL).

33. *Domestic Manners of the Americans,* by Frances Trollope (1832).

34. Harrison.

35. New York *Mirror*, October 21, 1832. Paulding's *Westward Ho* appeared a quarter century before the Charles Kingsley book of the same title.

36. New York *Mirror*, September 21, 1833. Payne had explained in his prospectus: "The proposed title of this journal

has been hinted by the story of the magical
cup . . . the famous cup of Jamshed, a
very ancient king of Persia . . . said to
have been discovered in digging the foundations of Persepolis, filled with the elixir
of immortality . . . supposed to possess
the strange property of representing the
whole world and all the things that were
then doing."

37. "List of Subscribers," published
June 1834 (NYPL). Three of the titles
here listed after the name of Philip Hone
have not been found elsewhere: "President
of the Clinton Hall Association for the
Cultivation of Literature, Science and the
Arts; president of the German Society;
vice-president of the New York Horticul-
tural Society; vice-president of the New
York Savings Bank."

38. Adams letter (L).

39. Foreword to "List of Subscribers."

40. Althea Bass, *Frontier and Midland*
(1933).

41. To Anna, January 11, 1835 (L).

42. Account of New Orleans adventure
from "John Howard Payne in New Orleans," by Lewis Leary and Arlin Turner,
Louisiana Historical Quarterly, June 1934.

43. New Orleans *Bee* (quoted by Leary
and Turner). The *Bee's* attacks on Payne
seem to be spread over most of March and
a part of April 1835.

44. Harrison and others.

45. Payne's letter to the New Orleans
Committee is here somewhat abridged and
consequently some of its passages have
been transposed. (Original in Pennsylvania Historical Society.)

46. To Thatcher from Mobile, July 25,
1835 (L).

47. To the family, from New Orleans,
June 15, 1835: "I am sending some trunks
and a live rattlesnake. I need not caution
you about His Highness. . . . If you don't
want him in the establishment, *chez vous*,
he may be deposited in Peale's Museum."
This letter has a marginal note, in the
handwriting of Payne's niece, apparently
added years later: "The rattlesnake came
and was sent to Peale's Museum" (L).

48. To J. R. Lambdin, from Pensacola,
May 16, 1835. Payne adds: "Have a wife
ready for me when I return!" (NYPL).

49. To Thatcher, September 12, 1835
(L).

50. The story of the visit to the Cherokees and of the Green Corn Dance is from

a very long letter of Payne to his sister
Lucy, August 1835. To Thatcher, on September 12, Howard referred to "a long
letter to Lucy, given to a stage passenger
to put in at the postoffice when he should
reach New York, as I did not think it
worth the postage." This letter, regarded
by ethnologists as unique and valuable,
was published in the *Continental Monthly*
(twelve two-column pages) January 1862
(ten years after Payne's death).

51. On July 25, 1835, from Montgomery,
Payne had written his sister Anna: "Chief
Apotheola has three daughters, and will
give $10,000, negro slaves and lands in
superabundance to the man who will marry
the girls. . . . To take all three at once
would be regarded as most complimentary"
(L).

52. Payne's idea of writing a Cherokee
history is mentioned in many later letters.
The Newberry Library of Chicago has
fourteen volumes of his handwritten notes
on the Cherokees, including not only political history, but also accounts of religious customs, myths, and legends.

53. Authorities for this résumé: *Indian
Removal*, by Grant Foreman, Norman,
Oklahoma, 1932; *The Cherokee Nation*,
by Marion Starkey, New York, 1944; also
general reference works and notes of
Payne.

54. Report of Committee on Indian Affairs to United States Senate, April 5,
1820. (This and other government publications, in economics division or American
history room, NYPL.) Chiles says that in
1802 Georgia ceded much territory to the
United States "on condition the Cherokees
would be removed from the state."

55. "The legislature of Georgia passed
a law making it penal for an Indian to dig
gold under Georgia" (Memorial and Protest of Cherokee Nation, to accompany
H.R. 695, 1836).

56. H.R. 287, February 24, 1820. The
other tribes removed were the Choctaws,
Creeks, Chickasaws, and Seminoles.

57. Jackson is said to have remarked:
"John Marshall makes the decision; let
him enforce it" (Starkey).

58. Payne's statement in the Knoxville
Register, December 2, 1835, contains the
entire story of his arrest and detention,
with Ross, by the Georgia Guard. On
December 24 it was reprinted in the
Georgia Constitutionalist of Augusta.

59. Knoxville *Register* statement.

60. "An act to authorize the issuing of grants by the State of Georgia to the fortunate drawers of lots," passed by the Georgia legislature in special session, December 21, 1834.

61. It is stated, not only in Payne's report after the event but also in a letter to his brother written before he went to see Ross, that he intended to stay but one day.

62. The first appeal written by Payne and printed at the end of his account of the arrest, was not used for the Cherokee signatures, but one dated February 22, 1838, was so used. That was sent to the Senate and House with 15,656 signatures.

63. Payne's account of the Council, apparently written for a northern newspaper, was among the papers seized by the Guard. It is printed in Senate Document 120, 25th Congress, 2nd session (p. 573).

64. Account of arrest and detention of Ross and Payne and their final release is from Knoxville *Register* statement.

65. This "Home, Sweet Home" story has been told in innumerable ways. This, Payne's own account, is of course the correct one.

66. Cassville (Georgia) *Pioneer*, November 13, 1835.

67. Knoxville *Register*.

68. Dr. Elizur Butler to Thatcher Payne, November 11 and 16, 1835 (L).

69. Thatcher to Howard, December 8, 1835 (L).

70. Resolutions of the two houses of Georgia Legislature, December 18, 1835 (copy L).

71. Payne to Myers (UC). On December 5, 1835 Payne wrote to General Edward Harden of Athens, Georgia: "I should not be surprised if those scoundrels make my journey a longer one than I have calculated upon. But no matter. If the worst happens, I shall not be the first . . . and unless the nation awakens, I shall not be the last" (Duke University).

72. General Harden wrote to Payne, December 18, 1835: "There is no doubt but that the President has been greatly deceived by his agents here" (L). President Jackson, in a letter to the Secretary of War, January 17, 1836 (copy, L) directed investigation of charges contained in a letter in the *Federal Union* of Georgia alleging that Payne had been "distributing Abolition tracts."

73. "Fully persuaded that an instrument so unwarranted would not be sanctioned by the Senate," Ross in 1836 presented a protest signed by 3,250 Cherokees. The transcript of proceedings of the Cherokee Nation at Red Clay, 1836, contains a memorial signed by "2245 male adults." Of the most eloquent of the memorials, Starkey, in *The Cherokee Nation* says: "Boudinot [a prominent Cherokee editor and writer] claims it was written by Payne." Others attribute it to Payne, but authorities do not agree as to which memorial it accompanied. These lines are famous:

"We are denationalized; we are deprived of membership in the human family! We have neither land nor home nor resting place that can be called our own. . . . We appeal with confidence to the justice, the magnanimity, the compassion, of your honorable bodies. . . . In truth, our cause is your own. It is the cause of liberty and justice. It is based on your own principles which we have learned from yourselves; for we have gloried to count your Washington and Jefferson as our great teachers."

74. John Ross to Payne, January 17, 1836: "I am truly sorry to hear of the heavy loss sustained by your brother in the late conflagration" (L).

75. "Thatcher Payne, after teaching in his father's and Mme. Chagery's schools, was offered the chair of languages and *belles-lettres* in Carlisle, and of *belles-lettres* in Columbia College, but declined both and was later admitted to the bar" (T. T. P. Luquer, *Scribner's Magazine*, December 1915). Joseph D. Fay wrote to Howard in 1816: "Thatcher is a noble fellow, his mind opens charmingly" (L). The New York *Mirror*, November 24, 1832, called Thatcher Payne "one of the most learned and eloquent of our young barristers."

76. Stokes, *Iconography*.

77. New York *Herald*, December 12, 1835. Other references to Payne's Cherokee adventure: *Evening Post*, December 12, 18, and 23; *Morning Courier*, December 17, 1835.

78. *North American Quarterly Magazine*, May 1836. It was Fairfield, the poet-editor, who first made the comment on Payne often quoted: "He is abused for opinions he did not utter and persecuted for errors he did

not commit. . . . The faults, moral and literary, of authors whom he translates, are always imputed to him, while the beauties are invariably assigned to the original writers" (New York *Mirror*, November 20, 1837).

79. The letter to Henry Clay on copyright, and the various literary and other proposed projects, are mentioned in letters of 1837 and 1838. About 1839 Payne submitted to Edwin Forrest the manuscript of *Romulus, the Shepherd King*, another drama on a half historical, half legendary theme. Forrest expressed interest in the play but it was never produced. Payne's Texas play and Texas novel both have disappeared. They may have been lost with other manuscripts in Tunis.

80. Stokes.

81. *Ladies' Companion*, August 1837. Besides the Keats article and the piece on adversity Payne's other signed contributions included a travel sketch, tributes to actors and writers of his acquaintance, and a scholarly historical sketch of Octavia, sister of Augustus Caesar.

82. To William Gwynn, January 4, 1838.

83. In addition to several long poems by Johnson, Payne quotes this short one: "Life Is a Jest."

Life is a jest—but Gay himself must own
A sadder jest on earth was never known;
The sides of Heav'n must split to see such fun,
In terrors ended and in tears begun.

Lo, there a wretch extended on the rack,
See his veins spout, and hear his sinews crack—
And if a keener jest is your desire,
Go, take his place—and laugh till you expire!

84. The *Democratic Review* was also called the *United States Magazine*. Payne's articles and the terms of payment are discussed in letters to O'Sullivan and his partner, S. D. Langtree, 1837.

85. J. Hingston, an Englishman, apparently a congenial friend, was a member of the firm of Pethrick and Hingston, piano manufacturers, Bleecker Street.

86. (L).

87. Boston *Evening Gazette*, May 29, 1852.

88. Payne's 1838 diary (L). On August 21, 1838, he wrote to Lucy, then in Newburgh: "We have lost old Mr. Da Ponte. He was buried yesterday. There was a service in the Cathedral. . . . Dr. Francis, Verplanck, and many others were there. We afterwards walked to the burying ground beyond Tenth Street" (L).

89. To "Little Eloise," September 3, 1839 (L).

90. Ross to Payne, February 10, 1838 (L).

91. Payne's first articles and public letters on Cherokee matters were published in the *Journal of Commerce* March 30, April 23, and May 1, 1838. Later others appeared in that paper as well as in the *National Intelligencer* of Washington and in Boston and Philadelphia papers. He purposely signed them with pseudonyms or faked initials. Original copies of some of them are in the 1838 Letterbooks (L).

92. To Thatcher, May 28, 1838. This letter also stated: "A document of 1000 pages has been printed on the treaty, by order of the Senate. It contains a number of notices of my adventure and also some very absurd lies; also your letter to Cass." (This is the famous Senate Document No. 120, 25th Congress, 2nd session.)

93. On his way to Washington in 1840 Payne stopped in Baltimore to call on his old friend William Gwynn, and reported to Lucy on May 14: "At Mr. Gwynn's I saw your portrait by Jarvis. Mr. G. did not say anything more about the sale of it. His circumstances are much narrowed, and as it is one of the few pictures he has been able to retain, I suppose he does not like the idea of its surrender. . . . It is barely possible that he may think the $20 you named as too little. . . . The picture is a very good one and an excellent likeness" (L).

94. Ross to Payne, January 8, 1840: "My long silence and neglect in not writing to you deserves the severest rebuke. . . . There has never been the slightest change in my warm feelings of friendship for you" (L).

95. Payne to the Reverend Mr. Evans of Madisonville, a missionary among the Indians, July 27, 1837 (L).

96. (UC).

97. The New Orleans *Picayune* of September 15, 1840, reported Payne's presence in the city, enroute to the Indian reserva-

tion, in company with John Ross, Lewis Ross, Elijah Hicks, and other Cherokee leaders.

98. To Watterston, September 1, 1840 (Library of Congress).

99. To E. Kingman (Library of Congress).

100. *Journal of Commerce*, January 19, 1841.

101. Payne to "Sister Elizabeth" (his sister-in-law) December 2, 1840.

102. To Watterston, December 2, 1840 (Library of Congress).

103. From Salem, North Carolina, where the United Brethren mission school was located, Ross wrote August 9, 1836: "Arrived here and found my daughter doing well in her studies" (L).

104. December letter to Watterston.

105. To Thatcher, December 1, 1840 (L).

106. To Watterston.

107. Payne's account of the Cherokee murder trial was published in two long installments in the *Journal of Commerce*, April 17 and 29, 1841. In 1932 it appeared in book form, under the title, *Indian Justice*, with notes by Grant Foreman.

108. "John Howard Payne and the Cherokees," by Grant Foreman, *American Historical Review*, July 1932.

109. Payne's story of Sequoyah's visit to Park Hill is told in the December letter to Watterston.

110. "Talking Stones, John Howard Payne's Story of Sequoya," edited by Althea Bass, *Colophon*, 1932 (NYPL).

111. To Watterston, December letter.

112. Ross wrote Payne from Salem, North Carolina in 1836 of having called in "the principal men of the Society of United Brethren, who would furnish all in their power [for Payne's history] and would have German documents translated. To the Reverend Mr. Chandler of Salem (June 27, 1837) Payne wrote: "Nothing remains for the Cherokees but to look to history for justice. . . . I shall render service with alacrity and pride, but cannot write history without adequate material" (L).

113. Quoted by Grant Foreman, *American Historical Review*.

114. President William Henry Harrison was inaugurated March 4 and died April 4, 1841.

115. (DAB).

116. *Leslie's Magazine*, June 1883.

117. NYPL manuscript division. On March 24, 1842 Payne wrote to his London friend, Mrs. James Kenney: "I am on extremely friendly terms with President Tyler and his family, and while he continues in power, I shall not, probably, be forgotten" (L).

118. *American Historical Review*, July 1832.

119. Chiles.

120. New York *Evening Post*, February 15, 1842.

121. To Dickens, January 10, 1842 (NYHS).

122. *Charles Dickens* by Edgar Johnson (New York, 1952).

123. Lucy wrote to Howard November 15, 1842: "The horror has somewhat passed away from my feelings for that fellow, Colt, whose brother you were intimate with. That you had ever been intimate with a brood like that makes me shudder" (L).

124. From Washington May 13, 1840, Payne wrote his brother: "I am constantly helping [Samuel] Colt, without any compensation: want written security upon some of the projects he is pursuing, and he promises great gains. I promise to profit from Colt's inventions" (L). According to DAB Samuel Colt's business failed in 1842, and he lost his patent rights to others. He then turned his attention to the submarine batteries, of which a demonstration (probably arranged by Payne) was held, with President Tyler, Cabinet and Congress members in attendance (New York *Evening Post*, August 20, 1842).

125. Adams was killed by blows on the head with a hammer that Colt had been using in packing some books, and the body was placed in a box for shipment to New Orleans (according to contemporary newspapers). In his self-justification Colt declared that when he struck Adams "he had his hand in my neck handkerchief, twisting it so that I could scarcely breathe . . . had lost all power of reason" (*National Intelligencer*, January 31, 1842).

126. New York *Evening Post*, March 12, 1842.

127. Letterbook, 1839 (L).

128. New York *Evening Post*, January 24, 1842.

129. *An Authentic Life of J. C. Colt* by S. N. Dickerson (Boston, 1842).

130. Payne, shortly before sailing for Tunis, sent his sister Anna the letter of

Colt to his infant son, of which the Reverend Mr. Anthon had had copies made. Here is part of it: "My dear Son: When you are old enough to read this, and learn and comprehend my sad and melancholy fate, your young heart will weep with sorrow. But let it not trouble you. . . . I am doomed to die an ignominious death tomorrow. But I die full of faith in a better and juster world. . . . Be kind and charitable. Strive to do good. Be honest. . . . And may the God of the fatherless protect you, oh my child" (L).

131. The Reverend Henry Anthon, rector of St. Mark's Episcopal Church, New York.

132. New York *Evening Post*, November 18, 1842.

133. NYPL (Berg Collection).

134. Payne's report to the Secretary of State (National Archives, Washington).

135. *Carthage and Tunis, Past and Present*, by Amos Perry (Providence, 1869). Italy began to take an interest in Tunis in 1862; Tunisia became a French protectorate in 1881.

136. W. B. Hodgson, Payne's immediate predecessor, "spent his time in Italy; only thrice visiting Tunis" (Payne to his brother, 1843) (L).

137. Perry.

138. Letters with account of journey, description of house and surroundings, and account of arrival and of call on the Bey, are to Payne's sister, brother, and sister-in-law (L).

139. "The little city which serves as the port of Tunis is called by Europeans the Goletta. . . . The northern part of the Goletta embraces the town, the castle, the royal bathing house . . . the southern part, the palaces of the Bey, the prison, the arsenal and docks" (Perry).

140. Dispatch to State Department, May 18, 1843. All of Payne's official reports on work in Tunis are in the National Archives.

141. Description of consular uniform supplied by National Archives and Records Service; also *Diplomatic Law Digest* by John Bassett Moore, Vol. IV.

142. "The population of Tunis, the city, is about 120,000" (*Shores of the Mediterranean*, by Francis Schroeder, New York, 1846).

143. (NA).

144. Schroeder.

145. To State Department, October 10, 1843 (NA).

146. To State Department, January 25, 1844 (NA).

147. Perry's report in Providence *Evening Press*, July 12, 1873 (American Antiquarian Society) of a reputed celebration of completion of work on the consulate was based on legends built up in Tunis years after Payne's death. It may be somewhat confused with stories of Payne's party for the ship's officers. It has been accepted by Harrison and others.

148. Payne to his niece, January 4, 1845 (L).

149. Schroeder (see note 142).

150. To Calhoun, Payne wrote August 25, 1844: "On receiving sad intelligence of a calamity in Washington, which in a moment swept away so many distinguished citizens, have caused flag to be placed at half mast. England's flag also was put at half mast" (NA).

151. To State Department, November 25, 1843 (NA).

152. To Secretary of State, May 30 and June 6, 1843 (NA).

153. To Calhoun, October 30, 1844 (NA).

154. To Thatcher, January 4, 1845 (L).

155. Statement found in newspaper and other accounts. "In 1810 Dr. Heap married Margaret Porter, a sister of Commodore Porter" (DAB).

156. The case of Hadj Khil was reported by Payne in three official dispatches to Calhoun: November 30, 1844; December 2, 1844 (123 pages); January 4, 1845 (37 pages) (NA).

157. To Calhoun, December 2.

158. To Anna, December 17, 1844 (L).

159. To Calhoun, January 4, 1845 (NA).

160. To Anna, December 4, 1844 (L).

161. To Buchanan, September 1, 1845 (NA).

162. To Buchanan, July 15, 1845 (NA).

163. About Gaspary and Allegro, to Upshur, May 18, 1843; to Buchanan July 15, 1845 (NA).

164. To Anna from Palermo, December 17, 1845 (L).

165. From Palermo, to Sir Thomas Reade, November 18, 1845 (Weidenthal Collection).

166. From Paris, to Edward Slosson of New York, October 26, 1846 (NYPL).

167. The Bey's letter was copied by Payne and sent to his brother (L).

168. To Thatcher, August 25, 1847 (L).

169. Thatcher to Howard, August 27, 1847. On April 3 Thatcher had written for "some direction in relation to things sent from Palermo. There are 17 or 18 trunks and cases in storage in Broad Street, at a considerable expense . . . besides two trunks in the Customs House store . . . which I cannot get out for want of invoice or accompanying letter. After twelve months they will be sold" (L). Howard replied that Prosper Wetmore, an old friend who had become a customs official, might offer assistance.

170. To Thatcher, from Paris July 22, 1846 (L).

171. Writing from New York July 10, 1848, to R. L. Delaware, a prosperous Cherokee who had remained in the East, Payne proposed a plan for bringing out the first volume of his Cherokee history, which he stated was "ready for the press," provided Delaware would supply the means (L). Apparently Delaware did not.

172. To Prosper Wetmore, 1849 (Weidenthal).

173. To Thatcher, March 25, 1849: "Address me simply Washington. They know me at the post office" (L).

174. Marcy testimonial, November 25, 1848 (UC).

175. To Joan Miller of East Hampton, August 6, 1849 (L).

176. To Thatcher, March 25, 1849 (UC).

177. Corwin testimonial, March 26, 1849 (UC).

178. Irving testimonial, April 14, 1849 (UC).

179. Among the papers "methodized" at this time were the Von Harten letters.

180. Payne to his sister-in-law May 3, 1850.

181. New York *Evening Post:* Benton's speech, November 18; Payne's reply, November 26, 1850.

182. Payne had referred to the Tunis consulate as "a two-penny post." He had written several letters seeking appointment as secretary to the Ambassador to Russia (L).

183. New York *Evening Post*, December 18, 1850.

184. The New York Public Library Music Room has several faded clippings with this Jenny Lind story, but the names and dates of the newspapers have not been preserved. There is variation in the wording, but the facts are the same. The story is also found in the *New England Magazine,* November 1891.

185. To sister-in-law, January 31, 1851 (L).

186. To Daniel Webster, March 17, 1851 (NA).

187. To Anna, from St. Louis, December 21, 1834 (L).

188. To Thomas Isaacs, October 6, 1848 (L).

189. Diary, January 2 and 3, 1849 (Berg Collection).

190. (NYHS).

191. (L).

192. To Daniel Webster from Havre, May 19, 1851: "Arrived on steamer *Humboldt,* which left New York May 9th."

193. Paris diary, June 8, 1851: "Out to tailor's concerning my official costume. . . . Planning ornaments for pantaloons by trying first two narrow bits of lace with blue between, then with cord. The former much approved" (L).

194. Mrs. Joshua Bates (see note 1 of Part II).

195. To State Department, July 3, 1851 (NA).

196. To Eliza Watterston, July 3, 1851 (Library of Congress).

197. To State Department, July 17, 1851 (NA).

198. To Eliza Watterston, December 17, 1851 (Library of Congress).

199. To Francis Markoe, a clerk in the State Department, December 15, 1851.

200. To Lucy, March 3, 1852 (L).

201. To Markoe (NA).

202. To sister-in-law, December 3, 1851 (L).

203. To Lucy.

204. (NA).

205. "Last Days of John Howard Payne," by A. Chapelie, *American,* April 25, 1885.

206. Harrison and others; traced to Father Abram Ryan, the "poet-priest," quoted in *Irish Monthly,* 1889.

207. Perry, Providence *Evening Press.*

208. To Eliza Watterston, from New York, May 4, 1851 (Library of Congress).

209. Chapelie.

210. Harrison, Perry and others.

211. Perry.

212. Providence *Press.*

213. The Baltimore *Patriot* of May 19, 1852 carried a notice of Payne's death, and apparently it was through this that the news belatedly reached his family. A telegram to the State Department, dated May 24 and signed Thatcher Payne, reads: "Have you received late information respecting Consul Payne, Tunis?" On the same date Thatcher wrote to William Hunter, acting Secretary of State, referring to "a paragraph in the Baltimore Patriot, announcing death of my brother, John Howard Payne, U. S. consul at Tunis" (NA).

214. New York *Evening Post*, May 22, 1852. The *Times* of May 24, reporting the large audience at this Lind concert, added: "'Home, Sweet Home' almost brought the house about their ears."

215. Springfield *Republican*, May 1852 (day of month not stated) (L).

216. Palfrey to Thatcher Payne, May 31, 1852 (L).

217. Boston *Evening Gazette*, May 29, 1852. Other parts of Palfrey's tribute have been quoted at various points in this book.

218. *The Reign of Patti*, by Herman Klein (New York, 1920).

219. F. Lauriston Bullard, *The Musician*, April 1913.

220. O'Dell, *Annals*.

221. *Monthly Musical Record*, London, May 1895.

222. Klein.

223. Grove, *Dictionary of Music and Musicians*.

224. Corcoran to Frelinghuysen (Library of Congress).

225. Family records (L).

226. Brainard, Biographical Sketch (Washington, 1885).

227. New York *Tribune*, February 11, 1883.

228. Brainard. Worthington apparently thought Payne had been buried in the uniform of a colonel of the New York militia. But that it was his consular uniform seems more likely and is especially indicated by the mention of bits of lace found in the coffin.

229. Contemporary newspapers.

230. Article by Milton F. Ailes in *Leslie's Popular Monthly*, December 1899, based on an interview with Horace A. Taylor.

231. New York *Times*, March 23 and 24, 1883.

232. *The Critic*, Boston, January 16, 1883.

233. New York *Times*, June 10, 1883.

234. Robert Smith Chilton served the Department of State in Washington and Ontario from 1852 to 1902. The Tunis headstone, with his quatrain, was brought back with Payne's remains and placed beside the monument in the Oak Hill Cemetery.

235. Brainard prints all of the Oak Hill oration.

236. To pay for the Prospect Park bust, the Faust Club put on a "dramatic festival" consisting chiefly of Payne plays and including, of course, *Clari*, in which the title role was acted and sung by Phillis Glover, a granddaughter of the illustrious Mrs. Glover, Payne's old friend of the London stage.

237. For DeWitt's complete address, see Harrison.

The reburial of Payne occasioned several brief articles based on recollections of persons who had known him. One, by Rosalie Miller of East Hampton, appeared in *Lippincott's Magazine* September 1883. Joan and Rosalie Miller had been among Payne's legendary sweethearts, though "Miss Rosalie," who survived her sister, does not claim that distinction in her pleasant little reminiscence of the East Hampton visits.

Payne, throughout his life, was notably susceptible. His sister Anna, writing to him in 1829, says that Robert Sedgwick "is to marry a Miss Ellery. She remembers you and says you were her first lover, but as you have stood in that relation to so many it is hardly to be expected that you shall remember her" (L). A letter of Payne to George Watterston (1840) says: "I am sending a letter and some trifles to the young ladies" (Watterston's daughters); and the letter to the girls declares that he misses them despite "all the local lovelies in one's path. . . . There are a great many young ladies in the world, and every step I go I see pretty and smiling faces multiply" (Library of Congress). What was probably the last romance of Payne's life is revealed in letters exchanged (in 1848 and 1849) between him and Anna Mary Freeman, an artist, to whom apparently he had proposed marriage (Huntington Library).

APPENDIX: SPECIMENS OF PAYNE'S WRITING

EARLY VERSE

Home, Dear Home

Where burns the lov'd hearth brightest
Cheering the social breast?
Where beats the fond heart lightest,
Its humble hopes possess'd?
Where is the smile of sadness,
Of meek-eyed Patience, born,
Worth more than those of gladness
Which Mirth's bright cheek adorn?
Pleasure is marked by fleetness
To those who ever roam;
While grief itself has sweetness
At Home! dear Home!

There blend the ties that strengthen
Our hearts in hours of grief,
The silver links that lengthen
Joy's visit, when most brief;
There eyes in all their splendor
Are vocal to the heart,
And glances, gay and tender,
Fresh eloquence impart;
Then dost thou sigh for pleasure?
O! do not widely roam,
But seek that hidden treasure
At Home! dear Home!

Does pure religion charm thee
Far more than aught below?

Woulds't thou that she would arm thee
Against the hour of woe?
Think not she dwelleth only
In temples built for prayer;
For Home itself is lonely
Unless her smiles be there;
The devotee may falter,
The bigot blindly roam;
If worshipless her altar
At Home! dear Home!

Love over it presideth
With meek and watchful awe,
Its daily service guideth
And shews its perfect law.
If there thy faith shall fail thee,
If there no shrine be found,
What can thy prayers avail thee,
With kneeling crowds around?
Go, leave the gift unoffered,
Beneath religion's dome,
And be the first fruit proffer'd
At Home! dear Home!

Written at Union College, 1806.
Probably first published in Hanson's
Early Life of John Howard Payne, 1913.

UNTITLED VERSES

On the deck of the slow-moving vessel, alone,
     As I silently sat, all was mute as the grave;
It was night—and the moon brightly beautiful shone,
     Lighting up with her soft smile the quivering wave.

So bewitchingly gentle and pure was its beam,
     In tenderness watching o'er nature's repose,
That I liken'd its ray to Christianity's gleam
     When it mellows and soothes, without chasing, our woes.

And I felt such an exquisite wildness of sorrow
    While entranced by the tremulous glow of the deep,
That I longed to prevent the intrusion of morrow,
    And stay there forever, to wonder and weep.

        Probably written on Hudson River trip, 1806, at fifteen.
        Published in the *Literary Visitor*, Baltimore, 1813.

Fragment "Found at Falls of Mt. Ida"

        . . . shunning the noisy haunts of men
He lov'd to wander here . . .
      . . . he joy'd to mark
The silver stream, swift gliding, 'twixt banks
Which seemed to smile in ecstasy to see
Their lovely foliage in the polish'd wave!
The distant waters, torn up by the crags,
Rippling and sparkling as they sprang in air;

Then traced with hasty steps the forest path,
Till, sudden bursting on the astonish'd sight,
The stream, impetuous, plunges the abyss;
Then flows along, exulting to be free,
With roar at which earth trembles. Here he paus'd:
For inspiration liv'd in every wave,
And the aw'd soul was mute.

        Written about 1807, at sixteen, at Troy, New York.
        Published in *Lispings of the Muse*, London, 1815.

VERSES FROM PLAYS

Mary's Song

    Oh, not when other tongues may read
        My heart upon my cheek,
    Oh, not when other ears may hear
        Dare I of love to speak:
    But when the stars rise from the sea,
    Oh, then I think of thee, dear love,
        Oh, then I think of thee!

When o'er the olives of the dell
    The silent moonlight falls,
And when upon the rose, the dew
    Hangs scented coronals,
And buds close on the chestnut tree,
Oh, then I think of thee, dear love,
    Oh, then I think of thee!

From *Charles II* (1824). Published in the
Literary Gazette, London, May 29, 1824.

Silently

Silently, silently
Manage this affair for me!
    Be discreet. Don't let a word
    By a single soul be heard!
Favors, to be kind, must be
Ever granted silently.

    Silently, silently
Do the deeds of amity!
    They are balms whose virtue rare
    Dies, when open'd to the air!
Would you earn a smile from me?
Win and wear it—silently!

From *Woman's Revenge* (1832). Published with the
play in *America's Lost Plays,* Vol. 5 (Princeton, 1940).

Virginia to Her Nurse

Would it were morn! There is a charm in light,
It cheers the sorrowing, and seems an emblem
Of Heaven's benignity. Yet, why should I
Droop and be mournful? I have not liv'd long—
The little life, I think, too, has been guiltless;
But they say falsely, who pretend that guilt
Alone, is rest's disturber; for I feel
A sickness of the heart which, sure, remorse
Cannot exceed—

Virginius to the Soldiers

But how I lov'd my girl! Attend me all—
Yet give me first a little leave to drain
A few red drops (for soldiers should weep blood)
. . . but when I saw her pulled
By Appius's lictors to be made a slave . . .
To sate the passion of a treacherous judge;
There, then, oh soldiers, this hand stabbed her—
Stabbed her for honor, for paternal pity!

> From *Virginius* (1820). Published in
> *Gold's London Magazine and*
> *Theatrical Inquisitor*, December 1820.

LATER POEMS

Star Gazing

Like thee, I love the stars. In distant climes
I've stood alone and watch'd them, and have thought
I saw the spirit of departed friends
Smile in their loveliness; and then would dream
That some, not yet departed, but far off
Gazed with me on them; and that I could feel
Their glance of kindness in the gentle light
Which cast its sweet spell 'round me.

Like thee, I love the stars—and thou hast made
Their radiance dearer yet. The poetry
Of thy imaginings, like sunbeams flung
Upon the waterfall, has wrapped those stars
In colors new and beautiful; and now
O'er me bring visions of a deeper power.

They call the mighty from their monuments,
They fill the sky with old, historic wonder;
And all commingling with the thoughts of her
Whose wand has waked this witchery, my soul
Swells with the blended glories, and I thrill—
Like thee, to love the stars!

Like thee, I love the stars, and yet my fortunes
Have often seem'd to tell me, "Do not love them,
But give them hate for hate." They never bless me:
They hurl'd me forth on thwarted hopes, false friends,
And left me to those triumphs of the little
Which make the spirit wither up in scorn.

But I can have no quarrel with them now,
Since one has risen o'er me in the west
Whose gentle beauty speaks for all the rest.
Shine on, sweet star! Still let me feel thy light;
For though I know that light is not for me,
I would not have thy pity cloud the spell,
Whate'er its peril, which has taught me here,
In thee, to love the stars.

> Published in Harrison's biography of Payne,
> first and second editions, 1875 and 1885.

Face to Face with Death

Hast thou stood by when first the spirit felt
    The certainty its hour was come to part
    From its frail tenement for untried spheres?

Hast thou stood by, amid the fierce convulsion
    Which tells the soul is from the body breaking
    And straight must be divorc'd: Say, hast thou mark'd
The first glance of the dying, as the marble
    Uprose to show him the dark, narrow house
    In which he did not dream so soon to dwell?

For oft as he has taken lease of life,
Each time he thought that he *must* see the morrow,
    And need not die today—no, not today!

When the strange chill that tells him Death is real,
Wakes the wretch'd wanderer from the world's wild Dream,
Does there not, sometimes, if but for an instant,
Flit o'er his mind a consciousness
Whose quick grasp, more than human, seems an earnest
Of the unknown powers to which his mind is changing?

The clouds all vanish, and, its ken inspired
With quick and more than human grasp, proclaims
The mystic sphere where all is intellectual:

And from the mighty pinnacle, it looks
With outstretched wings, just ready for its flight,
Beyond the globe it loved so, and confesses
Its less than nothingness; and sees with wonder
Its once poor pathway strew'd with broken hopes
And mad ambition's ruins:—while the forms
Of slighted friends, hours murder'd; and the voice
Of warning, spurn'd, and long forgotten guilt
Call from their graves and ride in rushing hosts,
With hideous mien, led by the fiend, Remorse,
To fright the trifler, who a little moment
Feels how he should have lived, then lives no more!

In manuscript, Luquer collection. Not previously published.

The Blind Girl Listening to Her Lover

The gentle brook babbling its music,
The sward whose smooth green seem'd the hurt mind's valor,
The clear blue sky, as pure as angels' voices,
These, though not seeing, I saw—I saw them
In his eloquence.

The Deaf Seeing Dancing

The unexcited looker-on of love
Is like the deaf seeing dancing.—Withheld
The inspiration that appears to make
The floor the light toe touches, spring to meet
Its kiss, the wild bound looks like madness.—So
The heart's dance seems, of the heart's music robb'd,
A reel of bacchanals.

In manuscript, Luquer collection. Not previously published.

BIBLIOGRAPHY

(In this listing are included books and articles found of concrete value in the preparation of this work. Other valuable published works read or consulted have been mentioned in the footnotes. Manuscript sources are listed at the end.)

ABOUT PAYNE

Books

Brainard, Charles, *John Howard Payne, a biographical sketch, with a narrative of the removal of his remains from Tunis to Washington, D. C.,* Washington, 1885.

Chiles, Rosa Pendleton, *John Howard Payne, American poet, actor, playwright, consul and author of "Home, Sweet Home."* Washington, 1930.

Hanson, Willis Tracy, Jr., *The Early Life of John Howard Payne,* Boston, 1913.

Harrison, Gabriel, *The Life and Writings of John Howard Payne,* Albany, 1875.

Sanborn, Franklin Benjamin (annotator), *The Romance of Mary W. Shelley, John Howard Payne and Washington Irving* (letters), Boston, 1907.

Articles

Ailes, Milton F., "John Howard Payne, a strange, eventful history," *Frank Leslie's Popular Monthly,* December 1889.

Bass, Althea, "From the notebooks of John Howard Payne," *Frontier and Midland* (Missoula, Montana), 1933.

Blakeley, Sidney H., "New York's First Theatrical Magazine," *Studies in Philology,* Chapel Hill, N. C., October 1949.

Boston Evening Gazette, "John Howard Payne, a biographical sketch," March 6, 1833.

Duffee, F. H., "Reminiscences of John Howard Payne," *Boogher's Repository,* April 1883.

Fairfield, Sumner Lincoln, "Character of John Howard Payne," *New York Mirror,* March 24, 1827.

——— "The Payne Benefit," *North American Magazine,* November 1832.

Fairfield, Sumner Lincoln, "Memoirs of John Howard Payne," *North American Magazine*, May 1833.

────── "The Captivity of John Howard Payne," *North American Quarterly Magazine*, January 1836.

Fay, Theodore Sedgwick, "A Sketch of the Life of John Howard Payne," *New York Mirror*, November 24 and December 1, 1832.

Foreman, Grant, "John Howard Payne and the Cherokees," *American Historical Review*, New York, July 1932.

Hutton, Laurence, "John Howard Payne, the Actor," *Magazine of American History*, May 1883.

Leary, Lewis and Turner, Arlin, "Payne in New Orleans," *Louisiana Historical Quarterly*, New Orleans, January 1948.

Luquer, Thatcher Taylor Payne, "Letters from Paris," *Scribner's Magazine*, December 1910.

────── "When Payne Wrote 'Home, Sweet Home,'" *Scribner's Magazine*, December 1915.

────── "Extracts from the Diary of John Howard Payne," *Scribner's Magazine*, January-February 1921.

Mirror of Taste and Dramatic Censor, The, Philadelphia, March 1810, November 1810, January 1811.

Palfrey, John Gorham, "A Tribute to John Howard Payne," *Boston Evening Gazette*, May 29, 1852.

Polyanthos, The, Boston, 1812.

Portfolio, The, Philadelphia, February 22, 1806.

Sterns, Bertha Monica, "John Howard Payne as an Editor," *American Literature* (Durham, N. C.), May 1933.

Vedder, Morris Gilbert, "Stage Career of John Howard Payne," *Northwest Ohio Quarterly*, Toledo, Winter, 1950–51.

Wegelin, Oscar, "The Writings of John Howard Payne," *The Literary Collector*, Greenwich, Conn., 1905.

Wood, Clarence Ashton, "Birthplace of John Howard Payne," *Long Island Forum*, Amityville, N. Y., October 1948.

ABOUT THE SONG

Bullard, F. Lauriston, "The Story of 'Home, Sweet Home,'" *The Musician*, April 1913.

Corder, Frederick, "The Works of Sir Henry R. Bishop," *Musical Quarterly*, Winter, 1918.

Duncan, Barbara, "Home, Sweet Home," *University of Rochester Library Bulletin*, Winter, 1949.

Engle, Carl, *Discords Mingled*, New York, 1931.

Haddon, J. Cuthbert, "History of 'Home, Sweet Home,' " *The Metronome*, February 1920.
Monthly Musical Record, London, 1880 and 1895.
Musical America, New York, February 25, 1938.
Northcott, Richard, *The Life of Sir Henry R. Bishop*, London, 1920.
Quarterly Musical Magazine and Review, London, 1823.
The Theatrical Observer and Daily Bills of the Play, London, May 15, 1823.

COLLATERAL WORKS—THEATRICAL

American

Anderson, John, *The American Theatre*, New York, 1938.
Blakeley, Sidney H., *John Howard Payne, Dramatic Craftsman*, PH.D. dissertation, Chapel Hill, N. C., 1947.
Clapp, W. W. Jr., *A Record of the Boston Stage*, Boston, 1853.
Crawford, Mary Caroline, *The Romance of the American Theatre*, Boston, 1925.
Dunlap, William, *A History of the American Theatre*, New York, 1832.
Fox, Dixon Ryan, "The Development of the American Theatre," *New York History*, September 1936.
Gilder, Rosamond, *Enter the Actress*, Boston, 1931.
Hislop, Codman and Richardson, W. R. (eds.), *Trial Without Jury and Other Plays by John Howard Payne*, Vol. 5 of *America's Lost Plays*, Princeton, 1941.
——— *The Last Duel in Spain and Other Plays by John Howard Payne*, Vol. 6 of *America's Lost Plays*, Princeton, 1941.
Hoole, William Stanley, "Old Charleston Theater from 1793 to 1883," *Southwest Review*, Dallas, Texas, January 1940.
——— "Two Famous Theaters of the Old South," *South Atlantic Quarterly*, Durham, N. C., July 1937.
Ireland, J. W., *Records of the New York Stage*, New York, 1866.
Massachusetts Historical Society Proceedings, 1925–26, "A Boston Dramatic Critic of a Century Ago," Boston, 1926.
Matthews, Brander and Hutton, Laurence, *Actors and Actresses of Great Britain and the United States*, New York, 1886.
Moses, Montrose J., *Representative American Plays*, New York, 1930.
O'Dell, George C., *Annals of the New York Stage*, New York, 1927.
Phelps, Henry Pitt, *Players of a Century*, Albany, 1880.
Quinn, Arthur Hobson, *A History of the American Drama from the Beginning to the Civil War*, New York, 1923.
Schoenberger, Harold William, *American Adaptations of French Plays*, Philadelphia, 1924.

Seilhamer, George O., *A History of the American Theatre During the Revolution and After*, Philadelphia, 1889.
Wemyss, F. C., *A Chronology of the American Stage*, New York, 1852.
Winter, William, *The Prompt Book*, New York, 1878.
Wood, William, *Personal Recollections of the Stage*, Philadelphia, 1855.

Also many New York and Boston newspapers of 1805 to 1852, and some of later dates. A few from other American cities.

British

Baker, H. Barton, *The London Stage, its History and Traditions*, London, 1904.
Doran, John, *Annals of the English Stage*, New York, 1865.
Foreman, W. Corthope, "Sadler's Wells," *Notes and Queries*, London, 1945.
Genest, John, *Some Account of the English Stage*, London, 1832.
McQueen-Pope, W., *The Theatre Royal, Drury Lane*, London, 1946.
Nicoll, Allardyce, *The Development of the Theatre*, London, 1927.
—— *A History of the Nineteenth Century Drama*, Cambridge, 1930.
—— *The English Theatre, a Short History*, New York, 1936.
Nicholson, Watson, *The Struggle for a Free Stage in London*, Boston and New York, 1906.
Scott, Clement W., "Joey Grimaldi and Sadler's Wells," *English Illustrated Magazine*, December 1895.

(periodicals and newspapers containing theatrical news and criticisms)

Bell's Weekly Messenger, 1820–24
Court Journal, The, 1829–32
European Magazine, The, 1818–25
Gentleman's Magazine, The, 1814–17
John Bull, 1821, 1822, 1829
Knight's Quarterly Magazine, 1823–24
Literary Gazette, The, 1820–27
Literary Magnet, The, 1820–24
London Magazine, The, 1820–24
London Times, The, daily, 1813–32
London Weekly Examiner, The, 1820–24
New Monthly Magazine, The, 1820–27
Quarterly Review, The, 1822–26
The Drama, or Theatrical Pocket Magazine, May 1823–April 1825
Theatrical Inquisitor, The, 1812–30
　　　(In early 1820's called *Gold's London Magazine and Theatrical Inquisitor*; in 1829 called *The Stage or Theatrical Inquisitor*)

The Theatrical Observer and Daily Bills of the Play (official publication of Drury Lane and Covent Garden), 1823–32

Weekly Dramatic Register, The, 1823–24

Periodicals Edited by Payne
(devoted wholly or in large part to theatrical matters)

Boston, *The Fly, or Juvenile Miscellany* (ed. by Payne and Samuel Woodworth), Tufts College, complete file. October 16, 1805–April 2, 1806.

New York, *The Thespian Mirror,* 14 issues, December 1805–May 1806. New York Public Library, complete file.

Schenectady, *The Pastime,* 37 issues, February 21, 1807–June 25, 1808. Union College, complete file.

Boston, *The Boston Mirror,* late 1808–early 1809, New York Historical Society.

London, *The Opera Glass,* 26 issues. 1826–27. East Hampton Library, complete file.

COLLATERAL WORKS—BIOGRAPHICAL
Books and articles

About Americans

Dunlap, William, *The Life of Charles Brockden Brown,* Philadelphia, 1813; London, 1815.

Irving, Pierre M. (ed.), *The Life and Letters of Washington Irving,* New York, 1862.

Luquer, Thatcher Taylor Payne, *An Unconscious Autobiography (Diary and Letters of William Osborn Payne),* New York, 1938.

Quinn, Arthur Hobson, *Edgar Allan Poe, A Critical Biography,* New York, 1941.

Rotundo, Joseph, "Eliphalet Nott," *New York History Magazine,* September 1932.

Taft, Kendall B., *Samuel Woodworth,* Chicago, 1938.

Trent, William P. and Hellman, George S. (eds.), *The Journals of Washington Irving, 1814–1842,* Boston, 1919.

Van Santvoord, C., *Memoirs of Eliphalet Nott,* New York, 1878.

Williams, Stanley T. (ed.), *Journal of Washington Irving, 1823–1828,* Cambridge, 1931.

—— *The Life of Washington Irving,* New York, 1935.

About Britons

Dunlap, William, *Memoirs of the Life of George Frederick Cooke*, New York, 1813; London, 1815.

Howe, Will D., *Charles Lamb and His Friends*, Indianapolis, 1944.

Jones, Frederick L. (ed.), *Letters of Mary Shelley*, Norman, Okla., 1944.

—— *Mary Shelley's Journal*, Norman, Okla., 1947.

Lucas, E. V., *The Letters of Charles Lamb, to which are added those of his sister, Mary Lamb*, London, 1935.

Moore, Helen, *Mary Wollstonecraft Shelley*, Philadelphia, 1886.

Moore, Thomas (ed.), *Letters and Journals of Lord Byron*, London, 1832.

Morris, Muriel, "Mary Shelley and John Howard Payne," *London Mercury*, September 1930.

Nitchie, Elizabeth, *Mary Shelley, Author of Frankenstein*, New Brunswick, N. J., 1953.

Raymond, George, *The Life and Enterprise of Robert W. Elliston*, New York, 1857.

Russell, Lord John (ed.), *Memoirs, Journal and Correspondence of Thomas Moore*, Boston, 1853.

Wardle, Ralph, *Mary Wollstonecraft*, Lawrence, Kansas, 1951.

COLLATERAL WORKS—HISTORICAL

Davis, William Thomas, *Plymouth Memories of an Octogenarian*, Providence, 1906.

Drake, Samuel Adams, *Old Landmarks and Historical Persons of Boston*, Boston, 1900.

Dunbar, Seymour, *A History of Travel in America*, Indianapolis, 1915.

Earle, Alice M., *Stage Coach and Travel Days*, New York, 1900.

Francis, John W., *Old New York*, New York, 1857.

Haswell, Charles H., *Reminiscences of an Octogenarian*, New York, 1857.

Hedges, Henry P., *A History of the Town of East Hampton, New York*, Sag Harbor, N. Y., 1897.

Holmes, Oliver W., "Levi Pease, Father of New England Stage Coaching," *Journal of Economic and Business History*, February 1931.

Old New York, "The City in 1805," New York, 1889.

Ross, Peter, *A History of Long Island*, New York, 1913.

Seabury, Samuel, *Two Hundred Years of East Hampton*, New York, 1926.

Stokes, I. N. Phelps, *Iconography of Manhattan Island*, New York, 1928.

Thompson, Benjamin Franklin, *A History of Long Island*, 1887.

Valentine's Manual, "New York Fifty-two Years Ago," 1859.

Wilson, James Grant, *The Memorial History of the City of New York*, New York, 1893.

About the Cherokees

Foreman, Grant, *Indian Removal,* Oklahoma City, 1932.

Memorials and Protests to Congress, 1836 and 1838.

Payne, John Howard, "Ancient Cherokee Traditions and Religious Rites," *American Quarterly Review,* December 1849.

—— Articles in *Journal of Commerce,* New York, March 30, April 7 and 23, 1838; January 19, March 11 and 21, April 17 and 19, 1841.

—— Articles in *National Intelligencer,* Washington, 1840, 1841, and 1843.

—— *Indian Justice (a Cherokee Murder Trial),* with foreword by Grant Foreman, Oklahoma City, 1932.

—— "Talking Stones, the Story of Sequoya," with foreword by Althea Bass, *Colophon,* Cambridge, February 1932.

—— "The Green Corn Dance," *Continental Monthly,* New York, January 1862.

Resolutions of the Georgia Legislature, December 18, 1835.

Starkey, Marion, *The Cherokee Nation,* New York, 1946.

United States Senate Document, No. 120, 25th Congress, Second session, 1836.

MANUSCRIPT SOURCES

Harvard Theatre Collection

  Nine letterbooks, 1809, 1810, 1814, 1825, 1834, 1835, 1836, 1839.

  Correspondence with Drury Lane Committee, 1816–17.

  Correspondence with Drury Lane Committee about *Brutus,* 1819–20.

  Plays in Payne's handwriting: *The Magpie and the Maid, Mazeppa, Romulus, Woman's Revenge.*

  Scrapbooks containing programs, critiques, etc.

Huntington Library (San Marino, Calif.)

  Correspondence with Emelia Von Harten, 200 pages.

  Correspondence with Anna Mary Freeman, 106 pages.

  Letters to friends and business associates.

Library of Congress

  Letters to George Watterston, Eliza Watterston, W. L. Marcy, Henry R. Schoolcraft, Francis Markoe, others.

Luquer Collection (Bedford Hills, N. Y.)

  Family records—dates and places of birth of family members.

  Letters of William Payne to his children, 1802–12.

  "A History of the Family," by Lucy Taylor Payne Osborn (written about 1861).

Letters of Eloise Richards Payne to William Ellery Channing, Susan Channing, Catharine M. Sedgwick, Thomas Warner, and others, arranged by Anna B. Z. Payne (five letterbooks, about 1820).

Letters of Lucy, Eloise, Anna, and Thatcher Payne to John Howard and other family members.

Letters of Payne to his father and other members of family, and to friends and business associates (unbound and in letterbooks).

Twenty letterbooks (J. H. Payne, business and personal), 1825–40.

Diary kept by Payne in debtor's prison, 1821.

Diary kept by Payne in Paris, 1826.

Diary kept by Payne in New York, 1838.

Letters of John Ross to Payne, 1836–40.

List of subscribers to *Jam Jehan Nima* (with signatures).

Letters to Payne from Washington Irving (about 70, mostly 1825–26).

Letters to Payne from John Quincy Adams, Washington Allston, Baring Brothers, Henry Brevoort, James Buchanan, Charlotte Cushman, George W. P. Custis, Charles Kemble, Fanny Kemble, Charles Lamb, Charles R. Leslie, Samuel F. B. Morse, William Macready, W. L. Marcy, Daniel O'Connell, John Gorham Palfrey, Lord Palmerston, J. R. Poinsett, John Trumbull, Benjamin West, and others.

National Archives

Official records and correspondence of Payne from U. S. Consulate, Tunis, to Department of State, Washington, 1842–44, 1850–52 (including letters to James Buchanan, John C. Calhoun, Daniel Webster).

Newberry Library (Chicago)

Payne's notes for a proposed history of the Cherokees, 1835–38 (14 volumes).

New York Historical Society

Twelve letters to and from Payne, mostly of London period and later.

Letter of Eloise Payne to John Howard (1814).

New York Public Library

Berg Collection

Letters of Payne to friends, mostly of 1849.

Diary kept in New York January 1–March 3, 1849.

Plays in Payne's handwriting: *Adeline* and *Richelieu* (with dedication to Irving).

Manuscript Division

Ten letters to and from Payne.

Pennsylvania Historical Society
  Letters of Payne to Jonathan Meredith, S. L. Fairfield, managers of New
    Orleans benefit, and others.

Union College
  Hatch collection of letters and manuscripts, including letterbook (London),
    1818–20.
  Also letters of William Payne, Eliphalet Nott, and early letters of John
    Howard Payne.

Others
  Some manuscript letters in libraries of Brown University, Duke University,
    Princeton, Yale; also Maryland Historical Society, East Hampton Li-
    brary, Weidenthal Collection (Cleveland).

INDEX

Abolition issue, 306, 307, 308, 309, 409
Accusation, 147, 148, 149, 150, 151, 152, 153, 154, 179, 191, 397
Adams, John Quincy, 292, 408
Adams, Samuel, 333, 334, 411
Adelgitha, 156, 157, 398
Adeline; or, the Victim of Seduction, 204, 208, 401
Air, Mrs. James (Rebecca Power), 96, 137, 394
Albany, 68, 72
Alexandria Index, 334
Ali Pacha, 206, 207, 208
Allegro, Ambrose, 352, 368, 412
Allston, Washington, 115, 395
American Antiquarian Society, 412
American Citizen, 46, 60, 83, 391
"American Plutarch," 72
"American Roscius," name applied to Payne, 83, 109, 110, 116, 119, 146, 398
Anna Bolina, 221
Annals of the New York Stage (O'Dell), 64, 407, 414
Anne Boleyn; or, Virtue Betrayed, 182
Anthon, Rev. Henry, 335, 412
Appius and Virginia, 187
Appleton, Mrs. Nathan (Maria Theresa Gold), 390
Armistice, The, 209
Arnold, Samuel J., 145
Arthur, Chester A., 382
Aspinwall, Thomas, 227, 403
Association of Teachers (N. Y.), 104, 105
Audubon, John James, 324
Authors' Rights, 295, 296 (see also Copyright)
Azendai, 226, 227, 228, 232

Baerer, Henry, 385
Baker, H. Barton, 394, 399, 400
Baltimore, 41, 42, 87, 89, 90, 96, 105, 111, 127, 138, 394, 410
Baltimore American, 393
Baltimore Federal Republican, 393
Baltimore Patriot, 76, 414
Banished Son, The, 314
Barbarossa, 82
Barbary Powers, 337
Baring Brothers, 109, 366, 394
Bates, Mrs. Joshua, 366, 394, 413
Bath (England) theaters, 146, 156, 206
Battle of New Orleans, 139, 396
Bayly, Thomas Haynes, 220
Beazley, Samuel, 199
Beethoven, 205, 268, 375, 385, 400
Bell's Weekly Messenger, 215
Benefits, theatrical, custom of, 61, 87, 101, 132, 281, 285
Benton, Thomas Hart, 358, 359, 360, 413
Berg Collection, 396, 405, 412, 413

Berry Street Academy, 33, 34, 35, 36, 39, 68, 75, 98, 266, 390
Betterton, Julia (see Mrs. Glover)
Betty, William Henry West ("Master Betty"), 37, 83, 91, 92, 113, 119
Bey of Tunis, 338, 341, 342, 344, 345, 349, 350, 352, 353, 362, 365, 367, 368, 370, 412, 413
Biggs, James, 120, 123, 125, 127, 129, 130, 395
Birmingham Royal Theatre, 172, 173, 177
Bishop, Anne Revere, 222
Bishop, Henry Rowley, 202, 205, 213, 216, 217, 218, 219, 220, 222, 227, 229, 401, 402
Bixby, William K., 404
Blaine, James G., 382
Bleecker, Harmanus, 392
Blue laws respecting theater, 26, 88, 390
Boieldieu, F. A., 269
Bond Street, N. Y., 291, 312, 319, 364
Booth, Edwin, 165
Booth, Junius Brutus, 391
Booth, Sarah, 124, 395
Boston, 33, 34, 35, 36, 37, 38, 41, 47, 49, 50, 75, 84, 85, 95, 103, 284, 285
Boston Atlas, 284
Boston Daily Advertiser, 407
Boston Evening Gazette, 43, 284, 285, 292, 373, 374, 390, 391, 398, 400, 407, 410, 414
Boston Globe, 284
Boston Mirror, 76, 393
Boston Patriot, 393
Boston Polyanthos, 395
Boston Sentinel, 284
Boston Symphony Orchestra, 390
Boston Transcript, 284, 292, 407
Boudinot, Elias, 409
Bowery Theatre, 279, 286
Brady, Matthew, 385
Brainard, Charles, 414
Brevoort, Elias, 391
Brevoort, Henry, 49, 72, 110, 112, 136, 319, 391, 398
British Monitor, 209
Broadway, 29, 77, 87, 278, 363, 381
Brooklyn Public Library, 397
Brougham, Lord Henry P., 273
Brown, Charles Brockden, 66, 67, 255, 391
Brutus, a Tragedy (Voltaire), 161
Brutus; or the Fall of Tarquin (Payne), 159-172, 173, 186, 187, 191, 196, 241, 271, 273, 279, 282, 287, 313, 398
Bryant, William Cullen, 283, 287, 319, 332, 373
Buchanan, James, 349, 352, 412
Buek, Gustave, 24
Buell, Samuel, 21, 25
Burr, Aaron, 291
Burroughs, Watkyns, 205, 217, 401
Butler, Elizur, 309, 409

433

Byron, George Gordon, 110, 143, 145, 159, 160, 254, 397

Caesar, Julius, 161
Calas, 180, 181, 193
Caldwell, J. H., 294
Calhoun, John C., 349, 351, 412
California gold rush, 356
Carthage, 339, 343, 345, 348, 366, 370, 371
Carthage and Tunis, Past and Present (Perry), 412
Cass, Gen. Lewis, 309, 360
Catalani, Angelica, 234
Catlin, George, 297
Censorship in England, 405
Chandler, W. P., 372, 396, 404
Channing, William Ellery, 34, 35, 103, 394, 395
Chapelie, A., 372, 413
Charles De Moor, Payne as, 182, 183
Charles II (King of England), 111, 180, 229, 399
Charles II, 228, 229, 231, 233, 234, 241, 265, 271, 281, 287, 295, 403, 407, 419
Charleston Theatre, 93
Cherokee Indians, 298–311, 320, 321, 322, 325, 332, 386, 408, 409
Cherokee Nation, 301–303, 324, 325, 327, 408, 409
Chiles, Rosa Pendleton, 64, 392, 401, 402, 408, 411
Chilton, Robert Smith, 372, 383, 414
Cholera epidemic, 278, 279, 314
Cibber, Colly, 399
City Hall, N. Y., 45, 381
Civil War, 135, 165, 307, 374, 376
Clapp, W. W., 392
Clari, the Maid of Milan, 202, 207, 210–223, 227, 228, 229, 234, 271, 282, 294, 318, 332, 401, 402, 403, 414
Clari; or, the Promise of Marriage, 205, 401
Clark, William, 293
Clay, Henry, 280, 314, 360, 410
Clayton, John M., 358
Clinton Academy, 19, 25, 26
Coleman, William, 51, 52, 53, 54, 57, 391
Coleridge, Samuel Taylor, 110
Colman, George, 362
Colt, John C., 333, 334, 335, 411, 412
Colt, Samuel, 333, 335, 411
Columbia College, 25, 291, 391, 409
Comédie française, 140, 397
Congress, 36, 96, 99, 301, 311, 314, 321, 332, 361
Continental Congress, 390
Cooke, George Frederick, 99, 100, 101, 159, 160, 394
Cooper, James Fenimore, 243
Cooper, Thomas Abthorpe, 81, 82, 83, 84, 87, 88, 90, 97, 100, 165, 286, 336, 392, 393, 398
Copyright, 144, 215, 314, 333, 410
Corcoran, William Wilson, 93, 376, 379, 382, 384, 385, 393, 414
Corlaer's Hook, 98, 99, 102, 105, 277
Corwin, Sen. Tom, 357, 361, 413
Così fan tutte, 247, 287
Court Journal, 272, 274, 406, 407
Covent Garden, 111, 125, 144, 145, 146, 154, 155, 157, 158, 180, 186, 187, 189, 199, 205, 206, 208, 211, 217, 218, 229, 233, 234, 249, 259, 269, 271, 273, 386, 397, 398, 399, 400
Crafts, Caroline, 393
Creek Indians, 298, 299, 300, 330
Crocker, Philander, 23
Curran, Amelia, 405
Cushman, Charlotte, 314

Daily Gazette and General Advertiser (N. Y.), 46
D'Anglade (see *Accusation*)
Da Ponte, Lorenzo, 286, 287, 291, 407, 410
D'Arcy, J. N., 127, 396, 397, 398, 399
Davenant, Sir William, 399
de Begnis, Giuseppina, 248
Declaration of Independence, 22
Delaware, R. L., 413
Democratic-Republicans, 356
Democratic Review, 317, 410
De Staël, Mme., 140
De Witt, William C., 386, 414
Dibdin, Charles, 179, 181, 184
Dibdin, Thomas, 149, 179, 397
Dickens, Charles, 214, 332–333, 411
Dido and Aeneas, 343, 399
Diplomatic Law Digest, 412
Domestic Manners of the Americans (Trollope), 407
Don Giovanni, 287
Donizetti, Gaetano, 221, 222, 405
Douglas, The Tragedy of, 77, 80, 113, 115, 116, 132, 182, 392
Dramatic Censor (see *Mirror of Taste and Dramatic Censor*)
Drury Lane Sub-Committee, 150, 169, 170, 397, 398, 399
Drury Lane Theatre, 111, 112, 113, 115, 123, 143, 144, 145, 147, 150, 152, 153, 155, 157, 159, 160, 161, 165, 166, 173, 179, 180, 186, 193, 196, 198, 199, 200, 201, 204, 206, 208, 216, 233, 245, 249, 271, 273, 338, 386, 396, 399, 401
Ducange, Victor H. J. B., 180, 193 (see also M. Victor)
Dunlap, William, 48, 78, 79, 81, 101, 255, 285, 286, 394, 395
Duval, Alexander, 229

Earl of Dysart, 22, 389
Eastham, Mass., 22
East Hampton, 19–29, 31, 99, 317, 327, 377, 389
Eastman School of Music, 222, 403
Edinburgh Review, 110
Elliston, Robert William, 116, 118, 173, 193, 194, 195, 196, 199, 201, 202, 204, 233, 248, 269, 395, 400, 401, 404
English Illustrated Magazine, 399, 400
"Eugenius, Gent," a Payne pseudonym, 55, 61, 62, 65
European Magazine, 148, 149, 165, 199, 215, 397
Eustaphieve, Alexis, 406
Evening Post (see New York *Evening Post*)
Examiner (see *London Weekly Examiner*)

Fairfield, Sumner Lincoln, 313, 409
Fairlie, Mary, 336, 391
Fall of Algiers, 406
Falstaff, 160
Faust Club of Brooklyn, 385, 414
Fawcett, John, 214, 229, 403, 405
Fay, Joseph D., 79, 136, 146, 392, 398, 409
Fay, Theodore S., 282
Federal Street Band, 37, 38, 49
Federal Street Theatre, 36
Fennell, James,·47, 90, 100, 101, 394
Fillmore, Millard, 356, 358, 361
Fleet Prison, 190, 400
Fly, The, 38, 39, 42
Forbes, Ralph B., 42, 44, 45, 51, 52, 390
Forbes, Robert B., 390
Forman, W. Courthope, 399
Forrest, Edwin, 165, 200, 282, 287, 321, 407, 410

Francis, John W., 390, 391, 410
Frankenstein, 239
Fraunce's Tavern, 30
Freeman, Anna Mary, 414
Free school movement, 28
Freischütz, Der, 226, 233, 290
Frelinghuysen, Frederick, 376, 377, 414
French Libertine, The, 263
French Revolution, 140, 141, 193, 210
Fricandeau, 272
Frontier and Midland, 408

Gale, W. R. B., 340, 341, 342, 345
Galignani's Messenger, 260, 366, 368
Galli-Curci, Amelita, 403
Garrick, David, 83, 100, 115
Gaspary, Joseph, 352, 367, 371, 372, 412
Genest, John, 171, 399
"Geoffrey Crayon," an Irving pseudonym, 272
George II (King of England), 179
George III, 110, 115, 162, 183
George IV, 184, 204
Georgia Guard, 303, 305, 306, 307, 408
Georgia Legislature, 310, 311, 409
Globe Theatre, 178
Glover, Julia B. (Mrs. Glover), 118, 147, 165, 191, 192, 194, 195, 201, 202, 400, 414
Glover, Molly, 271, 406
Glover, Phillis, 414
Gluck, Alma, 385
Godwin, William, 239, 251, 256, 404
Godwin, William Jr., 191, 200, 240, 259
Gold, Maria Theresa (see Appleton, Mrs. Nathan)
Gold's London Magazine or Theatrical Inquisitor, 187, 400 (see also *Theatrical Inquisitor*)
Goody Two-Shoes, 180, 181
Goulding, D'Almaine Company, 402
Gracie, Archibald, 283, 407
Grecian Daughter, The, 36
Green Corn Dance, 298, 300, 330, 408
Grimaldi, Joey, 181, 182, 185, 399
Guedalla, Philip, 396
Guess, George (see Sequoyah)
Gwynn, William, 394, 410

Hackett, James, 314
Hale, Philip, 393
Hallem family, 57, 131
Hamilton, Alexander, 46, 51, 53
Hamlet, Payne as, 85, 87, 89, 92, 93, 118, 132, 393, 397
Handel, George Frederick, 400
Hannibal, 339
Hanson, Willis Tracy Jr., 89, 96, 391, 392, 393, 394
Harden, Gen. Edward, 409
Harris, Henry, 154, 155, 156, 157, 158, 160, 189, 398
Harrison, Gabriel, 28, 39, 64, 78, 132, 149, 168, 274, 344, 385, 389, 390, 395, 397, 398, 400, 402, 407, 408, 412, 413, 414
Harrison, William Henry, 330, 331, 411
Harvard College, 23, 25, 31
Harvard Theatre Collection, 392, 393, 395, 396, 397, 398, 399, 401, 405
Haymarket Theatre, 47, 180, 216, 271, 272
Hazlitt, William, 401
Heap, Dr. Samuel, 350, 352, 354, 358, 359, 365, 368, 372, 412
Hedges, Mary (see Isaacs, Mrs. Aaron)
Hedges, Stephen, 21, 22
Hedges, William, 21
Henry VIII, 178
"Heyward, J.," name used by Payne, 227, 228, 243

Higginson, Henry Lee, 390
Higginson, Stephen, 33, 390
History of the American Drama (Quinn), 64, 398, 399
History of the American Theatre (Dunlap), 286, 395, 397
History of the Cherokees, Payne's plan for, 301, 319, 320, 323, 356, 408, 413
History of the Family, A (Lucy Payne Osborn), 26, 389, 390
History of New York (Martha J. Lamb), 394
Hodgson, W. B., 359, 412
Holbrouke, Rev. Theophilus, 395
Home, Rev. John, 77, 392
"Home, Dear Home," 71, 415
"Home, Sweet Home," 19, 23, 24, 29, 71, 202, 206, 207, 213, 214, 216, 223, 229, 231, 234, 282, 305, 306, 313, 333, 348, 361, 372, 376, 379, 381, 383, 386, 400, 405, 409, 414
Hone, Henry, 280, 291
Hone, Isaac, 280, 283, 291
Hone, Philip, 279, 280, 283, 291, 408
Honegger, John Baptist, 345, 346, 352
Horn, Charles, 201
Howard, Dr. John, 27
Humboldt, S.S., 365, 413
Hundred Days, 143
Hunter, William, 414
Huntington Library, 394, 404, 414

Inchbald, Elizabeth, 87
Iconography of Manhattan Island (see Stokes, Isaac N. Phelps)
Indian Territory, 323, 325, 327, 331
Ireland, 131, 132, 134, 414
Irish Monthly, 413
Irving, Ebenezer, 264
Irving, Peter, 46, 57, 112, 225, 228
Irving, Pierre, 265, 401, 403, 404
Irving, Washington, 46, 49, 90, 136, 160, 168, 189, 190, 203, 204, 209, 210, 224, 228, 230-239, 241, 250-267, 272, 281, 283, 291, 317, 318, 319, 357, 373, 393, 398, 400, 401, 403, 404, 405, 413
Isaacs, Aaron, 20, 21, 24, 25, 27, 31, 378, 389
Isaacs, Mrs. Aaron (Mary Hedges), 21, 22
Isaacs, Esther, 31, 99, 137, 174, 175, 312
Isaacs, Harriet, 390
Isaacs, Thomas, 363, 413
Italy, 220, 355

Jackson, Andrew, 280, 302, 311, 408, 409
Jam Jehan Nima, 289, 290, 296, 315, 317
Jarvis, John Wesley, 136, 410
Jefferson, Thomas, 51, 409
Jeffrey, Francis, 110
Joconde, 152, 153
Johnson, Edgar, 411
Johnson, Ellen, 221
Johnson, Mrs. John, 47, 221
Johnson, William Martin, 317, 410
Jones, Mrs. Granger, 47, 57, 61, 77, 391, 392
Journal of Commerce (N. Y.), 330, 331, 410, 411
Julia; or, the Wanderer, 54-65, 77, 391

Kean, Charles, 401
Kean, Edmund, 159, 160, 161, 164, 165, 166, 167, 173, 186, 187, 338, 384, 386, 398, 399, 405
Keats, George, 315, 316
Keats, John, 315, 316, 317, 318, 410
Kelly, Fanny, 147, 196, 197, 198, 214, 273, 397, 400, 401
Kelly, Michael, 397

Kemble, Charles, 125, 157, 160, 200, 206, 217, 228, 231, 232, 233, 252, 279, 287, 400, 401, 402
Kemble, Mrs. Charles, 214
Kemble, Fanny, 279, 287
Kemble, John Philip, 48, 110, 132, 158, 159, 160, 384, 395
Kemble, Stephen, 160, 164, 165, 167, 219
Kenney, James, 147, 205, 214, 217, 218, 401, 404
Kenney, Mrs. James, 241, 401, 411
Killarney, 134
Killigrew, Thomas, 399
King Lear, 101
King's Bench Prison, 200
Kingsley, Charles, 407
Kingston Academy, 25
Kinnaird, Douglas, 143, 144, 147, 150–154, 160, 169, 182, 397, 398
Klein, Herman, 414
Knickerbocker's History of New York, 98
Knowles, John Sheridan, 186, 187, 188, 288, 405, 407
Knoxville Register, 310, 313, 409
Koran, the, 362
Kotzebue, August, 87
Kreutzer, Rodolph, 205, 401
Kubla Khan, 110

La Dame Blanche, 269, 270 (see also *The White Maid*)
Ladies' Companion, 316, 317, 393, 410
La Gazza Ladra (see Magpie plays)
La Jeunesse de Henri V, 229
Lalla Rookh, 192
Lamb, Charles, 147, 205, 207, 208, 230, 240, 250, 317, 394, 395, 400, 401, 403, 404
Lamb, Martha, 394
Lamb, Mary, 111, 205, 208, 240, 394, 401, 404
Lancers, The, 271, 407
Last Days of John Howard Payne, The (Chapelie), 413
Last Days of Shelley and Byron, The (Trelawny), 404
Lee, Gideon, 291
Lee, Nathaniel, 161
Leslie, Charles, 115, 122, 168, 226, 395
Le Vol; ou la Famille D'Anglade (see *Accusation*)
Lewis, James, 391, 392
Life of Jesus, 318
Lincoln, Abraham, 375
Lincoln, Robert, 382
Lincoln's Inn Fields, 111
Lind, Jenny, 222, 360, 361, 373, 375, 413, 414
Lionel Lincoln, 243
Lippincott's Magazine, 414
Lispings of the Muse, 392, 400
Literary Gazette, 159, 179, 399, 406
Literary Magnet, 401
Liverpool, 43, 109, 116, 118, 122, 125, 137, 395
Liverpool *Mercury*, 118
Livingston, Mrs. Luther, 402
Livius, Barham, 226, 233
Livy, 171, 399
Lodoiska, 86
London, 37, 47, 110, 113, 116, 125, 127, 135, 139, 143–150, 152, 155, 156, 183–186, 205, 206, 211, 216, 223, 227, 228, 233, 239, 240, 241, 248, 261, 267, 269, 338, 386
London *Courier*, 215, 396
London *Day*, 114, 395
London *Dispatch*, 395
London *Globe*, 114
London *Literary Journal*, 168
London Magazine, The, 179, 187, 188, 399, 400

London Red Cross, 376
London Stage, The (Baker), 399
London *Sun*, 395
London *Times*, 181, 207, 215, 218, 233, 261, 263, 268, 270, 397, 398, 400, 403, 405, 406
London Weekly Examiner, 268, 270, 272, 406
London theaters, 142, 166, 178, 180
Longfellow, Henry W., 390
Long Island, 19, 20, 21, 27
Long Island Sound, 20, 27
Longworth, David, 65
Longworth's Directory and Almanac, 391, 392
Louis XIII, 209
Louisiana Advertiser, 294
Love in Humble Life, 204, 208, 407
Love in a Village, 201
Lovers' Vows, 86, 87, 132, 393
Lowell, James Russell, 377
Ludwig, Emil, 396
Luquer, Mrs. Lea (Eloise Elizabeth Payne), 312, 319, 330, 377, 410
Luquer, Thatcher Taylor Payne, 385, 390, 400, 409
Luquer collection, 389–414

Mabie, Hamilton Wright, 385
Macready, William Charles, 187
Madison, Dolly Payne, 95, 96, 136, 313, 394
Madison, James, 82, 95
Magpie plays, 143, 145, 146, 154, 397
Mahomet, the Impostor, 156
Mahomet, The Tragedy of, 82, 85, 113, 152
Malta, 352, 353
Manchester, 119, 137
Manchester *Herald*, 395
Manfred, 159
Manhattan Island, 30, 66
Marcy, W. L., 291, 355, 356, 357, 358, 359, 361, 394, 413
Markoe, Francis, 413
Man of the Black Forest, 151, 152, 153, 182
Marine Band, 376, 383
Marriage of Figaro, 171, 287
Married and Single, 226, 227, 228
Marshall, John, 408
Marshall, Mrs. Julian, 402
"Master Betty" (see Betty, William Henry West)
"Master Payne," 76, 79, 81, 82, 89, 90, 91, 115
Matthews, Brander, 397
Mayo, Maria, 94, 95, 137, 394
Mazeppa, the Wild Horse of Tartary, 406
McCullough, John, 165
Melodies of Various Nations, 220, 402
Mercier, L. Sebastian, 229
Mercure de France, 141, 397
Meredith, Jonathan, 146, 313, 394, 397, 407
Mexican War, 356
Meyers, Mordecai, 310, 409
Miller, Joan, 413, 414
Miller, John, 191, 216, 217, 227, 228, 233, 400, 401
Miller, Rosalie, 414
Milon, Louis, 205, 401
Miranda's Expedition, 395
Mirror of Taste and Dramatic Censor, 91, 393
Mohammed, 152, 398
Molière, J. B. P., 397
Monastery, The, 269
Monthly Musical Review, 414
Moore, John Bassett, 412
Moore, Thomas, 168, 192, 225, 241, 397, 403, 404
Morgan, Commodore, 351, 365
Morris, George Pope, 283, 407
Morse, Samuel F. B., 115, 321, 395

Mother's Curse, The, 228
Mountaineers, The, 82, 85, 133, 182
Mozart, 197, 287, 397
Murray, John, 145, 318
Music and Letters, 403

Napoleon, 37, 110, 118, 135, 139, 140, 143, 338, 396
National Archives and Records Service, 403, 412, 413, 414
National Institute, 313
National Intelligencer, 331, 410, 411
Newberry Library, 400, 408
New England Magazine, 413
New Monthly Magazine, 195, 207, 215, 263, 274, 396, 397, 405, 406
New Orleans, 293, 294, 296, 297, 324
New Orleans *Bee*, 294, 408
New Orleans *Picayune*, 410
Newton, Gilbert Stuart, 168, 241, 404
New York *Advocate*, 406
New York *American Citizen*, 83, 391, 392, 393
New York City, 19, 26, 29, 31, 41, 47, 55, 56, 65, 67, 71, 77, 81, 87, 89, 98, 100, 101, 136, 165, 200, 221, 264, 274, 277, 278, 287, 289, 290, 291, 310–314, 318, 319, 324, 330, 332, 333, 363, 380, 381
New York *Commercial Advertiser*, 46, 62, 389, 391, 392
New York *Evening Post*, 45, 46, 51, 53, 54, 57, 62, 83, 104, 280, 282, 286, 287, 313, 359, 390, 391, 406, 407, 409, 411, 413, 414
New York *Herald*, 313, 409
New York *Journal and Patriotic Register*, 28
New York *Mirror*, 221, 278, 280, 285, 288, 290, 389, 392, 397, 398, 400, 405, 406, 407, 410
New York *Morning Courier*, 45, 57, 313, 389, 409
New York *Times*, 381, 382, 383, 399, 404, 414
New York *Tribune*, 378, 380, 381, 414
New York University, 314, 364
Nicholson, Watson, 399
Nicklin, Philip, 102
Nicol, George, 167, 168
Niew Amsterdam, 29
Noah, Mordecai, 406
Noblet, Mlle., 216
Norah; or the Maid of Erin, 260
North American Quarterly Magazine, 313, 409
North American Review, 318
Notable Irishwomen, 396
Notes and Queries, 399
Nott, Dr. Eliphalet, 69, 70, 72, 74, 391, 392

Oak Hill Cemetery, Washington, 382, 385, 414
Oberon, 268
O'Dell, George, 64, 398, 400, 402, 407, 414
"Old Oaken Bucket," 38, 390
Oliver Twist, 332
Olympic Theatre, 172, 173
O'Neill, Eliza, 131, 132, 133, 134, 136, 156, 157, 396
Opera Glass, The, 267, 268, 269, 270, 405
Osborn, John Cheever, 175, 405
Osborn, Mrs. John Cheever (Lucy Taylor Payne), 23, 26, 27, 31, 32, 34, 36, 40, 99, 104, 105, 137, 175, 177, 277, 278, 279, 287, 312, 318, 319, 332, 362, 377, 389, 390, 394, 399, 406, 408, 410, 411, 413
Osborn, Joseph, 391
O'Sullivan, John Louis, 317, 410
Otis, H. G., 407
Outlook, The, 385
Oxford University, 119, 218

Paine, Robert Treat, 22, 35, 51, 390

Paine, Robert Treat Jr., 84, 85, 391, 392, 393, 394
Paine, Thomas, Payne ancestor, 22
Palais Royal, 209, 223, 226, 261, 400
Palermo, 353, 355, 412
Palfrey, John Gorham, 34, 43, 76, 176, 265, 318, 373, 374, 390, 391, 414
Paris, 139, 140, 142, 145, 146, 147, 149, 155, 165, 203, 204, 209, 210, 216, 223, 224, 225, 234, 260, 338, 413
Paris, Catherine Irving, 225
Parish, David, 397
Park Theatre, 45, 54, 77, 79, 81, 83, 84, 88, 111, 254, 281, 284, 285, 288, 332, 381, 391, 392, 406
Pasta, Guidetta, 221, 248, 249, 405
Pastime, The, 50, 71, 72, 74
Patti, Adelina, 222, 375, 386, 414
Paulding, James, 290, 319, 407
Payne, Anna Bevan Zeagers, 23, 26, 32, 99, 105, 136, 175, 176, 181, 210, 223, 268, 278, 279, 287, 293, 296, 312, 318, 335, 337, 351, 362, 363, 377, 394, 396, 399, 403, 405, 408, 411, 412, 413, 414
Payne, Eloise Elizabeth ("little Eloise") (see Luquer, Mrs. Lea)
Payne, Eloise Richards, 23, 26, 31, 32, 50, 70, 99, 102, 103, 105, 133, 135, 136, 137, 138, 139, 141, 158, 175, 176, 362, 377, 390, 392, 394, 396, 398, 399
Payne, John Howard
    birthplace, controversy concerning, 19, 23, 26, 28, 29, 389
    editorial ventures, 38, 39, 46, 47, 48, 50, 53, 54, 71, 72, 76, 267, 270, 289–297, 405
    financial management, 68, 69, 71, 75, 88, 100, 153, 176, 235, 237, 266, 355, 404
    health, 31, 41, 42, 50, 52, 82, 268, 352, 358, 369, 370, 371
    personal appearance, 50, 66, 81, 92, 241, 280, 347, 391
    plays by, 54, 55, 86, 87, 145–148, 151, 152, 159, 172, 186, 187, 188, 193, 202, 226, 228, 230, 249, 259, 260, 269, 270, 271, 272, 273, 393, 406
    religious faith, 177, 318, 319, 363, 371
    romances and women friends, 95, 96, 97, 119–131, 133, 134, 192, 238–257, 391, 414
    stage roles, 36, 39, 74, 77, 79, 80, 82, 85, 86, 87, 89, 92, 93, 112, 113, 116, 118, 124, 132, 133, 156, 157
Payne, Lucy Taylor (see Osborn, Mrs. John Cheever)
Payne, Sally, 23, 26, 32, 75
Payne, Thatcher, 27, 32, 99, 103, 105, 133, 136, 137, 138, 146, 173, 174, 175, 177, 279, 287, 309, 310, 312, 319, 320, 322, 332, 333, 355, 362, 364, 374, 377, 396, 397, 399, 407, 408, 409, 410, 411, 412, 413, 414
Payne, William, 20, 22, 23, 25, 28, 29, 30, 33, 34, 35, 36, 39, 42, 52, 72, 74, 75, 79, 98, 99, 103, 104, 175, 389, 390, 391, 392
Payne, Mrs. William (Sarah Isaacs), 20, 22, 23, 42, 73, 266
Payne, William Osborn, 23, 26, 28, 31, 36, 37, 40, 42, 44, 53, 73, 390
Peake, Richard, 401
Peale's Museum, 408
Pearl Street, 28, 29, 30, 44, 49, 277, 381
Pearman, William, 221, 402
Pendleton, Nathaniel, 53
Perkins, Thomas Handasyd, 33, 390
Perry, Amos, 272, 273, 412, 413
Petit-Méré, Frederic du, 147
Phelps, Samuel, 185
Philadelphia, 29, 36, 50, 73, 81, 103, 165, 200, 312
Philadelphia theater, 47, 90, 91, 92, 115, 146, 393

Pickwick Papers, 332
Pie Voleuse, La (see Magpie plays)
Pinkney, Bishop, 383
Pisani, M., 372, 378
Pitt, William, 37
Pizarro, 82
Placide, Alexander, 92
Pocock, Isaac, 145, 146, 155
Poe, David, 85, 393
Poe, Edgar Allan, 85, 393
Poe, Elizabeth, 85, 86, 87, 97, 132
Poe, Sam, 393
Poinsett, Joel R., 323
Political Justice (Godwin), 239
Polk, James K., 349, 356, 359
Pollock, Thomas C., 393
Porter, David, 350, 412
Port-Folio, The, 50
Powell, Mrs. F. P. R., 113, 394
Power, Rebecca (see Air, Mrs. James)
Price, Stephen, 81, 84, 88, 150, 254, 257, 258, 259, 264, 269, 271, 392, 393, 397, 405
Prince Regent, 110, 135, 184
Princeton, S.S., 349
Procrastination, 271, 272, 406
Procter, Bryan Waller, 200
Prospect Park, Brooklyn, 385
Prospectus of a New Periodical, 289, 407
Protestant Cemetery of St. George's, Tunis, 371, 372, 378
Providence, R. I., 89, 96, 97, 394
Providence *American*, 393
Providence *Evening Press*, 412, 413
Pulaski, Count Casimir, 74
Pulaski (the play), 74, 86, 138

Quarterly Journal of the New York Historical Association, 391
Quarterly Musical Review, 214, 215, 401
Queen Caroline, 184, 400
Queen Charlotte, 161
Queen Victoria, 124, 218, 344, 375
Quinn, Arthur Hobson, 64, 171, 398, 399

Randolph, David Meade, 133, 134
Randolph, Edmund, 331
Reade, Sir Thomas, 348, 353, 378, 412
Reade, Thomas Fellows, 378
Reese, James, 402
Repository of Arts, Literature and Fashions, 399
Revolution, American, 20, 22, 23, 27, 30, 36, 38, 66, 70, 74, 115, 301
Richelieu, Cardinal, 209, 261
Richelieu (the play), 226, 227, 228, 229, 260, 261, 262, 264, 265, 405
Richmond, Va., 92, 97, 133, 331, 394
Richmond *Enquirer*, 97
Richmond Hill Theatre, 279, 286
Robbers, The, 182, 183
Robertson, Henry, 208
Robinson, Crabb, 241, 401, 404
Robinson, Leigh, 383
Rochester, Earl of, 229, 230
Rome, ancient, 161, 162, 164, 166
Romeo, Payne as, 82, 86, 92, 116, 124, 132
Romulus, the Shepherd King, 410
Roscius, Gallus Quintus, 393
Roscoe, William, 117, 393
Ross, John, 301, 302, 303, 305, 306, 307, 308, 310, 311, 320–326, 328, 350, 357, 409, 410, 411
Rossini, Gioacchino, 145, 219
Royal Coburg Theatre, 199, 216, 399
Royal Philharmonic Orchestra, 218, 268

Rue Richelieu, 224, 225, 226, 234, 255, 267
Ryan, Abram, 413

Sadler's Wells, 177, 178, 179, 184–190, 193, 216, 254
Sadler's Wells Ballet, 177, 399
Santillano, Moses, 371
Schenectady, N. Y., 66, 67, 68, 69, 76
Schermerhorn, John, 304, 305, 311
Schiller, John Christophe Friedrich von, 399
School for Scandal, 194
Schroeder, Francis, 347, 412
Scipio, 339
Scott, Clement, 399, 400
Scott, Sir Walter, 110, 269, 270, 399
Scott, Gen. Winfield, 291, 361
Scribe, Eugène, 269
Seaman, John E., 53, 54, 65, 67, 68, 69, 72, 75, 79, 392
Sedgwick, Catharine Maria, 35, 50, 68, 104
Sedgwick, Henry, 104
Sedgwick, Robert, 68, 414
Sedgwick and Bleecker, 72, 392
Seine River, 140, 203, 209
Semmes, John, 393
Senate, 311, 322
Sequoyah, 301, 328, 329, 330, 411
Shakespeare, 39, 47, 132, 142, 160, 186, 360, 386, 404
Shelley, Mary, 238–259, 404, 405
Shelley, Percy Bysshe, 239, 240
Shelley, Percy Florence, 243, 404
Sheridan, Richard Brindsley, 47
Sherman, Gen. William T., 382
Siddons, Mrs., 77, 131, 159, 160
Singleton, Esther, 389
Sinnett, J. H. W., 235
Smart, Sir George, 269, 400, 405
Snowden, W. W., 315, 316
Society Library, 102
Solitary of Mount Savage, 208
Sousa, John Philip, 383
Southey, Robert, 110
Spanish Husband, The, 252
Springfield *Republican*, 414
St. Helena, 140
St. Louis, 293, 359, 360
St. Vitus' dance, 42, 52
State Department, 309, 344, 349, 353, 360, 365, 367, 372, 373, 378, 379, 383, 412, 413, 414
Stokes, Isaac N. Phelps, 389, 391, 394, 406, 409, 410
Stokes, Olivia E. Phelps, 396
Struggle for a Free Stage in London, 399
Stuart, Gilbert, 390
Supreme Court, 302
Surrey Theatre, 202, 205, 206, 209

Tales from Shakespeare, 404
Tallis Dramatic Magazine, 405
Talma, 140, 141, 142, 151, 158, 161, 203, 268, 397, 398, 400, 405
Talmadge, Experience, 22
Talmadge, Thomas, 22
Taming of the Shrew, 132, 282
Tancred and Sigismunda, 82
Taylor, Bayard, 361
Taylor, Horace A., 380, 414
Taylor, Lucy, 23
Taylor, William, 31, 32, 36, 41, 42
Taylor, Zachary, 356, 357, 358, 359
Theatre Alley, N. Y., 77, 100
Théâtre Français, 210, 397
Théâtre de la République de France, 141, 397
Theatrical Inquisitor, 146, 158, 179, 182, 184, 187, 188, 397, 398, 399, 403

Theatrical Observer, 272, 402, 406
Thérèse; or the Orphan of Geneva, 180, 193, 194, 197, 200, 220, 295, 400, 407
Thespian Mirror, 46, 47, 48, 50, 53, 54, 61, 65, 71, 72, 83, 286, 391
Thieving Magpie (see Magpie plays)
Thorndike, Dame Sibyl, 392
Tragedy of the Fatal Marriage, The, 36
Travel conditions, 27, 93, 94, 116, 117, 139, 298, 320, 338, 339, 365
Treaty of Ghent, 139, 396
Tree, Ann Maria, 214, 216, 229, 234, 401
Tree, Ellen, 401
Trial Without Jury; or, the Magpie and the Maid (see Magpie plays)
Trinity Church, 175, 318, 399
Tripler Hall, 373
Trollope, Frances, 289, 407
Trumbull, John, 117, 119, 283, 291, 395
Tunis, appointments to, 335, 358, 362
Tunis, city and county of, 339, 343, 349, 412
Tunis, U.S. consulate house, 340, 344, 346, **347**, 348, 367
Tunis in 1883, 378, 379
Twaits, William, 79, 393
Twaits, Mrs. William, 77, 79
'Twas I, 259, 269
Two Galley Slaves, 206, 207
Tyler, John, 331, 335, 356, 359, 411
Tyler, John, Jr., 331
Tyler, Mrs. Robert, 336

Union College, 66, 67, 70, 138, 304, 382, 385, 392, 398, 399, 401, 407
United Brethren Mission School, 411
United Nations, 325
United States Magazine, 410
Upshur, A. P., 349, 412

Van Buren, Martin, 291, 320, 321, 322, 323
Van Corlaer, Antony, 95, 394
Venice Preserved, 157
Verplank, Eliza, 104
Verplank, Gulian, 283, 410
Versailles, 205, 223, 224, 227
Vestris, Mme., 259, 269, 273
Victor, M. (see Ducange, H. J. B.)
Vindication of the Rights of Woman, A. 240
Virgil, 339, 343
Virginius; or the Patrician's Folly, 172, 186, 187, 188, 189, 288, 400, 407, 420
Visitandines, 151, 152
Voltaire, 82, 113, 152, 161, 398
Von Harten, Emelia, 119–130, 133, 134, 136, 148, 158, 395, 396, 415
Von Harten, George, 119–130, 133, 395

Waggoners, The, 228
Wagner, Richard, 213, 401
Wallack, Henry, 47, 116, 402
Wallack, James, 47, 116, 147, 196, 197, 282, 314
Wall Street, 30, 40, 43, 44, 49, 277, 314
Waltham, W., 183, 187, 188
War Department, 323, 331, 335
War of 1812, 77, 109, 136, 139
Warner, Henry, 74, 138, 396
Warner, Susan, 396
Warner, Thomas, 138, 176
Warren, Dr. Joseph, 23
Washington, George, 30, 99, 331, 370, 409
"Washington City," 93, 320, 322
Washington, D. C., 136, 305, 330, 341, 349, 356, 357, 358, 382, 393
Washington Monument, 370
Waterloo, 140, 142, 143
Watterston, Eliza, 370, 413
Watterston, George, 324, 411, 414
Weber, Carl Maria von, 226, 233, 268
Webster, Daniel, 283, 358, 360, 361, 362
Webster, John, 187
Webster, Noah, 46
Welch, James, 201
West, Benjamin, 115
Westminster Abbey, 111
West Point, 138
Westward Ho!, 290, 407
Wetmore, Prosper M., 283, 407, 413
Whig Party, 331, 356
Whitbread, Samuel, 112, 143, 394
White, Col. Maunsell, 297
White House, 95, 320, 336, 356, 394, 396
White Maid, The, 269, 270, 285, 405
Wide, Wide World, The, 396
Willett, Marinus, 66, 68, 99, 137, 391
Williams, Jane, 243, 249
Williams, Helen Maria, 140
Windsor Castle, 168, 375
Winter, William, 171, 399
Woffington, Peg, 77
Woman's Revenge, 273, 274
Wood, Dr. Clarence Ashton, 389
Wood, William, 146, 165, 397
Woodworth, Samuel, 38, 288, 390
World War I, 376
Worthington, John, 378, 379, 414
Wyndham, Henry S., 394

Yale, 25, 407
Young Norval, Payne as, 77, 79, 80, 93, 96, 101, 113, 114
Young Roscius, name applied to Payne, 83, 84, 87, 88, 92, 116, 122, 126, 129, 134, 331